SIMULATING AN AGEING POPULATION:
A MICROSIMULATION APPROACH APPLIED TO SWEDEN

CONTRIBUTIONS
TO
ECONOMIC ANALYSIS

285

Honorary Editors:
D. W. JORGENSON
J. TINBERGEN[†]

Editors:
B. BALTAGI
E. SADKA

Emerald

United Kingdom – North America – Japan
India – Malaysia – China

SIMULATING AN AGEING POPULATION: A MICROSIMULATION APPROACH APPLIED TO SWEDEN

ANDERS KLEVMARKEN
Department of Economics, Uppsala University, Uppsala, Sweden

BJÖRN LINDGREN
Lund University Centre for Health Economics (LUCHE), Lund, Sweden

Emerald

United Kingdom – North America – Japan
India – Malaysia – China

Emerald Group Publishing Limited
Howard House, Wagon Lane, Bingley BD16 1WA, UK

First edition 2008

CH

British Library Cataloguing in Publication Data
A catalogue record for this book is available from the British Library

ISBN: 978-0-444-53253-4
ISSN: 0573-8555

Contents

CHAPTER 1   **AN AGEING ECONOMY IN AN INTERNATIONAL PERSPECTIVE**   1
Anders Klevmarken and Björn Lindgren

CHAPTER 2   **DYNAMIC MICROSIMULATION FOR POLICY ANALYSIS: PROBLEMS AND SOLUTIONS**   31
Anders Klevmarken

CHAPTER 5   SICKNESS ABSENCE FROM WORK   115
Kristian Bolin, Sören Höjgård and
Björn Lindgren

CHAPTER 6   EARLY RETIREMENT   143
Kristian Bolin, Matias Eklöf, Daniel Hallberg,
Sören Höjgård and Björn Lindgren

CHAPTER 7   GEOGRAPHICAL MOBILITY AND TENURE CHOICE
Urban Fransson and Matias Eklöf

CHAPTER 8   THE INCOME OF THE BABY BOOMERS
Lennart Flood, Anders Klevmarken and Andreea Mitrut

Introduction to the Series

This series consists of a number of hitherto unpublished studies, which are introduced by the editors in the belief that they represent fresh contributions to economic science.

The term "economic analysis" as used in the title of the series has been adopted because it covers both the activities of the theoretical economist and the research worker.

Although the analytical method used by the various contributors are not the same, they are nevertheless conditioned by the common origin of their studies, namely theoretical problems encountered in practical research. Since for this reason, business cycle research and national accounting, research work on behalf of economic policy, and problems of planning are the main sources of the subjects dealt with, they necessarily determine the manner of approach adopted by the authors. Their methods tend to be "practical" in the sense of not being too far remote from application to actual economic conditions. In addition, they are quantitative.

It is the hope of the editors that the publication of these studies will help to stimulate the exchange of scientific information and to reinforce international cooperation in the field of economics.

The Editors

Preface

Many Western countries now experience population ageing when the large post World War II birth cohorts retire and age. The future consequences of ageing are an issue of research that might have far-reaching policy implications. Although the Swedish dependency ratios will not increase as much as in some of the South and Central European countries, Sweden will share the experience of a major increase in the number of elderly and in particular in the number of old-olds with most other European countries. Some 7 years ago, a group of Swedish social scientists of different disciplines started a research project, which got the nickname "The Old Baby-boomers". Among our research issues were:

- How much health care and social care will the future big generations of elderly use?
- Can they count on the same amount of assistance from spouses, children, and other relatives as today?
- How much will the (public) expenditures for health care and social care increase?
- Will the tax revenues from households increase in proportion to the increase in expenditures for care (with the current tax system)?
- Will future elderly have incomes and assets such that they can pay for the care they will need?
- Will poverty among the elderly increase or decrease?
- Is it possible to get a better balance between the demand for care and the resources that can be made available for this purpose by stimulating working generations to retire later, by welcoming more immigrants or by improving the health status of the population?

Micro-simulation was the approach, which we found most useful for finding answers to our research questions. Although we were fortunate to start from an already existing dynamic micro-simulation model, SESIM, the model needed extensions and modifications to fit our purposes. We have, hence, completed a number of empirical studies in order to develop and estimate new models to be incorporated into SESIM. They include:

- Changes in the health status of the population.
- Utilization of sickness benefits, hospital care, and social care of the elderly.

- The mechanisms behind early retirement in Sweden.
- Migration within Sweden and closeness to kin.
- The incomes of the elderly relative to the working population.
- Changes in the distribution of wealth as the population ages.

Thus, this volume reports on our empirical studies, our model development, and the results of our scenario simulations. It further presents our experience from the micro-simulation approach and discusses the results of our simulations.

Among our key results are the following:

- If the same share of elderly as today was to get access to health care and old age care in the future, the supply of these services would have to increase at the same rate as the relevant age groups, which implies about 70 percent for inpatient hospital care, 50 percent for home help, and 80 percent for institutionalized care for the elderly. The public sector costs for these services would then increase more than the tax revenues from the household sector, if tax rates were kept unchanged.
- The income standard of the elderly relative to that of the working generations will decrease with increasing age. Younger generations of retired will have relatively lower incomes, unless they postpone retirement.
- The share of income poor old-olds will increase, but the old baby-boomers are relatively wealthy and not expected to deplete their stocks of wealth as they age. Our simulations show, however, that we will get a group of old-olds who both have small incomes and no assets.
- Regional migration and changes in the age distribution imply that the share of elderly that lives close to a child will decrease. Thus, there seems to be little hope for children and other relatives taking an increasing share of the future burden of care for the elderly.
- An increase in the average pension age would reduce the future care burden, while increased immigration would have only very small effects.
- Our simulations are sensitive to what we assume about mortality risks. If the health status of the population of young elderly increases and, consequently, their mortality risks decrease we might get an agglomeration of very old people, who will be in need of very much care, toward the middle of the century.

We would like to thank the Swedish Ministry of Finance for giving us access to SESIM, and in particular Tomas Pettersson, who has been instrumental as a link between the SESIM team at the Ministry and our research group. He has also contributed greatly to our project by implementing our models into SESIM, running tests, and giving good advice.

We would also like to thank our group of advisors: Uno Davidson, Per-Anders Edin, Leif Johansson, Bettina Kashefi, Mårten Palme, Edward Palmer, and Annika Sundén, as well as the demographic research group at Lund University and members of the Department of Economics at Lund University for valuable discussions, useful comments, and constructive suggestions on previous drafts.

Anders Klevmarken
Björn Lindgren
Uppsala and Lund
September 2007

List of Contributors

Kristian Bolin	LUCHE, Lund University, Lund, Sweden
Matias Eklöf	Department of Economics, Uppsala University, Uppsala, Sweden
Lennart Flood	Department of Economics, School of Business, Economics and Law, Gothenburg University, Gothenburg, Sweden
Urban Fransson	Institute for Housing and Urban Research, Uppsala University, Gävle, Sweden, and Department of Human and Economic Geography, School of Business, Economics and Law, Gothenburg University, Gothenburg, Sweden
Daniel Hallberg	Department of Economics, Uppsala University, Uppsala, Sweden
Sören Höjgård	LUCHE, Lund University, Lund, Sweden, and Swedish Institute for Food and Agricultural Economics, Lund, Sweden
Anders Klevmarken	Department of Economics, Uppsala University, Uppsala, Sweden
Mårten Lagergren	Stockholm Gerontology Research Center, Stockholm, Sweden
Björn Lindgren	LUCHE, Lund University, Lund, Sweden
Andreea Mitrut	Department of Economics, School of Business, Economics and Law, Gothenburg University, Gothenburg, Sweden

List of Figures

Chapter 4

Chapter 5

List of Tables

Chapter 6

Chapter 7

Chapter 8

An Ageing Economy in an International Perspective

Anders Klevmarken and Björn Lindgren*

1. Background

The challenge of an ageing population is a major concern to policymakers and researchers all over the world. As evident in Figure 1, the percentage of people aged 60 and above will increase substantially between 2000 and 2050 in all parts of the world. Europe has the highest proportion; only Japan has a similar age structure. The already high proportion of older people in Europe is expected to rise to an even higher level by 2050, from currently 19 percent to an estimated 34 percent.

Although the populations in all European countries are ageing, they differ substantially in their basic demographics. Thus, they differ where they are today and they differ in the speed at which their populations are ageing, depending on differences both in fertility rates and in life expectancies. Figure 2 shows the population "pyramids" in 12 European countries in 2000. There is a striking difference between Sweden (and Belgium and France) on one hand and Germany, Greece, Italy, and Spain on the other, due to markedly lower fertility rates in the latter countries. The young generations in these countries are only about half the size of the largest baby-boom cohorts of the 1940s.

By 2050, the "diamond" shape of the European population pyramids of 2000 will all have turned "urn-shaped" (see Figures 3 and 4). Still, there are large differences among the countries. Toward 2050, Sweden and France

---

* Corresponding author.

CONTRIBUTIONS TO ECONOMIC ANALYSIS
VOLUME 285   ISSN: 0573-8555
DOI:10.1016/S0573-8555(07)00001-6

Anders Klevmarken and Björn Lindgren

Figure 1. People aged 60 and above as shares of total population by region, 2000–2050. Percent (UN, 1998)

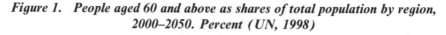

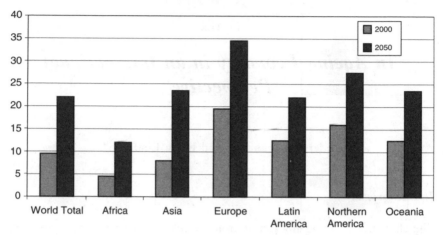

will have a much more favorable age distribution than most other European countries. The other extreme is Italy.

There are equally striking differences among the European countries for life expectancy (Figure 5). A newborn Swedish girl is expected to live for 82 years, a few months less than a newborn French, Italian, Spanish, or Swiss girl, but 3 years longer than her counterpart in neighboring Denmark. A newborn Swedish boy is expected to live for 78 years, which is longer than his counterpart in all other countries in Europe. The gender gap is also closer in Sweden, only 4 years. France seems to have the largest, 8 years between the female and male life expectancies.

The approaching demographic transition faced by many countries will give rise to a number of effects, some of which are more foreseeable than others. Due to the predictable nature of cohort life cycles, the relationship between demographic structure and macroeconomic variables, such as inflation and gross domestic product (GDP), appears to be both strong and stable (McMillan and Baesel, 1990; Lenehan, 1996; Lindh and Malmberg, 1998, 2000b). Dependant groups, such as children and pensioners, have a negative effect on growth and a positive effect on inflation, while working age groups show reverse correlations (Lindh, 2004). A comparatively large group of people around the age of 50 generally increases GDP growth; the long-life experience of the cohort provides the country with a high level of human capital. Also, people at the top of their career will save money, affecting investments positively. Even when countries are at a stage with many young pensioners, resulting in low savings, the level of investments has proved to remain high, possibly due to growing inflation. Taking Sweden as a typical example, the next decade would, according to this scenario, be characterized by high growth followed by stagnation and,

Figure 2. Population pyramids in 12 European countries in 2000

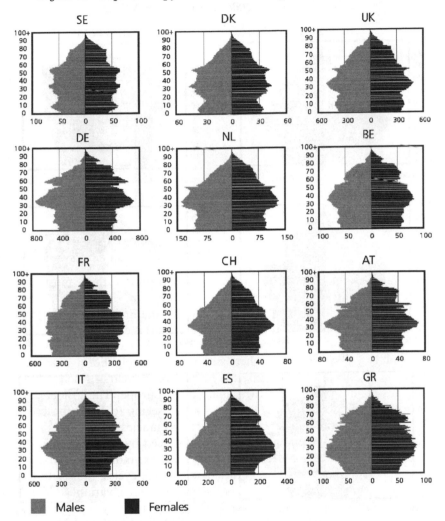

Males   Females

Source: Eurostat (Population by sex and age on 1st January of each year)

later, when the old-age pensioners make out a fairly high percentage of the population, a decrease in growth (Lindh and Malmberg, 2000a). Still, since the economic and social situation within a birth cohort varies widely, these macroeconomic perspectives tell quite little about the situation at the household level.

When the large birth cohorts of the 1940s retire from the labor market, the support burden of the working generations will increase. In Figure 6, this is expressed by the actual and expected old-age dependency ratios in

Figure 3. **Population ageing in the European Union, France, and Italy, 2000–2050**

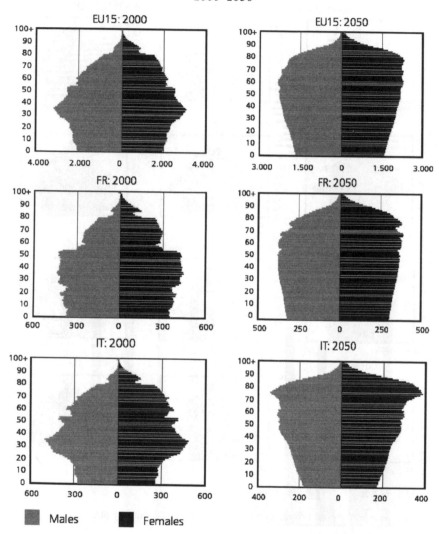

| Males | Females |

Source: Eurostat (Eurostat projections 1995, revision 1999)

2000 and 2050 for the same 12 European countries as above. The old-age dependency ratio is here defined as the number of inhabitants aged 60 and over (the "elderly") divided by the number of inhabitants aged 20–59 (people of "working age"); the choice of age limits is, of course, somewhat arbitrary but follows a rather widespread convention. Presently, Sweden, together with Germany, Greece, and Italy, has the highest dependency ratio (around 40 percent) among these 12 European countries; the

Figure 4. Population ageing in Sweden, 2000–2050

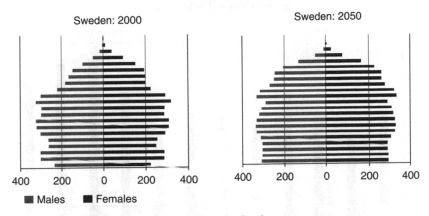

Source: Statistics Sweden

Figure 5. Life expectancy at birth, 2001

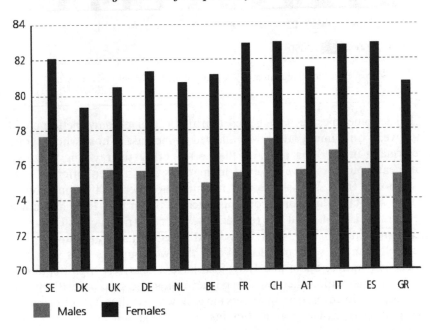

Source: OECD Health Data 2004

Netherlands has the lowest (around 30 percent). The old-age dependency ratio will increase fast in countries with low mortality and fertility rates. By 2050, the dependency ratio is expected to rise to 65 percent in Sweden, but to 90 percent in Italy and Spain.

Figure 6. *Old-age dependency ratio, 2000 and 2050 (population 60 and over to population 20–59 years)*

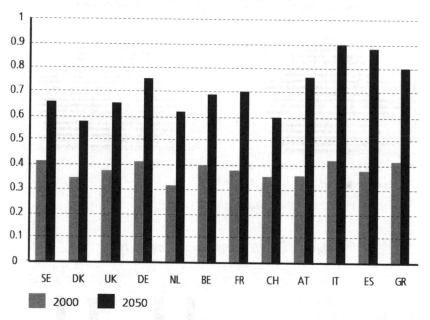

Source: Eurostat (Population by sex and age on 1st January of each year)

It has sometimes been suggested that this rather gloomy picture could improve, if only immigration was allowed to increase. Those who migrate are usually in working age and they often bring their young children. European countries have received immigrants at a rather different rate. A snap-shot from 2004 shows that net migration per 1000 population to EU-25 was 4.0, while some countries such as Spain and Italy had much higher rates, i.e., 14.3 and 9.6, respectively, and countries such as Denmark, Germany, France, the Netherlands, and Sweden had rates lower than average.[1] It might seem paradoxical that the two countries with very high dependency ratios, Spain and Italy, also have a relatively high migration, while countries with rather low dependency ratios also receive relatively few immigrants. However, demographers have shown that the effect of increased immigration is rather modest. For instance, Bengtsson and Scott (2005) demonstrated that the share of the Swedish population aged 65+ would have increased from 18 to 21 percent, i.e., had been only 3 percentage points

---

[1] Eurostat, Population Statistics 2006, Table b-5: Population change, 2004.

**Table 1.   GDP per capita in PPS (purchasing power standards),
EU-25 = 100**

	1997	1998	1999	2000	2001	2002	2003	2004	2005	2006	2007
EU-25	100	100	100	100	100	100	100	100	100	100	100
EU-15	109	109	110	110	109	109	109	108	108	107	107
Denmark	124	123	127	126	125	121	120	121	123	123	123
Germany	116	114	114	112	110	109	108	109	108	108	107
Greece	71	70	71	71	73	77	80	82	83	84	85
Spain	87	89	92	93	93	95	97	98	98	98	97
France	114	114	114	114	114	112	111	109	109	108	108
Italy	113	113	113	112	109	107	105	103	101	101	100
Netherlands	118	119	119	120	127	125	125	124	124	123	124
Austria	124	123	126	126	122	120	121	123	122	122	121
Sweden	115	114	118	119	115	114	116	117	118	119	119
UK	112	112	112	113	113	116	116	116	116	116	116
Switzerland	139	138	134	133	128	130	131	131	132	131	130
US	152	153	155	153	149	146	148	151	152	153	152

Source: Eurostat (Economy and Finance: National Accounts).

higher in year 2000, had there been no net migration to Sweden at all after 1930. The explanation is that even immigrants age and that they tend to adjust their fertility rather quickly to that of their new country. One might also note that it is not sufficient to keep net migration at a high level. In fact, net migration would have to increase in order to drive down the dependency ratio.

Economic conditions also vary substantially among the European countries. According to Table 1, average income, or GDP per capita, is now highest in Switzerland (30 percent above the average of the EU-25 countries) and lowest in Greece (15 percent lower). The relative positions of countries have changed, however, during the last 10 years, reflecting differences in growth rates (Table 2). If they continued, the low growth rates in Germany and Italy would make the fast increasing support burden for their working generations even worse. On the other hand, the more modestly increasing support burdens in Sweden and the United Kingdom would be moderated by high economic growth rates.

Even though conditions for increases in general productivity and for economic growth may vary, all countries have to consider whether incentives need to be built into the pension and tax systems to make people postpone their retirement and increase their average age of retirement in order to ease the burden of the younger generations. This is a change quite opposite to the trend that has been observed in the past few decades. Survey data on people's retirement plans generally show no signs of an increased interest in postponing retirement, rather these surveys indicate that early retirement has become ever more desirable over the years. However, if such a policy were successful, it would not only stimulate the

Anders Klevmarken and Björn Lindgren

Table 2. *Average and expected real GDP growth rate (constant prices, 2000)*

	Average GDP growth 1996–2005	Expected GDP growth 2006	Expected GDP growth 2007
EU-25	2.1	2.1	2.4
EU-15	2	2	2.2
Denmark	1.8	2.3	2.1
Germany	1.3	1.2	1.6
Greece	3.6	3.4	3.4
Spain	3.4	3.2	3
France	2.1	1.8	2.3
Italy	1.3	1.5	1.4
Netherlands	1.9	2	2.4
Austria	1.9	1.9	2.2
Sweden	2.6	3	2.8
UK	2.5	2.3	2.8
Switzerland	1.5	1.6	1.5
US	2.9	3.2	2.7

Source: Eurostat (Economy and Finance: National Accounts).

growth of the economy but also imply that on average these cohorts would become better off financially.

However, to what extent incentives to increase employment rates and to postpone retirement among the middle aged and elderly might seem workable depend on the current situation, which differs substantially among the 12 European countries that we are comparing. As is evident from Figure 7, the employment rate for workers aged 55–64 is highest (close to 70 percent) in Sweden and in Switzerland; less than 50 percent in Austria, Italy, France, Germany, Greece, the Netherlands, and Spain; lowest in Belgium (25 percent). The gender gap has more or less been eliminated in Sweden; in Austria, Belgium, Italy, Greece, and Spain, the employment rate among men is more than double the female one, though. The latter countries, hence, have a potential to compensate their population ageing by increased female labor force participation.

The average exit age from labor force also varies but not quite as much as the employment rates (Figure 8). True, Sweden is still among the countries with the highest average exit age – 62 – but Denmark and the United Kingdom have equally high exit ages, several other countries around 60, France 58, and Belgium 57.

Until recently, newly retired cohorts have been both healthier and wealthier than previous generations. The healthier and wealthier are likely to show a strong demand for leisure activities, travel services, good housing, etc. The trend toward ever-healthier elderly seems now to have been broken, however. As can be seen in Figures 9 and 10, the share of young and middle-aged Swedish men and women, reporting "very good"

Figure 7. Employment rates of workers aged 55–64, 2001, and the employment targets according to the Lisbon and Stockholm summits

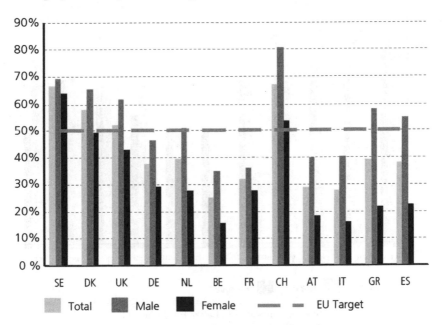

Source: Eurostat (EU Labor Force Survey)

or "good" health status to the Survey of Living Conditions (ULF), started to decline already in the early 1990s. As a consequence, as the cohorts are graying, the share of elderly people, reporting "very good" or "good" health status, has now started to decline, too. Using a different health measure, this has been shown also by Burström *et al.* (2003). Moreover, this is not just a Swedish phenomenon. Figures 11 and 12 show corresponding trends for the entire EU-15 countries, even though the data only cover the years 1996–2001. Similar trends have also been reported for the United States (Lakdawalla *et al.*, 2004). Part of the explanation seems to be the growth at young ages in allergy, asthma, diabetes, other long-standing illness, and health problems associated with obesity (Lakdawalla *et al.*, 2004). Understanding the factors behind the health, or ill health, trends among the young and middle-aged provides insights into future health, or ill health, trends among the elderly.

There are substantial individual differences in health among the elderly (Crimmins *et al.*, 1997; Manton *et al.*, 1997; Waidman and Manton, 1998). Ageing with preserved good health to a high age is associated with good income and education level, good social network and support, health-enhancing living habits — no smoking, moderate alcohol, normal weight, etc. — and an active physical, social, and cultural life (Maxson *et al.*, 1997;

Figure 8. *Average exit age from labor force, 2001*

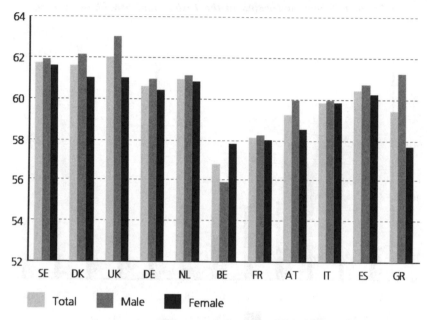

Source: Eurostat (EU Labor Force Survey)

Figure 9. *Percentage of men in Sweden with good and very good self-perceived health by age*

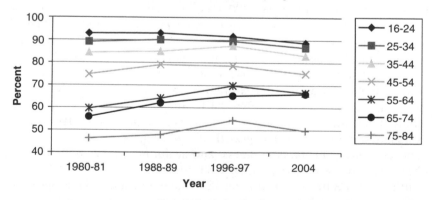

Source: Statistics Sweden

Rowe and Kahn, 1987; Guralnik and Kaplan, 1989; Deeg *et al.*, 1989; Sundberg and Jansson, 1998).

As the newly retired cohorts grow older, their demand for health- and social care will increase. Whether provided for publicly or privately, it is

Figure 10. Percentage of women in Sweden with good and very good self-perceived health by age

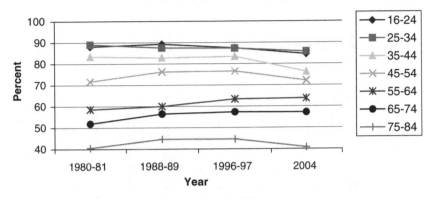

Source: Statistics Sweden

Figure 11. Percentage of men in EU-15 with good and very good self-perceived health by age

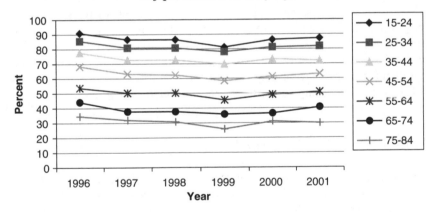

Source: Eurostat

important to be able to estimate its magnitude and timing to understand what measures are needed to meet this new demand. New health technologies will be available, some of which will increase the costs, while others may well reduce the costs of health care and related services. For various reasons, out-of-pocket charges may be raised, so it will also become interesting to analyze and predict what economic means the elderly can use to pay, at least partly, for these services (other than through the tax bill and other mandatory contributions).

Related to these issues is the issue of leaving a bequest. Do elderly plan for leaving their assets as bequests to their children or do they see their

Figure 12. **Percentage of women in EU-15 with good or very good self-perceived health by age**

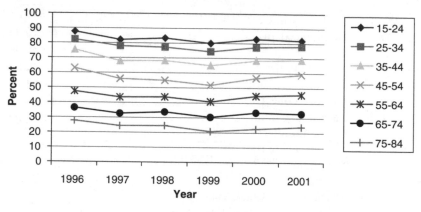

Source: Eurostat

wealth primarily as a safe guard against bad health and the need for care, while any bequest becomes residual? Changes in out-of-pocket charges may alter the incentives for wealth accumulation, i.e., reduce the importance of the bequest motive in favor of savings for health services and old-age care, but also increase inter-vivo gifts to sons, daughters, and grandchildren (premature bequests) in an attempt to reduce charges and still transfer something to younger generations.

2. The project "old baby-boomers"

The perspectives of ageing populations in most Western countries have raised issues such as how fast will the ageing process go, when will we reach the peak of the dependency ratio, how severe will the burden of the large baby-boom cohorts of the 1940s become to the younger cohorts, and, perhaps most interesting, who will pay for the pensions, the health care, and the social care of the baby-boom cohorts? These issues motivated the project "old baby-boomers," the results of which are reported in this volume. Even if Sweden might have less severe problems than many other countries – the Swedish fertility rate was relatively high also after the baby-boom cohorts were born and the dependency ratios have thus not become as high as in other countries – the dependency ratios will increase and Sweden will face large cohorts of very old, who most likely will be in need of care. If one side of an ageing population is increased pension payments and increased care, the other side is the size of the population in working age and its labor force participation. Even if labor force and work effort increase, will they increase enough to balance the increase in resources that will go to the baby-boom cohorts? If not, are there policy measures that could be taken either to increase the growth of the economy or reduce the need for care?

Particular policy issues are whether pensions, health care, and social care should be financed privately or by taxes, and if the services to the elderly should be produced privately or publicly. Different countries have sought different solutions. In Sweden, private pensions play a relatively minor role while most pension arrangements are collective, either through social security or collective labor market agreements. Almost all institutional care is tax financed and also provided by the public. There are an increasing number of private providers, but they still play a relatively small role. There is no market mechanism, which makes the price of care adjust to changes in demand and supply, but excess demand results in queues, which may or may not be met by increased supply, all depending on political decisions.

Our project cannot address all these issues, but we will estimate the size of health- and social care, using the assumption that utilization of the services for elderly will have approximately the same "pattern" as in the 1990s and the early 2000. These simulations should not be seen as predictions of what will happen, but rather as the consequences of an ageing population given that politicians adjust to a changing demand in about the same way they did in the 1990s and early 2000. We will, however, analyze how changes in health status might influence the demand for care as well as labor supply.

We will take the pension system as it was in the first years of the twentieth century after the major reform in the 1990s for granted and, hence, not assume any future changes.

Our study includes a rather detailed analysis of the retirement decisions and the resulting model is used to analyze the relative importance of "golden hand shakes" and the consequences of an increase in the stipulated maximum retirement age. Most Swedish labor market contracts stipulated that the upper retirement age was 65. A few years ago, Parliament overruled these contracts and lifted the upper retirement age to 67. Subject to common rules, which regulate the dismissal of employees, this law implies that everyone has the right to remain at a job until 67. In our analysis we will lift this age even further, to 70.

To evaluate the future burden of increased health- and social care, we should ideally be able to simulate future incomes and expenditures of the public sector. Our approach does not permit this. All we can do is to estimate the expenditures for health care and social care and compare to total direct taxes paid by the household sector, and to disposable income and assets owned by households.

We do not only aim at an analysis of averages but rather focus also on distributional issues. Which groups are likely to become heavy users of care? Will there be large groups of poor elderly with low incomes and/or wealth? To what extent will those who are in great need of care belong to the poor? These issues are not only of importance for the design of the pension system, but also for the choice between publicly and privately financed care. If there are large groups of elderly who have no means to pay for the services that they need, their provision must to a large extent be tax financed.

Our focus on distributional issues implies that we will have to consider heterogeneity in behavior and choose an approach, which accommodates heterogeneity. We also need an approach, which to the extent possible models the interdependence of all household decisions. Individuals and families make plans for their future by implicitly or explicitly taking decisions with long-term consequences. Decisions concern education, entering and leaving the labor market, job carriers, marriage and divorce, the number of children to raise and how, health and expected length of life by choosing healthy or unhealthy lifestyles, where and how to live, savings, loans and insurance to name some of the most important decisions. All decisions are more or less interrelated; a decision in one area cannot be taken without affecting all other areas. A new and better paid job for one family member may imply that the whole family moves to a new city and that all other family members have to adapt to the new situation as well; a higher income may lead to more savings, better housing, and/or more children; a new job for husband and/or wife may also imply new health hazards, which sooner or later may restrict the opportunities to take part in various leisure and labor market activities, etc.

All these decisions may be seen as parts of an optimization process, in which individual preferences and various resource constraints play the leading roles. Plans are not always realized. Bad luck and miscalculations as well as unforeseen opportunities may change the preconditions more or less drastically, and plans have to be revised accordingly. The preconditions which affect individuals' or families' life plans are to a large extent determined by political measures, and changes in these measures will also alter people's plans. Thus, changes in pension schemes and the availability of health- and social care for the elderly will certainly alter the decisions people (of almost all ages) will make about health, retirement age, wealth accumulation, and housing.

It is difficult to capture this complicated web of decisions and consequences in a model. An approach, which allows it, is the micro-simulation approach. It is not practical to build a large interdependent model, and data shortage will certainly in many cases restrict us to estimate reduced-form type distributions of target variables, but by choosing an insightful hierarchy of household decisions, it might be possible to capture the most important properties of this cob web.

To build a large-scale dynamic micro-simulation model is a major project, which requires large resources, a large team of scientists and other specialists, and takes a long time. Not having these resources, we explored the possibilities to start with an already existing model, which we could modify and expand for our purposes. The dynamic micro-simulation model SESIM developed by the Swedish Ministry of Finance met our requirements as a platform for further developmental work, and we were able to reach an agreement of co-operation with the Ministry of Finance. In focusing on the behavior of middle-aged and elderly and following the ageing of the baby-boom cohorts, we have supplemented SESIM with a number of new models. They simulate (a) the progression of health as people age, (b) sickness absence, (c) early retirement with disability benefits, (d) old-age retirement, (e) geographical mobility and tenure choice, (f) incomes of the elderly, (g) wealth of the elderly, (h) utilization of hospital care, and (i) utilization of old-age care. Part of the contribution of this volume is the specification and estimation of these models. The following section gives a brief review of the theory and previous results we have relied on in this work.

3. Theory and previous empirical results

3.1. Health

Health status is one of the most important indicators of individual well being and population welfare. As such, it is also a target for public policy-making. Health status is a major determinate behind many decisions during the course of an individual's life. It affects decisions on education, labor market career, marriage and divorce, fertility among other things. It predicts to a large degree expenditures on health- and social services, but it is also reciprocally affected by social and health policies and programmes. Health status can be maintained or improved by health promotion and disease prevention programs, and the negative impact of disease reduced by effective health services.

Grossman's (1972) demand for health model is a theoretical framework for studies on individual behavior related to health. This dynamic life-cycle model has been extended theoretically in several ways and empirically estimated with data from a number of countries. For instance, the model has been extended to incorporate the influence of family members, social network, and employer interests, as well as various forms of uncertainty in health on the demand for health (Liljas, 1998; Jacobson, 2000; Bolin *et al.*, 2001, 2002a–c, 2003; Bolin and Lindgren, 2002).

The original SESIM model did not include health. Individual health was not predicted, nor were the consequences of good or bad health considered. The importance of health to the ageing processes made it obvious that we had to include health as a driving factor in SESIM and to model the effects of ill health on sickness absence, early retirement, the utilization of health care and old-age social care, and a number of other health-related decisions.

Some SESIM modules are more sensitive to the inclusion of health as a determinant than others. Some modules are also more relevant than others when it comes to simulating scenarios for an ageing population. Therefore, existing modules in SESIM were examined and evaluated from the perspective of how the inclusion of individual health might contribute most to the development of SESIM in these respects. Empirical studies suggested that the following already existing modules might be candidates: (1) the cohabitation module, (2) the divorce module, (3) the education module, (4) the income (and working time) module, (5) the early retirement due to health problems module, and (6) the sickness absenteeism module. For our purposes, it seemed most important to develop the sickness absenteeism and the early retirement due to health problems modules. In addition, obvious candidates for our purposes were health care and old-age social care; completely new modules were created for these two areas, important as they were for aged people and ageing populations. Another potentially important module, which we did not modify, is the mortality module. The number of deaths by age and gender is in SESIM aligned to the projections of Statistics Sweden and we have chosen to implement any changes in the death rates through the alignment procedure. There is though one exception. We explicitly model the excess mortality among elderly with all-day surveillance (see Chapter 11).

These modifications of SESIM necessitate the addition of a new module, a health module. This new module (1) imputes a health measure into the database that is used by SESIM and (2) updates the health measure each year.

3.2. Sickness absence

Sickness absence is important, when studying ageing, for at least two reasons. First, there is a high probability that long spells of sickness absence lead to early retirement (disability pension), and second, sickness benefits lower than labor income will reduce disposable income and, if there are long spells of sickness, also reduce future pensions.

The original SESIM model simulated sickness absenteeism, without considering individual health. The theoretical and empirical reasons for including health as an explanatory variable in this module are obvious – general health affects the probability of being struck by illness, temporarily or permanently.

Though the labor economics literature has analyzed sickness absence as a labor supply problem over which the individual has at least some control, most empirical studies include a variable to control for the effects of differences in health status. Examples from the sickness absence literature include: Allen (1981), Leigh (1983), Barmby *et al.* (1991), Johansson and Palme (1996), Delgado and Knieser (1997), Primoff Vistness (1997), Barmby and Stephane (2000), Henrekson and Persson (2004), and

Broström *et al.* (2004). A general finding is that absence is negatively related to health status. The literature is less clear as to the significance of the size of benefits, in particular for long-term sickness, but some studies find both that the frequency of spells and their length increase with increasing benefits.

Data give us observations on the number of days reported sick in a year. Because a large share of the population has no days reported at all, we have chosen to work with a model, which handles the selection into sickness as a process separate from that which determines the duration of a sickness once having become sick.

3.3. Withdrawal from the labor market

Studies of retirement behavior may be grouped into two broad categories: studies using structural models and studies using reduced-form type of models. The former ones are based on the theory of labor supply and assume that a utility function is being maximized, subject to a budget constraint. The analysis of retirement is usually based on a life-cycle model in which the discounted stream of future utilities is maximized subject to a budget constraint including present and future income and consumption streams. In some of these approaches, the retirement decision is conditioned on previous work, while others permit joint decisions about work and retirement. Hansson-Brusewitz (1992) is an example of the latter approach, using Swedish data.

In the reduced-form approach, no assumption of utility maximization is usually made. Instead, a probability model is specified to explain transitions from work to non-work. (It is possible, though, that a reduced-form probability model is consistent with utility maximization.) Transition probabilities are assumed to depend on wage rates, pension benefits, wealth, age, sex, occupation, etc. Surveys of this literature can be found, for instance, in Hansson-Brusewitz (1992), Hurd (1992), Gustman and Juster (1996), and Hakola (2003).

Much attention has been given to the problem of explaining the decline in labor force participation and hours of work among older men (and, to a lesser extent, women). Economists have tried to ascribe a large share of this decline to the social security system. Hurd (1992), for instance, concluded: "In my view, these are solid reasons for thinking that social security has been responsible for a substantial part of the decline in participation" (p. 606), although he had to admit that "models based on standard theory of labor supply extended to a dynamic setting have found small effects" (p. 606). In a more recent evaluation, Anderson *et al.* (1999) found that at most about a quarter of the reduction in full-time work by US men in their early sixties can be explained by changes in pension plans and social security. Other factors must then have played a major role in explaining the decline in labor supply. To these factors might belong a general increase in wages and earnings (an income effect), an increase in private pensions and other assets, a perceived decrease in health status (perceived because objective measures of health rather indicate a general improvement), and changes in the taste for leisure (retirement). Survey data from the Swedish 1984–1998 panel surveys HUS[2] (Klevmarken and Olovsson, 1993; Flood *et al.*, 1997) show that about 50 percent of working men and women in the age bracket 50–64 would like to reduce their work effort partly or completely before normal retirement age. If anything, this share seems to have increased in the period investigated, and in particular so for women (Klevmarken, 1986; Sjöström, 2000).

For couples, retirement is a joint decision, and pension rules and other constraints imposed on one spouse will in general also influence the behavior of the other spouse. This interdependence partly comes from relatively strong preferences for joint leisure and partly from the fact that changes in the family budget set will influence both spouses. There are few studies, which have analyzed retirement within a household context. One example is Zweimüller *et al.* (1996) that survey the standard models of family labor supply and examine their predictions about retirement before such a model is applied to Austrian data. A bivariate probit model is estimated to analyze the effects of an increase in the minimum retirement age for women. They find a strong jointness in the behavior of the spouses but also an asymmetry in the response to a minimum retirement age. Men reacted more strongly to a change in the minimum retirement age of women than women reacted to that of men. If the minimum retirement age of women were increased, not only women but also men would work longer. Hernaes and Ström (2000) is another example, analyzing the effect of a decrease in the minimum retirement age in Norway. A similar problem is the effect of a change in the maximum (compulsory) retirement age. Such an analysis would have to consider the choice opportunity set for every sample individual and the corresponding economic reward. Pension rules will determine when an individual is eligible for a pension, if it is possible to take another job and still keep the pension, and the gross compensation rates. Taxes and benefits will then transform pensions and earnings into a net reward. Most economic models treat rules about a minimum and a maximum age as constraints on free choice, and predictions from these models are, hence, generated as adjustments toward an unconstrained optimum. Another hypothesis is that a common mandatory retirement age will work as a social norm to which people adjust.

---

[2] www.handels.gu.se/econ/econometerics/hus/husint.htm

In the choice between a structural- and a reduced-form approach, it has been argued that the structural approach is preferable if one wants to isolate the effects of changes in the budget set – like changes in the pension rules and in taxes – from those of preferences. In the reduced-form approach, the estimated parameters are believed to be a mixture of preferences and budget-set parameters. Changes in pension rules and in the tax system would then make the estimated reduced-form parameters unstable. However, in the structural approach, one conditions the analysis on a particular usually oversimplified structure, which might have a decisive influence on the results, and furthermore there is no guarantee for stability of the structural (preference) parameters. Structural approaches usually produce complex econometric models, which are difficult to handle empirically. If it is a serious disadvantage not to be able to separate all preference and budget-set parameters in the reduced form depends on the particular model and on the scientific problem at focus. Sometimes, the reduced form contains all the information needed.

In SESIM, as the model was developed at the Ministry of Finance, it was assumed that everyone retired at the age of 65 (or at another exogenously determined age) with the only exception of early retirement caused by disability. This assumption reflected that most labor-market contracts stipulated a mandatory retirement age of 65, but it missed the fact many employees retired before this age. In 2003, the mean retirement age in Sweden was 62.8 for females and 63.5 for males.[3] We have thus developed a behavioral model that explains early retirement taking various economic incentives into account (Chapter 6). We have also re-specified and re-estimated the previous model for disability pension. In particular, health status has been introduced to explain the incidence of disability pensions.

In simulating future retirement, and in particular an increase in the average retirement age, there is a methodological problem, which follows from the fact that retirement in Sweden to a large extent was determined by the rules of the occupational pension agreements that forced people to take retirement at a certain age, usually at the age of 65. Even if Parliament now has overruled the agreements and given everyone the right to continue work until the age of 67, there is very little empirical basis for a study of retirement after 65. We either have to base estimates of the propensity to retire on the behavior of those who have retired early (before 65), and extend those results beyond the age of 65, taking into account the differences in characteristics of the two groups, or we would have to work

---

[3] Source: Statistics Sweden (www.gis.scb.se). Table: Nyckeltal för EU-25 länder efter land, nyckeltal och tid.

with alternative assumptions about retirement behavior after 65, possibly guided by results from other countries.

3.4. Geographical mobility and tenure choice

It is useful to distinguish between regional migration and residential mobility. Although the former will always imply the latter, the reverse is not necessarily true.

The frequency of migration decreases with increasing age. Currently, mobility is very low at the age of 60. At the time of retirement, the frequency of long-distance migration increases slightly, probably a result of migration to secondary homes, to former home districts, and to the neighborhood of children. Short-distance migration increases among the very old, i.e., above the age of 80. Presumably, people move closer to children and kin and into nursing homes. Migration figures suggest that some parts of Sweden are more attractive than other parts to older migrants, for instance, Dalarna, Österlen, and Båstad (Öberg *et al.*, 1993). According to studies from other countries, where migration in connection with retirement is common, couples are more likely than singles to move to resorts. The migration to resorts is partly an effect of class, income, and wealth, but also a result of increased pleasure traveling that makes people aware of the attractiveness of resorts (Cribeir, 1987). There is thus also among Swedes an increasing population of elderly that lives at least part of the year in Mediterranean countries. We also find that former immigrants to Sweden return to their countries of origin after retirement. There are, however, few studies of the mobility of the elderly and we know relatively little about motives, incentives, and driving forces.

About 65 percent of retired couples live in detached houses, while single pensioners usually live in multi-family houses. Housing tenure also varies with age. The very old more frequently live in small apartments, while it is more common among those who have retired more recently to live in detached houses. There are at least two reasons why the very old live in small apartments. One is that many widows and widowers cannot afford a house or a large apartment, despite housing allowances for pensioners. Another reason is that those who are very old today belong to cohorts who could never afford and never got used to more spacious housing. Mobility to smaller and less expensive housing is lower among those who have their own house or live in a co-operative compared to those who rent (Borgegård, 1991; Lundin, 1991).

Ageing and deteriorating health will make it difficult for many elderly to manage their home and to take care of themselves. Several studies have shown that most people prefer to remain in their old home and neighborhood (Tinker, 1997). Depending on the support from children and kin, the organization of community care, the extent of needs for care, different forms of care and assistance are used in ordinary or special housing (Lundin and Turner, 1995). There are several forms of special housing for elderly in Sweden all of which provide 24 h surveillance: home for elderly (ålderdomshem), institutions for long-term sick (sjukhem), group housing for elderly (gruppboende), and other forms of housing. In 2004, 27 percent of those who were 85 or older lived in special housing, 9 percent of those aged 80–84, and for the whole age group 65 + the share was 7 percent.

A number of interesting issues are related to the mobility and housing of the elderly. Our project and our model focus on (a) the mechanisms that determine if and when elderly homeowners sell their home and move to a smaller home or a rented flat, (b) what determines the demand for special housing for the elderly, and (c) regional migration, in particular, migration to/from children and kin.

Both residential and geographical mobility have been modeled as a reaction to a gap between desired housing services and current services, see, for instance, Edin and Englund (1991) and Ermisch and Jenkins (1999). Desired services is a function of preferences, which may depend on age, the size and composition of the household, education, social background, income, and wealth, etc. Retirement as such might change desired services, because there is no longer any need to live close to a work place, but the accompanying decrease in incomes might be even more important. If a household member becomes ill, disabled, or dies, this will also change the preferences and the needs of the household. A change in desired services will, however, translate into a move, only if the gap between desired and current services is so large that it balances the cost of moving.

Primarily for practical reasons, residential mobility has sometimes been modeled in two steps. The first step captures the decision to move, and the second step determines the kind of dwelling conditional on the decision to move. In the literature, one, hence, finds probit- and logit-type models used in the first step. The second step could also be a model for discrete choice (tenure choice) or a regression-type model, if the target variable is the size or market value of the dwelling.

For our purposes, we had to formulate models, which are able to simulate residential mobility, including moves into special housing for elderly. We also model proximity to children and kin, because the availability of informal care influences the demand for publicly or privately provided institutional care. Unfortunately, data did not permit us to estimate the strength of this relation.

Proximity to children and kin depends on regional migration, which was one reason to include it in our model. Another reason was regional differences in taxes, benefits, and charges and in principle also in the supply of health care and social services. Depending on the characteristics of a household and its members, changes in household composition and on regional attributes, the household is assumed to take decisions about moving to another region as well as about the region of destination. Multinomial models have been estimated to capture this kind of behavior.

3.5. Incomes and wealth of the elderly

Modeling the income- and wealth processes is an important part of the micro-simulation project for several reasons. First, income and wealth are the best available indicators of individual or household standard of living. For this reason, we are interested in studying the distribution of income and wealth for the retired population. Our focus is on the comparison with the standard of living of the working population and on the incidence of poverty. Second, personal wealth, pensions, and incomes from work are important determinants of decisions to retire. Third, there is also an issue about elderly people having the means to pay for the health- and social services that they will need or demand, regardless of whether these services will be provided by private or public producers. Fourth, real estate including condominiums makes up a large share of the assets of most households, but this kind of asset is rather illiquid and cannot be used for other consumption purposes, unless the house is sold or the mortgage is increased. Thus, it is of great scientific interest and political relevance to analyze if and when retirees increase their liquidity by selling their houses or increasing their mortgages in order to help finance consumption. There is a new and increasing market for reversed mortgages.

The income streams of the elderly have three major components: pensions, incomes of capital, and earnings. Palme and Svensson (1997) showed that the relative importance of these income sources in Sweden depends on the age of the household head. On average public pensions contribute by 60–75 percent, occupational pensions about 10 percent, private pension policies just a few percent, and capital income 10–15 percent. Other transfers and earnings make the remaining few percentages. In Sweden, pensions are determined by previous earnings history, pension rules, and if the retiree has saved in any private pension policy. In modeling the earnings history and the pension rules, we have to a large extent relied on current developments of the SESIM project in the Swedish Ministry of Finance. When it comes to income of capital, including interests, dividends, and any realized capital gains (losses), we have supplemented SESIM with new models (Chapter 8). There are new models of financial assets, debts, and models that simulate sales and purchases of new homes. Thus, in order to model the flow of capital income, we start from observed stocks of assets in the base year 1999 and then model any changes as the household ages. In the simulations, young people are assumed to start out with no assets, while wealth is transferred from old to new households formed by separation, death, and marriage according to rules explained in Chapter 9.

There is a large literature, covering both theoretical and empirical studies on wealth accumulation and the distribution of wealth. Much work has focused on the explanatory power of the life-cycle hypothesis, which suggests that people accumulate before retirement and dis-save after retirement. Empirical results have not always confirmed this age-wealth pattern, but suggested the influence of complementary hypotheses, such as hedging for uncertainty about the length of life itself and about the costs for health care at the end of life, and the desire to bequeath to one's heirs. Using previous results, we argue that life-cycle savings have been rather weak in Sweden while much of this kind of saving has been done in collective forms. The private wealth of Swedish households is relatively small in an international comparison, but the share of financial assets is large as is the debt ratio. In estimating new models of wealth accumulation we do not try to discriminate between these hypotheses mentioned above but estimate models that replicate changes in wealth as people age using panel data of wealth. We focus on a few major aggregates of assets: financial assets, private pension accounts, own homes, other real estate, and debts (Chapter 9).

3.6. Utilization of health- and social care

Elderly generally consume more health care than younger age groups. This fact is particularly emphasized when it comes to inpatient care, i.e., hospital care that requires at least one night's stay in a hospital bed. Patients aged 65 and above account for 45 percent of all hospital stays in Sweden. Thus, a large share of hospital resources goes to the elderly. Inpatient care is also expensive, and it accounts for almost 50 percent of total health-care expenditures in Sweden (nursing homes not included). There are large variations in inpatient utilization even among the elderly, though. Thus, many elderly do not use any inpatient care at all during a year. For these reasons, we have chosen to develop a module, which explains the probability of becoming hospitalized and the number of days in hospital, if hospitalized (Chapter 10).

Empirical studies on the utilization of inpatient care have been done for a number of reasons (Cameron *et al.*, 1988; Nolan, 1993; Gerdtham, 1997; Holly *et al.*, 1998; Harmon and Nolan, 2001; Gravelle *et al.*, 2003; Iversen and Kopperud, 2003; Lindström *et al.*, 2003; Höfter, 2006). Results on the determinants of inpatient-care utilization then come more or less as a by-product to the main objective of the study. There is evidence that ill health is a strong positive (and the most important) determinant. Positive effects are also reported for age, women, and being married, while negative associations have been reported for income, education, and living single.

Research concerning the availability of social networks and their role for providing informal care is still in its infancy despite its importance. About two-thirds of the total number of hours of care that elderly people receive in Sweden is provided by spouse, children, other kin, or by neighbors and friends (Johansson, 1991). The propensity to provide informal care does not seem to have changed over time, and there is no evidence that formal care tends to crowd out informal care as long as the elderly person stays in his or her own home (Daatland, 1990). Extensive burden of care − especially in relation to dementia − forces transfer to institutional care (Poulshock and Deimling, 1984). Swedish municipalities provide both help to elderly in their own homes and, when there is a need for all-day surveillance, special housing. Using a multinomial model, we model the "choice" of care mode as a function of ADL score, age, and marital status. We also model the excess death risk of elderly with care (Chapter 11).

4. A dynamic micro-simulation model

SESIM is a dynamic micro-simulation model that ages the Swedish population using demographic models of fertility, household formation, and death. It is possible to align the demographic changes simulated by the model to the official forecasts of Statistics Sweden. The statistical basis of the model is the large longitudinal database of individual register data LINDA.[4] All simulations start from the 1999 wave of LINDA which in our version of the initializing data set has about 112 000 individuals and 59 000 households. In addition to demographics, the basic version of SESIM at the Ministry of Finance includes models, which simulate schooling, labor force participation, earnings, other incomes, and taxes. In particular, it includes all essential parts of the income tax and benefit codes. For a more detailed description, see Chapter 3.

It is a great advantage to estimate behavioral models from the same data that constitutes the basis of the simulation model. Panel data from LINDA have thus been used whenever possible to estimate new models added to SESIM. However, even this rich data set has limitations and in a few cases we had to go to other sources, both sample surveys, and register data, see Chapter 3.

It is obvious that many of the issues discussed above in this chapter are closely connected in the sense that a policy change in one part of the system will have repercussions in other parts. For instance, new incentives to postpone retirement will not only change people's retirement behavior and their income streams. New incentives may also influence their health capital, their demand for housing, and their demand for health- and social care. These interrelated mechanisms are very difficult to capture without a micro-simulation approach.

A benchmark scenario was created by using the model as estimated and with "average" assumptions about changes in exogenous indicators.

---

[4] http://www.scb.se/templates/Product____34427.asp

Its properties are explained at the end of Chapter 3. This benchmark scenario has been used in all empirically oriented chapters of this book to evaluate each sub-model and explain how the simulation model works. In chapter 12, a number of alternative scenarios have been compared to the base scenario to investigate the sensitivity of the model to alternative assumptions and to evaluate the consequences of alternative policy measures.

In summary, this volume provides:

- an analysis of the behavior of the elderly in our chosen focus areas;
- a formalization of these results in a simulation model;
- the results from policy-relevant simulation experiments, assessing the impact of alternative health scenarios, pension rules, and growth assumptions on the market work, income, and wealth of the elderly, on their mobility in the housing market, and on their utilization of health- and social care; and
- the experience from building and using a large-scale micro-simulation model.

References

Anderson, P.M., A.L. Gustman and T.L. Steinmeier (1999), "Trends in male labor force participation and retirement: some evidence on the role of pensions and social security in the 1970s and 1980s", *Journal of Labor Economics*, Vol. 17, pp. 757–783.

Allen, S.G. (1981), "An empirical model of work attendance", *Review of Economics and Statistics*, Vol. 60, pp. 77–87.

Barmby, T. and G. Stephane (2000), "Worker absenteeism: why firm size may matter", *Manchester School*, Vol. 68, pp. 568–577.

Barmby, T.A., C.D. Orme and J.G. Treble (1991), "Worker absenteeism: an analysis using microdata", *Economic Journal*, Vol. 101, pp. 214–229.

Bengtsson, T. and K. Scott (2005), "Varför åldras Sverige befolkning? Vad kan vi och vad kan vi inte göra åt det?", *Sociologisk Forskning*, Vol. 3.

Bolin, K., L. Jacobson and B. Lindgren (2001), "The family as the health producer – when spouses are Nash-bargainers", *Journal of Health Economics*, Vol. 20, pp. 349–362.

Bolin, K., L. Jacobson and B. Lindgren (2002a), "Employer investments in employee health. Implications for the family as health producer", *Journal of Health Economics*, Vol. 21, pp. 563–583.

Bolin, K., L. Jacobson and B. Lindgren (2002b), "The demand for health and health investments in Sweden 1980/81, 1990/91 and 1996/97", pp. 93–112 in: B. Lindgren, editor, *Individual Decisions for Health*, London: Routledge.

Bolin, K., L. Jacobson and B. Lindgren (2002c), "The family as the health producer – when spouses act strategically", *Journal of Health Economics*, Vol. 21, pp. 475–495.

Bolin, K. and B. Lindgren (2002), "Asthma and allergy – the significance of chronic conditions for individual health behaviour", *Allergy*, Vol. 57, pp. 115–122.

Bolin, K., B. Lindgren, M. Lindström and P. Nystedt (2003), "Investments in social capital – implications of social interaction for the production of health", *Social Science and Medicine*, Vol. 56, pp. 2379–2390.

Borgegård, L.E. (1991), "Äldreboende i Västerås. Sammanfattning av ett forskningsprojekt", *Research Report SB:35*, Statens Institut för Byggnadsforskning, Gävle.

Broström, G., P. Johansson and M. Palme (2004), "Economic incentives and gender differences in work", *Swedish Economic Policy Review*, Vol. 11, pp. 33–61.

Burström, K., M. Johannesson and F. Diderichsen (2003), "The value of the change in health in Sweden 1980/81 to 1996/97", *Health Economics*, Vol. 12, pp. 637–654.

Cameron, A.C., P.K. Trivedi, F. Milne and J. Piggott (1988), "A microeconometric model of the demand for health care and health insurance in Australia", *Review of Economic Studies*, Vol. LV, pp. 85–106.

Cribeir, F. (1987), "Retiring to the seaside: a housing perspective", *Housing Studies*, Vol. 2, pp. 42–56.

Crimmins, E.M., Y. Saito and S.L. Reynolds (1997), "Further evidence on recent trends in the prevalence and incidence of disability among older Americans from two sources: the LSOA and the NHIS", *Journal of Gerontology: Social Sciences*, Vol. 52B, pp. S59–S71.

Daatland, S.O. (1990), "What are families for? On family solidarity and preference for help", *Ageing and Society*, Vol. 10, pp. 1–15.

Deeg, D.J.H., R.J. van Zonneveld, P.J. van der Maas and J.D.F. Habbema (1989), "Medical and social predictors of longevity in the elderly: total predictive value and interdependence", *Social Science and Medicine*, Vol. 29, pp. 1271–1280.

Delgado, M.A. and T.J. Knieser (1997), "Count data models with variance of unknown form: an application to a hedonic model of worker absenteeism", *Review of Economics and Statistics*, Vol. 79, pp. 41–49.

Edin, P.A. and P. Englund (1991), "Moving cost and housing demand: are recent owners really in equilibrium?", *Journal of Public Economics*, Vol. 44, pp. 299–320.

Ermisch, J.F. and S.P. Jenkins (1999), "Retirement and housing adjustment in later life: evidence from the British Household Panel Survey", *Labour Economics*, Vol. 6, pp. 311–333.

Eurostat. http://epp.eurostat.ec.europa.eu

Flood, L., N.A. Klevmarken and P. Olovsson (1997), *Household Market and Nonmarket Activities*, Vol. III–VI, Uppsala: Department of Economics, Uppsala University.

Gerdtham, U.G. (1997), "Equity in health care utilization: further tests based on hurdle models and Swedish micro data", *Health Economics*, Vol. 6, pp. 303–319.

Gravelle, H., M. Sutton, S. Morris, F. Windmeijer, A. Leyland, C. Dibben and M. Muirhead (2003), "Modelling supply and demand influences on the use of health care: implications for deriving a needs-based capitation formula", *Health Economics*, Vol. 12, pp. 985–1004.

Grossman, M. (1972), "On the concept of health capital and the demand for health", *Journal of Political Economy*, Vol. 890, pp. 223–255.

Guralnik, J.M. and G.A. Kaplan (1989), "Predictors of healthy ageing: prospective evidence from the Alameda County Study", *American Journal of Public Health*, Vol. 79, pp. 703–708.

Gustman, A.L. and F.T. Juster (1996), "Income and wealth of older American households: modeling issues for public policy analysis", in: E. Hanushek and N.L. Maritato, editors, *Assessing Knowledge of Retirement Behaviour*, Washington, DC: National Academy Press.

Hakola, T. (2003), "Alternative approaches to model withdrawals from the labour market – a literature review", Working Paper 2003:4, Department of Economics, Uppsala University, Uppsala.

Hansson-Brusewitz, U. (1992), "Labour Supply of Elderly Men. Do Taxes and Pension Systems Matter?" PhD thesis, Department of Economics, Uppsala University, Uppsala.

Harmon, C. and B. Nolan (2001), "Health insurance and health services utilization in Ireland", *Health Economics*, Vol. 10, pp. 135–145.

Henrekson, M. and M. Persson (2004), "The effects on sick leave of changes in the sickness insurance system", *Journal of Labor Economics*, Vol. 22, pp. 87–113.

Hernaes, E. and S. Ström (2000), *Family labour supply when the husband is eligible for early retirement*, Oslo: Department of Economics, University of Oslo.

Höfter, R.H. (2006), "Private health insurance and utilization of health services in Chile", *Applied Economics*, Vol. 38, pp. 423–439.

Holly, A., L. Gardiol, G. Domenighetti and B. Bisig (1998), "An econometric model of health care utilization and health insurance in Switzerland", *European Economic Review*, Vol. 42, pp. 513–522.

Hurd, M.D. (1992), "Research on the elderly: economic status, retirement, and consumption and saving", *Journal of Economic Literature*, Vol. 28, pp. 565–637.

Iversen, T. and G.S. Kopperud (2003), "The impact of accessibility on the use of specialist health care in Norway", *Health Care Management Science*, Vol. 6, pp. 249–261.

Jacobson, L. (2000), "The family as the producer of health – an extension of the Grossman model", *Journal of Health Economics*, Vol. 19, pp. 611–637.

Johansson, L. (1991), "Caring for the next of kin. On informal care of the elderly in Sweden", PhD thesis, Department of Social Medicine, Uppsala University, Uppsala.

Johansson, P. and M. Palme (1996), "Do economic incentives affect work absence? Empirical evidence using Swedish micro data", *Journal of Public Economics*, Vol. 59, pp. 195–218.

Klevmarken, N.A. (1986), "Höj och sänk pensionsåldern", *Socialmedicinsk Tidskrift*, Vol. 6.

Klevmarken, N.A. and P. Olovsson (1993), *Household Market and Nonmarket Activities. Procedures and Codes 1984–1991*, Stockholm: Almquist & Wiksell International.

Lakdawalla, D., J. Bhattacharya and D. Goldman (2004), "Are the young becoming more disabled?", *Health Affairs*, Vol. 23, pp. 168–176.

Leigh, J.P. (1983), "Sex differences in absenteeism", *Industrial Relations Review*, Vol. 22, pp. 349–361.

Lenehan, A. (1996), "The macroeconomic effects of the postwar baby boom: evidence from Australia", *Journal of Macroeconomics*, Vol. 18, pp. 155–169.

Liljas, B. (1998), "The demand for health with uncertainty and insurance", *Journal of Health Economics*, Vol. 17, pp. 153–170.

Lindh, T. (2004), "Medium-term forecasts of potential GDP and inflation using age structure information", *Journal of Forecasting*, Vol. 23, pp. 19–49.

Lindh, T. and B. Malmberg (1998), "Age structure and inflation – a Wicksellian interpretation of the OECD data'", *Journal of Economic Behavior and Organization*, Vol. 36, pp. 19–37.

Lindh, T. and B. Malmberg. (2000a), 40-talisternas uttåg – en ESO-rapport om 2000-talets demografiska utmaningar. Ds 2000:13, Ministry of Finance, Stockholm.

Lindh, T. and B. Malmberg (2000b), "Can age structure forecast inflation trends?", *Journal of Economics and Business*, Vol. 52, pp. 31–49.

Lindström, K., S. Engström, C. Bengtsson and L. Borgquist (2003), "Determinants of hospitalisation rates: does primary health care play a role?", *Scandinavian Journal of Primary Health Care*, Vol. 21, pp. 15–20.

Lundin, L. (1991), "Movers and stayers on the housing market in the post-parental stage: the Swedish case", *Scandinavian Housing & Planning Research*, Vol. 8, pp. 19–24.

Lundin, L. and B. Turner (1995), "Housing frail elders in Sweden", in: J. Pynoos and P.S. Liebig, editors, *Housing Frail Elders: International Policies, Perspectives and Prospects*, Baltimore and London: The Johns Hopkins University Press.

Manton, K.G., L. Corder and E. Stallard (1997), "Chronic disability trends in elderly United States populations: 1982–1994", *Proceedings of the National Academy of Sciences (Medical Sciences)*, Vol. 94, pp. 2593–2598.

Maxson, P.J., C. Hancock Gold and S. Berg (1997), "Characteristics of long-surviving men: results from a nine-year longitudinal study", *Ageing Clinical and Experimental Research*, Vol. 9, pp. 214–220.

McMillan, H.M. and J.B. Baesel (1990), "The macroeconomic impact of the baby boom generation", *Journal of Macroeconomics*, Vol. 12, pp. 167–195.

Nolan, B. (1993), "Economic incentives, health status and health services utilisation", *Journal of Health Economics*, Vol. 12, pp. 151–169.

Öberg, S., S. Scheele and G. Sundström (1993), "Migration among elderly, the Stockholm case", *Espace Population Societies*, Vol. 3, pp. 503–514.

Palme, M. and I. Svensson (1997), "Social security, occupational pensions and retirement in Sweden", NBER Working Paper 6137, National Bureau of Economic Research, Cambridge, MA.

Poulshock, S.W. and G.T. Deimling (1984), "Families caring for elders in residence: issues in the measurement of burden", *Journal of Gerontology*, Vol. 39, pp. 230–239.

Primoff Vistness, J. (1997), "Gender differences in days lost from work due to illness", *Industrial and Labor Relations Review*, Vol. 50, pp. 304–325.

Rowe, J.W. and R.L. Kahn (1987), "Human ageing: usual and successful", *Science*, Vol. 237, pp. 143–149.

Sjöström, M. (2000), *Mot en högre pensionsålder? D-essay*, Uppsala: Department of Economics, Uppsala University.

Sundberg, C.J. and E. Jansson (1998), "Regelbunden fysisk aktivitet hälsosamt för alla åldrar (Regular physical activity healthy for all ages)", *Läkartidningen*, Vol. 95, pp. 4062–4067.

Tinker, A. (1997), *Older People in Modern Society*, London and New York: Longman.

UN (1998), *World population prospects, the 1998 revision, volume II: sex and age.* The Population Division, Department of Economic and Social Affairs, United Nations Secretariat.

Waidman, T.A. and K.G. Manton, (1998), *International Evidence on Disability Trends Among the Elderly*, Urban Institute, Duke University, Mimeo.

Zweimüller, J., R. Winter-Ebmer and J. Falkinger (1996), "Retirement of spouses and the social security reform", *European Economic Review*, Vol. 40, pp. 449–472.

CHAPTER 2

Dynamic Microsimulation for Policy Analysis: Problems and Solutions

Anders Klevmarken*

1. What is microsimulation?

Microsimulation is a technique that uses the capacity of modern computers to make microunits act and interact in such a way that it is possible to aggregate to the level of interest. A microsimulation model can be seen as a set of rules, which operates on a sample of microunits such as individuals, households, and firms. Each microunit is defined and characterized by a set of properties (variables) and as the model is simulated these properties are updated for each and every microunit. The model might simply be a set of deterministic rules such as the income tax rules of a country operating on a sample of taxpayers, and used to compute the distribution of after-tax income, the aggregate income tax revenue, or other fiscal entities of interest. But the model could also include behavioral assumptions usually formulated as stochastic models. Examples are fertility models, models for household formation and dissolution, labor supply, and mobility.

In microsimulation modeling there is no need to make assumptions about the average economic man. Although unpractical, we can, in principle, model every individual in the population. It is no simple task to model the behavior of single consumers and firms, but it is an advantage to model the decisions of those who actually make them and not the make believe decisions of some aggregate. It stimulates the researcher to

---

* Corresponding author.

CONTRIBUTIONS TO ECONOMIC ANALYSIS
VOLUME 285   ISSN: 0573-8555
DOI:10.1016/S0573-5555(07)00002-8

pay attention to the institutional circumstances that constrain the behavior of consumers and firms. It also, in a straightforward way, suggests what data should be collected and from whom. Similarly, in a microsimulation model it is possible to include the true policy parameters and the rules which govern their use, such as tax rates, eligibility rules, tax thresholds, etc. One is not confined to using average tax rates applied to everyone. This makes microsimulation especially useful for policy analysis.

The development of microsimulation can be traced to two different sources. One is Guy Orcutt's idea about mimicking natural experiments also in economics and his development of the behavioral dynamic microsimulation model DYNASIM (Orcutt, 1957; Orcut *et al.*, 1961, 1976) that later was further developed by Steven Caldwell into the CORSIM model (Caldwell, 1993, 1996). Another source is the increased interest among policy makers for distributional studies. Changes in the tax and benefit systems of many Western economies have developed a need for a tool that analyzes who will win and who will loose from changes in the tax and benefit systems. As a result many governments now have so-called tax-benefit models. Examples are the Danish LAW model, the UK model POLIMOD (Redmond *et al.*, 1996), STINMOD in Australia (Lambert *et al.*, 1994; Schofield and Polette, 1996), SWITCH in Ireland (Callan *et al.*, 1996), and FASIT[1] in Sweden. At the European level EUROMOD is an ambitious attempt to build a tax-benefit model for all of EU (Sutherland, 1996, 2001). These models usually do not include behavioral relations but only most details of the tax and benefit rules. These rules are then applied to a sample of individuals for which one knows all gross incomes and everything else needed to compute taxes and benefits. For every individual in the sample one is thus able to compute the sum of all (income) taxes due and the disposable income for each household. The output becomes, for instance, the distribution of disposable income. It is then possible to change the tax rates or anything else in the tax code and run the model once again and compare to the previous result. In this way one can analyze who will gain and who will loose from a tax change, and estimate the aggregate budget effects of tax and benefit changes. The simulation model will, however, only give the first-order effect of a tax change, because household composition, work hours, and incomes are assumed unchanged and not influenced by the taxes. This is both strength and weakness of the tax-benefit models. It is strength because it is easy to understand what the model does and no controversial assumptions are needed. There is also no difficult inference problem. All the analyst needs to do is to draw an inference from the random sample of taxpayers to the population of

---

[1] http://www.scb.se/befovalfard/inkomster/iof/ioffasit.asp

taxpayers, which is something we know from sampling theory.[2] The weakness is of course that we do not know the relative size of any adjustments of behavior to the tax and benefit changes. Many tax reforms aim at changing the behavior of taxpayers. The first-order effect might then become a bad approximation. As a result attempts have been made to enlarge the tax-benefit models with behavioral models to capture these adjustments. Duncan and Weeks (1997) gives an example of a tax-benefit model amended with a labor supply model. Additional examples can be found in Table 3 of Klevmarken (1997). In this way, the tax-benefit models approach Orcutt's DYNASIM and its successors.

Large-scale dynamic microsimulation models with behavioral adjustments typically include demographic models that move the population forward, models that simulate earnings and labor supply, and sometimes also models for geographical mobility, demand for housing, etc. Most models of this kind have been developed in academic environments and have rarely been used to advice governments on policy issues. Examples are the Swedish MICROHUS (Klevmarken and Olovsson, 1996; Klevmarken, 2001, Appendix), the Dutch NEDYMAS (Nelissen, 1994), and the German Sfb3-MSM (Helberger, 1982; Galler and Wagner, 1986; Hain and Helberger, 1986; Galler, 1989, 1994). Among the few models of this kind that have been used for policy purposes are CORESIM and its Canadian sister model DYNACAN (Morrison, 1997), the Swedish Ministry of Finance model SESIM (Flood *et al.*, 2005 and www.sesim.org), and the microsimulation model used by the Swedish National Insurance Board (RFV) to simulate the future of the Swedish public pension system. The latter model is probably one of the oldest policy-driven microsimulation models that are still in operation. It was developed in the beginning of the 1970s (Eriksen, 1973; Klevmarken, 1973).

Most of the models mentioned above are not very explicit and detailed about the path economic subjects follow to reach a decision. These models usually take the form of conditional distributions or transition matrices that only describe the outcome of the decisions taken. There is a class of microsimulation models, sometimes called "agent-based models" that, for instance, model the search behavior of agents in the market and when a transaction takes place, rather than just the distribution of transactions. The data requirements for these models are even more demanding than those of more conventional microsimulation models and as a result there are rather few models of this kind and they are experimental in character, see for instance, Eliasson (1996).

---

[2] However, there is sometimes a problem when the sampling frame does not apply to the current year target population. If the sample used was drawn a few years ago it is not obvious how one can use it for an inference to the current population.

A number of conference volumes give good surveys of the microsimulation territory, for instance Orcutt *et al.* (1986), Harding (1996), Gupta and Kapur (2000), and Mitton *et al.* (2000).

2. Modeling for microsimulation

Most microsimulation models are built for policy analysis. One can see a microsimulation model as a laboratory in which it is possible to evaluate alternative policies in a constant environment, see for instance Rake (2000) who used a common microsimulation model to compare the properties of the pension systems of France, Germany, and the UK.[3] This particular focus of microsimulation raises a number of issues related to model building.

First, as already mentioned microsimulation models can relatively easily accommodate real life policy parameters when, for instance, tax, eligibility, and benefit rules are programmed into a model. There is no need to apply average tax rates to aggregates of individuals.

Tax rules and rules that determine who is eligible for various benefits are usually highly non-linear and sometimes have discontinuous jumps. Microsimulation models have the advantage of relatively easily accommodating such functional forms. One is thus not confined to functions with smooth properties. Sometimes we have policy problems, which require that these discontinuities are modeled at an individual level where an aggregate approach is impossible. For instance, in the Swedish ATP pension system pensions were based on the 15 best years of earnings and studies of the properties of this pension system required simulations of individual earnings profiles to determine the 15 best years. Another example is a study of the cost for old age care in the United Kingdom, see Hancock (2000). In this case the liability for charges was related to income and wealth in a complicated non-linear way.

Some policy issues are related to the behavior of relatively small and sometimes extreme groups of the population. This is, for instance, the case when we analyze poverty or study how a new tax will work on various subgroups of the population. The models needed in these situations are models that simulate the whole distribution of outcomes well. It is not sufficient to simulate means or conditional means but we also have to

---

[3] Some authors have extended the applicability of a microsimulation model even further. Caldwell and Morrison (2000, p. 216) suggest that "Just as simulation in astronomy are used to 'observe' processes which are difficult or impossible to observe with other methods ..., so microsimulation can be used to 'observe' processes and outcomes for which no respectable data exist from other sources." This idea appears analogous to that of estimating the cells of a contingency table just knowing the marginal distributions and using minimal assumptions about the joint distribution.

replicate the tails of the distributions. This focus has obvious implications for model building: heterogeneity in behavior must be reflected in the model structure and the properties of residual variation must be carefully considered. But it also has implications for estimation and validation. Criterions for estimation and validation should agree with the general purpose of microsimulation and not just aim at estimating conditional means (see below).

In building microsimulation models we are thus primarily interested in models that simulate well while the interpretation of model parameters are of secondary interest. Good predictors or simulators use all available information at the time the simulation is done. Suppose, for instance, that we are interested in simulating a variable y_{ti}, $t = 1, 2, 3,...$ for every individual $i = 1,...n$. Assume also that we know y_{0i} (and possibly also a longer history) for every individual. We will then need a model structure that uses the information y_{0i} to simulate the future of each individual. Economic models are not always derived on this form. It is often the case that these models have been adapted to cross-sectional applications and implicitly assume that a new decision is taken at every new time point without being influenced by past decisions. Such models are not very useful in dynamic microsimulation. They tend to introduce too much mobility and too quickly decaying autocorrelations. Consider for instance a labor supply model. In a dynamic microsimulation context labor supply should not only be a function of the wage rate, non-labor income, and the income tax system but also of the current and possibly past labor supply, episodes of non-work, etc. Most people who have a job do not change their hours very much from one year to another.

Similarly, simulated tenure choice should depend on current tenure choice and possibly also on when the family moved into their current house or apartment. A family which has recently moved into a new house has a low probability to move again. From a theoretical point of view it would seem quite natural that decisions depend on the current situation of the decision maker. One could, for instance, think of habits, cost associated with a change or a move, and of decisions about durables covering more than one period.

Dynamic microsimulation models thus often take the form of conditional distributions, distributions that are conditioned on past history, and recent changes in key variables that influence a new decision.[4]

---

[4] The simulation context puts constraints on the choice of model. For instance, in studying the evolution of variables such as fertility, income, and wealth, models which assume specific period or birth cohort effects are sometimes used. Circumstances which as associated with a particular year or a particular birth cohort are assumed to influence the variable of interest. Models of this kind are not suitable for microsimulation because one would have to extrapolate exogenously the estimated period and birth cohort effects into the future.

Microsimulation models have sometimes been criticized because they do not have the character of structural relations but rather that of reduced forms. As a consequence, one has questioned the autonomy and stability of the model structure under policy changes. This is a discussion that goes back at least to Haavelmo's famous supplement to *Econometrica* (Haavelmo, 1944) in which he discussed the concepts of an autonomous model and an empirically stable model structure, a discussion that became revitalized through the Lucas' critique. With the microsimulation focus on policy evaluation this is an important issue. If the model structure is not autonomous to policy changes (within ranges of interest) it is not possible to use the model for this purpose. It is, however, not easy to know if a model is sufficiently stable to permit the analysis of a certain change in policy.

Consider the following example. Frequently we need to model the presence of a property or an event and if the individual has the property or experiences this event we have to simulate an intensity or an amount. For instance, we might like to simulate if an individual has a job or not and if he/she is working we also need the number of work hours. A common model is a two-equation selection model with a probit equation for the participation decision and a regression model capturing the number of hours. If there is correlation between the two equations they are usually estimated jointly or by the Heckit approach to capture the endogenous selection into the group of working individuals. The estimated-hours equation then applies unconditionally to the entire population. In a simulation context the two equations have to be simulated jointly. An alternative approach is to estimate the distribution of hours worked conditional on having a job. The model for the probability to get a job and the hours model can then be simulated sequentially. This second approach can be criticized because the properties of the conditional hours equation might depend on who is selected into having a job. Any policy change that influences employment may then also change the hours equation. On the other hand, only those who get or have a job have a choice of hours, while those who do not have a job might not even think about how many hours they would work had they had a job. An equally plausible model is thus to assume that it is the fact that an individual has a job that determines the decision about hours. This does not exclude that individuals choose different hours and that the composition of the group of employed will determine the total number of hours and even the dependence of hours on wage rates and non-labor incomes. To get a model that is robust to policy changes the factors that determine heterogeneity in the responses to wage rates and income changes would then have to be included in the hours equation.

It is certainly not sufficient for autonomy to have a model that is derived through some kind of optimization such as a utility maximization and includes the "deep" parameters of a utility function. Although many economists think of preferences as something stable, there is not much empirical evidence to support this notion. In particular, there are good reasons to think that preferences change as people age. There are very few if any economic fix points and a humble attitude toward the autonomy of economic models seems justified. In the end, it is an empirical issue to find out if a model structure is stable and not influenced by policy changes.

3. Data problems

Good data are needed for three different purposes: data that give individual start values of the simulations, data for estimation, and data for validation. In dynamic microsimulation one would ideally have a longitudinal data set that can serve all three purposes. This is rarely the case. In practice, the data set that gives the start values is usually a cross-sectional sample or at best a short panel that can also be used to estimate some of the relations needed in the microsimulation model. For this project we have been able to use the rich longitudinal register data of the LINDA database from Statistics Sweden. Start data were taken from the 1999 wave, but amended with information from other sources.[5] Quite frequently behavioral relations have to be estimated using other data sources than the start data set because the variables needed are not included (with the accompanying problems of differences in the definitions of units of analysis and the variables being used). The set of variables included in the data set that gives start values thus sets limits as to which variables one can use to explain behavior. Not only the target variables of the microsimulation analysis need to be simulated but also all explanatory variables, and they also have to be assigned start values. To some extent this problem can be circumvented. An example from our work on the simulation model SESIM can explain this. LINDA does not include any health data, but health status is an important variable both in its own right and to explain various processes related to aging such as retirement and the demand for health care and social care. There was thus a need to introduce a model that imputed health status for the base year and then simulated any changes in health status as people aged. This model was estimated from an external data source but recognizing that the variables driving the

---

[5] Although rich in coverage and usually of good quality, Swedish register data lack complete information on who lives in the same household. Unmarried cohabiting couples without common children are considered singles and adult children living with their parents are also considered independent single households. To get around this problem and obtain a useful household concept data from another non-register-based survey of Statistics Sweden were used to pair some of the singles in the 1999 wave of LINDA into new households, see Chapter 3.

health status model, such as age, gender, marital status, schooling, area of residence, and if born in Sweden, had to be included in the data set of start values.

Extending a microsimulation model with new submodels to simulate both target variables and non-target explanatory variables obviously introduces a lot of noise into the simulated distributions. There is a tradeoff between theory-driven modeling and the desire to avoid simulation errors introduced when data or theory are weak. Suppose theory suggests that the distribution of a variable y depends on another variable x, while it is difficult to formulate and estimate a good model for x because there is no good theory to explain x or because we do not have access to all the data needed to estimate such a model. Depending on the context it might then be better to simulate y unconditionally of x, or use a proxy for x if possible, than to use a poor model to simulate x. In evaluating these alternatives one again has to consider the possibility that a change in policy might change the unconditional distribution of y while the conditional distribution might be more stable (cf. above).

Most microsimulation models are fixed period models, i.e., the time period between events is fixed to, for instance, a year. The possibility of multiple changes in individual status in this time span is usually not accounted for. Dynamic models condition on the status attained in the previous period (and possibly also in earlier periods). To estimate such models one needs annual panel data. In building the SESIM model we encountered a problem in estimating the health status model mentioned above. The data we could use had a longer time span than a year. In this particular case, we had to use data with a lag of 8 years. Assuming that the true model has a lag of 1 year and that the parameters were known, then it would be possible to simulate health status paths for 8 years and compare to observed data. It is thus possible to estimate such a model from data with a lag of more than 1 year using simulation-based estimation (see Chapter 4 and Eklöf (2004) for a discussion).

Exploring micro data usually reveals observations that deviate from the behavior suggested by theory or common sense. There are almost always outliers and sometimes there are groups of outliers that are so numerous that it is hard to ignore them when modeling. For instance, to simulate the tax base for the tax on income from capital we needed a function that simulated interest paid on mortgages and loans. One might think that nobody would pay interest unless one has a loan and that it would be natural to model interest paid not in kronor but as a rate on the sum of all mortgages and loans. In this way we could also avoid the problem of indexing an amount by the CPI or another index. However, it turned out that some of these rates came out with missing values and some rates were unrealistically high. Our annual data included mortgages and loans at the end of a year and the sum of all interest paid during a year.

Closer inspection showed that 25% of the sample households had paid interest in a year without having any loan or mortgage at the end of the year and 10% had paid interest without having any loans or mortgages either in the beginning of the year or at the end. The probability of misreported data is very low, because they were register data originating from banks, insurance companies and brokers, and not self-reported data. A reasonable explanation is that some people take up a loan and repay it in the same calendar year and thus they had no loan in the beginning nor at the end of the year, but they had to pay interest. The unrealistically high estimated rates had a similar explanation. People had taken a loan or increased their mortgage in a year but repaid most of it before the end of the year. In these cases the liability both in the beginning of the year and at the end was small relative to the interest paid. Our solution in this particular case was to stick to the idea of an interest rate function but censor the data before the model was estimated and only use observations with liabilities of at least 1000 SEK (111 euro) at the end of the year. The convenience of this solution has the price that our simulations will underestimate the interest paid a little because households with no liabilities will in the simulations never pay interest, but the amounts paid by these households are after all rather small.

4. Macro chocks, feedback, and markets in microsimulation models

Most individual and household microsimulation models simulate the behavior of consumers and households but have no supply side and no market clearance mechanisms. Macro entities such as the CPI, interest rates, the increase in the average wage rate, and the unemployment rate are usually fed into the microsimulation model exogenously. This is a simple solution in already rather complex models, but there are at least two problems: First, the macro assumptions must be made internally consistent and consistent with the path of the household sector simulated by the model. Second, it is usually very difficult to have an opinion about the values of these macro indicators in the future. Most analysts thus assume constant rates possibly after a few years of variation close to the base year. This convention has the disadvantage of not exposing the microsimulation model to normal business cycle variations. A more realistic approach, which still makes the macro indicators exogenous to the microsimulation model, is to generate swings in the macro indicators mimicking business cycles by, for instance, a VAR model.

More ambitious attempts to merge a microsimulation model with a general equilibrium model can be found in the literature, but merging two so complex models into one model must still be seen as experimental (one example is Cameron and Ezzeddin, 2000). One can, however, think of situations in which a market feedback is of key importance for the microsimulation analysis. Returning to our experiences of the model SESIM, when we introduced geographical mobility into the model, we also had to consider its potential impact on house prices. Housing wealth is a major share of the wealth of Swedish households and the market values of houses and apartments show considerable variation across the country. While there is not much of a trend in the real house price index for the whole country, only cyclical swings, the prices in the major metropolitan areas have increased dramatically in the last decades. If the model would simulate continued migration to these areas house prices would most certainly increase even more and at the same time shift wealth from households living in urban areas to households in the major cities, but probably also cool off the migration process unless the building of new homes in these areas could accommodate the new migration. In this case, it would thus be in line with one purpose of SESIM – to simulate the future distribution of wealth for the elderly – to include the market, at least in the form of a price mechanism.[6] Until this is accomplished, we have to forward house prices exogenously.

There are thus a few macro indicators fed exogenously into SESIM. In our base scenario, we use observed values for the period 1999–2005 and assumed values thereafter. In this case, we have not introduced any assumptions about business cycles but built up our macro series around a steady increase in real wages of 2% and a general increase in prices also of 2% (for additional details see Chapters 3 and 12). In this scenario, we will thus be able to study the steady state properties of the model when it is unaffected by business cycles.

In its adjustment to a steady state, a dynamic microsimulation model can sometimes initially show a rather dramatic change in key variables. This can be a result of changes in exogenous macro variables. For instance, prices on the financial markets might show a high volatility and the few initially observed values might deviate much from the assumed long-term values. It can also be a result of the dynamic model structure, in particular, if it is such that the simulated path is sensitive to the start values. Another possible explanation is lack of coherence between the data used to estimate the model and the start data set. It is thus not always obvious how one should look upon the first few years of simulated values, do they give a realistic picture of the economy or is the adjustment phase primarily the result of data problems?

---

[6] A simple but useful solution to an analogous problem was recently suggested in Creedy and Kalb (2005).

5. Estimation

If the relations of a microsimulation model are estimated using large micro data sets, efficiency is of a less concern than consistency. But many economic variables have non-standard distributions. They are often heavily skewed and have a high kurtosis. Sometimes a variable transformation is helpful, but it is not always easy to find one. Data might also be censored from below or from above. Variables capturing assets and other wealth items sometimes show extreme outliers. OLS-based estimation is not such a good idea in these situations because the extreme tails will tend to dominate the estimates to the extent that the model might not simulate well even in the center of the distribution. In our work with SESIM, we have sometimes preferred to work with robust estimation methods (robust regression) that weight down the extreme tails and thus limit their influence. As a consequence residuals to the estimated relation must be simulated from the empirical distribution of the residuals from the robust regression. We have chosen to estimate the percentiles of this distribution and interpolate linearly between them. In the last percentile, one might have to deviate from a linear interpolation between the 99th percentile and the maximum value in order to avoid excessively many very large draws.

Most microsimulation models have a recursive or block recursive structure for the simple reason that it is not practical and technically feasible to simulate all variables jointly. A usual sequence might, for instance, start the simulation with demographics, and then continue with schooling, wage rates, labor force participation and hours of work, incomes, wealth, and finally taxes. All previously simulated variables may influence later simulated variables but not vice versa. If the system is recursive also in a statistical sense, the relations of each block can be estimated independently of the rest of the model. If it is not, the implied stochastic dependence must be accounted for.

The recursive model structure is something the model builder will have to accept for technical reasons and because of shortage of data, even if there are no strong theoretical reasons to think that this structure represents reality. In theory one might shorten the time unit of the model to make the recursive property more realistic (cf. the old discussion about interdependent systems versus recursive systems, Bentzel and Hansen, 1954; Bentzel, 1997), but in practice data will usually not allow it.

As pointed out by the Panel of Retirement Income Modeling of the U.S. National Research Council (Citro and Hanushek, 1997), one of the major problems in microsimulation work is the shortage of good micro data. Although the supply of micro data has increased a great deal in the last 20–30 years it is still hardly possible to find one data source or one sample, which will contribute all the information needed for a typical micro-simulation model. In fact many model builders have found it necessary to use guestimates of model parameters and then try to calibrate the model against known benchmarks. Calibration is nothing but an attempt to tune the unknown parameters such that the model is able to simulate reasonably well the distributions of key variables. In this respect there is a similarity between microsimulation modeling and general equilibrium modeling. Both rely too often on the calibration technique. Hansen and Heckman (1996) criticized this approach because they found too little emphasis on assessing the quality of the resulting estimates. In fact the properties of the estimates are usually unknown and *mutatis mutandis* the same is true for the simulated entities. The calibration techniques also tend to hide a more serious problem, namely that typically calibration involves only one year's data or a single average or total. Because this reliance on a single or just a few points of benchmark data they do not always identify a unique set of model parameter values.

However, even if all unknown parameters are estimated calibration is still used to make the model "stay on track." Policy analysts sometimes require simulations to replicate known benchmarks such as the age and gender distribution of the population, known unemployment rates, etc. In SESIM a number of demographic variables, such as the number of deaths, immigrants, emigrants, and the number of newborn children, are calibrated to agree with the official population forecasts of Statistics Sweden. Calibration to official statistics is also applied to the number of new graduates at various educational levels. Labor income is calibrated such that its rate of change agrees with the exogenously assumed rate of change. In a few cases the model is also calibrated to the expected outcome of a variable, i.e., the mean of a simulated variable is forced to agree with its expected value. This is done to reduce the Monte Carlo variability of the simulations. This applies, for instance, to the number of youths who leave their parent's home, the number of women who start cohabitation, and the inflow to and outflow from disability retirement.[7]

If simulated distributions and statistics deviate from observed distributions and statistics more than the random properties of the model allow, this is a clear indication that data reject either the particular set of estimates and/or the model structure as such. The model then needs re-specification and not alignment. However, if data do not reject the

---

[7] In SESIM, the calibration is achieved using one of three different approaches. Let $\hat{\pi}_i$ be the estimated probability of an event, and let u_i be a random draw from a standard uniform distribution. Assume that the calibration benchmark is T, i.e., the simulated process must result in T cases. Then in "uniform calibration" the T cases with the smallest differences $u_i - \hat{\pi}_i$ are selected, while in "logistic calibration" the T cases with the smallest differences $\log it(u_i) - \log it(\hat{\pi}_i)$ are selected, $\log it$ is the logistic function $\log (x/1-x)$. A third approach is just to rescale $\hat{\pi}_i$ to give the desired expected number of cases. In the latter case there is no reduction in simulation variability.

model but it still does not replicate benchmark distributions and statistics well enough alignment is an approach to increase the precision of the simulations. Alternatively one could adjust the parameter estimates so the model reproduces the benchmarks. One can thus see alignment as estimation subject to the constraints of satisfying the benchmarks. It is, however, not immediately obvious how the parameter estimates should be adjusted. In the case of a linear model and OLS estimation, it is a simple case of constrained estimation as demonstrated in Klevmarken (2002), and it is also possible to derive explicit expressions for the alignment factors if one prefers to adjust the simulated values rather than the parameters. This exercise demonstrated that efficient alignment is not equivalent to the proportional adjustment that is commonly used. It also showed that in general all variables will need alignment, not only those who are constrained to satisfy the benchmarks.

It is less obvious how alignment should be done in a non-linear model. Given that all parameter estimates before alignment are consistent estimates, one approach is to find new estimates that deviate as little as possible from the consistent estimates but make the model satisfy the benchmarks. Write the microsimulation model in the following form,

$$y_{it} = g(y_{i0}, \ldots, y_{it-1}, x_{i0}, \ldots, x_{it}; \theta); \tag{1}$$

where y_{it} is a vector of k endogenous variables for an individual i at time period t, x_{it} a vector of exogenous variables including any unobserved random variates, and θ a vector of p parameters. Let Y_T be the $k \times n$ matrix $\{y_{1T}, \ldots y_{iT}, \ldots, y_{nT}\}$ of simulated values for n individuals in a period T outside the sample period and write the benchmark constraints in the following form,

$$\overline{Y}_T = R(Y_T); \tag{2}$$

where $\overline{Y}_T$ is a matrix of benchmarks for period T with dimensions less than those of Y_T. R is a matrix function. Let the number of implied constraints be c. Typically $c < p$. For instance, if $\overline{Y}_T$ is a vector of totals, then $R(Y_T) = Y_T J(N/n)$ where J is a $n \times 1$ vector with unit elements and N the population size.[8] Alignment can now be achieved by minimizing the following Lagrange expression with respect to θ,[9]

$$(\theta - \hat{\theta})' V^{-1} (\theta - \hat{\theta}) + \lambda'(\overline{Y}_T - R(Y_T)); \tag{3}$$

where V is the covariance matrix of $\hat{\theta}$. To simplify the exposition let us reformulate the constraint as $A(\theta) = 0$, where A is a vector of c non-linear

---

[8] It is assumed that the sample was obtained with simple random sampling.

[9] The quadratic distance function is a natural choice, but alternatives are possible. In a different context, calibration estimators in survey sampling, Deville and Särndal (1992) gave examples of several useful distance functions.

functions. This is possible because Y is a function of θ through the function g of Eq. (1) and conditional on a given set of x vectors. The alignment criterion now becomes,

$$(\theta - \hat{\theta})' V^{-1}(\theta - \hat{\theta}) + \lambda' A(\theta); \tag{4}$$

The first-order conditions are,

$$\theta - \hat{\theta} = -\frac{1}{2} V \frac{\partial A'}{\partial \theta} \lambda; \tag{5}$$

We assume that the constraints are unique in the sense that rank $(\partial A / \partial \theta) = c$. Using a first-order Taylor expansion of the constraints $A(\theta)$ around $\hat{\theta}$ and inserting the first-order conditions (5) makes it possible to solve for λ,

$$\lambda = 2 \left[\frac{\partial A}{\partial \theta} V \frac{\partial A'}{\partial \theta} \right]^{-1} A(\hat{\theta}); \tag{6}$$

where $\partial A / \partial \theta$ is evaluated at $\hat{\theta}$. Substituting expression (6) into (5) gives the aligned parameter estimates,

$$\tilde{\theta} = \hat{\theta} - V \frac{\partial A'}{\partial \theta} \left[\frac{\partial A}{\partial \theta} V \frac{\partial A'}{\partial \theta} \right]^{-1} A(\hat{\theta}); \tag{7}$$

Given that $\hat{\theta}$ is a consistent estimator, θ satisfies the constraints and that $\partial A / \partial \theta |_\theta$ has full rank, it follows that $\tilde{\theta}$ is consistent too. In practice, the covariance matrix V is unknown and must be replaced by a consistent estimate. The aligned values of Y_T, say $\tilde{Y}_T$ are obtained if the aligned estimates $\tilde{\theta}$ are used in model (1) jointly with the same history of the lagged endogenous variables and same xs that gave the non-aligned simulated Y_T.[10] Due to the non-linearity of the model and the constraints it is not possible to obtain an explicit expression for the aligned Y, but the same general conclusions as in the linear case still hold.

Before the model is aligned the constraints should be tested. A test can be obtained from a comparison of the aligned and non-aligned estimators. To simplify the notation, reformulate Eq. (7) in the following form

$$\tilde{\theta} - \hat{\theta} = BA(\hat{\theta}); \tag{8}$$

---

[10] Note that this implies that the same realisations of all random variables have to be used. This follows from the assumption that it is the simulated values using $\hat{\theta}$, a single realisation of the model, that is aligned. Although this is what is most often done in practice, an alternative approach is to constrain the expected value of the simulated realizations to satisfy the constraint.

If the constraints hold, the covariance matrix of this difference becomes,

$$E(\tilde{\theta} - \hat{\theta})(\tilde{\theta} - \hat{\theta})' = BE[A(\hat{\theta})A(\hat{\theta})']B' = B\left[\frac{\partial A}{\partial \theta} V \frac{\partial A'}{\partial \theta}\right]B'$$

$$= V\frac{\partial A'}{\partial \theta}\left[\frac{\partial A}{\partial \theta} V \frac{\partial A'}{\partial \theta}\right]^{-1}\frac{\partial A}{\partial \theta}V; \tag{9}$$

A χ^2-test is obtained in the following way,

$$\chi_k^2 = (\tilde{\theta} - \hat{\theta})'\left[V\frac{\partial A'}{\partial \theta}\left[\frac{\partial A}{\partial \theta} V \frac{\partial A'}{\partial \theta}\right]^{-1}\frac{\partial A}{\partial \theta}V\right]^{-1}(\tilde{\theta} - \hat{\theta})$$

$$= A(\hat{\theta})'\left[\frac{\partial A}{\partial \theta} V \frac{\partial A'}{\partial \theta}\right]^{-1}\frac{\partial A}{\partial \theta}V\left[V\frac{\partial A'}{\partial \theta}\left[\frac{\partial A}{\partial \theta} V \frac{\partial A'}{\partial \theta}\right]^{-1}\frac{\partial A}{\partial \theta}V\right]^{-1} \tag{10}$$

$$\times V\frac{\partial A'}{\partial \theta}\left[\frac{\partial A}{\partial \theta} V \frac{\partial A'}{\partial \theta}\right]^{-1}A(\hat{\theta});$$

In practice, V and $\partial A/\partial \theta$ will have to be estimated using consistent estimates of θ.

If all parameters had been jointly estimated from a common data source an estimate of V had been available. In practice, subsets of the parameter vector have been estimated from different data sources and thus there is no estimate of the complete covariance matrix. The best one can do is to use the information available and form a block diagonal matrix, say $\hat{V}$. The resulting new aligned estimates will still be consistent if $\hat{V}$ tends in probability to a positive definite matrix, but a χ^2 distribution might not approximate the distribution of the corresponding test statistic well.

The whole approach builds on the first-order Taylor expansion of the constraints $A(\theta)$. If the model is highly non-linear a first-order approximation might not be good enough. An alternative approach then is to minimize the first term of Eq. (4) with numerical methods subject to the constraints. If there are too many constraints, in particular if the number of constraints exceeds the number of parameters, a set of parameters that satisfies the constraints might not exist. In this case, a solution is to reduce the number of constraints and, for instance, only align to marginal distributions. It might also be possible to make separate alignments for selected subsamples.

This approach was used to check the estimates of the imputation model for old age care. The start data set of SESIM does not include any information about old age care and we thus had to impute it. Using an external data source from a study of elderly aged 75+ and living in a parish of Stockholm, a multinomial logit model was estimated for the probability to have, respectively, public assistance in one's own home or to live in a dwelling/institution with professional help available all day and night (see Chapter 11). Because data came from such a small and rather special area and only applied to those who were at least 75 years old, while we wanted to use the model also for the age group 65–74, it was desirable to check the predictions from the estimated model against national estimates of old age care. Such estimates were obtained by age and gender from the relatively large survey HEK of Statistics Sweden.[11]

In this case, it turned out that the first-order Taylor approximation was not good enough for the multinomial logit model. Instead we have maximized the criterion function using numerical methods subject to the side constraint that the model will replicate the HINK frequencies.[12] In doing so with 36 constraints (6 age groups for each gender and for each combination of age group and gender, 3 possible outcomes: no help, help at home, and 24 h surveillance) and 12 parameters we encountered the problem that there were no parameter combination that satisfied the constraints. To avoid this problem the model was aligned for males and females separately but only to the totals of the three groups of care for the age group 65–74. For each gender there were thus only three constraints. Although the model was estimated for males and females jointly we in this way got separate estimates of the parameters for each gender. The original estimates are compared to the aligned estimates in Table 1 and the originally simulated and the aligned frequencies of care form are compared in Table 2.

In Klevmarken (2002) it was suggested that the simulated method of moments is a natural and convenient estimation method in the context of microsimulation, because the model is built as a simulator and it usually includes a complex structure non-linear in parameters as well as in variables, and it is thus difficult to estimate with more traditional methods. Certain kinds of alignment constraints can easily be accounted for in the method of simulated moments. Suppose one of the moment conditions is

$$E(y_t - E(g(x_t, \varepsilon_t, \theta_0))) = 0; \tag{11}$$

The empirical correspondence to the expression to the left of the equality sign is

$$\bar{y} - \frac{1}{n} \sum_{t=1}^{n} \tilde{k}(x_t, \varepsilon^s, \theta_0); \tag{12}$$

where $\tilde{k}$ is an unbiased simulator of $E(y)$. Suppose now that we know the finite sample mean $\bar{Y}$. How could we use this information? If we also knew the x_t values for all individuals in the finite sample, we could substitute $\bar{y}$ in Eq. (12) for $\bar{Y}$ and extend the summation in the second term of Eq. (12) to N, and thus get an empirical correspondence to Eq. (11) for the whole finite

---

[11] We could not use the HEK survey to estimate the model because HEK does not have ADL measures, which are good predictors of old age care.

[12] The GAUSS program CO was used.

Table 1. **Aligned and original estimates of a MNL model for social care**

Variable	Aligned (females)	Aligned (males)	Original ML-estimates
Help at home			
Age	0.2096	0.2127	0.119
If man	–	−1.6894	−0.749
ADL1	1.4968	1.6456	1
ADL2	2.6648	2.7901	2.12
ADL3	3.2562	3.3229	2.86
Intercept	−20.1854	−20.3627	−11.8
Special housing			
Age	0.1474	0.1610	0.171
If man	–	0.0029	−0.769
ADL1	−0.9949	−1.2447	0.684
ADL2	1.3713	1.1473	2.97
ADL3	4.7634	4.4460	6.5
Intercept	−14.8972	−15.9354	−18.8

Note: The comparison state is no help.

Table 2. **Aligned and originally simulated relative frequencies of social care (%)**

Form of care	Aligned (HINK)			Simulated without alignment
	Males	Females	All	All
No help	98.9	98.3	98.6	98.1
Help at home	0.1	0.6	0.4	1.9
Special housing	1.0	1.1	1.0	0.1

population. In practice, this is of course not possible. One only knows the x observations of the sample, but with known selection probabilities p_t they can be used to compute the following estimate,

$$\overline{Y} - \frac{1}{N}\sum_{t=1}^{n}\frac{1}{p_t}\tilde{k}(x_t, \varepsilon^s, \theta_0); \tag{13}$$

The covariance matrix of the resulting estimate $\hat{\theta}$ should now have a third component, which reflects the sampling from the finite population.

6. Model validation

An important part of any model building effort is testing and validation. Validation involves two major issues. First the choice of criterion and validation measure, and second the derivation of the stochastic properties of this measure taking all sources of uncertainty into account. The choice of criterion for validation is of course closely related to that for estimation. As already mentioned, we are not only interested in good mean predictions but also in good representations of cross-sectional distributions and of transitions between states. When events occur is also important in any dynamic microsimulation exercise. A microsimulation model is likely to have a number of simplifying assumptions about lack of correlation and independence, both between individuals and over time. For this reason one might expect more random noise in the simulations and faster decaying correlations compared to real data. In addition to model wide criteria one might thus be interested in criteria that focus on these particular properties. Work is needed to develop such measures with known properties.

For a model not to big and complex in structure it might be feasible to derive an analytic expression for the variance–covariance matrix of the simulations, which takes all sources of uncertainty into account: random sampling, estimation, and simulation errors. For an example see Pudney and Sutherland (1996). In general microsimulation models are so complex that analytical solutions are unlikely. Given the parameter estimates, the simulation uncertainty can be evaluated if simulations are replicated with new random number generator seeds for each replication. There is a tradeoff between the number of replications needed and the sample size. The bigger sample the fewer replications.

To evaluate the uncertainty that arises through the parameter estimates one approach is to approximate the distribution of the estimates with a multivariate normal distribution with mean vector and covariance matrix equal to that of the estimated parameters. By repeated draws from this normal distribution and new model simulations for each draw of parameter values, an estimate of the variability in the simulation due to uncertainty about the true parameter values can be obtained.

To avoid the normal approximation one might use sample re-use methods. For instance, by bootstrapping one can obtain a set of replicated estimates of the model parameters. Each replication can be used in one or more simulation runs, and the variance of these simulations will capture both the variability in parameter estimates and the variability due to simulation (model) errors. If the bootstrap samples are used not only to estimate the parameters but also as replicated bases (initial conditions) for the simulations, then one would also be able to capture the random sampling errors. In practice, this advice will become difficult to follow for large models. To re-estimate all relations using many data sets is likely to become burdensome. Depending on model structure this approach could, however, be applied to submodels or blocks of submodels.

Much of the total error in simulated values will come from the choice of a particular model structure. Sensitivity analysis is an approach to assess the importance of this source of error. As pointed out in Citro and Hanushek (1997, p. 155) "sensitivity analysis is a diagnostic tool for ascertaining which parts of an overall model could have the largest impact on results and therefore are the most important to scrutinize for potential errors that could be reduced or eliminated". If simple measures of the impact on key variables from marginal changes in parameters and exogenous entities could be computed they would potentially become very useful.

7. End remark

The size and complexity of a typical microsimulation model makes it hard to understand its properties intuitively. This is one reason why microsimulation has received a rather cool interest by the economics profession. Given the main tradition of working with small, stylized models, and the relative failure of the large macro models of the 1960s and 1970s many economists are now skeptical about the usefulness of large models. In order to change this, microsimulation modeling has to rely on good economic theory and use sound econometric inference methods, but economist also have to learn what scientists in other disciplines already know, namely how to examine the properties of large simulation models.

Contributing to the skeptics of the economics profession is also the view that the science of economics has not yet given us knowledge such that it is meaningful to build large microsimulation models for policy analysis and policy advice. For instance, in their assessment of the needs for data, research, and models the Panel of Retirement Income Modeling of the U.S. National Research Council concluded (Citro and Hanushek, 1997, p. 163):

> To respond to immediate policy needs, agencies should use limited, special-purpose models with the best available data and research findings to answer specific policy questions. Although such models may not provide very accurate estimates, the alternative of developing complex new individual-level microsimulation or employer models in advance of needed improvements in data and research knowledge has little prospect of producing better results and will likely represent, in the immediate future, a misuse of scarce resources.

This was a recommendation to government agencies as policy makers concerned with retirement behavior. It should not be interpreted as general recommendation against microsimulation. On the contrary they also suggested (p. 153):

> The relevant federal agencies should consider the development of a new integrated individual-level microsimulation model for retirement-income-related policy analysis as an important long-term goal, but construction of such a model would be premature until advances are made in data, research knowledge, and computational methods.

This evaluation is almost 10 years old. Do we take a different stand today? The supply of good data has certainly increased and the computing capacity has increased as well. Simulation is much faster today and simulation-based estimation is feasible. What about economic theory and our understanding of how society works?

References

Bentzel, R. (1997), "Ekonomporträttet: Herman Wold 1908–1992", *Ekonomisk Debatt*, Vol. 25(8), pp. 473–479.

Bentzel, R. and B. Hansen (1954), "On recursiveness and interdependency in economic models", *Review of Economic Studies*, Vol. 22, pp. s153–s168.

Caldwell, S. (1993), "Content, validation and uses of CORSIM 2.0, a dynamic microanalytic model of the United States", Paper presented at the IARIW conference on Micro-Simulation and Public Policy, Canberra, Australia.

Caldwell, S. (1996), "Health, wealth, pensions and lifepaths: the CORSIM dynamic microsimulation model (Chapter 22)", in: A. Harding, editor, *Microsimulation and Public Policy*, Amsterdam, North-Holland: Elsevier Science Publishers.

Caldwell, S. and R.J. Morrison (2000), "Validation of longitudinal dynamic microsimulation models: Experience with CORSIM and DYNACAN", in: L. Mitton, H. Sutherland and M. Weeks, editors, *Microsimulation in the New Millennium: Challenges and Innovations*, Chapter 9, Cambridge, UK: Cambridge University Press.

Callan, T., C. O'Donoghue and M. Wilson (1996), "Simulating welfare and income tax changes: the ESRI tax-benefit model", ESRI, Dublin.

Cameron, G. and R. Ezzeddin (2000), "Assessing the direct and indirect effects of social policy: integrating input–output and tax micro-simulation models at Statistics Canada", in: L. Mitton, H. Sutherland and M. Weeks, editors, *Microsimulation Modelling for Policy Analysis. Challenges and Innovations*, Cambridge, UK: Cambridge University Press.

Citro, C.F. and E.A. Hanushek (eds.) (1997), *Assessing Policies for Retirement Income. Needs for Data, Research, and Models*, Washington, DC: National Research Council, National Academy Press.

Creedy, J. and G. Kalb (2005), "Evaluating policy reforms in bahaviour tax microsimulation models", Paper presented at the 34th meeting with the Economic Society of Australia, September 26–28, Melbourne.

Deville, J.-C. and C.-E. Särndal (1992), "Calibration estimators in survey sampling", *Journal of the American Statistical Association*, Vol. 87(418), pp. 376–382.

Duncan, A. and M. Weeks (1997), "Behavioral tax microsimulation with finite hours choices", *European Economic Review*, Vol. 41, pp. 619–626.

Eklöf, M. (2004), "Estimation of a Dynamic Ordered Probit Model with Time Gaps Within Observations", Mimeo Department of Economics, Uppsala University.

Eliasson, G. (1996), "Endogenous economic growth through selection", in: A. Harding, editor, *Microsimulation and Public Policy*, Amsterdam: Elsevier Science Publishers.

Eriksen, T. (1973), *En prognosmodell för den allmänna tilläggspensioneringen*, Stockholm: Riksförsäkringsverket.

Flood, L., F. Jansson, Th. Pettersson, T. Pettersson, O. Sundberg and A. Westerberg (2005), "SESIM III – a Swedish dynamic micro simulation model", www.sesim.org

Galler, H. (1989), "Policy evaluation by microsimulation-the Frankfurt model", 21st General Conference of the International Association for Research in Income and Wealth, Lahnstein, August 20–26.

Galler, H. (1994), "Mikrosimulationsmodelle in der Forschungsstrategie des Sonderforschungsbereich 3", pp. 369–379 in: R. Hauser, N. Ott and G. Wagner, editors, *Mikroanalytischer Grundlagen der Gesellschaftspolitik*, Vol. 2, Berlin: Akademie Verlag.

Galler, H.P. and G. Wagner (1986), "The microsimulation model of the Sfb 3 for the analysis of economic and social policies", pp. 227–247 in: G.H. Orcutt, J. Merz and H. Quinke, editors, *Microanalytic Simulation Models to Support Social and Financial Policy*, Amsterdam: North-Holland.

Gupta, A. and V. Kapur (2000), *Microsimulation in Government Policy and Forecasting*, Contributions to Economic Analysis 247, Elsevier, ISBN 0-444-50174-6.

Haavelmo, T. (1944), "The probability approach in econometrics", *Econometrica*, Vol. 12(Suppl.), pp. 1–118.

Hain, W. and C. Helberger (1986), "Longitudinal microsimulation of life income", in: G.H. Orcutt, J. Merz and H. Quinke, editors, *Microanalytic Simulation Models to Support Social and Financial Policy*, Amsterdam: North-Holland.

Hancock, R. (2000), "Charging for care in later life: an exercise in dynamic microsimulation (Chapter 10)", in: L. Mitton, H. Sutherland and M. Weeks, editors, *Microsimulation Modelling for Policy Analysis*, Cambridge: Cambridge University Press.

Hansen, L.P. and J.J. Heckman (1996), "The empirical foundations of calibration", *Journal of Economic Perspectives*, Vol. 10(1), pp. 87–104.

Harding, A. (1996), *Microsimulation and Public Policy*, Amsterdam: North-Holland, Elsevier Science B.V.

Helberger, Chr. (1982), "Auswirkungen öffentlicher Bildungsausgaben in der BRD auf die Einkomensverteilung der Ausbildungsgeneration", *Gutachten im Auftrag der Transfer-Enquete-Kommission*, Kohlhammer, Stuttgart.

Klevmarken, N.A. (1973), "En ny modell för ATP-systemet", *Statistisk Tidskrift (Statistical Review)*, Vol. 5, pp. 403–443.

Klevmarken, N.A. (1997), "Behavioral modeling in micro simulation models. A survey", Working Paper 1997:31, Department of Economics, Uppsala University.

Klevmarken, N.A. (2001), "Microsimulation – a tool for economic analysis", Working Paper 2001:13, Department of Economics, Uppsala University.

Klevmarken, N.A. (2002), "Statistical inference in micro simulation models: incorporating external information", *Mathematics and Computers in Simulation*, Vol. 59(1–3), pp. 255–265.

Klevmarken, N.A. and P. Olovsson (1996), "Direct and behavioral effects of income tax changes – simulations with the Swedish model MICROHUS", in: A. Harding, editor, *Microsimulation and Public Policy*, Amsterdam: Elsevier Science Publishers.

Lambert, S., R. Percival, D. Schofield and S. Paul (1994), "An introduction to STINMOD: a static microsimulation model", NATSEM Technical Paper No 1, University of Canberra, Australia.

Mitton, L., H. Sutherland and M. Weeks (2000), *Microsimulation Modelling for Policy Analysis*, Cambridge: Cambridge University Press.

Morrison, R.J. (1997), "DYNACAN, the Canadian pension plan policy model: demographic and earnings components", Proceedings of the Microsimulation Section at the International Conference on Information Theory, Combinatorics, and Statistics, Portland, Maine, July 1997.

Nelissen, J.H.M. (1994), *Towards a payable pension system. Costs and redistributive impact of the current Dutch pension system and three alternatives*, The Netherlands: TISSER, Tilburg Institite for Social Security Research, Department of Social Security Studies.

Orcutt, G.H. (1957), "A new type of socio-economic system", *Review of Economics and Statistics*, Vol. 58, pp. 773–797.

Orcutt, G.H., S. Caldwell and R. Wertheimer (1976), *Policy Explorations Through Microanalytic Simulation*, Washington, DC: The Urban Institute.

Orcutt, G.H., M. Greenberger, J. Korbel and A. Rivlin (1961), *Microanalysis of Socioeconomic Systems: A Simulation Study*, New York: Harper and Row.

Orcutt, G.H., J. Merz and H. Quinke (eds.) (1986), *Micronalystic Simulation Models to Support Social and Financial Policy*, Amsterdam: Elsevier Science Publishers B.V.

Pudney, S. and H. Sutherland (1996), "Statistical reliability in microsimulation models with econometrically-estimated behavioural responses (Chapter 21)", in: A. Harding, editor, *Microsimulation and Public Policy*, Amsterdam: Elsevier Science Publishers.

Rake, K. (2000), "Can we do better comparative research using microsimulation models? Lessons from the micro analysis of pension systems", in: L. Mitton, H. Sutherland and M. Weeks, editors, *Microsimulation in the New Millennium. Challenges and Innovations*, Cambridge, UK: Cambridge University Press.

Redmond, G., H. Sutherland and M. Wilson (1996), "POLIMOD: an outline", 2nd edition, Microsimulation Unit MU/RN/19, DAE, University of Cambridge, Cambridge.

Schofield, D. and J. Polette (1996), "A comparison of data merging methodologies for extending a microsimulation model", NATSEM Technical Paper No 11, University of Canberra, Australia.

Sutherland, H. (1996), "EUROMOD: a European benfit-tax model", Microsimulation Unit MU/RN/20, DAE, University of Cambridge, Cambridge.

Sutherland, H. (2001), "EUROMOD: an integrated European benefit-tax model. Final report", EUROMOD Working Paper No. EM9/01, DAE University of Cambridge, Cambridge.

CHAPTER 3

SESIM: A Swedish Micro-Simulation Model

Lennart Flood*

1. Introduction

In 1997, SESIM was developed as a tool at the Swedish ministry of finance to evaluate the Swedish system to finance higher education. Part of that work was documented in Ericson and Hussénius (2000). We refer to this as version I of SESIM. Focus then shifted from education to pensions. SESIM was used to evaluate the financial sustainability of the new Swedish pension system. This new application implied that SESIM was developed into a general micro-simulation model (MSM) that can be used for a broad set of issues. We refer to this as the second version of SESIM and the documentation is presented in Flood (2003). The present version, SESIM III, maintains the focus on pensions but extends the analyses to include health issues, regional mobility, and wealth.

SESIM II has recently been used in several studies: Flood (2007) calculated the replacement rates of the Swedish pension system; Pettersson and Pettersson (2003, 2007) studied income redistribution over the life cycle; and Pettersson et al. (2006) analyzed inter-generational transfers.

2. The structure of SESIM

SESIM is a mainstream dynamic MSM in the sense that the variables (events) are updated in a sequence, and the time span of the updating processes is a year. The start year is 1999 and every individual included in

---

* Corresponding author.

CONTRIBUTIONS TO ECONOMIC ANALYSIS
VOLUME 285   ISSN: 0573-8555
DOI:10.1016/S0573-8555(07)00003-X

the initial sample of about 100 000 individuals goes through a large number of events, reflecting real life phenomena, like education, marriage, having children, working, retirement, etc. Every year individuals are assigned a status, reflecting their main occupation in that year. A status is related to a source of income, working gives earnings, retirement gives pensions, etc. The tax and benefit systems are applied to simulated incomes and after tax income is calculated. If the simulations are repeated for a long time period individual life-cycle incomes can be generated.

The sequential structure of SESIM is presented in Figure 1. The first part consists of a sequence of demographic modules (mortality, adoption, migration, household formation and dissolution, disability pension, and rehabilitation). There is also a new module that simulates regional mobility (cf. Chapter 7). Then comes a module for education (compulsory school, high school (gymnasium), municipal adult education (komvux), and university).

The next module deals with the labor market including the retirement decision. The date of retirement can be decided according to a retirement model, see Chapter 6 for details, but it is also possible to choose a specific age of retirement. The labor market module also includes models for sick leave (see Chapter 5) and unemployment, and a model that imputes labor market sector. A sector is required for the calculations of occupational pensions. In SESIM, we have implemented the rules for occupational pensions as well as the choice of labor market sector. We also allow for change of sector. The occupational pension is then adjusted in accordance to the rules of the new sector.

Having gone through the sequence this far, the next step is to simulate a status for each individual. There are nine different statuses. Each individual can only have one status in a year (the status "emigrated" is an exception). These statuses reflect the main occupation in a year. This is of course a simplification, because in reality an individual can have many occupations in a year. One can be a student in one part of the year and work the other part, or one can have several occupations at the same time. The list of statuses is

1. child (0–15 years old)
2. old age retired: individuals with income from old age pension
3. student: individuals who study at gymnasium, adult education, or university
4. disabled: individuals who have disability/sickness benefits
5. parental leave: women who give birth during the year
6. unemployed: individuals with income from unemployment insurance or from labor market training
7. miscellaneous
8. employed: individuals in market work
9. emigrated: individuals living abroad with Swedish pensions rights. Note, this classification is not unique since they can also have income from early or old age pensions.

Figure 1. *Structure of SESIM*

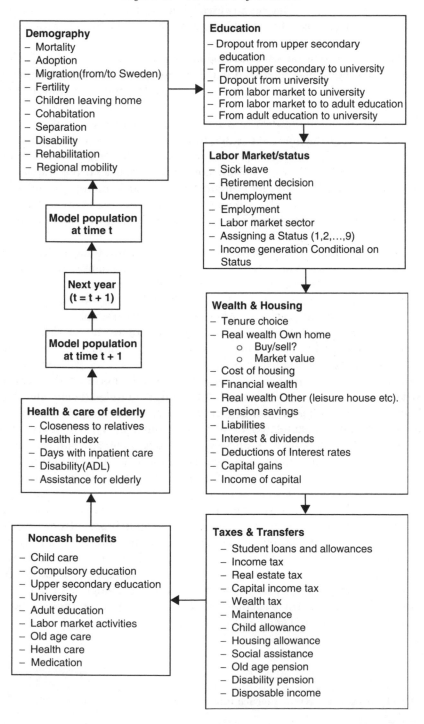

Status determines income. For employed (status 8) the earnings equation presented in Chapter 8 is used to determine income. Unemployed get unemployment benefits, disabled get disability benefits, etc., following the statutory rules.

After the income module, a module which simulates wealth, capital income, and housing is entered. A detailed description is given in Chapter 9. After the wealth/housing module a large module applies all relevant tax, transfer, and pension rules. For the old age pension system, the rules for public and occupational pensions have been implemented in all relevant details. After all incomes and taxes have been computed the household disposable income can be obtained. Next, a module for public consumption is entered.[1] We have, however, not updated and used this module in our study. Instead we have implemented a new health module. It simulates health status (Chapter 4), sickness absence from work (Chapter 5), inpatient care (Chapter 10) and the proximity of parents to their children, and social care (Chapter 11).

Obviously, an important characteristic of the SESIM model is the notion of full-time status. The model assumes that being employed, retired, student, etc., is full-time. This has implications for the income generation. For instance, income from work is calculated based on an estimated equation for full-time earnings. Alternatively a labor supply model could have been used in order to impute yearly hours of work and then yearly income could be obtained using a model for an hourly wage rate. The advantage of this alternative approach is that earnings for part-time work can be calculated. However, simplicity is the advantage of the present structure, which only considers full-time status. Once part-time status is allowed for this, it has to be implemented in a consistent way. For example, if an individual is simulated to work part-time, then there must be a complementary part-time status, say part-time pensioner or part-time student and obviously this would complicate the structure. However, there is one exception from the principle that income is generated conditional on status. Students have income from study benefits but also from earnings. Thus, even if the status is (full-time) student we allow for some additional earnings from part-time or temporary employment. Income from work is simulated using a so-called two-part model. First the probability of working is predicted and then conditional on working and earnings are calculated.

It is important for many purposes to get a good representation of the household composition. Many stochastic models use household information, and some benefit systems too. For instance, to compute social assistance, housing and child allowances, one needs to know who lives in a

---

[1] Details are discussed in Pettersson and Pettersson (2003).

household. In SESIM the model population lives in households. Like in reality the household composition can change. New households are formed and households split. In the base population households are real observed households (with some modifications). During the course of simulation household formations and dissolutions are simulated using the demographic models of SESIM.

An illustration of a SESIM-created life is given in Figure 2. Household size, income, and status are displayed each year for a woman. After having been classified as a child up to the age of 15, she studies between 16 and 24. There is a short interruption in her studies when she is working. At the age of 22 she moves from her parents, forms a new household and marries. At 24, she gives birth to her first child and stays on parental leave, but later she returns to work. Her second child is born when she is 32 years old. Two years later she gets the status "Miscellaneous," which in this case can be interpreted as being housewife. After that she returns to market work and stays in the market with a few interruptions until she retires at the age of 65. Her earnings profile is also displayed. There is an increasing trend, but a considerable variation. When she is a student and a "housewife" her income is quite low. After retirement her income is given by the pension rules, which explains the lack of volatility. When she is 43, her first child leaves the household and 10 years later also the second child leaves. Her husband dies when she is 90, 2 years before her.

During lifetime a large amount of information is generated for each individual in the model population. Totally about 300 variables are stored, in Figure 2 only three of them are displayed.

Figure 2.   A SESIM-created life path

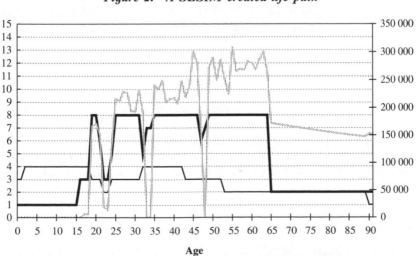

Age

━━ Status ━━ Household size ┈┈┈ Income (right hand axis)

A summary description of all statistical models included in SESIM is given in the Appendix.

3. Data sources

This section gives a brief description of the main data sources for estimation and construction of the model population. We also discuss some corrections or adjustments that have been made to this population.

3.1. LINDA: a panel database[2]

LINDA is the main source of information used in SESIM. This panel data set covers about 3.5 percent of the Swedish population. For year 1999 this implies that 308 000 individuals were randomly selected. For each of them all household members were added. In total the sample size became 786 000 individuals in 1999. This is the primary database of SESIM for the estimation of models as well as the construction of the model population.

The selected individuals are followed backwards and forwards and data from a number of registers are collected. Some information, for instance pension rights, can be traced back as long as to 1960. Selected individuals who disappear from the data by death or emigration are replaced by newly selected individuals in such a way that each cross section is a random sample from the Swedish population of the same year.

Note that the database is completely created from administrative registers. Thus, no interview is needed and therefore a major advantage is that there are no problems of attrition. The registers used cover income and wealth, earnings, pension rights, sickness and unemployment benefits, schooling, and census data.

The base population used in SESIM is formed by a random draw of 104 000 individuals from the 1999 LINDA. To this sample 8000 individuals have been added from a register for pension rights at the National Social Insurance Board. This additional sample includes individuals living outside Sweden, but with Swedish pension rights.

In the construction of the base population in SESIM two major adjustments have been made in order to obtain a model population consistent with the definitions used in SESIM. They are described below in Section 4.

---

[2] Longitudinal Individual Data for Sweden. For documentation see Edin and Fredriksson (2000).

3.2. Other data sources

In addition to LINDA a few data sources have been used for estimation or imputation. They are HINK/HEK, GEOSWEDE, the Kungsholmen study, and ULF. HINK/HEK[3] is a sample survey to which Statistics Sweden has administered telephone interviews and then merged the survey data with register information. In the interview it is possible to obtain the data needed to use a meaningful household definition for economic analysis. This is in contrast to LINDA, which essentially is limited to a household definition used for taxation purposes. Apart from being used in the creation of useful households in SESIM, HINK/HEK has also been used to estimate models of public consumption, housing area, and the cost of housing.

Models of regional mobility and tenure choice were based on GEOSWEDE, a research database created from a number of administrative registers covering the whole Swedish population (see Chapter 7). The health and care module is based on data from the Kungsholmen study, ULF, and HINK/HEK. The Kungsholmen study is a small study of old age care in a parish of Stockholm (see Chapter 11). The Survey of Living Conditions in Sweden (ULF) is a sample survey covering a number of welfare components including health status (see Chapters 4, 5, and 10).[4]

4. Initial adjustments

4.1. Adjustments to a meaningful household definition

To define a household in LINDA one uses information from the population registers (RTB) and the so-called inter-generational register. The latter register links parents with children. This implies that all individuals are assumed to live in the municipality where they are recorded according to the national tax registry, and that adults living together without being legally married or having common children are considered separate households. A comparison with the HINK/HEK surveys shows that there are two problems in LINDA. First, the number of youngsters between 18 and 29 who still live in their parents' household are over reported. Many children who have moved are still tax registered in their old household. Second, the number of cohabitants without children is underestimated, especially for young couples.

---

[3] The income distribution survey of Statistics Sweden, a yearly sample survey of about 30 000 individuals merged with administrative data.

[4] The expenditure survey of Statistics Sweden, HUT, have been used for calculation of indirect taxes in SESIM, but the corresponding modules have not been used in our study.

4.1.1. Older children living with parents

Figure 3, compares the share of young individuals, 18–29, living with their parents according to LINDA and HINK/HEK in 1999. The comparison confirms that the share of youngsters living with their parents is overestimated in LINDA. The difference is largest for males aged 21 years. The share from LINDA is 57 percent compared with only 42 percent in HINK/HEK. In order to correct for this a model for the probability to move from parents was estimated based on HINK/HEK data for those in the age bracket 18–29.[5] This model was used in the following way to impute in 1999 which kids had left the home of their parents. All individuals at risk were ranked according to the predicted probability of moving, and the individuals with highest probabilities were chosen such that the HINK/HEK frequencies were matched.

4.1.2. Cohabitation

In Figure 4 the share of married or cohabiting women in LINDA is compared by age with the shares in HINK/HEK. As expected, the largest difference is found among young individuals. For this reason, a correction is made only in the age group 18–29. When children move away from their parents, in SESIM they are classified as singles by default. This results in an even larger underestimation of non-single households, see Figure 5 which shows the share of married/cohabiting women after having corrected the move from parents.

In order to solve this problem, a model was estimated for the probability of being married/cohabiting in the age group 18–29 among women without children in /HINKHEK.[6] Based on the estimated model, the probability of being cohabiting/married was calculated for 18–29 years old females without children in LINDA. The individuals were ranked after the predicted probabilities. A number of women with highest probabilities were matched with single males 2 years older than the female and at the same level of education. The number of couples created in this way was chosen to coincide with the HINK/HEK frequencies.

---

[5] The probabilities are estimated by a logit regression. The explanatory variables are gender, age, square of age, born in Sweden (dummy), study allowance/1000, earnings/1000, highest education (dummys compulsory school and upper secondary school), interaction age, and education.

[6] The probabilities were estimated by a logit regression. The explanatory variables were gender, age, square of age, born in Sweden (dummy), study allowance/1000, earnings/1000, highest education (dummys compulsory school and upper secondary school), interaction age, and education.

Figure 3. **Share of youngsters living with their parents in LINDA and HEK**

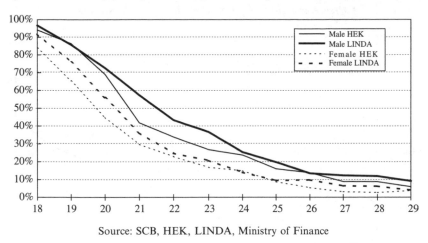

Source: SCB, HEK, LINDA, Ministry of Finance

Figure 4. **Comparison of married/cohabiting women in LINDA and HEK 1999**

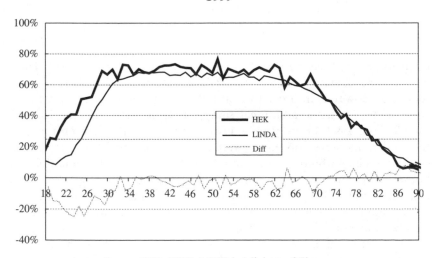

Source: SCB, HEK, LINDA, Ministry of Finance

4.2. Adding emigrants with pension rights

Individuals with Swedish pension rights will keep these entitlements regardless of country of residence, and after retirement the pension is paid out also if they live outside Sweden. Thus, in order not to underestimate the cost of pensions we must keep track of all individuals with pension rights.

Because LINDA does not include individuals living outside Sweden, another data source has been used. Information comes from a sample from

Figure 5. Share of married/cohabiting women in LINDA and HEK (after correction of youngsters living with parents)

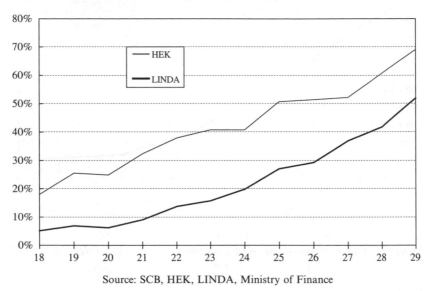

Source: SCB, HEK, LINDA, Ministry of Finance

the pension point database of the National Social Insurance Board. These data include all individuals with Swedish pension rights regardless of where they live. However, in order to merge these data some adjustments have been made. First, the additional sample is from 1995 and the LINDA sample from 1999. In order to compensate for this, the pension rights of the emigrants were moved forward 4 years. Second, the sample of emigrants has no household information. In order to overcome this, the household composition was imputed from HINK/HEK. Because many emigrants were born outside Sweden, the imputation of a household composition was based on those households in HEK for which at least one member was born outside Sweden.

After these adjustments the emigrants were merged with the base population. Note, however, that the emigrants are treated somewhat differently from other population members in the simulations. For instance, for these individuals no change in household composition is modeled. For most of our analysis in the project "The old baby-boomers" we have focused on the population resident in Sweden, while emigrants have been excluded.

5. SESIM: a stochastic simulation model

SESIM is a *stochastic simulation model*, which means that the statistical models include random components. In the simulation, a *Monte Carlo* technique is used to generate a stochastic process. Consider the typical case in SESIM, and in dynamic MSM, with a binary dependent variable. This variable then have a Bernoulli distribution, i.e., $Y_i \sim$ Bernoulli(π_i), where $Pr[Y_i = 1] = \pi_i$ and $Pr[Y_i = 0] = 1 - \pi_i$.

As an illustration, let $Y_i = 1$ denote that individual i is unemployed and $Y_i = 0$ that i is in work. π_i denotes the probability that the individual is unemployed in a year. This event is simulated by comparing π_i with a uniform random number. If $u_i < \pi_i$ the event is realized and individual i becomes unemployed.

By allowing π_i to be a function of individual or household attributes these attributes also determine the probability of unemployment. This is typically accomplished by a logit or probit regression. The logit model is given as $\pi_i = [1 + \exp(-X_i\beta)]^{-1}$, where X_i is a vector of individual or household characteristics (or any other characteristic relevant for explaining unemployment, i.e., rate of regional unemployment) and β a vector of parameters.

Due to the Monte Carlo simulation, the number of generated events in repeated simulation does not have to be the same.[7] Let T denote the total number of individuals in a population of size N that experience the simulated event, that is, $T = \sum_{i=1}^{N} Y_i$. If the individuals are simulated independently of each other, the expected number of events is $E(T) = \sum_{i=1}^{N} \pi_i$ and the variance Var$(T) = \sum_{i=1}^{N} \pi_i(1 - \pi_i)$. If N is large enough, and π_i not too close to zero or one, T is approximately normally distributed. Assume an event with a 10 percent probability (and for simplicity that all individuals face the same probability). For a population size of 10 000 individuals and a large number of repeated simulations, the number of individuals that experience the event is between 941 and 1059 in 95% of the replications.[8]

The Monte Carlo variation can be problematic in evaluating the results from an experiment. If, for instance, a change in a tax rate is evaluated, then due to the Monte Carlo variation, it is difficult to isolate the pure tax effect from the stochastic Monte Carlo effect. One approach could be to repeat the simulations a number of times and use the average result, since this reduces the effect of the stochastic simulation.

An alternative approach is to use methods that reduce the Monte Carlo variance. In SESIM, a method is used which is directly related to calibration. Calibration is a technique used in order to predict according to an a priori defined target. In the binary model this implies that the expected number of predicted events have to be adjusted in order to

---

[7] Given that the seed used for generating random numbers is changed in each simulation.

[8] If number of events is approximately normally distributed a 95% interval is defined as: $10\,000 \times 0.1 \pm 1.96\sqrt{0.1 \times 0.9 \times 10\,000}$.

coincide with a given target. This is accomplished by adjusting the predicted probabilities. A simple, and quite common, technique is a proportional adjustment $\pi_i^* = \alpha \pi_i$, where π_i^* is the adjusted probability and α is the factor of adjustment. A problem with this technique is that it does not restrict π_i^* to be in the [0,1] interval. If instead $\pi_i^* = \min(1, \alpha \pi_i)$ is used, this implies that individuals with $\pi_i^* = 1$ with certainty will experience the event. This can produce unrealistic results, for instance all individuals with the same set of attributes might die. Alternatively, the adjustments can be made using a different scale. In SESIM, an additive adjustment on the logit scale is used, this is equivalent to adjusting the intercept term in the estimated logit model. Thus, SESIM uses $\text{logit}(\pi_i^*) = \alpha + X_i \beta$, or $\pi_i^* = [1 + \exp(-\alpha - X_i \beta)]^{-1}$, where the logit function is $\text{logit}(x) = \log[x/(1 - x)]$. This implies $\pi_i^* \in [0, 1]$.

Regardless of approach, the adjustment factor α must be calculated. In the first approach this is simple (given that the frequency of truncated probabilities are low) but in the second it is a bit more complicated. Even if the techniques discussed above ensure that the expected number of events corresponds to the desired, the Monte Carlo variance can still produce discrepancies. The method for variance reduction that is used in SESIM, eliminates these discrepancies by using the α that, given the random values of u_i, generates the exact number of events n. The problem of calculating α is solved by the fact that this is equivalent with sorting the variable $v_i = \text{logit}(u_i) - \text{logit}(\pi_i)$ in an ascending order and letting individuals with the lowest rank obtain a positive event.

Even if calibration is a common method in dynamic MSM there have still been some critique (see Klevmarken, 2002). If the discrepancy from the expected result is due to an incorrectly specified model, then this should be corrected for, and not solved by calibration. However, calibration can also be motivated by a desire to replicate exactly well-known statistical benchmarks or predictions to avoid a discussion about the meaning of random deviations from a targeted benchmark. Alternatively calibration can be viewed as a method of implementing different scenarios in a simulation, for instance, the effect of two different assumptions about immigration flows (cf. Chapter 11). As discussed in Chapter 2 an alternative to calibrate the simulated values is to calibrate the parameter estimates of the model, but this approach might be much more difficult to implement due to the complexity of the model.

The different models/processes in SESIM that use calibration or variance reduction are mentioned in the Appendix.

Monte Carlo variance is not the only source of random variability in a dynamic MSM. Since the sample used for simulation is a random sample from a population, this introduces another source of randomness. Further, because the estimated parameters are random they also introduce a source of randomness.[9] Thus, a proper inference should incorporate all possible sources of randomness, but due to the complexity of a dynamic MSM it is quite difficult to derive analytical results for simulated entities of interest. However, methods based on replicated simulation could be used, such as the *bootstrap*.[10]

6. Assumptions about exogenous variables

SESIM is not linked to any general equilibrium model or macro model, which could give feedback from market adjustments to changes simulated in SESIM. The macro-economic scenario is instead fed into SESIM through a number of macro indicators such as the general growth in wage rates, the rate of inflation, and the return on real and financial assets. These indicators are exogenous to SESIM. From the base year 1999 until 2005, we have used already observed values on these exogenous variables. After 2010, we have assumed constant rates and in the interim period 2005–2010 we allow the rates to adjust from the last observed rates to the assumed constant rates. There is no technical reason to assume constant rates. The model is quite flexible and can take any assumed time path, but we have limited our simulations to alternative scenarios with constant future rates to get "clean" alternatives. There is, for instance, one alternative with high wage rate growth and one with low growth. Throughout the analysis in this book we have used a main or base scenario toward which new submodels are evaluated and alternative scenarios are compared. This is a scenario, which is close to the medium-range predictions of the Ministry of Finance. More specifically, the base scenario uses the following assumptions after 2010:

Annual rate of change in inflation (CPI)	2.00%
Annual real general increase in wage rates	2.00%
Short-term interest rate	4.00%
Long-term interest rate	5.00%
Dividends	2.50%
Rate of change in prices on stocks and shares	3.75%

The demographic changes in the base scenario are aligned to the main projection of Statistics Sweden as explained above and detailed in the Appendix of this chapter. The properties of alternative scenarios are explained in the succeeding chapters as they are introduced and in particular in Chapter 12.

---

[9] However, due to the large sample size that is used for estimation in SESIM this source of error is presumably rather small.

[10] For a general reference to the bootstrapping technique (see Davison and Hinkley, 1997).

References

Davison, A.C. and D.V. Hinkley (1997), *Bootstrap Methods and Their Application*, Cambridge, MA: Cambridge University Press.

Edin, P.A. and P. Fredriksson (2000), "LINDA – longitudinal individual data for Sweden", Working Paper 2000:19, Uppsala Universitet, Nationalekonomiska Institutionen.

Ericson, P. and J. Hussénius (2000), "Studiebidragen i det långa loppet", Rapport till Expertgruppen för studier i offentlig ekonomi (ESO). Ds 2000:19.

Flood, L. (2003), "Formation of wealth, income of capital and cost of housing in SESIM", SESIM Working Paper, www.sesim.org

Flood, L. (2007), "Can we afford the future? An evaluation of the new Swedish pension system", in: A. Harding and A. Gupta, editors, *Modelling our Future*, Oxford: Elsevier.

Klevmarken, A. (2002), "Statistical inference in micro-simulation models: incorporating external information", *Mathematics and Computers in Simulation*, Vol. 59, pp. 255–265.

Pettersson, T. and T. Pettersson (2003), "Fördelning ur ett livscykel perpektiv", Appendix 9, Long Term Survey, Swedish Ministry of Finance, Stockholm.

Pettersson, T. and T. Pettersson (2007), "Lifetime redistribution through taxes, transfers and non-cash benefits", in: A. Harding and A. Gupta, editors, *Modelling our Future*, Elsevier.

Pettersson, T., T. Pettersson and A. Westerberg (2006), "Generationsanalyser – omfördelning mellan generationer i en växande välfärdsstat", ESS 2006:6, The Swedish Ministry of Finance.

SCB's demographic forecast [BE18SM0201], Swedish population until year 2050.

Appendix

Stochastic models in SESIM

Below, a short summary is provided of all stochastic models in SESIM, we concentrate on the following characteristics:

Event/outcome: The event or the outcome variable

At risk: Individuals or household at risk, i.e., they are affected of the outcome of the model

Model: A crude classification of the statistical model used. In SESIM, the typical ones are linear regression for continuous dependent variables and logit/probit models for binary dependent variables

Covariates: The independent variables used to explain the variation in the dependent variable. We only list the variables not their functional form

Comment: General comments, for instance about calibration

Algorithm: Sometimes the process is a combination of stochastic models and rules or algorithms

Mortality

At risk: Individuals of age 0–29 years

Model: Yearly death risks in accordance to SCB population forecast

Comment: Due to the very low death risks in these ages, it is difficult to specify a statistical model. For this reason, the average risks for each age/sex are used. These are constructed based on observed risks for the total population, in the relevant age range

At risk: Individuals of age 30–64 years

Model: Logistic regression

Covariates: Sex, age, indicator for early retirement, pensionable income (quintile), marital status

At risk: Individuals older than 64 years

Model: Logistic regression

Covariates: Sex, age, indicator for early retirement at 64 years of age, marital status, highest level of education

Comment: For mortality a calibration is done for gender and age group in accordance to SCB long-term population forecast[11]

Adoption (orphans)

Event/outcome: Household adopting a child is drawn at random from all households with an age between 24 and 51 years

At risk:

1. Children (younger than 18 years) that have become orphans during the year
2. Adopting household, where the lowest age among the spouses is 24 and the highest 51

---

[11] See SCB's demographic forecast [BE18SM0201], Swedish population until year 2050.

Model: Regression

Covariates: Indicator for household type (single female, single male, non-single), female age (male age for single male)

Algorithm: Number of children are simulated for adopting households (using the estimated model) and compared with the actual number of children. Orphans are adopted by these households with the largest difference between simulated and actual children

Emigration

At risk: Household that has immigrated

Model: Logistic regression

Covariates: Householder's highest age, number of children, number of adults, household's highest education, time since immigration

At risk: Swedish born household

Model: Logistic regression

Covariates: Household's highest age, number of children, number of adults, household's highest education

Comment: The total number of simulated emigrants is calibrated to total number emigrants according to SCB's demographic forecast

Immigration

At risk: Household/individuals that have emigrated

Model: Hazard model

Covariates: Time since emigration

At risk: First-time immigrants

Algorithm: Existing households in the model population are "cloned" and considered as first-time immigrants. The selection of household for the matching is done such that the immigrated household achieves a reasonable composition according to the highest age and size of the household

Comment: Total immigration from the model is calibrated to total immigration according to SCB forecast. This is done by adjusting the number of first-time immigrants within the sample of total immigration

Fertility

At risk: Women 18–49 years of age, who moved from their parents and have not given birth to a child

Model: Logistic regression

Covariates: Age, marital status, pensionable income (quartiles), indicator for market work, highest education

At risk: Women 18–49 years of age, who moved from their parents and have given birth to at least one child

Model: Logistic regression

Covariates: Age, marital status, pensionable income (quartiles), indicator for market work, highest education, age of youngest child

Comment: Separate models have been estimated for women who have given birth to one, two, and three children, respectively; more than four births are not modeled

Comment: The total number of births are calibrated against total number of children born each year, according to the SCB forecast

Moving from parents

At risk: Individuals older than 17 years and living with their parents

Model: Logistic regression

Covariates: Age, highest education, indicator for ongoing studies, indicator for taxable income greater than zero, nationality[12]

Comment: Separate models estimated for males and females. The model is calibrated against the observed share of movers per sex and age according to HEK 1999

Creation of new households

At risk: Adult (not living in the parent's household) females and males who are single

Model: Logistic regression

Covariates: Age

Algorithm: The women who will form the new household during the year are drawn at random from the estimated probabilities. For every female, from the sample of "selectable" males, the first male selected is 3 years older and in the same region as the female is picked from. If no match is found the process is repeated but now the selected male is 4 years older and if necessary the process can be repeated until a match is found

Dissolution of households

At risk: Non-single male

Model: Logistic regression

Covariates: Age

---

[12] Nationality is set to one if the individual is born in Sweden, else zero.

Algorithm: Based on estimated probabilities of leaving the household, males are drawn at random

Disability pension

At risk: Individuals between 16 and 29 years of age who are not disability pensioners
Model: Logistic regression
Covariates: Health, sector, age
At risk: Individuals between 30 and 60 years of age who are not disability pensioners
Model: Logistic regression
Covariates: Health, highest education, sector, age, nationality, gender, pensionable income (quartiles)

At risk: Individuals between 61 and 64 years of age who are not disability pensioners
Model: Logistic regression
Covariates: Health, highest education, sector, age, gender, pensionable income (quartiles)

Rehabilitation from disability pension

At risk: Individuals who are disability pensioners
Model: Logistic regression
Covariates: Age, time as disability pensioner, highest education

Regional mobility

Event/outcome: Household moving
At risk: All households
Model: Logistic regression
Covariates: Age, region, income, unemployment

Event/outcome: Choice of region
At risk: Households who move
Model: Conditional logit
Covariates: Age, region, income, unemployment

Event/outcome: Tenure choice (owned/rented)
At risk: Households who move
Model: Conditional logit
Covariates: Age, region, income, unemployment
Comment: Two models

Education

Event/outcome: Starting gymnasium (high school)
At risk: Sixteen-year-old who is not a disability pensioner
Algorithm: All individuals start gymnasium at 16 years of age
Comment: At most 3 years of studies are required in order to obtain a gymnasium degree

Event/outcome: Exit from gymnasium
At risk: Students at gymnasium
Model: Logistic regression
Covariates: Sex, parent's highest education, parent's highest age, nationality, indicator for divorced parents, household's income (quartiles), number of children in household
Comment: For those individuals who are predicted to exit, a time for this exit is also predicted by a random draw

Event/outcome: Starting university studies directly after gymnasium
At risk: Nineteen years old who finished their gymnasium degree the preceding year and who are not disability pensioners or on parental leave
Model: Logistic regression
Covariates: Sex, nationality, indicator for living with parents, indicator for own children, indicator for living in big city, rate of unemployment

Event/outcome: Exit from university studies before a degree
At risk: Students at the university
Model: Logistic regression
Covariates: Sex, nationality, marital status, age, number of children, indicator for living in big city
Comment: University studies are assumed to continue for 3 or 4 years. Students that exit after the third year obtain a degree, after the forth year they obtain a degree by default

Event/outcome: Transition from labor force to university studies
At risk: Individuals with a degree from gymnasium who do not have a student status
Model: Logistic regression
Covariates: Sex, nationality, GNP growth, time since the gymnasium degree, age, marital status, number of children

Event: Transition from labor force to "komvux" (gymnasium for adults)
At risk: Individuals between 20 and 64 years of age without a degree from gymnasium, who are not disability pensioners or on parental leave

Model: Logistic regression

Covariates: Sex, nationality, GNP growth, marital status, time since the gymnasium degree, number of children, age

Comment: Studies at "komvux" are assumed to continue for three years, this gives a gymnasium degree

Event/outcome: University studies directly after "komvux"

At risk: Individuals who finished "komvux" the preceding year and who are not disability pensioners or on parental leave

Model: Logistic regression

Covariates: Sex, nationality, age, marital status, number of children, indicator for living in big city, GNP growth

Market work

Event/outcome: Market work/no market work during the year

At risk: Individuals older than 15 years who are not old age pensioners, disability pensioners, students, on parental leave, or unemployed

Model: Logistic regression

Covariates: Indicator for market work the preceding year, age, highest education, indicator for current studies

Comment: Separate models estimated for male and female

Unemployed

Event/outcome: Unemployed/not unemployed during the year

At risk: Individuals older than 15 years who are not old age pensioner, disability pensioner, student, or on parental leave

Model: Logistic regression

Covariates: Indicator for unemployment the preceding year, age, age group, highest education

Comment: Separate models estimated for male and female. Calibration to exogenously unemployment rates is possible

Early retirement

Event/outcome: Permanent exit from market work to old age pension

At risk: Individuals in the age group 60–64 years, who had worked the previous year and are not classified as old age or disability pensioners

Model: Bivariate probit with partial observability

Covariates: Social security wealth and its accrual, highest education, marital status, indicator for working spouse, nationality, qualifying wage, sector

Occupational sector[13]

At risk: Individuals in labor force without an occupational sector
Model: Multinomial logit
Covariates: Age, sex, highest education, nationality

At risk: Individuals in labor force with an occupational sector
Model: Multinomial logit
Covariates: Age, sex, highest education, nationality
Comment: Separate models estimated for each occupational sector

Housing/wealth

Event/outcome: Probability of financial wealth
At risk: Households without financial wealth, who did not change real wealth $\geq 100\,000$ SEK between 1999 and 2000
Model: Logistic regression
Covariates: Age group (5-year intervals), quartiles and percentiles for taxable income (p25, p50, p75, p90, p95, >p95)

Event/outcome: Financial wealth
At risk: Households with a positive financial wealth predicted from the preceding model
Model: Robust regression (M-estimation), logarithm of response variable
Covariates: Age group (5-year intervals), quartiles and percentiles for taxable income (p25, p50, p75, p90, p95, >p95)
Comment: No Monte Carlo simulation

Event/outcome: Financial wealth
At risk: Households with a positive financial wealth (the previous year), no change in household composition, not sold or bought a house
Model: A dynamic random effect model
Covariates: Lag of financial wealth, interaction with lag financial wealth and age and income, and finally a variable for general index on Stockholm stock exchange

Event/outcome: Probability of other real wealth
At risk: Households without other real wealth, who did not change real wealth $\geq 100\,000$ SEK between 1999 and 2000

---

[13] The sectors are, blue-collar workers in the private sector, white-collar workers in the private sector, central government employees, local government employees, and self-employed.

Model: Logistic regression
Covariates: Age group (5-year intervals), marital status, quartiles and percentiles for taxable income (p25, p50, p75, p90, p95, >p95)

Event/outcome: Other real wealth
At risk: Households with a positive other real wealth predicted from the preceding model
Model: Robust regression (M-estimation), logarithm of response variable
Covariates: Age, quartiles and percentiles for taxable income (p25, p50, p75, p90, p95, >p95)
Comment: No Monte Carlo simulation

Event/outcome: Other real wealth
At risk: Households with a positive other real wealth (the previous year), no change in household composition, not sold or bought a house
Model: A random walk

Event/outcome: Probability of private pension savings
At risk: Individuals between 18 and 64 years without private pension savings
Model: Logistic regression
Covariates: Age, age square, sex, education, marital status, nationality, quartiles and percentiles for taxable income (p25, p50, p75, p90, p95, >p95)

Event/outcome: Private pension savings
At risk: Households with a positive private pension savings predicted from the preceding model
Model: Regression private pension savings/1000
Covariates: Age, sex, education, nationality, quartiles and percentiles for taxable income (p25, p50, p75, p90, p95, >p95)
Comment: In forecasting accumulated pension savings we have to estimate the probability and the amount saved first time. Then we assume that the individual save the same amount (adjusted by KPI) each year until the age of 64

Event/outcome: House area
At risk: Household who bought a house during the year
Model: Regression
Covariates: Age group for oldest spouse, indicator for married/cohabiting, number of children below 18, quartiles for taxable income, indicator for living in Stockholm, Göteborg, or Malmö dense areas (H-region)

Comment: No Monte Carlo simulation, i.e., the variance is assumed equal to zero

Event/outcome: Market value of house/apartment
At risk: Household who bought house/apartment during the year
Model: Regression, log-transformed response variable
Covariates: Age group for oldest spouse, indicator for married/cohabiting, number of children below 18, quartiles for taxable income, indicator for living in dense areas (H-region), quartiles for households financial wealth

Event/outcome: Probability of debt
At risk: Households without debt
Model: Random effect probit
Covariates: Age group, household taxable income/median, household gross wealth/median, and household gross wealth/median squared

Event/outcome: Debt
At risk: Households with a positive debt predicted from the preceding model
Model: Robust regression (M-estimation), logarithm of debt
Covariates: Age group, household taxable income/median (lag of household debt)

Event/outcome: Debt
At risk: Households with a debt (the previous year) and a reduction in market value of house more than 100 000 SEK

- Model 1: Probit for probability of debt
- Model 2: Robust regression for level

Covariates: Age group, marital status, household taxable income/median, household gross wealth/median, and household gross wealth/median squared

Event/outcome: Debt
At risk: Households with a debt (the previous year) and no large changes in market value of house

- Model 1: Probit for probability of debt
- Model 2: Robust regression for level

Covariates: Age group, marital status, household taxable income/ median, household gross wealth/median, and household gross wealth/ median squared

Event/outcome: Debt
At risk: Households with a debt (the previous year) and an increase in market value of house more than 100 000 SEK

- Model 1: Probit for probability of debt
- Model 2: Robust regression for level

Covariates: Age group, marital status, household taxable income/ median, household gross wealth/median, and household gross wealth/ median squared

Event/outcome: Interest/dividends
At risk: All households
Model: Tobit
Covariates: Schooling, age, a dummy variable for marital status, and the mean value of the assets as explanatory variables
Comment: Interest and dividend incomes are defined as a rate of return on financial assets. To avoid excessively high return rate estimates all households with less than 1000 SEK of financial assets were dropped from the sample

Event/outcome: Capital gains on owned house
At risk: All households who sell their owned house
Comment: Eighty per cent of capital gain is added to taxable income. If the household buys a new house it is possible to defer whole or part of the gain

Event/outcome: Probability of income of capital (excluding capital gain on owned house)
At risk: All households
Model: Probit
Covariates: Age group, marital status, reduction in real estate value, increase in real estate value, reduction in financial wealth, increase in financial wealth, household gross wealth/median

Event/outcome: Income of capital (excluding capital gain on owned house)
At risk: Households with a positive value predicted from the preceding model
Model: Robust regression (M-estimation), logarithm of income of capital

Covariates: Age group, marital status, reduction in real estate value, increase in real estate value, reduction in financial wealth, increase in financial wealth, household gross wealth/median

Event/outcome: Probability of capital loss (excluding capital loss on owned house)
At risk: All households
Model: Probit
Covariates: Age group, marital status, reduction in real estate value, increase in real estate value, reduction in financial wealth, increase in financial wealth, household gross wealth/median

Event/outcome: Capital loss (excluding capital loss on owned house)
At risk: Households with a positive value predicted from the preceding model
Comments: No model instead random draws from the empirical distribution

Event/outcome: Probability of interest deductions
At risk: Households without interest deductions *t*–1
Model: Random effects probit
Covariates: Age group, education, debt ratio, dummy if debts>total wealth, market value of owned house/median value, household taxable income/median

Event/outcome: Interest deductions
At risk: Households with a positive debt predicted from the preceding model
Model: Random effects GLS
Covariates: Age group, education, debt ratio, dummy if debts>total wealth, market value of owned house/median value, household taxable income/median, household financial wealth/median, change in market value of house/median

Event/outcome: Probability of interest deductions
At risk: Households with interest deductions *t*–1
Model: Random effects probit
Covariates: Age group, education, debt ratio, dummy if debts>total wealth, market value of owned house/median value, household taxable income/median

Event/outcome: Interest deductions
At risk: Households with a positive value predicted from the preceding model

Model: Random effects GLS

Covariates: Age group, education, debt ratio, dummy if debts > total wealth, market value of owned house/median value, household taxable income/median, household financial wealth/median, change in market value of house/median

Earnings[14]

Event/outcome: Earnings
At risk: Individuals in labor force
Model: Regression (mixed regression), log-transformed response variable
Covariates: Working experience, highest education, occupational sector, nationality, marital status, random intercept
Comment: A separate model for each gender and separate estimations of the variance components for each occupational sector

Event/outcome: Probability of earnings
At risk: Students
Model: Probit regression
Covariates: Age, sex, nationality

Event/outcome: Earnings
At risk: Students predicted to have earnings from previous model
Model: Regression, log-transformed response variable
Covariates: Age, sex, nationality

Event/outcome: Probability of earnings
At risk: Individuals classified as other (status = 7)
Model: Probit regression
Covariates: Age, sex, nationality, highest education

Event/outcome: Earnings
At risk: Individuals classified as other and predicted to have earnings from previous model.
Model: Regression, log-transformed response variable
Covariates: Age, highest education

---

[14] The earnings equation was discussed in Section 4.1.

Compensated sickness days

Event/outcome: Number of compensated sickness days

At risk: Individuals between 30 and 64 years of age who are not disability or old age pensioners or on parental leave

Model: Negative binomial corrected for sample selection

Covariates: Previous sickness absenteeism, current health, age, sex, marital status, indicators for whether or not the respondent had a child below the age of one, perceived cost of being absent from work because of sickness

Comments: Two models were estimated, an imputation equation and a model for yearly changes

Take-up social assistance[15]

At risk: Household with an adult whose income is below the norm for social assistance

Model: Logistic regression

Covariates: Age, sex, number of children, number of children under 7 years of age, highest education, indicator for unemployment, the difference between disposable income and the norm for social assistance, working experience, indicator for ongoing studies, nationality, indicator for living in big city, indicator for any earlier divorce

At risk: Household with two adults and a disposable income below the norm for social assistance

Model: Logistic regression

Covariates: Male age, female age, number of children, number of children below 7 years of age, male highest education, female highest education, indicator for male unemployment, indicator for female unemployment, the difference between disposable income and the norm for social assistance, male working experience, female working, male nationality, female nationality, indicator for living in big city

Health and care of elderly

Event/outcome: Probability that a relative lives in the same labor market region

---

[15] Take-up denotes the propensity to apply for a benefit given that the individual/household is entitled to it. In social assistance it is quite common that a large portion of eligible household do not apply.

At risk: Individuals 65 or older

Model: Logistic regression

Covariates: Region, marital status, own/rent, nationality, age group, income, and education

Comment: The model is applied in 1999 or then the individual enters the population at risk

Event/outcome: Probability that a relative lives in the same labor market region

At risk: Individuals aged 65 years or older

Model: Dynamic logistic regression

Covariates: Region, marital status, own/rent, nationality, age group, income, education, and closeness to relative $t-1$

Comment: The model is applied after 1999

Event/outcome: Health index ($0 =$ unknown, $1 =$ severe illness, $2 =$ some illness, $3 =$ not full health, and $4 =$ full health)

At risk: All individuals

Model: Ordered probit

Covariates: Region, marital status, own/rent, nationality, age group, taxable income, education, number of children, and sex

Comment: The model is applied during 1999–2006 or if the individual enters the population at risk. Different model depending on if the individual is older or younger than 50

Event/outcome: Health index ($0 =$ unknown, $1 =$ severe illness, $2 =$ some illness, $3 =$ not full health, and $4 =$ full health)

At risk: All individuals with a value on health index $t-8$

Model: Ordered probit

Covariates: Region, marital status, own/rent, nationality, age group, taxable income, education, number of children, sex, and health index $t-8$

Comment: The model is applied from 2007 for individuals with a value on health index $t-8$. Different model depending on if the individual is older or younger than 50

Event/outcome: Number of days in patient care

At risk: All individuals older than 60 years

Model: Zero-inflated negative binomial

Covariates: Health index, age, taxable income/mean, education, marital status, number of children, region, sex, and nationality

Comment: The model is applied in 1999 and for new individuals. Different model depending on if the individual is aged between 16 and 49 years or older than 50 years

Event/outcome: Number of days in patient care

At risk: All individuals older than 60 years

Model: Zero-inflated negative binomial

Covariates: Health index, age, taxable income/mean, education, marital status, number of children, region, sex and nationality, days in patient care $t-1$

Comment: The model is applied after 1999 and for new individuals. Different model depending on if the individual is aged between 16 and 49 years or older than 50 years

Event/outcome: ADL (0 = unknown, 1 = non-disabled, 2 = slightly disabled, 3 = moderately disabled, and 4 = severely disabled)

At risk: All individuals 65 years or older

Model: Ordered logit

Covariates: Health index, age group, and sex

Event/outcome: Assistance elderly (0 = no assistance, 1 = assistance at home, and 2 = special accommodations)

At risk: All individuals aged 75 years or older

Model: Multinomial logit

Covariates: ADL, previous level of assistance, number of years since the individual became 75, closeness to relative

Comment: The initial level of assistance is imputed based on observed frequencies per age, sex, and ADL level

CHAPTER 4

Changes in the Health Status of the Population

Kristian Bolin, Matias Eklöf, Sören Höjgård and Björn Lindgren*

Health status is one of the most important indicators of individual well being and population welfare. As such, it is also a target for public policy-making. Health status is a major determinate behind many decisions during the course of an individual's life. It affects decisions on education, labor market career, marriage and divorce, fertility among other things. It predicts to a large degree expenditures on health and social services, but it is also reciprocally affected by social and health policies and programs. Health status can be maintained or improved by health promotion and disease prevention programs, and the negative impact of disease reduced by effective health services.

Policy concerns relate to the distribution of health in the population, not least among elderly people. Policy concerns also relate to the future viability of pension-, healthcare-, and social insurance schemes; how long can people be expected to be physically and mentally capable to continue working, paying taxes, and saving? Policy concerns, furthermore, relate to the fact that public policies primarily addressed to health and health services often have important implications for and complex interactions with other sectors of the economy.

Despite its great importance, individual health-related behavior was not included in the SESIM model in 2002, when our project commenced. Individual health was not predicted and the consequences of good or bad health were not considered in any of the modules. Simulations that had been performed had not been able to account for the effects on health of various determining factors, nor for the effects of ill health on the demand for healthcare, early retirement, sickness absence, or on a number of other

* Corresponding author.

CONTRIBUTIONS TO ECONOMIC ANALYSIS
VOLUME 285   ISSN: 0573-8555
DOI:10.1016/S0573-8555(07)00004-1

health-related decisions. The objectives of our including health status in the dynamic micro-simulation model were, hence, both (a) to improve the predictions of individual decisions that depend on health status and (b) to improve the predictions of the consequences of changes in health status on the demand for health and social services as well as for the distribution of health in the population. Modules that seemed most sensitive to the inclusion of health status and most relevant in this context were sickness absence (Chapter 5), early retirement (Chapter 6), inpatient care (Chapter 10), and old-age care (Chapter 11).

The purpose of this chapter is to estimate the determinants of individual health and, subsequently, to simulate over time, the development of the chosen health measure, which will be used in estimations and simulations of health-related behavior in the modules mentioned above. We will (1) provide some additional information on the development of health in Sweden during the last 20 years, (2) present our theoretical framework and some previous empirical research on the determinants of individual health, (3) introduce our econometric model, (4) describe the data employed, including our chosen empirical measure of health, (5) present and discuss our estimation strategy, (6) report and interpret the estimates, and (7) present and discuss the simulations obtained from SESIM of the evolvement of health in the population.

1. Health trends in Sweden

As summarized in our introductory Chapter 1, the trend toward ever-healthier elderly seems to have been broken (Figures 8 and 9). The share of young and middle-aged Swedish men and women, reporting very good or good health status to the Survey of Living Conditions, started to decline already in the 1980s. As a consequence, as the cohorts are graying, the share of elderly people, reporting very good or good health status, has also begun to decline. Increasing health problems among Swedish oldest old have also been reported from the SWEOLD (SWEdish panel of living conditions of oldest OLD) study (Parker *et al.*, 2004). Similar trends have been reported for the United States and for the entire EU-15. Part of the explanation appears to be the growth at young ages in allergy, asthma, diabetes, other long-standing illness, and health problems associated with obesity. In the time perspective of our simulations, these trends in long-standing health problems might have less impact on the health of the elderly (and their demand for healthcare and old-age care or their life expectancy) than on the health of people in their middle ages but still be important. In this section, we will present some additional information on the development of health status during the last 20 years or so for the Swedish population.

According to Figure 1, the share reporting bad or very bad health status in Sweden is higher among women than among men; the difference seems to widen over time. Furthermore, women report bad or very bad health

Figure 1. Shares with bad or very bad self-assessed health among Swedish men and women 16–84 years old, 1980/81–2002/2003 (age-standardized)

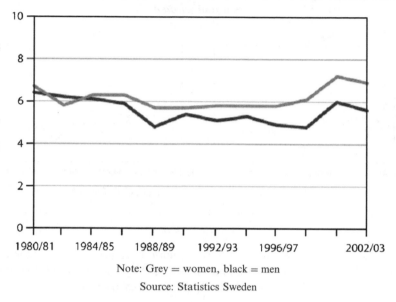

Note: Grey = women, black = men

Source: Statistics Sweden

Figure 2. Distribution of self-assessed health by age group among Swedish men and women, 2002/2003 men and women

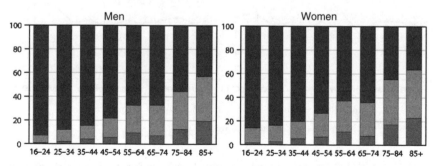

Note: Black = good or very good, light grey = in between, and dark grey = bad or very bad

Source: Statistics Sweden

more often than men in all age groups (Figure 2). For both sexes, the share reporting bad or very bad health increases with age. Still, among the 85+, slightly more than 40 percent of the men and slightly less than 40 percent of the women reported good or very good health in 2002/2003. Education is also important. According to Figure 3, bad or very bad self-reported health is more frequent among both men and women with low education. Differences do not seem to diminish over time, either. Another important

Figure 3. *Shares with bad or very bad health by educational level among Swedish men and women 16–84 years old, 1982/83–2002/2003, men and women*

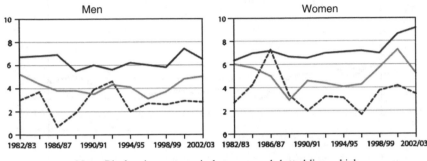

Note: Black = low, grey = in between, and dotted line = high

Source: Statistics Sweden

Figure 4. *Shares with bad or very bad health by country of birth (Swedish or foreign) among Swedish men and women 16–84 years old, 1982/83–2002/ 2003 (age-standardized) men and women*

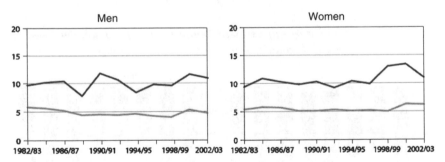

Note: Black = born in other country and grey = born in Sweden

Source: Statistics Sweden

factor is Swedish or foreign background. According to Figure 4, bad or very bad self-reported health is substantially more frequent among both men and women with foreign as opposed to Swedish background.

Figures 5 and 6 show the presence of long-standing illness and seriously affected work capacity due to long-standing illness in the Swedish population 16–84 years old. During the 20-year period 1980/1981–2002/ 2003, the share reporting long-standing illness has increased from 43 to 52 percent for women and from 42 to 46 percent for men. During the same time period, the share reporting that their long-standing illness seriously affects their work capacity has increased from 12 to 15 percent for women, but has remained the same, about 11 percent, among men during the

Figure 5. Shares with long-standing illness and severely affected work capacity, respectively, among Swedish men and women 16–84 years old, 1980/81–2002/2003 (age-standardized)

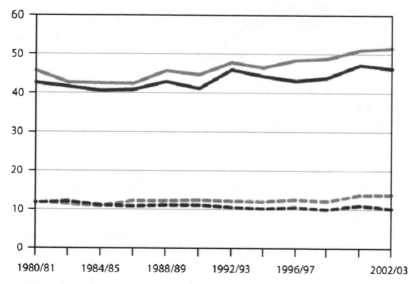

Note: Grey = long-standing illness, women; black = long-standing illness, men; dotted grey = severely affected work capacity, women; and dotted black = severely affected work capacity, men

Source: Statistics Sweden

Figure 6. Shares with severely affected work capacity due to long-standing illness by age and sex, 2002/2003

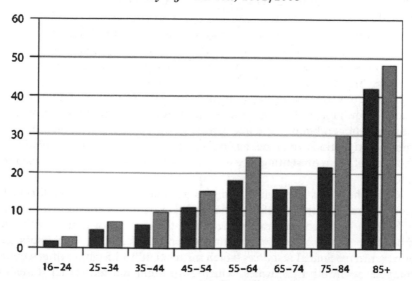

Note: Black = men and grey = women

Source: Statistics Sweden

whole period. The share reporting that their long-standing illness seriously affects their work capacity increases markedly with age, and women dominate in all age groups. For pensioners, the data reflect to what extent long-standing illness obstructs "normal activities."

According to the results of the first wave of SHARE (Survey of Health, Ageing, and Retirement in Europe), the 50 + population in Sweden reports higher self-perceived health than their counterparts in most of the 11 countries participating in SHARE. Moreover, lifestyle health risks are less prevalent among Swedes. The consumption of alcohol and tobacco is lower, the share of overweight- and obese people is lower, and the share of physically active people is higher in Sweden than in most other countries (Börsch-Supan *et al.*, 2005).

2. *Theoretical framework and our choice of explanatory variables*

The theoretical framework for our empirical work is the demand-for-health model (or the individual-as-producer-of-health model), developed by Grossman (1972). It is the dominating theoretical model within health economics and an important contribution to micro-economic theory, extending the human capital theory (Becker, 1964) to individual health behaviour. The original model has recently been extended in a number of ways (see, for instance, Liljas (1998), Jacobson (2000), and Bolin *et al.* (2001, 2002b)).

The demand-for-health model comprises two types of human capital: education and health; health is endogenous whereas education is exogenous. Health capital is determinate for the amount of productive time while education determines the productivity of that time. Each individual is born with a certain amount of health capital, which depreciates with age and as a response to exogenous factors, such as the environment, accidents and diseases, and endogenous factors, such as the lifestyle chosen by the individual. The individual, however, is able to invest in his or her health by combining own time and market goods; market goods are, for instance, healthcare, but also wholesome food and exercise equipment. The amount of education determines the individual's efficiency in combining time and goods in order to invest in health. Some goods and actions may be hazardous to health and might, hence, by thought of as representing negative investments in health, for instance, smoking.

Good health is demanded for two reasons in the demand-for-health model. First, health is welfare enhancing per se – the consumption aspect of health – and, second, health determines the amount of time available for productive purposes – the investment aspect of health. The individual, however, have limited resources which means that health-improving activities compete with other activities which also improve individual's welfare.

The balance between the individual's different preferences determines the individual's demand-for-health, which, in turn, determines his or her demand for healthcare and other kinds of health investments, such as to give-up or never start smoking, to consume moderate amounts of alcohol, and to exercise regularly.

The most important predictions of the original theoretical model are that, under some plausible conditions, (a) age should be negatively correlated with health capital but positively correlated with health investments; (b) the individual's wage rate should be positively correlated both with the demand for health and with the demand for health investments; and (c) education should be positively correlated with health capital but negatively correlated with expenditures on health investments (Grossman, 1972). Recent extensions of the model to include the family as the producer of health suggest that the demand for health should be (d) positively correlated with marriage or cohabitation, (e) negatively correlated with divorce, (f) negatively correlated with widowhood, and (g) undetermined when it comes to the presence of children (Jacobson, 2000; Bolin *et al.*, 2001, 2002b). Thus, the demand-for-health model explains variations in health status (besides the exogenously given initial levels of health) and health investments among individuals.

Empirical estimations of the demand-for-health model on general population data comprise Grossman's (1972) own study on US data, Muurinen (1982) on Finnish data, Wagstaff (1986) on Danish data, and Bolin *et al.* (2002a) on Swedish data. Bolin and Lindgren (2002) and Bolin *et al.* (2003, 2006) estimated the demand-for-health model, taking into account the effects of specific chronic conditions, social interactions, and a specific health-risk factor, obesity, respectively. The results of these empirical studies have by and large supported the predictions of the demand-for-health model.

Our choice of variables reflecting the main determinants of individual health (beside genetic inheritance) – age, education, wage rate, marriage, divorce, widowhood, presence of children is, hence, well founded in both theoretical and empirical studies. The theoretical model does not predict any correlation between sex and health status. Since all empirical observations indicate that health status is lower among women, we include sex as a determinant. The theoretical model does not predict any correlation between health status and the country in which the individual was born, either. Empirical evidence shows that health status is substantially higher among people who are born in Sweden, why we also include a variable for being born in Sweden or not. Furthermore, the number of working hours and individual earnings are certainly endogenously determined in the theoretical model. However, since the SESIM model does not contain this information elsewhere, we chose income (and not the wage rate) as the independent variable in our empirical analysis.

3. Modeling the evolution of health

Health status is a multi-dimensional and unobservable individual quality. Self-assessed health, long-standing illness, healthcare consumption, sickness absence, physical mobility, grip-strength, etc., are all (more or less) related but not synonymous to individual health. They are observable proxies but imperfect measures of true health states.

Intuitively, there are strong inter-temporal correlations between (true) health states in subsequent time periods, which should be accounted for in the specification of the evolution of health. Although the correlation relates to the unobserved health state, most econometric models actually introduce correlation by including lagged observable measures as determinants of current health. One could argue, however, that this is an incorrect way of introducing inter-temporal dependence, when the observable proxies are imperfect measures of true health states.

In our model of health and its determinants, we explicitly introduce inter-temporal correlation in the latent health variable as follows:

$$h_{it}^* = \rho h_{it-1}^* + \mathbf{x}'_{it}\beta + \varepsilon_{it} = V_{it} + \varepsilon_{it}, \tag{1}$$

where h_{it}^* denotes latent health of individual i in period t, ρ the autoregressive coefficient, $\mathbf{x}_{it}$ a vector of observable variables influencing health with associated weights β, and ε_{it} reflects stochastic health shocks in period t.

The interpretation of the model parameters here is slightly different compared to "standard" models. As we have an autoregressive component in the evolution of health, the model parameter β reflects the marginal effect on health conditional on lagged health h_{it-1}^*, i.e., $dE(h_{it}^*|h_{it-1}^*, \mathbf{x}_{it})/d\mathbf{x}_{it} = \beta$. However, the marginal effect of the unconditional expectation is inflated by $1/(1-\rho)$ such that $dE(h_{it}^*|\mathbf{x}_{it})/d\mathbf{x}_{it} = \beta/(1 - \rho)$. The autoregressive coefficient ρ reflects the persistence of the idiosyncratic shocks captured by ε_{it}; the higher the ρ, the higher persistence in shocks. Note that in the case of finite life, there is no reason to assume that $\rho < 1$. Furthermore, note that the coefficients β and ρ are dependent on the frequency chosen for the model, i.e., β and ρ will depend on whether the model is "running" on annual or bi-annual frequency.

4. Our health measure

4.1. Options

As emphasized above, individual health is a multi-dimensional and unobservable individual quality, which may be empirically represented in several seemingly appropriate ways of which none can be assumed a priori to perform better than the others. There is no objective measure of individual health and no general solution to the problem of choosing an empirical representation. Nor is there any consensus among researchers how to handle this problem in practice.

There are two principles according to which it may be possible to obtain an empirical measure of individual health; either one chooses a single indicator of health, or one constructs composite measures. Single-indicator candidates are, for instance, self-assessed health, mobility, presence of long-term illness, working capacity, or personal discomfort. Composite measures consist of measurements in several dimensions, which are weighted in order to establish a single number. Health-related quality-of-life indices are all examples of composite measures; for a general treatment and overview, see, for instance, Brooks (1995).

The choice of health measure for the SESIM health module is certainly most important, but our options are confined to the information contained in available Swedish data sets. There are two possible sets of Swedish data on health and its determining factors that might be used: (1) LNU (Levnadsnivåundersökningarna; the Swedish Level of Living Surveys) and (2) ULF (Undersökningar om levnadsförhållanden; the Swedish Surveys of Living Conditions). We also need to connect individual data on health and its determining factors with data on the utilization of inpatient care, sickness absenteeism, and early retirement, available in Swedish national registers. Such a data set already exists, HILDA (Health and Individuals. Longitudinal Data and Analysis), linking ULF and register data, and created for the purpose of analyzing individual health behavior.

HILDA (and ULF) contains individual information on self-assessed health; self-assessed mobility; ability to perform activities of daily living; presence of long-standing illness by diagnosis; working capacity; discomfort and frequency of symptoms due to illness; anxiety; utilization of pharmaceuticals, outpatient care, and inpatient care; health-risk factors such as obesity and alcohol and tobacco consumption, etc. Thus, we can either use a single indicator or a composite measure based on more than one of these indicators. There are two options among the latter that seem relevant: (1) a composite measure based on an interpretation of the EQ-5D health-related quality-of-life index suggested by Burström *et al.* (2001), using ULF data, and (2) a composite measure based on ULF data suggested by Statistics Sweden (1992). Self-assessed health, EQ-5D, and the Statistics Sweden Health Index seem to produce roughly the same results for the non-elderly, but the Statistics Sweden Health Index is more sensitive to changes in health status among the very old. Thus, simulations of the development of health status and the demand for old age and inpatient care for this group will be more reliable, if they are based on this measure.

4.2. Our measure of health

The health index suggested by Statistics Sweden has four dimensions: self-assessed health, mobility, long-standing illness, and working capacity (Statistics Sweden, 1992).

Self-assessed health reflects the individual's own assessment of his or her health. In the 1996/1997 ULF Survey, the variable was reported with five levels: 1 very good, 2 good, 3 less good, 4 bad, and 5 very bad. In order to obtain an index for 1996/1997, which is comparable to the corresponding ones for 1980/1981 and 1988/1989, Statistics Sweden also combines levels 5 and 4, and 2 and 1, respectively, in the construction of a three-level health index.

Mobility reflects the individual's own assessment of his or her mobility. It has three levels (numeric value within parentheses) – heavily reduced mobility (1), somewhat reduced mobility (2), no reduced mobility (3) – constructed from the survey variables described below. The individual was defined as having heavily reduced mobility, if he or she answered "no" to question (a) below; "no" to at least one of questions (b) and (c); and "yes" to question (d). The individual was defined as having somewhat reduced mobility, if he or she answered "no" to question (a); "no" to at least one of questions (b) and (c); and "no" to question (d). The individual was defined as having no reduced mobility if he or she answered "yes" to both questions (b) and (c) and "no" to question (d) – irrespective of the answer to question (a). Questions (a)–(d) are:

a. Whether or not the respondent *is able to run* 100 m if in a hurry. The variable is reported as a binary variable: Yes/No.
b. Whether or not the respondent *is able to effortlessly climb a bus*. The variable is reported as a binary variable: Yes/No.
c. Whether or not the respondent *is able to take a quick walk* for 5 min. The variable is reported as a binary variable: Yes/No.
d. Whether or not the respondent *needs aid or personal assistance* in order to move indoors. The variable is reported as a binary variable: Yes/No.

Long-standing illness reflects whether or not the respondent answers that he or she suffers from at least one *diagnosed* long-standing illness. This dimension has two levels: the individual does not suffer from long-standing illness (2) and the individual does suffer (1).

Working capacity reflects to what extent long-standing illness has affected the individual's working capacity. For pensioners, the variable reflects to what extent long-standing illness obstructs normal activities. In the Survey, this question is only asked to individuals who have responded "yes" to the question about the presence of long-standing illness above. It has three levels: working capacity is unaffected (3); working capacity is somewhat affected (2); and working capacity is strongly affected by long-standing illness (1).

There are 36 different combinations of levels in the four dimensions. They were all allotted to one of four states of health: full health, not full health, some illness, and severe illness. Appendix A gives a detailed description of how the Statistics Sweden Health Index was constructed from the dimensions and levels described above.

5. Data

We used the longitudinal part of HILDA for the estimation, i.e., health status, and other data measured for the same individual repeatedly with 8-year intervals. The part that we used comprises 4696 individuals, who were between 16 and 76 years of age in 1988/1989 and between 24 and 84 in 1996/1997. The Statistics Sweden Health Index is our measure of health (the dependent variable). Our choice of explanatory variables – age, income, education, marriage, divorce, widowhood, presence of children, born in Sweden, and sex – was motivated in Section 2.

Descriptive statistics are given in Tables 1 and 2.

Table 1.   Descriptive statistics 1988/1989

Variable	Mean/percentage	SD	Minimum	Maximum	Cases
All observations in current sample					
HI88	3.47	0.78	1.00	4.00	4696
AGE	42.09	16.53	16.00	76.00	4696
SEX	0.48	0.50	0.00	1.00	4696
RELINC	0.77	0.50	0.00	10.23	4696
COLLEGE	0.44	0.50	0.00	1.00	4696
UNIV	0.22	0.41	0.00	1.00	4696
MARITAL	0.66	0.47	0.00	1.00	4696
DIVORCED	0.69E-01	0.25	0.00	1.00	4696
WIDOW	0.07	0.25	0.00	1.00	4696
CHILD	0.26	0.62	0.00	4.00	4696
SWED	0.93	0.26	0.00	1.00	4696

Table 2.   Descriptive statistics 1996/1997

Variable	Mean/percentage	SD	Minimum	Maximum	Cases
All observations in current sample					
HI96	3.29	0.91	1.00	4.00	4696
AGE	50.09	16.53	24.00	84.00	4696
SEX	0.48	0.50	0.00	1.00	4696
RELINC	1.23	1.03	0.00	42.68	4696
COLLEGE	0.45	0.50	0.00	1.00	4696
UNIV	0.26	0.44	0.00	1.00	4696
MARITAL	0.71	0.45	0.00	1.00	4696
DIVORCED	0.10	0.31	0.00	1.00	4696
WIDOW	0.10	0.31	0.00	1.00	4696
CHILD	0.29	0.67	0.00	4.00	4696
SWED	0.92	0.28	0.00	1.00	4696

5.1. Dependent variables

- HI96 is a discrete variable, which reflects health in 1996/1997. The respondent's health status is represented by one of four categories: 1, 2, 3, or 4, where 4 is the category with highest health status. (All dependent discrete variables are later re-scaled so that the ordinal scale begins at 0.)
- HI88 is a discrete variable, which reflects health in 1988/1989. The respondent's health status is represented by one of four categories: 1, 2, 3, or 4, where 4 is the category with highest health status. (All dependent discrete variables are later re-scaled so that the ordinal scale begins at 0.)

5.2. Explanatory variables

- SPLINE_AGE0 is a discrete variable indicating the age of the respondent in 1988/1989.
- SPLINE_AGE25 is defined as AGEDUM*(AGE88-25), where AGEDUM is a dummy variable, which takes the value 1 if the respondent's age is above the age of 25 in 1988/1989.
- SPLINE_AGE50 is defined as AGEDUM*(AGE88-50), where AGEDUM is a dummy variable, which takes the value 1 if the respondent's age is above the age of 50 in 1988/1989.
- SPLINE_AGE75 is defined as AGEDUM*(AGE88-75), where AGEDUM is a dummy variable, which takes the value 1 if the respondent's age is above the age of 75 in 1988/1989.
- RELINC is a continuous variable for the ratio between the respondent's income and the mean income.
- COLLEGE is a dummy variable, which takes the value 1, if the respondent's attained educational level is college level in 1996/1997, and 0 otherwise (corresponds to levels 31, 32, and 40 in Statistics Sweden's educational measure, SUN86).
- UNIV is a dummy variable, which takes the value 1, if the respondent's attained educational level is university level in 1996/1997 and 0 otherwise (corresponds to levels 50, 60, and 70 in Statistics Sweden's educational measure, SUN86).
- MARITAL is a dummy variable, which takes the value 1, if the respondent was either married or cohabiting in 1996/1997, and 0 otherwise.
- DIVORCED is a dummy variable, which takes the value 1, if the respondent was divorced in 1996/1997, and 0 otherwise.
- WIDOW is a dummy variable, which takes the value 1, if the respondent was a widow or widower in 1996/1997, and 0 otherwise.
- CHILD is a discrete variable indicating the number of children below 7 years of age in 1996/1997.

- SWED is a dummy variable, which takes the value 1, if the respondent was born in Sweden, and 0 otherwise.
- SEX reflects sex: 0 corresponds to the respondent being a female and 1 corresponds to the respondent being a male.

6. Estimation strategy

There is a formal description of the estimator in Appendix B. Here we provide a brief outline of the estimation procedure. Two distinct problems need to be handled: (a) lagged latent variables imply unobserved variables in both the left- and right-hand side variables, and (b) available health data are only collected every 8 year, while the simulation model, nevertheless, presumes that the health module be able to predict health profiles on a 1-year frequency.

First, the estimation of a model with lagged latent variables such as Eq. (1) is complicated by the fact that one does not have access to the latent health h_{it}^* as this implies that we have unobserved variables in both the left- and right-hand side variables. The unobserved left-hand side variable is handled by assuming a link function between the unobserved latent variable h_{it}^* and some observed function of the variable denoted by h_{it}. Here we assume that h_{it} represents a categorization of h_{it}^* such that

$$h_{it} = j \text{ iff } \tau_{j-1} < h_{it}^* \leq \tau_j, \tag{2}$$

where h_{it} denotes the discrete health index with J possible outcomes and τ_j denotes the upper threshold of category j with $\tau_0 = -\infty$ and $\tau_j = \infty$. With the additional assumption that the error term ε_{it} is normally distributed, an ordered-probit model with lagged latent variables emerges.

In a standard setting, i.e., without lagged latent variables, the estimation would be completely straightforward using, e.g., maximum likelihood techniques. In this case, however, it is more complex as the lagged latent variable enters the right-hand side. This means that we need to integrate out the lagged latent variable in order to calculate the sample likelihood contribution for an individual given a candidate vector (β, ρ, τ). Using the normality assumption of the error term, this implies that we need to integrate a multi-dimensional normal distribution for which there are no closed forms. Furthermore, the recursive structure implied by the lagged latent variable also means that the multi-dimensional integral will not collapse to a product of univariate integrals, even if the error terms are serially uncorrelated. We, therefore, need to retreat to either numerical or Monte Carlo techniques to evaluate the sample likelihood contribution. Unless the dimensionality is very small (<4), the standard numerical integration techniques (e.g., Gaussian quadrature) are very time consuming and, hence, impractical. Monte Carlo techniques are feasible, though, if we could simulate the probability to observe a given sequence of health states conditional on a candidate vector. The GHK simulator (discussed in Appendix B) gives us exactly this possibility.

For a given candidate vector of model parameters $(\beta, \rho, \tau, \sigma_0)$, we can use the GHK simulator to simulate a sequence of latent health observations $(h_{i1}^{r*}, ..., h_{iT}^{r*})$ that translates to a sequence of health indices $(h_{i1}^r, ..., h_{iT}^r)$ via the link function. In principle, we could make draws from the assumed normal error distribution, calculate the sequence of latent health states and the corresponding sequence of health indicators, and check if the observed sequence is identical to the simulated one. Repeating this procedure, a large number of times would enable us to calculate the probability of the observed sequence as the average of replications where the simulated sequence conforms to the observed. However, if the number of time periods is larger than 3, this would be very time consuming. The GHK simulator offers a more efficient procedure by focusing on the probabilities rather than the outcomes. In the GHK simulator, we draw only sequences of error terms that guarantee conformity between simulated and observed sequences of health indices. The GHK simulator hence produces the probability p^r to observe a sequence such as $(h_{i1}^{r*}, ..., h_{iT}^{r*})$. Averaging over R such draws produces an estimate of the true contribution of the individual and this estimate will serve as the sample likelihood contribution

$$\widehat{\Pr}((h_{i1}, ..., h_{iT})|\beta, \rho, \tau, \sigma_0, \mathbf{X}_i, h_{i0}^*) = \frac{1}{R}\sum_{r=1}^{R} p_i^r, \tag{3}$$

where $\mathbf{X}_i$ denotes the matrix of independent variables for individual i over periods $t = 1, ..., T$. As the process including lagged latent variables requires an initial value h_{i0}^*, we cannot use this dynamic specification for the first period. Here, we estimate a standard ordered-probit model, where the slope coefficients β_0 and the error variance σ_0^2 are allowed to vary freely. The initial-period order-probit model is linked to the dynamic model by the threshold parameters $(\tau_0, ..., \tau_j)$, which are assumed time invariant. Thus, the initial-period model and the dynamic model are estimated simultaneously. There are also some technical issues on the assumption about the initial value h_{i0}^* that are discussed in Appendix B.

Second, data are collected in 8-year intervals, whereas the required model should run on an annual frequency. In principle, one could specify the model, using the 8-year intervals, $h_{it}^* = \rho h_{it-8}^* + \mathbf{x}_{it}'\beta + \varepsilon_{it}$, and then translate the estimated model parameters $(\beta, \rho, \sigma_\varepsilon)$ to an annual frequency. Another approach is to keep the annual frequency in the model specification and explicitly account for the fact that the latent variable is unobserved in intermediate periods. The only modification required in the estimation strategy is that the latent variable is allowed to vary freely in the periods where it is not observed. In order to estimate the model on annual frequencies, we also need to impute values of the independent variables in the intermediate years. Here we use linear interpolation of the x-variables for which additional information is lacking.

7. Results

Results from the estimations are presented in Table 3. The table is separated into six panels: A presents the estimates of the initial-period ordered-probit, B the estimates of the dynamic model, C the estimated thresholds and sample log-likelihood, D and E the estimated initial-period error variance and autocorrelation coefficients, respectively, and F some sample statistics. Note that both the initial-period and dynamic-model parameters are estimated simultaneously. "*" and "**" mark significance at 10 and 1 percent levels, respectively. The age splines are defined such that the age spline coefficients reflect the additional slope going from a lower segment to a higher. For example, the age slope of the latent health of the initial-period model at age 30 equals $-0.113 + 0.057 = 0.057$.

As for *initial latent health*, there are several expected results. Male, higher income, longer education, married/cohabiting, born in Sweden, and having children are all correlated with better health, and divorced are less healthy than never been married/cohabiting. The estimates suggest that initial latent health is decreasing in age, which is in accordance with expectations. The estimates further suggest that this takes place at a decreasing rate. This may seem counterintuitive, but there is nothing in the original formulation of the demand-for-health model that presumes or predicts an increasing (or a decreasing) rate of deterioration of health over the life cycle. The "natural" depreciation of health with age may be more or less offset by the individual's own "investments" in health over time. Still, people do die and, hence, the rate of deterioration of health cannot decrease too fast, since that would allow for eternal life. Also note that the estimate of the additional age slope in health for the very old (75+) is highly insignificant and poorly estimated. The estimated standard deviation in the initial period is about 2.5 times higher than the standard error in the dynamic model (normalized to unity).

Turning to the *dynamic process*, the results indicate that the most important factor of current health is lagged health. The lagged latent variable is here interacted with age dummies, which implies that the autocorrelation coefficient is age dependent. In panel E, one should observe that the autocorrelation coefficient is highly significant and increasing in age (the autocorrelation coefficient for a 30-year old is $0.884 + 0.049 = 0.993$). This implies that health shocks in ε_{it} become more permanent with age, which should be expected. According to panel B, most independent variables become insignificant when we control for lagged health. Age, relative income, and a university degree still turns out significant and with expected signs, though. Remaining coefficients still have the expected signs, but they are not significant. Recall that the

Table 3. *Simulated maximum-likelihood estimates of latent health (standard errors within parentheses)*

A. Initial period

$\mathbf{1}(\text{age} > 0)(\text{age} - 0)$	−0.113**
	(0.030)
$\mathbf{1}(\text{age} > 25)(\text{age} - 25)$	0.057*
	(0.034)
$\mathbf{1}(\text{age} > 50)(\text{age} - 50)$	0.004
	(0.015)
$\mathbf{1}(\text{age} > 75)(\text{age} - 75)$	0.666
	(0.506)
Sex (male = 1, female = 0)	0.046
	(0.102)
Taxinc/med(taxinc)	0.504**
	(0.090)
College degree	0.198*
	(0.113)
University degree	0.666**
	(0.144)
Married	0.187
	(0.145)
Divorced	−0.408*
	(0.242)
Widow	−0.059
	(0.258)
Has children	0.220*
	(0.092)
Born in Sweden	0.449**
	(0.174)

B. Dynamic process

$\mathbf{1}(\text{age} > 0)(\text{age} - 0)$	−0.013**
	(0.003)
$\mathbf{1}(\text{age} > 25)(\text{age} - 25)$	0.012**
	(0.004)
$\mathbf{1}(\text{age} > 50)(\text{age} - 50)$	−0.001
	(0.002)
$\mathbf{1}(\text{age} > 75)(\text{age} - 75)$	−0.008
	(0.016)
Sex (male = 1, female = 0)	0.012
	(0.015)
Taxinc/med(taxinc)	0.060**
	(0.014)
College degree	0.014
	(0.018)
University degree	0.041*
	(0.021)
Married	0.017
	(0.023)
Divorced	−0.033
	(0.035)
Widow	−0.022
	(0.035)

(*Continued on next page*)

Table 3.   (Continued)

Has children	0.019
	(0.018)
Born in Sweden	0.038
	(0.028)
C. Thresholds	
τ_1	-7.825^{**}
	(0.674)
τ_2	-5.822^{**}
	(0.668)
τ_3	-3.172^{**}
	(0.662)
D. Initial period SE	
$\sigma_0, \text{age} > 0$	2.539^{**}
	(0.141)
$\sigma_0, \text{age} > 25$	0.128
	(0.141)
$\sigma_0, \text{age} > 50$	0.000
	(0.107)
$\sigma_0, \text{age} > 75$	-0.020
	(0.320)
E. Autocorrelation coefficients	
$\mathbf{1}(\text{age} > 0)h_{it-1}^*$	0.884^{**}
	(0.016)
$\mathbf{1}(\text{age} > 25)h_{it-1}^*$	0.049^{**}
	(0.016)
$\mathbf{1}(\text{age} > 50)h_{it-1}^*$	0.015^{*}
	(0.006)
$\mathbf{1}(\text{age} > 75)h_{it-1}^*$	0.005
	(0.013)
F. Sample statistics	
LogLik	-8591.135
Observations	4696
R	100

*significance at 10 percent level.
**significance at 1 percent level.

coefficients in the dynamic model represent marginal effects *conditional* on lagged health. In order to compare the marginal effects in panels A and B, one needs to inflate the coefficients by $1/(1 - \rho)$.

By definition, latent health cannot be observed, but we can compare predicted and observed sample shares by health category. This is done in Figure 7. The bold solid lines represent observed sample shares in 5-year age groups for 1988 (black) and 1996 (gray). For each individual in the sample, we have simulated a single latent health profile and calculated the corresponding health category. The predicted sample shares are represented by the thin lines for 1988 (black) and 1996 (gray). The four panels each give the sample share in the health category indicated by the panel title.

Figure 7. *Observed and predicted sample shares by health category 1988 and 1996*

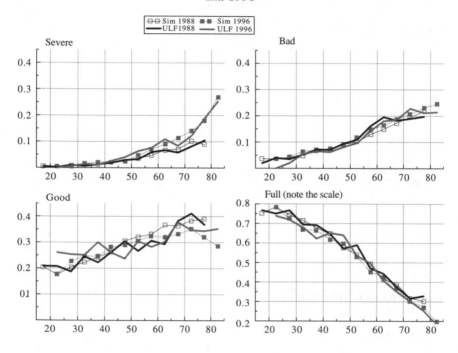

The overall impression is that the model predicts the cross-section age profile quite well. The predicted shares follow the observed quite closely. One can note that the predictions pick up the increases in observed sample shares, conditional on age, with severe and bad health conditions between 1988 and 1996. This trend is not unique for Sweden, as we have emphasized, but seems to be a more general phenomenon, closely linked to the increase in long-standing illness such as asthma, allergy, diabetes, and conditions related to obesity. The divergence starts at fairly young ages and is most prominent for individuals in their early 60s. (There are only few observations, though, in the right-hand tail of the age distribution, which may produce inaccurate estimates.) The results are more mixed for the "Good" and "Full" categories. The most problematic category is "Good" where both the observed and predicted shares are rather volatile, and the model seems to over-estimate the share of "Good."

8. Simulations

In this section, we present the results of our simulations for the baseline scenario described at length in Chapter 3. The simulations are based on a 100 percent sample in SESIM. Since men generally have higher health status than women, regardless of whether the health indicator is subjective or "objective," we present our simulation results separately for men and women.

8.1. Cross-sectional age–health profiles

Figures 8 and 9 reproduce simulated cross-sectional age profiles of the population shares by health category for 2000 (average for 1999–2001), 2020 (2019–2021), and 2040 (2039–2041) for men and women, respectively. Health status continues to be worse for women, but the general shapes of the graphs are similar for men and women: the share in full health declines by age, the shares in severe and bad health increase, whereas the shares in good health first increase, then decrease (more so for women). Over time, the cross-sectional age–health profiles change in a similar way for men and women. Thus, by 2020 and 2040, the shares of men and women, respectively, in good health are predicted to decline, while the shares in severe health are predicted to increase. The simulations provided no substantial changes in the predicted cross-sectional age profiles for people in full or bad health.

8.2. Cohort age–health profiles

Note that the age profiles above are cross-sectional representations and, hence, mix cohort-specific and time effects. So, next, in Figures 10 and 11,

Figure 8.** **Simulated cross-sectional age–health profiles 2000, 2020, and 2040 (men)

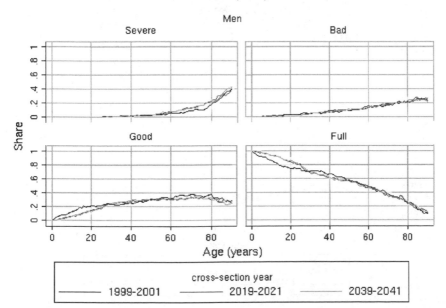

Figure 9. Simulated cross-sectional age–health profiles 2000, 2020, and 2040 (women)

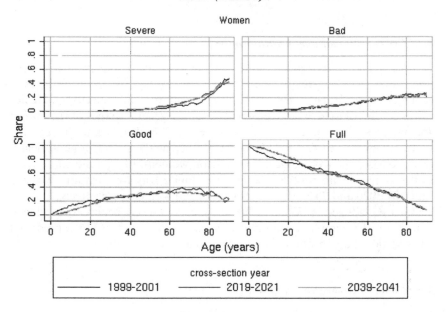

Figure 10. Simulated cohort age–health profiles for the birth-cohorts of 1930, 1940, and 1950 (men)

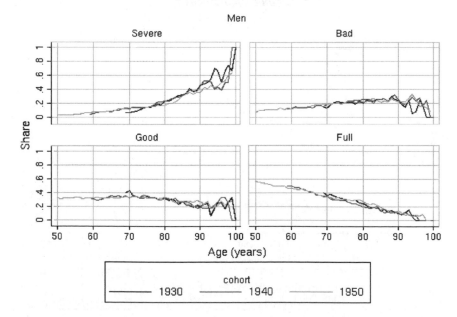

Figure 11. Simulated cohort age–health profiles for the birth-cohorts of 1930, 1940, and 1950 (women)

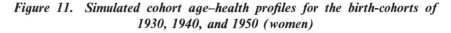

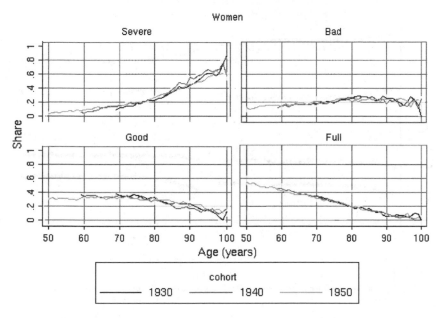

we present simulated age–health profiles for the three birth-cohorts of 1930, 1940, and 1950 for men and women, respectively. The age–health profiles of the three cohorts have similar shapes for both men and women. There seem to be differences between men and women, though, when it comes to the levels of the profiles. For men, the 1940 and 1950 cohorts have lower shares in severe health status than the 1930 cohort, higher shares in bad and good health, but apparently also in full health. For women, the 1940 and 1950 cohorts have lower shares in full health than the 1930 cohort. The 1940 female cohort seems to have a higher share in severe health than the 1930 cohort, but the 1950 cohort, on the other hand, seems to have a lower share in severe health than the 1930 cohort. In all, there seem to be a decrease in the overall health level for the 1940 and 1950 female cohorts, while there is not such a marked tendency for the male cohorts.

8.3. Population-shares time series

Finally, we present the development of the simulated population shares for each health category from 2000 to 2040; in Figure 12 for the 50–74 years old and in Figure 13 for the 75 +. As for the 50–74 years old, the shares in full or good health are decreasing for both men and women, while the

Figure 12. Simulated population 50–74 shares for each health category, 2000–2040

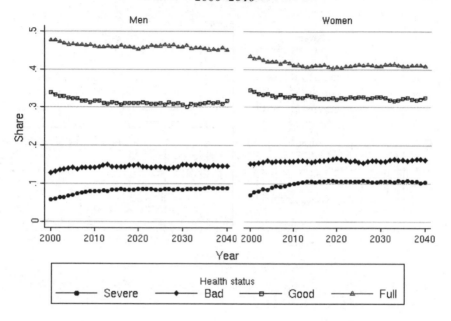

Figure 13. Simulated population 75+ shares for each health category, 2000–2040

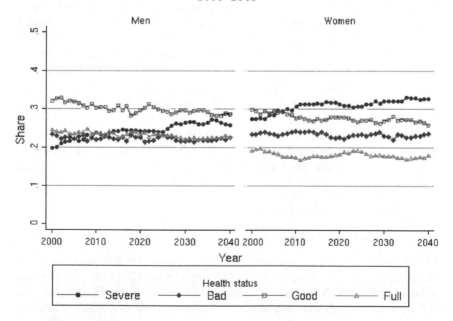

shares in bad or severe health are increasing. It should be noted, though, that at least part of the increase in health categories "severe" and "bad" are influenced by increased longevity and changes in the demographic structure. As for the 75+, the differences between men and women are more marked. While the share in severe health would increase to be the most common health status for women in 2020 and 2040 with some 32–33 percent of the female population 75+ belonging to this health status group, the most common health status for men would be good health; the share in severe health in the male population would be some 25–26 percent – an increase from some 20 percent in 2000. The share in full health would be around 17–18 percent for women and 22–23 percent for men. For both men and women, the shares in severe health would increase and the shares in good health decrease from 2000 to 2020 and 2040, while the shares in full health and bad health would fluctuate but show no clear trend.

9. Conclusion

We have developed a module, which simulates health in four categories: full health, good health, bad health, and severe health problems. Determining factors are age, gender, education, relative income, civil status, the presence of children, and nationality (born in Sweden or not).

According to the simulations, following the base case scenario, presented in this chapter, women will continue to have higher shares in severe and bad health states and lower in full health than men. There is also a trend toward decreasing shares in full health and increasing shares in severe and bad health for both men and women aged 50–74. This trend seems to accumulate and be stronger for the 75+. Differences between men and women seem to be even more marked for the 75+; they even get larger from the year 2000 to 2020 and 2040.

The simulated development of health states among men and women, presented here, will be an essential input into the modules that simulate sickness absence (Chapter 5), disability pension (Chapter 6), inpatient care (Chapter 10), and social care for the elderly (Chapter 11). Since the major changes in the distribution of health states from 2000 to 2020 and 2040 seem to be among the 75+ females, who are large consumers of care, the simulated development of health will certainly have a substantial impact on inpatient care and social care for the elderly.

References

Becker, G.S. (1964), *Human Capital*, New York: Columbia University Press (for the National Bureau of Economic Research).

Bolin, K., L. Jacobson and B. Lindgren (2001), "The family as the health producer – when spouses are Nash-bargainers", *Journal of Health Economics*, Vol. 20, pp. 349–362.

Bolin, K., L. Jacobson and B. Lindgren (2002a), "The demand for health and health investments in Sweden 1980/81, 1990/91 and 1996/97", pp. 93–112 in: B. Lindgren, editor, *Individual Decisions for Health*, London: Routledge.

Bolin, K., L. Jacobson and B. Lindgren (2002b), "The family as the health producer – when spouses act strategically", *Journal of Health Economics*, Vol. 21, pp. 475–495.

Bolin, K. and B. Lindgren (2002), "Asthma and allergy – the significance of chronic conditions for individual health behaviour", *Allergy*, Vol. 57, pp. 115–122.

Bolin, K., B. Lindgren, M. Lindström and P. Nystedt (2003), "Investments in social capital – implications of social interactions for the production of health", *Social Science and Medicine*, Vol. 56, pp. 2379–2390.

Bolin, K., B. Lindgren and S. Rössner (2006), "The significance of overweight and obesity for individual health behaviour – an economic analysis based on the Swedish surveys of living conditions 1980/81, 1988/89, and 1996/97", *Scandinavian Journal of Public Health*, Vol. 34, pp. 422–431.

Börsch-Supan, A., A. Brugiavini, H. Jürges, J. Mackenbach, J. Siegrist and G. Weber (eds.) (2005), "Health, ageing, and retirement in Europe, first results from the survey of health, ageing, and retirement in Europe (SHARE)", Mannheim Research Institute for the Economics of Aging, Mannheim.

Börsch-Supan, A., V. Hajivassiliou, L. Kotlikoff and J. Morris (1992), "Health, children, and elderly living arrangements: a multiperiod-multinominal probit model with unobserved heterogeneity and autocorrelated errors", pp. 79–107 in: D.A. Wise, editor, *Topics in the Economics of Aging*, Chicago and London: University of Chicago Press.

Brooks, R.G. (1995), *Health Status Measurement. A Perspective on Change*, London: Macmillan.

Burström, K., M. Johannesson and F. Diderichsen (2001), "Health-related quality of life by disease and socio-economic group in the general population in Sweden", *Health Policy*, Vol. 55, pp. 51–69.

Grossman, M. (1972), *The Demand for Health: A Theoretical and Empirical Investigation*, New York: Columbia University Press (for the National Bureau of Economic Research).

Jacobson, L. (2000), "The family as producer of health – an extension of the Grossman model", *Journal of Health Economics*, Vol. 19, pp. 611–637.

Liljas, B. (1998), "The demand for health with uncertainty and insurance", *Journal of Health Economics*, Vol. 17, pp. 153–170.

Muurinen, J.M. (1982), "An economic model of health behaviour – with empirical applications to Finnish Health Survey Data", Ph.D. thesis, Department of Economics and Related Studies, University of York, York.

Parker, M.G., K. Ahacic and M. Thorslund (2004), "Health changes among Swedish oldest old: prevalence rates from 1992 and 2002 show increasing health problems", *Journal of Gerontology Medical Sciences*.

Statistics Sweden (1992), *Hälsoindex för den svenska befolkningen. Rapport från ett utvecklingsprojekt*, Stockholm: Statistics Sweden.

Wagstaff, A. (1986), "The demand for health: some new empirical evidence", *Journal of Health Economics*, Vol. 5, pp. 195–233.

Appendix A. Illustration of the construction of the health index suggested by Statistics Sweden

	Self-assessed health	Self-assessed mobility	Long-term illness	Working capacity
Full health (health level 4)	3	3	2	–
	3	2	2	–
Not full health (health level 3)	3	3	1	3
	3	3	1	2
	3	3	1	1
	3	2	1	3
	3	2	1	2
	3	1	2	–
	3	1	1	3
	2	3	2	–
	2	3	1	3
	2	2	2	–
	2	2	1	3
	2	1	2	–
Some illness (health level 2)	3	2	1	1
	3	1	1	2
	3	1	1	1
	2	3	1	2
	2	3	1	1
	2	2	1	2
	2	1	1	3
	2	1	1	2
	1	3	2	–
	1	3	1	3
	1	3	1	2
	1	2	2	–
	1	2	1	3
	1	2	1	2
	1	1	2	–
	1	1	1	3
	1	1	1	2
Severe illness (health level 1)	2	2	1	1
	2	1	1	1
	1	3	1	1
	1	2	1	1
	1	1	1	1

Source: Statistics Sweden (1992).

Appendix B. The estimator

Consider the following simple dynamic model of a latent variable,

$$h_{it}^* = \rho h_{it-1}^* + \mathbf{x}_{it}'\beta + \varepsilon_{it} = V_{it} + \varepsilon_{it}, \tag{B.1}$$

where h_{it}^* denotes the latent variable ρ of individual i in period t, $\mathbf{x}_{it}$ a vector of observable predetermined variables with associated coefficients β. Consider the following link function between the latent and observed variable,

$$h_{it} = j \text{ iff } \tau_{j-1} < h_{it}^* \leq \tau_j, \tag{B.2}$$

where h_{it} denotes the discrete health index with J possible outcomes and τ_j denotes the upper threshold of category j with $\tau_0 = -\infty$ and $\tau_j = \infty$. Under the assumption that ε_{it} is normally distributed, the model describes a dynamic ordered-probit process with a lagged latent regressor.

Consider $T + 1$ time periods $t = 0, ..., T$, where we assume that the initial value h_{i0}^* is exogenously given. The probability to observe $h_{it} = j$ is given by

$$\Pr(h_{it} = j | \mathbf{x}_{it}, h_{it-1}^*, \Omega) = \Pr(\tau_{h_{it}-1} < V_{it} + \varepsilon_{it} \leq \tau_{h_{it}})$$
$$= \int_{\tau_{h_{it}-1}-V_{it}}^{\tau_{h_{it}}-V_{it}} f(\varepsilon_{it} | \mathbf{x}_{it}, h_{it-1}^*, \Omega) \mathrm{d}\varepsilon_{it}, \tag{B.3}$$

where Ω denotes the set of model parameters $\{\rho, \beta, \tau\}$, $V_{it} = \rho' h_{it-1}^* + x_{it}'\beta$, and $f(\bullet | \mathbf{x}_{it}, h_{it-1}^*, \Omega)$ denotes the conditional density function of ε_{it}. Thus, the conditional probability to observe a sequence of outcomes $h_i' = (h_{i1}, ..., h_{iT})$ given initial latent condition h_{i0}^* is

$$\Pr(h_{i1}, ..., h_{iT} | h_{i0}^*) = \int_{\tau_{h1-1}-V_{i1}}^{\tau_{h_{i1}}-V_{i1}} ... \int_{\tau_{h_{iT}-1}-V_{iT}}^{\tau_{h_{iT}}-V_{iT}} f(\varepsilon_{i1}, ..., \varepsilon_{iT} | \mathbf{x}_{it}, h_{i0}^*, \Omega) \mathrm{d}\varepsilon_{iT}...\mathrm{d}\varepsilon_{i1}, \tag{B.4}$$

where $f(\bullet, ..., \bullet | \bullet)$ denotes the conditional multivariate distribution of the error vector $(\varepsilon_{i1}, ..., \varepsilon_{iT})$. Note that the integration limits are recursively defined such that $V_{it} = \rho(V_{it-1} + \varepsilon_{it-1}) + x_{it}'\beta$.

As the initial latent variable h_{i0}^* is unobserved, we need to condition the probability on the initial value of the observable categorical variable h_{it} rather than on the latent variable h_{it}^*. As the initial value h_{i0}^* is the outcome of an unobserved stochastic process predating period 0, we do not restrict the error variance to unity. The conditional probability can then be written as

$$\Pr(h_{i1}, ..., h_{iT} | h_{i0}) = \int_{\tau_{h_{i0}-1}-x_{i0}'\beta_0}^{\tau_{h_{i0}}-x_{i0}'\beta_0} \Pr(h_{i1}, ..., h_{iT} | h_{i0}^*) f_0(\varepsilon_{i0}) \mathrm{d}\varepsilon_{i0}, \tag{B.5}$$

where $f_0(\varepsilon)$ denotes the density function and $h_{i0}^* = \mathbf{x}_{i0}'\beta_0 + \varepsilon_{i0}$.

The latent model can be expressed in vector form as (including $t = 0$)

$$h_i^* = V_i \Psi + \varepsilon_i, \tag{B.6}$$

where

$$V_i = \begin{pmatrix} x_{i0} & 0 & 0 \\ 0 & h_{i1}^* & x_{i1} \\ \vdots & \vdots & \vdots \end{pmatrix} \tag{B.7}$$

and $\Psi = (\beta_0 \; \rho \; \beta)$. The error term is assumed multivariate normal $\varepsilon_i \sim \text{MVN}(0, \Sigma)$.

Let $D^h(\Omega, h_i)$ denote the subspace of $\Re^{T+1}$ such that the latent variable h_i^* is consistent with the observed outcome h_i, that is

$$D^h(\Omega, h_i) = \{h_i^* : \tau_{h_{it}-1} < h_{it}^* \le \tau_{h_{it}}, \quad t = 0, ..., T\}. \tag{B.8}$$

The indicator for the observed outcome is

$$\mathbf{1}(h_i^* \in D^h(\Omega, h_i)) = \mathbf{1}(V_i \Psi + \varepsilon_i \in D^h(\Omega, h_i)). \tag{B.9}$$

Let Γ denote the Cholesky decomposition of Σ such that $\Gamma\Gamma' = \Sigma$, and let η denote a $T + 1$ dimensional vector of iid standard normal random variables. The indicator can be written in a recursive form as

$$\mathbf{1}(h_i^* \in D^h(\Omega, h_i)) = \prod_{t=0}^{T} \mathbf{1}(\eta_{it} \in D_t^\eta(\Omega, \eta_{i, <t})), \tag{B.10}$$

where subscript "$<t$" denotes the sub-vector with elements predating period t.[1] The relevant subspaces can be expressed as

$$D_t^\eta(\Omega, \eta_{i, <t}) = \{\eta_{it} : a_{it} < \eta_{it} \le b_{it}\}, \tag{B.11}$$

where the boundaries are recursively given by

$$\begin{aligned} a_{it} &= \frac{\tau_{h_{it}-1} - \rho h_{it-1}^* - x_{it}'\beta - \Gamma_{t, <t}\eta_{i, <t}}{\Gamma_{tt}} \\ b_{it} &= \frac{\tau_{h_{it}} - \rho h_{it-1}^* - x_{it}'\beta - \Gamma_{t, <t}\eta_{i, <t}}{\Gamma_{tt}} \end{aligned} \tag{B.12}$$

and h_{it}^* is recursively updated according to

$$h_{it}^* = \rho h_{it-1}^* + x_{it}'\beta + \Gamma_{t, <t+1}\eta_{i, <t+1}. \tag{B.13}$$

---

[1] $\eta_{i, <1}$ is defined as the empty matrix.

Thus, individual i's contribution to the sample likelihood is

$$L_i = \Pr(h_i|\Omega) = \Pr(h_i^* \in D^h(\Psi, h_i)) = E[1(h_i^* \in D^h(\Psi, h_i))]$$

$$= E\left[\prod_{t=0}^{T} \Pr(\eta_{it} \in D_t^\eta(\Omega, \eta_{i,<t}))\right] = E\left[\prod_{t=0}^{T}(\Phi(b_{it}) - \Phi(a_{it}))\right] \quad \text{(B.14)}$$

As given in Eq. (B.4), the required probability involves a multi-dimensional integral, which generally cannot be evaluated using analytical methods. However, simulation assisted methods are applicable if we can simulate the probability for the observed vectors of outcomes. To do this, we modify the GHK simulated proposed by Börsch-Supan *et al.* (1992). The simulator approximates the expectation in Eq. (B.14), using recursive random draws from $\eta_{it} \in D_t(\Omega, \eta_{i,<t})$ such that

$$\eta_{it}^r = \Phi^{-1}((\Phi(b_{it}^r) - \Phi(a_{it}^r))u_{it}^r + \Phi(a_{it}^r)), \quad \text{(B.15)}$$

where u_{it}^r represents a uniform pseudo-random draw. Let u_i^r denotes a $(T+1) \times 1$ vector of uniform random draws. In the application, we use antithetic draws such that $u_i^{2r} = 1 - u_i^r$ for $r \leq R/2$. The simulated probability is calculated as follows:

1. Calculate a_{i0} and b_{i0} for $t = 0$ according to Eq. (B.12) with $\Gamma = 0$ and $\eta = 0$ and calculate

$$p_{i0} = \Phi(b_{i0}) - \Phi(a_{i0})$$
$$\eta_{i0}^r = \Phi^{-1}(p_{i0}u_{i0}^r + \Phi(a_{i0}))$$
$$h_{i0}^{*r} = x_{i1}'\beta_0 + \Gamma_{00}\eta_{i0}^r. \quad \text{(B.16)}$$

2. For $t = 1, ..., T$ and $r = 1, ..., R$ update a_{it}^r and b_{it}^r according to Eq. (B.12), calculate and store

$$p_{it}^r = \Phi(b_{it}^r) - \Phi(a_{it}^r)$$
$$\eta_{it} = \Phi^{-1}(p_{it}^r u_{it}^r + \Phi(a_{i1}^r))$$
$$h_{it}^{*r} = \rho h_{it-1}^* + \mathbf{x}_{it}'\beta + \Gamma_{t,<t+1}\eta_{i,<t+1}. \quad \text{(B.17)}$$

3. Calculate $p_i^r = \prod_{t=0}^{T} p_{it}^r$ and

$$\widehat{p}_i = \frac{1}{R}\sum_{r=1}^{R} p_i^r. \quad \text{(B.18)}$$

Individual i's approximated contribution to the sample likelihood is given then given by $\widehat{L}_i(\Omega) = \widehat{p}_i$ and the simulated sample

Kristian Bolin et al.

log-likelihood is

$$\ln \widehat{L}_N(\Omega) = \sum_{i=1}^{N} \ln \widehat{L}_i(\Omega) \tag{B.19}$$

The maximum simulated likelihood (MSL) estimator is based on the simulated sample log-likelihood given in Eq. (B.19) such that

$$\widehat{\Omega} = \arg\max_\Omega \ln \tilde{L}_N(\Omega). \tag{B.20}$$

The estimate is the argument that maximizes this simulated log-likelihood.

If we do not have observations of h_{is} for some $0 < s < T$ we cannot specify the integration limits for this observation. If there are no other restrictions on the latent variable, all we can do is to allow the latent variable to take on any value in period s.[2] Hence, for period we use the integral limits $-\infty$ and ∞, respectively, such that

$$\Pr(h_i|h_{i0}^*) = \int_{\tau_{h_{i0}-1}-x'_{i0}\beta}^{\tau_{h_{i0}}-x'_{i0}\beta} \cdots \int_{-\infty}^{\infty} \cdots \int_{\tau_{h_{iT}-1}-V_{iT}}^{\tau_{h_{iT}}-V_{iT}} \tag{B.21}$$
$$\times f(\varepsilon_{i0}, \ldots, \varepsilon_{is}, \ldots, \varepsilon_{iT}) d\varepsilon_{iT} \ldots d\varepsilon_{is} \ldots d\varepsilon_{i0}$$

for s being the unobserved period. This probability then replaces Eq. (B.4) in Eq. (B.5).

---

[2] If there were information on an absorbing state (e.g., death), this information could be included to restrict the limits in the intermediate periods.

CHAPTER 5

Sickness Absence from Work

Kristian Bolin*, Sören Höjgård and Björn Lindgren

The purpose of this chapter is to analyze and simulate sickness absence from work. We will provide a brief background, recapitulate the empirical research, briefly describe the Swedish sickness-benefits system, present the data, estimate the empirical model, interpret the estimates, and discuss the simulations obtained from SESIM regarding sickness absence from work. Due to data limitations, our analysis will be restricted to sickness-absence spells that last 15 days or longer. In another context, this might have caused a major problem. Since our focus is on the ageing baby-boomers, spells of sickness absence among the younger and middle-aged generations are not of particularly great interest or importance per se. Longer lasting spells, though, are positively correlated with the probability of receiving disability pension, which clearly belongs to our research priorities. This issue will be dealt with in Chapter 6, where the results from this chapter will be one of the inputs when predicting the development of disability pensions in Sweden.

1. Background

There are many factors that may explain the number of spells and the number of days of absence from work reported as due to sickness. Health problems seem to be the most natural candidate to include among the explanatory factors, but individual health behavior could enter the scene in several ways. A day of reported sickness might primarily be due to the

---

* Corresponding author.

CONTRIBUTIONS TO ECONOMIC ANALYSIS
VOLUME 285 ISSN: 0573-8555
DOI:10.1016/S0573-8555(07)00005-3

fact that a person's capacity to produce market goods and household commodities is so heavily reduced so the day is just spent at home with very little or no household commodities produced. It might also be a day when the person actively produces a restoration of his or her health, combining own time and healthcare of some kind. It might be a day when the person waits for a hospital treatment, for instance, a hip replacement, but his or her condition is an obstacle for taking part in market production (very much depending on the kind of job, in which the person would normally be involved).

Due to the fact that there is often no clear-cut borderline between illness and healthiness, days off work may well be reported as caused by some (minor) illness, difficult to diagnose, even though vaguely or not at all related to sickness. So, the number of spells and the lengths of spells certainly depend also on people's preferences and on the incentives that eligibility rules, the generosity of sickness-benefits schemes, and societal norms create. Part of "leisure time," reported as sickness absence, might still be health-related, if the time is used taking precautionary actions in order to invest in own health. This was the point of departure for our work on adding health as an explanatory variable to the already existing SESIM module on sickness absence.

2. Previous empirical research

In the labor-economics literature, sickness absence has been analyzed as a labor supply phenomenon. The underlying theoretical model for most empirical work is either a traditional utility maximizing labor-leisure trade-off model,[1] an efficiency-wage model,[2] or a hedonic-price model.[3]

Most empirical studies use cross-sectional or time-series data from a single country to analyze absence behavior. One exception is Drago and Wooden (1992), who utilized cross-sectional data on absence among employees of 15 paired establishments producing similar products (one in Australia and the other in another country) owned by the same company. Another is Barmby *et al.* (2002), who used cross-country data from the Luxemburg Employment study (including absence data from nine countries, not necessarily from the same year). Finally, Nyman *et al.*

---

[1] For instance, Allen (1981a), Leigh (1983), Paringer (1983), Drago and Wooden (1992), Johansson and Palme (1996), Winkelmann (1996), Barmby and Stephane (2000), Lindeboom and Kerkhofs (2000), Bridges and Mumford (2001), Broström et al. (2004), and Henrekson and Persson (2004).

[2] For instance, Drago and Wooden (1992), Barmby et al. (2001), and Barmby et al. (2002).

[3] For instance, Allen (1981b), Leigh (1983), Barmby et al. (1991), Drago and Wooden (1992), Delgado and Knieser (1997), and Primoff Vistness (1997).

(2002) used time-series data from the national labor force surveys of eight countries.

Most of the studies are also concerned with short-term absence. The underlying theoretical approach implies that absence is seen, at least partly, as a strategy, which the individual can use to increase leisure beyond what was agreed upon in the employment contract. Hence, the solution to the utility maximization problem allows for specifying the "demand for absence" as a function of characteristics such as non-labor income, the wage rate, the availability of sickness-benefit or sick-leave compensation and the compensation rate entailed, the number of contracted hours, the flexibility of the work schedule, the risk of loosing one's job (often approximated by the unemployment rate), work-place hazards, employer efforts to constrain absence, etc. It might be noted here that, according to the efficiency-wage model, absence may be controlled by employers differentiating wages according to the sickness-absence records of the employees. The hedonic-price model also assumes that workers are rewarded for not being absent through higher wages.

The majority of studies are, therefore, primarily concerned with analyzing the effects on sickness absence of economic incentives inherent in the wage schemes, the flexibility of the work schedules, and the sickness-benefit schemes. However, several studies also include some measure of the individual's health. This may be in the form of self-reported health (Allen, 1981a; Leigh, 1983; Paringer, 1983; Winkelmann, 1996; Primoff Vistness, 1997; Gilleskie, 1998; Barmby and Stephane, 2000), or some more objective measure such as whether the absence was due to hospitalization or serious medically certified illness (Barmby *et al.*, 1991; Delgado and Knieser, 1997), whether the individual suffers from some medically diagnosed condition, and the number of such conditions (Johansson and Palme, 1996; Winkelmann, 1996; Primoff Vistness, 1997; Broström *et al.*, 2004), or mortality (Henrekson and Persson, 2004).

The empirical specifications and the variables included vary (Table 1). In general, the empirical evidence suggests that short-term absence (a) increases with the generosity of the health insurance schemes, (b) is higher for individuals with poorer working conditions, (c) is higher for women than for men, (d) decreases during recessions, (e) is higher for individuals with poorer health (though Johansson and Palme (1996) showed conflicting results). The results regarding the effects of a higher wage rate are inconclusive.

There are, however, concerns regarding the interpretation of the results, particularly among authors that explicitly refer to an efficiency-wage or a hedonic-price model as their theoretical foundation. For instance, it is argued that the limited effect of wage differences may be attributed to endogeneity problems. That is, workers may sort themselves into high- and low-wage occupations (or firms) according to differences in their relative preferences for consumption of goods and leisure. In that case, the effects

Table 1. Empirical specifications and variables included in previous studies

Author	Dependent variable	Explanatory variables	Empirical specification
Thomas (1980), Country not stated, time-series, 1955–1975	Industry-specific number of absence days	*Industry*: Wage-rate, ratio of sickness benefit to wage. *Labor market*: Unemployment rate	Log-linear OLS
Allen (1981a), US data (Quality of Employment Survey). Cross-section, 1972	Individual absence rate	*Personal*: Wage-rate, number of contracted hours, flexibility of work-schedule, occupation, union membership, non-labor income, age, gender, marital status, education, and race. *Firm*: Work-hazards, industry, sick-leave availability. *Health*: Self-reported	Logit
Allen (1981b), US data (American Paper Institute Survey), time-series, 1974–1977	Firm absence rate	*Firm*: Wage-rate, pension, minimum disability payment, injury-rate, union at firm, number of employees, and regional dummies	Logit
Leigh (1983), US data (Quality of Employment Survey). Cross-section, 1974	Individual absence rate	*Personal*: Wage-rate, union-membership, tenure, age, marital status, number of children, education, race, non-labor income. *Firm*: Work-hazards, number of employees, paid sick-leave, paid vacation, repetitive job, physically demanding job, and regional dummies. *Health*: Self-reported, conditions, smoking habits, drinking habits, and obesity	Logistic
Barmby *et al.* (1991), UK data, source not stated. Monthly data, 1987–1988	Firm absence rate, absence duration	*Personal*: Sickness-benefit grade, proximity to loosing sickness-benefit grade, full-time employment, gender, marital status. *Firm*: Firm dummies. *Health*: Absence caused by hospitalization, absence caused by medically certified illness	Logit, survival analysis

Study	Dependent variable	Explanatory variables	Estimation method
Drago and Wooden (1992), cross-national data (Australian national Institute of Labour Studies). Cross-section, 1988	Individual absence rate	*Personal*: Wage-rate, number of contracted hours per week, type of job, number of contracted days per week, tenure, permanent contract, job-security, job-satisfaction, age, gender, whether the individual has dependents, education *Firm*: Promotion opportunities, annual number of days of sick-leave entitlement *Labor market*: Probability of alternative employment	Logit
Johansson and Palme (1996), Swedish data (Swedish Level of Living Survey). Cross-section, 1988	Absence days	*Personal*: Net earnings lost when absent, number of contracted hours, non-labor income, age, gender, marital status, number of children *Firm*: Work-hazards, punctuality requirements, use of punch clock *Health*: H1 and H2 (constructed from a principal component analysis of 11 diagnoses), disability *Labor market*: Unemployment rate	Binomial, binomial with mixture distribution
Winkelmann (1996), German data (German Socio-economic Panel). Cross-section, 1985	Absence days	*Personal*: Wage-rate, union membership *Firm*: Work-hazards, number of employees, advancement opportunities, degree of autonomy in work *Health*: Self-reported	Poisson, under-reported Poisson, negative binomial
Delgado and Knieser (1997) UK data, source not stated. Time-series, 1981–1985.	Absence spells	*Personal*: Pay-grade, tenure, age, gender, marital status *Firm*: Number of employees, distance from garage to town center *Health*: Number of absence days the preceding year, number of absence days 2 years ago, number of long-term absence spells, proportion of absence spells for which a doctor's certificate has been shown	OLS, Poisson, negative binomial, GLS

(Continued on next page)

Table 1. (Continued)

Author	Dependent variable	Explanatory variables	Empirical specification
Primoff Vistness (1997), US data (National Medical Expenditure Survey). Cross-section, 1987	Absence days	*Personal*: Wage-rate, number of contracted hours, type of occupation, union membership, tenure, sick-leave entitlement, health insurance, non-labor income, age, gender, marital status, number of children, type of child-care, education *Firm*: Number of employees, type of industry *Health*: Self-reported, number of chronic conditions, number of ambulatory visits, number of emergency visits, number of prescription drugs *Labor market*: Regional dummies	Hurdle model – Logit for absence probability, negativity binomial for number of absence days
Lindeboom and Kerkhofs (2000), Dutch data (Leiden Institute for Social Research). Time-series, 1987–1991	Time from work to absence, time from absence to work	*Personal*: Type of contract, tenure, type of teacher, class-size, age, gender, marital status *Firm*: Type of school, number of teachers, ease of replacing when absence anticipated, ease of replacing when absence not anticipated, increasing number of pupils, decreasing number of pupils, health services supplied at school	State-specific survival model with work-place fixed effect
Barmby and Stephane (2000), German data (German Socio-economic Panel). Longitudinal, 1984–1988, and 1990	Firm absence rate	*Personal*: Wage-rate, number of contracted hours, contracted minus desired hours, tenure, age, number of children, education *Firm*: Number of employees *Health*: Grade of disability	Random effects panel data model
Bridges and Mumford (2001), UK data (Family Expenditure Survey). Cross-section, 1993	Absence spells, absence days	*Personal*: Difference between individual wage and occupation-average wage, number of contracted hours, non-labor income, age, marital status, number of children, education	Probit

Study	Absence measure	Explanatory variables	Method
Barmby *et al.* (2001), UK data, source not stated. Cross-section, 1988	Absence days	*Personal*: Wage-rate, sickness-benefit grade, number of contracted hours, age, gender, marital status. *Firm*: Firm dummies	Negative binomial
Barmby *et al.* (2002), Labour Force Surveys from nine countries. Cross-section, but year depends on country	Absence rate	*Personal*: Number of contracted hours, type of industry, tenure, age, gender, marital status. *Country*: Country dummies	OLS
Nyman *et al.* (2002), Labour Force Surveys in nine countries. Time-series, 1985–2001	Absence rate	*Personal*: Age-group, gender. *Country*: Unemployment rate, employment rate, share of labor force with temporary contracts	OLS
Johansson and Palme (2002), Swedish data (Swedish level of Living Survey). Cross-section, 1990 and 1991	Time from work to absence, time from absence to work	*Personal*: Wage-rate, number of contracted hours, marginal tax rate, non-labor, income, gender. *Labor market*: Unemployment rate at local labor market	Survival analysis
Henrekson and Persson (2004), Swedish data (National Social Insurance Board). Time-series, 1955–1999. Longitudinal, 1983–1991	Absence days	*Institutional*: Reform dummies (compensation rate, number of mandatory waiting days). *Labor market*: Age-composition of labor force, gender-composition of labor force, labor force participation rate. *Health*: Mortality rate	OLS (time-series analysis), panel data model
Broström *et al.* (2004), Swedish data (Swedish Level of Living Survey). Daily work absence from 1990 to 1991	Time from work to absence, time from absence to work	*Personal*: Wage-rate, number of contracted hours, replacement rate in sickness benefit, non-labor income, age, marital status, number of children. *Personal*: Non-labor income, age, marital status, number of children. *Firm*: Noisy work environment, exposed to gas, dust, smoke, or vibrations, heavy lifting, physically exhausting work, mentally exhausting work, stressful work, repetitive work, monotonous work, unpleasant body positions, work accidents, work-related diseases, punctuality requirements, use of punch clock. *Health*: Selected conditions	Survival analysis

of financial incentives would be underestimated. It may be noted that health status could affect the relative preferences for income (goods consumption) and leisure, albeit in an indeterminate way. That is, a poor health status may have negative effects on earnings capacity (and hence increase the marginal utility of income) while, at the same time, make work more stressful (and hence increase the marginal utility of leisure for recuperative purposes).

Another concern relates to the measure to be used to control for the effect of differences in health status. It has been suggested that self-reported health may be endogenous for other reasons than its potential effect on relative utility of income and leisure. That is, absence for a worker in poor health may be less stigmatizing than absence for a worker in good health. Thus, workers with a large number of absence days might be induced to report a low-health status to gain social acceptance when interviewed for surveys. In that case, the effect of differences in health status would be overestimated. Accordingly, as reported above, some authors have attempted to use more objective measures to control for differences in health. However, objective health measures, such as the existence and number of medically diagnosed conditions, or mortality, may have no relation to the observed absence spells, and workers may suffer a temporary reduction in health status without being hospitalized or seeing a physician (i.e., persons with a flu or some other viral infection, where self-care is more or less equally efficient as medical care).

3. The Swedish sickness-benefits system

Sweden has had a comprehensive public sickness-benefits system since 1955 (Broberg, 1973; Lindgren, 1995; Henrekson and Persson, 2004). It compensates for income losses from work caused by ill health. It is tax financed and administered by the Swedish Social Insurance Administration (formerly the Swedish National Board of Social Insurance). Some key features of the system for the period 1974–2007 are briefly presented in Table 2. The amounts of compensation as well as the number of waiting days and other features of the system have been subject to several changes through the years.

Presently (March 2007), the sickness-benefits system covers all those who are *employed* and have been working for at least 14 days, as well as those who are *unemployed* (provided that they are registered as job seekers at the local employment office), and *persons participating in active labor market programs*. There is, in principle, no limitation to the duration of benefits, provided that the person is unable to work (alternatively, unable to seek work or participate in the labor market program) because of illness (Hogstedt *et al.*, 2004). Formally, this is assessed by the local social insurance office in the municipality to which a person belongs.

Table 2. Features of the Swedish sickness-benefits system 1974–2007

Year	Compensation rate (percent)	Income cap SEK (current prices)	Average annual wage SEK (current prices)	Mandatory waiting period	Employer pays	Doctor's certificate required from
1974	90	63000	45000	1 day	No	Day 8
1975	90	70000	53000	1 day	No	Day 8
1976	90	77000	59000	1 day	No	Day 8
1977	90	85000	64000	1 day	No	Day 8
1978	90	92000	72000	1 day	No	Day 8
1979	90	101000	78000	1 day	No	Day 8
1980	90	112000	86000	1 day	No	Day 8
1981	90	125000	93000	1 day	No	Day 8
1982	90	134000	99000	1 day	No	Day 8
1983	90	146000	105000	1 day	No	Day 8
1984	90	152000	117000	1 day	No	Day 8
1985	90	164000	127000	1 day	No	Day 8
1986	90	175000	135000	1 day	No	Day 8
1987	90	181000	145000	1 day	No	Day 8
1988	90	194000	156000	None	No	Day 8
1989	90	209000	172000	None	No	Day 8
1990	90	223000	—	None	No	Day 8
1991	65 (days 1–3) 85 (days 4–89) 90 (day 90…)	242000	185000	None	No	Day 8
1992	65 (days 1–3) 85 (days 4–90) 90 (day 91+)	253000	176000	None	First 2 weeks	Day 8
1993	65 (days 1–3) 85 (days 4–90) 80 (day 91+)	258000	179000	1 day	First 2 weeks	Day 8

(*Continued on next page*)

Table 2. (Continued)

Year	Compensation rate (percent)	Income cap SEK (current prices)	Average annual wage SEK (current prices)	Mandatory waiting period	Employer pays	Doctor's certificate required from
1994	65 (days 1–3) 85 (days 4–90) 80 (day 91 +)	264000	187000	1 day	First 2 weeks	Day 8
1995	65 (days 1–3) 85 (days 4–90) 80 (day 91 +)	268000	192000	1 day	First 2 weeks	Day 8
1996	75	271000	204000	1 day	First 2 weeks	Day 8
1997	75	272000	215000	1 day	First 4 weeks	Day 8
1998	80	273000	223000	1 day	First 2 weeks	Day 8
1999	80	273000	233000	1 day	First 2 weeks	Day 8
2000	80	275000	244000	1 day	First 2 weeks	Day 8
2001	80	277000	256000	1 day	First 2 weeks	Day 8
2002	80	284000	265000	1 day	First 2 weeks	Day 8
2003 Jan–June	77.6	290000	274000	1 day	First 2 weeks	Day 8
2003 July–Dec	77.6	290000	274000	1 day	First 3 weeks	Day 8
2004	77.6	294700	284000	1 day	First 3 weeks	Day 8
2005	80	295500	292000	1 day	First 2 weeks	Day 8
2006 Jan–June	80	297700	n.a.	1 day	First 2 weeks	Day 8
2006 July–Dec	80	397000	n.a.	1 day	First 2 weeks	Day 8
2007	79.12	302200	n.a.	1 day	First 2 weeks	Day 8

Source: Swedish Social insurance Act (compensation rates, waiting period, employer payment, doctor's certificate requirement). Swedish National Social Insurance Administration (2006a, 2006b), Statistics Sweden, SOS Löner (various years) (average wage rates – these refer to the average blue-collar wage for the period 1974–1990, and to the general average wage from 1992 and onwards).

Compensation is granted according to the degree of work incapacity, of which there are four levels (25, 50, 75, or 100 percent incapacity), in which case the individual is granted the corresponding percentage of compensation (Swedish Social Insurance Act, SFS 1962, p. 381). However, there is no requirement of a doctor's certificate to support that the person is ill, and therefore unable to work, until after the first week of absence. Hence, for short-term absence, the individual has a substantial amount of discretion in deciding whether or not she is eligible for compensation. In most cases, compensation is paid after one mandatory waiting day.

For *employees*, the employer is required to pay the compensation during the first 14 days of illness, subject to one mandatory waiting day. The rate of compensation is 80 percent (or rather 79.12 percent in 2007) of the income foregone, subject to a cap at an annual income of 7.5 basic amounts,[4] corresponding to SEK 302 200 in 2007.[5] There is also a lower cap at an annual income of 24 percent of one "basic amount," corresponding to SEK 9700 in 2007. If the sickness period continues for more than 4 weeks, the employer is required to investigate the individual's need for rehabilitation, and to make proper adjustments at the workplace to facilitate her return to work. By collectively bargained employment contracts, many employees will receive an additional 10 percent of the income forgone from their employers on top of the legally regulated compensation rate.

People, who are *openly unemployed* or *participating in labor-market programs*, when they fall ill, receive compensation from the health insurance scheme after 1 day of mandatory waiting. The rate of compensation is the same as that rendered by their unemployment benefits but subject to a cap (lower than the cap mentioned above).[6] *Private entrepreneurs* can choose between waiting periods of 1, 3, and 30 days. A longer waiting period implies a lower fee to the Swedish health insurance system.[7] The rate of compensation is the same as for employees.

---

[4] The basic amount is an entity used for regulating compensation from the various social insurance systems in the Swedish welfare sector. It is politically determined, but has in practice followed the consumer price index closely.

[5] The cap was lifted to 10 basic amounts, equivalent to SEK 397000, for a brief period, July–December 2006.

[6] Unemployment benefits formally have a maximum duration of 300 workdays in Sweden. However, unemployed for whom the compensation period expires may be granted a new period, or granted access to participation in active labor market programs (see the Swedish Unemployment Insurance Act (Lag om arbetslöshetsförsäkring) SFS, 1997, p. 238).

[7] A waiting period of 1 day results in a fee amounting to 11.12 percent of the firm's net revenue before tax, with a waiting period of 3 days the fee is 8.92 percent, and with a waiting period of 30 days the fee is 7.72 percent of the firm's net revenue (Swedish National Tax Board, 2005).

The annual income of the private entrepreneur is defined as the annual net revenue of the firm before taxes. Should the sickness period last for more than 4 weeks, the entrepreneur is required to let the local health insurance office investigate the need for rehabilitation and changes at the workplace.

Data on sickness absence from work available at the Swedish Social Insurance Administration are restricted to spells that last 15 days or longer, i.e., sickness-absence spells, which are compensated by social insurance. Thus, Tables 3 and 4 show the average number of days with sickness-cash benefit paid by social insurance (and *not* the average number of days off work due to sickness) per individual and year by age group in 1998–2006 for men and women, respectively. The average number of days

Table 3. *Average number of days with sickness-cash benefit paid by Social Insurance per individual and year by age group in 1998–2006 in men*

Age group	1998	1999	2000	2001	2002	2003	2004	2005	2006
16–19	0.2	0.2	0.3	0.4	0.3	0.3	0.2	0.2	0.2
20–24	1.8	2.2	2.7	3.5	4.0	3.9	3.3	2.9	2.7
25–29	3.6	4.1	4.7	5.6	6.4	6.3	5.7	5.0	4.5
30–34	5.2	6.2	7.1	8.2	8.9	8.6	7.4	6.4	5.7
35–39	6.8	8.2	9.7	11.1	11.9	11.3	9.6	8.1	7.2
40–44	8.2	9.7	11.3	13.2	14.5	14.1	12.2	10.4	9.1
45–49	9.8	11.7	13.7	15.7	16.8	16.0	13.8	11.9	10.9
50–54	12.3	14.5	16.6	18.7	19.8	18.7	16.1	14.0	12.6
55–59	16.8	19.8	22.0	24.0	24.7	22.8	19.5	16.8	15.6
60–64	15.7	19.7	22.9	26.0	26.5	24.9	21.2	17.9	16.4
All age groups	7.7	9.4	10.8	12.4	13.3	12.7	10.9	9.4	8.5

Source: Swedish National Social Insurance Administration, http://statistik.forsakringskassan.se

Table 4. *Average number of days with sickness-cash benefit paid by Social Insurance per individual and year by age group in 1998–2006 in women*

Age group	1998	1999	2000	2001	2002	2003	2004	2005	2006
16–19	0.2	0.3	0.3	0.5	0.5	0.5	0.3	0.2	0.2
20–24	2.9	3.6	4.4	5.8	6.6	6.7	5.7	4.9	4.2
25–29	6.8	8.1	9.8	11.8	13.3	13.1	11.5	9.9	8.9
30–34	9.9	12.3	15.0	18.1	19.9	19.3	17.2	14.6	12.9
35–39	11.7	14.6	18.1	22.0	24.2	23.6	20.6	17.9	15.8
40–44	12.8	16.0	20.1	24.0	26.6	25.4	22.4	19.2	17.2
45–49	15.3	19.0	23.3	26.9	28.5	27.3	23.8	20.5	18.5
50–54	18.6	22.9	27.5	31.1	31.9	30.1	26.1	22.1	20.1
55–59	22.4	27.8	32.9	36.2	36.4	33.2	28.1	23.7	21.9
60–64	17.3	23.2	28.1	33.2	34.6	32.5	27.8	23.6	21.8
All age groups	11.7	14.7	18.0	21.1	22.5	21.4	18.6	15.8	14.3

Source: Swedish National Social Insurance Administration, http://statistik.forsakringskassan.se

per individual and year is generally higher among women than among men. It also increases with age. Numbers increased in all age groups and for both sexes until 2002 and decreased between 2003 and 2006.

In Figure 1, Sweden is compared with Denmark, the Netherlands, and the EU-15 average, using data from the European Labour Force Surveys. Sickness absence is here defined in another way, though, in order to obtain comparable data. The data relate to interviews with a representative sample of the population in each country, and the question is whether the interviewee has been absent from work during the whole week in which he or she was interviewed. So, there is no information on shorter absence than 5 days, and there is no information on the total length of a spell above 5 days.

According to Figure 1, Sweden has a sickness-absence rate far above the EU-15 average (and its close neighboring country Denmark). The only country with similar rates seems to be the Netherlands, where the rate has declined, though, and quite substantially, since the year 2000. In contrast with all other European countries (the Netherlands also used to be an exception, but seems no longer), there appears to be a countercyclical pattern in the Swedish development; a high-unemployment rate has generally been associated with a low rate of sickness absence and vice versa.

A further picture as to the pattern of sickness-cash benefit paid by social insurance is obtained by examining the distribution of the number of days among individuals. Figure 2 shows a histogram of the frequencies of the number of days.

Figure 1.   Sickness absence among employees 20–64 years of age in Sweden, Denmark, the Netherlands, and the EU-15 in 1990–2004 (percent)

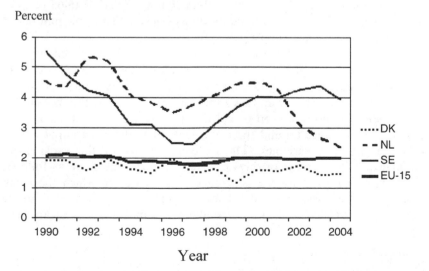

Source: Swedish National Social Insurance Administration (2005)

Figure 2.   The number of days for which sickness-absenteeism reimbursement was paid. Calculated from the data used in this chapter (HILDA). The categories include the following observations: 0, includes all zero observations; 1, includes 0<number of days≤25; 2, includes 25<number of days≤50;...;9, includes 200<number of days≤225; and 10, includes 225<number of days≤365

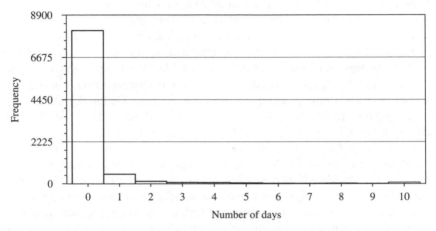

Source: Swedish survey of living conditions 1996/1997

4. Data

We used HILDA cross-section data for the years 1996/1997, supplemented with data on sickness absence for the year 1995.[8] Also, we restricted our sample to individuals who were older than 30 but younger than 65 years of age and who had not been granted disability pension. Thus, the number of individuals in our final sample was 9009.

Our choice of explanatory variables was been governed by the results choices of explanatory variables made in the empirical literature surveyed above. Sickness absenteeism during the examined period is determined by health during that same period. However, the measure of health used in this study only captures the typical health level for the period. The variance around the mean level of health is captured by the other explanatory variables. The expected effects of the explanatory variables on the number of days of sickness-cash benefit are as follows: (1) previous sickness absenteeism reflects the degree to which the mean level of health varies around its mean and is, hence, expected to be positively correlated with the dependent variable; (2) the mean level

---

[8] See Chapter 5 for a description of the HILDA data base.

of health declines with age and, hence, age is expected to be positively correlated to the dependent variable; (3) the cost accruing to the individual for sickness absenteeism is expected to be negatively correlated to the dependent variable. As regards the other explanatory variables, there are theoretical ground for expecting correlations between each one of them and the dependent variables; however, the sign of the correlation is indeterminate. Chosen dependent variables are described below.

4.1. Dependent variable

- ABSENT is a count variable for the number of days for which sickness-cash benefit was paid by social insurance in 1996/1997.

4.2. Explanatory variables

- ABSENTL is a dummy variable, which takes the value 1, if the respondent was paid any sickness-cash benefit from the public health insurance system in the year 1995/1996, and 0 otherwise (lagged dependent variable).
- Variables HI962, HI963, and HI964 are dummy variables, which take the value 1, if the respondent's health status, as measured by the health index described in Chapter 4, was 3, 2, and 1, respectively, in 1996/1997, and 0 otherwise. Comparison category: health index equal to 4.
- AGE96 is a discrete variable indicating the age of the respondent.
- CHILD is a dummy variable, which takes the value 1, if the respondent had any children below 7 years of age in 1996/1997.
- MARITAL is a dummy variable, which takes the value 1, if the respondent was either married or cohabiting in 1996/1997, and 0 otherwise.
- DIVORCED is a dummy variable, which takes the value 1, if the respondent was divorced in 1996/1997, and 0 otherwise.
- RELCOST is a continuous variable calculated as the respondent's cost of sickness absenteeism (COST) divided by median COST. COST is calculated as 25 percent of the taxable income for that part of the income which falls below 27 0000 SEK per year (the percentage which is not reimbursed), and as the difference between actual income and the threshold value 27 0000 SEK for that part of the income which falls above 27 0000 SEK per year.
- AGE > 40 is a dummy variable, which takes the value 1, if the respondent was older than 40 years of age, and 0 otherwise.
- SEX reflects sex: 0 corresponds to the respondent being a female and 1 corresponds to the respondent being a male.

- SEX_COST is the interaction SEX × COST.
- NEWBORN is a dummy variable, which takes the value 1, if the respondent had a child born within the year of the interview, and 0 otherwise.

5. Empirical model

We estimate two different models of sickness absence from work: (a) an imputation equation and (b) a year-to-year equation. Also in this case, we estimate both an imputation equation and a year-to-year equation. Both equations are estimated as sample selection models employing the cross-section for the years 1996/1997 complemented with data on sickness absenteeism for 1995.

5.1. Econometric specification

The dependent variable is the number of days for which sickness benefits were paid. We treat the observed number of days, for which reimbursement was paid as a two-stage choice. Thus, we estimated a negative binomial specification corrected for sample selection. The negative binomial specification is:

$$\Pr(Y_i = y_i) = \frac{e^{-\lambda_i}\lambda_i^{y_i}}{y_i!}, \quad y_i = 0, 1, 2, \ldots, \tag{1}$$

where y are observed frequencies and λ_i is defined as:

$$\text{Log}\lambda_i = \log(\beta' \mathbf{x}_i) + \log \varepsilon_i, \tag{2}$$

where $\varepsilon_i \sim \Gamma(1, \alpha)$ (for details, see, for instance, Greene, 1997, pp. 939–940). The sample selection equation is specified as a probit model:

$$z_i^* = \alpha' \gamma_i + u_i; \quad Z_i = 1 \quad \text{if } Z_i^* > 0; \quad Z_i = 0 \quad \text{if } Z_i^* \leq 0,$$

where $(\varepsilon_i, u_i) \sim N[0, 0, \sigma_u^2, \sigma_\varepsilon^2, \rho]$. The model was estimated by full information maximum likelihood.

6. Results

Estimated marginal effects are reported in Table 5.[9] First, variables appearing in both the selection- and the count data model are lagged

---

[9] An algorithm for calculating marginal effects, based on Green (2007) and using the LIMDEP computer programme, was developed by Dr. Anna Lindgren, Centre for Mathematical Sciences, Lund University. The algorithm for calculating marginal effects and the corresponding *p*-values is presented in Appendix A. We are grateful to Bill Greene for providing us with his working paper and to Anna Lindgren for developing the algorithm.

Table 5.   *The utilization of sickness-absenteeism*

Variable	Year-to-year
Both in sample selection and negative binomial part	
ABSENTL	20.200
	(0.000)
HI962	15.700
	(0.000)
HI963	50.400
	(0.000)
HI964	105.400
	(0.000)
SEX	−1.300
	(0.66)
RELCOST	7.800
	(0.060)
Only in negative binomial part	
CHILD	6.300
	(0.006)
MARITAL	−6.700
	(0.079)
DIVORCED	−11.800
	(0.050)
AGE > 40	−8.7
	(0.440)
Only in Selection part	
AGE96	0.012
	(0.45)
NEWBORN	0.300
	(0.480)

Note: Negative binominal model with sample selection. Marginal effects in the year-to-year equation (p-values within parentheses).

sickness absenteeism, which was reimbursed through the public health insurance system; the health dummies; sex; and the variable for the respondent's COST. Having been paid any sickness-cash benefit in the previous year increases the expected number of reimbursed days by approximately 20 days per year; assessed health in the second highest category increases the expected number of reimbursed days by almost 16 days compared to assessed health in the highest category – corresponding estimates for the second lowest and the lowest health levels are 50 and 105 days, respectively. Further, women are estimated to have about 1 day more than men with paid sickness-cash benefit (not significant at the 5 percent level). A surprising result is that the expected number of reimbursed days increases with the cost of absenteeism faced by the individual – an individual who has an income which is twice as high as the median income is expected to have almost 8 reimbursement days more than the median individual (not significant at the 5 percent level, though).

Second, variables appearing only in the count data model are the indicators for children, for whether or not the individual is married or cohabiting, for whether or not the individual is divorced, for whether or not the individual is more than 40 years of age; and the interaction term between sex and income. The marginal effects should be interpreted as the marginal effect *conditional* on having at least 1 day of reimbursement. Having children increases the expected number of reimbursed days by more than 6 days per year; being either married or cohabiting decreases the expected number of days for which reimbursement is paid by almost 7 days (not significant at the 5 percent level); being divorced increases the number of reimbursed days by almost 12 days; and being more than 40 years of age means that about half a day more per year is reimbursed (not significant at the 5 percent level).

Third, variables appearing only in the selection equation are the indicators for age and for whether or not the respondent has a newborn child. The marginal effects should be interpreted as the marginal effect of each of the (two) explanatory variables on the probability of having at least 1 day of reimbursement. Being 1 year older, or having a newborn child, increases the probability of having at least 1 day of reimbursement by 1.2 and 30 percent, respectively (neither of the marginal effects is significant at the 5 percent level).

Both first- and second-order effects of age and cost of absenteeism are incorporated in the estimated marginal effects and, hence, no separate marginal effect is reported for the interaction term (SEX_RCOST).

7. Simulations

In this section, we present the results of our simulations for the baseline scenario described comprehensively in Chapter 3. The simulations are based on a 100 percent sample in SESIM. Since women generally have a higher probability to be absent from work due to sickness and to have longer spells when absent, we present our simulation results separately for men and women. Doing so, we follow the same structure of presentation as for health status in Chapter 4.

7.1. Cross-sectional age profiles of average number of days of sick-leave

Figure 3 reproduces simulated cross-sectional age profiles of the average number of days with sick-leave in 2000 (average for 1999–2001), 2020 (2019–2021), and 2040 (2039–2041) for men and women, respectively. The general shapes of the graphs are similar for men and women: the average number of days of sick-leave increase with age, even though the averages

Figure 3. *Simulated cross-sectional average days of sick-leave by age 20–64 for 2000, 2020, and 2040 (men and women, respectively)*

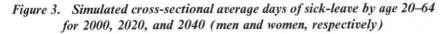
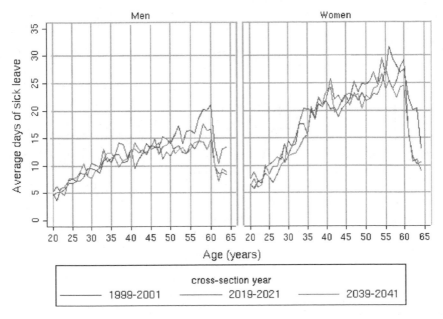

continue to be much larger among women. The average number of days of sick-leave seems to decline over the coming future years for both men and women.

7.2. Cohort age–health profiles

Simulated age profiles for sickness absence for the three birth-cohorts of 1930, 1940, and 1950 for men and women, respectively. Again, the age profiles of the three cohorts have similar shapes for both men and women, but the levels differ. No clear cohort effects can be detected, though (Figure 4).

7.3. Simulated development of the average number of days of sickness absence for the 50–64 population

The simulated development of the average number of days of sickness absence for the population is reproduced in Figure 5. According to our simulations, the average number of days of sickness absence will continue to be larger for women than for men; the gap does not seem to change.

Figure 4. **Simulated average number of days of sick-leave by age 50–64 for the birth-cohorts of 1940, 1960, and 1980 (men and women, respectively)**

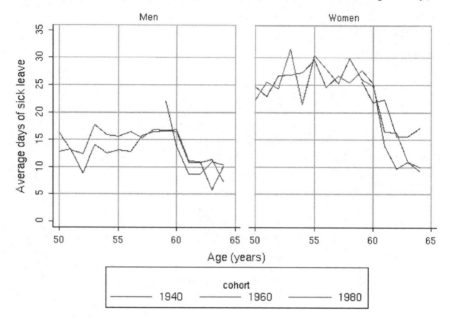

Figure 5. **Simulated annual average number of days of sick-leave for the 50–64 population, 2000–2040 (men and women, respectively)**

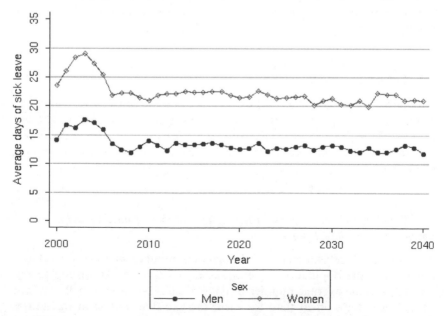

The number fluctuates over the years, but if there is a trend at all, it seems to be a downward-sloping one.

7.4. Simulated development of the total number of days of sickness absence for the 20–64 population

Finally, we present the development of the simulated development of the total number of days of sickness absence for the 20–64 population (Figure 6). The level is generally much higher for women, and the gap does not change over the years. The total number of days fluctuates, but there seem to be no clear trend toward an increase or a decrease, despite the fact that the population would be growing. The reason might be the downward trend in average number of days of sickness absence reported in Figures 3 and 4.

8. Conclusion

We have developed a module, which simulates the number of days of sickness absence, compensated by transfers from the Swedish Social

Figure 6. Simulated annual total number of days of sick-leave (in thousands) for the 20–64 population, 2000–2004 (men and women, respectively)

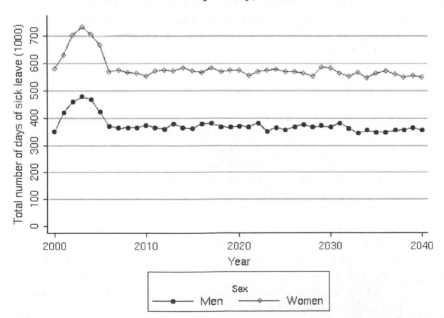

Insurance, i.e., for spells of sick-leave lasting more than 14 days. Determining factors are age, gender, health, civil status, the presence of children, the presence of a newborn child, the relative cost of sickness absence for the individual, and previous utilization of sickness-cash benefit payments from social insurance. According to our simulations, the total number of days of sickness absence, compensated by transfers from the Swedish Social Insurance, certainly fluctuates over the years 2000–2040, but apparently without any clear trend. Since the 20–64 population grows, though slowly, over these years, the average number of days of sickness absence will decrease to some extent. There is no indication that the gender gap will close or even diminish; women will continue to have a substantially larger number of days of sickness absence than men.

References

Allen, S.G. (1981a), "An empirical model of work attendance", *Review of Economics and Statistics*, Vol. 60, pp. 77–87.

Allen, S.G. (1981b), "Compensation, safety and absenteeism: evidence from the paper industry", *Industrial and Labor Relations Review*, Vol. 34, pp. 207–218.

Barmby, T., M. Nolan and R. Winkelmann (2001), "Contracted workdays and absence", *Manchester School*, Vol. 69, pp. 269–275.

Barmby, T. and G. Stephane (2000), "Worker absenteeism: why firm size may matter", *Manchester School*, Vol. 68, pp. 568–577.

Barmby, T.A., M.G. Ercolani and J.G. Treble (2002), "Sickness absence: an international comparison", *Economic Journal*, Vol. 112, pp. F315–F331.

Barmby, T.A., C.D. Orme and J.G. Treble (1991), "Worker absenteeism: an analysis using micro data", *Economic Journal*, Vol. 101, pp. 214–229.

Bridges, S. and K. Mumford (2001), "Absenteeism in the UK: a comparison across genders", *Manchester School*, Vol. 69, pp. 276–284.

Broberg, R. (1973), *Så formades tryggheten. Socialförsäkringarnas historia 1946–1972*, Stockholm: Försäkringskasseförbundet.

Broström, G., P. Johansson and M. Palme (2004), "Economic incentives and gender differences in work", *Swedish Economic Policy Review*, Vol. 11, pp. 33–61.

Delgado, M.A. and T.J. Knieser (1997), "Count data models with variance of unknown form: an application to a hedonic model of worker absenteeism", *Review of Economics and Statistics*, Vol. 79, pp. 41–49.

Drago, R. and M. Wooden (1992), "The determinants of labor absence: economic factors and workgroup norms across countries", *Industrial and Labor Relations Review*, Vol. 45, p. 778.

Gilleskie, D. (1998), "A dynamic stochastic model of medical care use and work absence", *Econometrica*, Vol. 66, pp. 1–45.

Greene, W.H. (1997), *Econometric Analysis*, 3rd edition, New York: Prentice Hall.

Greene, W.H. (2007), "Functional form and heterogeneity in models for count data", Stern School of Business Working Paper.

Henrekson, M. and M. Persson (2004), "The effects on sick leave of changes in the sickness insurance system", *Journal of Labor Economics*, Vol. 22, pp. 87–113.

Hogstedt, C., M. Bjurvall, S. Marklund, E. Palmer and T. Theorell (2004), *Den höga sjukfrånvaron – sanning eller konsekvens*, Stockholm: Statens Folkhälsoinstitut, (www.fhi.se).

Johansson, P. and M. Palme (1996), "Do economic incentives affect work absence? Empirical evidence using Swedish micro data", *Journal of Public Economics*, Vol. 59, pp. 195–218.

Johansson, P. and M. Palme (2002), "Assessing the effects of public policy on worker absenteeism", *Journal of Human Resources*, Vol. 37, pp. 381–409.

Leigh, J.P. (1983), "Sex differences in absenteeism", *Industrial Relations Review*, Vol. 22, pp. 349–361.

Lindeboom, M. and M. Kerkhofs (2000), "Multistate models for clustered duration data – an application to workplace effects on individual sickness absenteeism", *Review of Economics and Statistics*, Vol. 82, pp. 668–684.

Lindgren, B. (1995), "Health care in Sweden", in: A. Alban and T. Christiansen, editors, *The Nordic Lights. New Initiatives in Health Care Systems*, Odense: Odense University Press.

Nyman, K., E. Palmer and S. Bergendorff (2002), "Den svenska sjukan – sjukfrånvaro i åtta länder (Sickness in Sweden – sickness absence in eight countries)", *ESO Report* Ds 2002:49. Stockholm: Ministry of Finance.

Paringer, L. (1983), "Women and absenteeism: health or economics?", *American Economic Review*, Vol. 73, pp. 123–127.

Primoff Vistness, J. (1997), "Gender differences in days lost from work due to illness", *Industrial and Labor Relations Review*, Vol. 50, pp. 304–325.

Statistics Sweden (various years), "Löner inom privat och offentlig sektor. Statens Offentliga Statistik (SOS Löner)", Stockholm: Statistics Sweden.

Statistics Sweden (2007), "Stockholm: SCB", See the web address www.scb.se and the subsequent links to obtain a time series for the basic amount.

Swedish National Social Insurance Administration (2005) "Sjukfrånvaron i Sverige i ett europeiskt perspektiv 1983–2004". Stockholm: Försäkringskassan.

Swedish National Social Insurance Administration (2006a), "Social insurance. A general information about social insurance", FK 4002.06.05, Stockholm, See the following web address: www.forsakringskassan.se/sprak/eng/engelska.pdf

Swedish National Social Insurance Administration (2006b), "Förändringar 1968–januari 2005", Stockholm, See the following web address: www.forsakringskassan.se/omfk/socialforsakringen/historik/forandringar

Swedish National Tax Board (2005), "Stockholm: Skatteverket", See the following web address: www.skatteverket.se/infotext/arbetsgivare/ socialavgifter.html

Swedish Social Insurance Act (SFS 1962:381), "See the web address www.riksdagen.se for further details".

Swedish Uneployment Insurance Act (SFS 1997:238), "See the web address www.riksdagen.se for further details".

Thomas, R.B. (1980), "Wages, sickness benefits and absenteeism", *Journal of Economic Studies*, Vol. 7, pp. 51–61.

Winkelmann, R. (1996), "Markov chain Monte Carlo analysis of underreported count data with an application to worker absenteeism", *Empirical Economics*, Vol. 21, pp. 575–587.

Appendix A. An algorithm for bootstrap calculation of marginal effects and p-values in a negative binomial model with over dispersion, heterogeneity, and sample selection

An algorithm for calculating marginal effects and p-values, based on Greene (2007) and using the LIMDEP computer program, was developed by Dr. Anna Lindgren, Centre for Mathematical Sciences, Lund University, for the purposes of this chapter. We are grateful to Bill Greene for providing us with his working paper and to Anna Lindgren for developing the algorithm.

Sample selection part

$d_i^* = \mathbf{w}_i'\boldsymbol{\delta} + u_i$, where $u_i \in N(0, 1)$, $d_i = \mathbf{1}(d_i^* > 0)$, and $\Pr(d_i = 1|\mathbf{w}_i) = \Phi(\mathbf{w}_i'\boldsymbol{\delta})$.

Count data part

$$\Pr(y_i = y|\mathbf{x}_i, \varepsilon_i) = \frac{\Gamma(\theta + y)}{\Gamma(\theta + 1)\Gamma(\theta)} r_i^\theta (1 - r_i^\theta)$$

where

$$r_i = \frac{\theta}{\theta + h_i \lambda_i}, \quad \lambda_i = e^{\mathbf{x}_i'\boldsymbol{\beta}}, \ h_i = e^{\sigma \varepsilon_i}, \text{ and } \varepsilon_i \in N(0,1).$$

$$E(y_i|\mathbf{x}_i, \varepsilon_i) = h_i \lambda_i = e^{\mathbf{x}_i'\boldsymbol{\beta} + \sigma \varepsilon_i} \text{ and } E(y_i|\mathbf{x}_i) = e^{\mathbf{x}_i'\boldsymbol{\beta} + \sigma^2/2}.$$

Since $(u_i, \varepsilon_i) \in N_2((0,0),(1,1),\rho)$ we have $E(y_i|\mathbf{x}_i, \mathbf{w}_i, d_i = 1) = e^{\mathbf{x}_i'\boldsymbol{\beta} + (\rho\sigma)^2/2}(\Phi(\rho\sigma + \mathbf{w}_i'\boldsymbol{\delta})/\Phi(\mathbf{w}_i'\boldsymbol{\delta}))$.

Marginal effects

We want to estimate the marginal effects $g_k = \partial E(y|\mathbf{x}, \mathbf{w}, d = 1)/\partial v_k$, where $\mathbf{v} = \mathbf{x} \cup \mathbf{w}$, by $g_k = \sum_{i;d_i=1} g_{ki}/\sum_{i;d_i=1} 1$, where $g_{ki} = \partial E(y_i|\mathbf{x}_i, \mathbf{w}_i, d_i = 1)/\partial v_k$. In the case where v_k is a dummy variable, we use the differences $g_{ki} = E(y_i|\mathbf{x}_i, \mathbf{w}_i, d_i = 1, v_{ki} = 1) - E(y_i|\mathbf{x}_i, \mathbf{w}_i, d_i = 1, v_{ki} = 0)$ instead. We will also have to consider the cases where v_k is part only in $\mathbf{x}$, only in $\mathbf{w}$, and where v_k is part both in $\mathbf{x}$ and $\mathbf{w}$. A further complication arises with interaction terms, i.e., $v_k = v_l v_j$ for some l and j. In this particular case, we have an interaction term in $\mathbf{x}$ whose main factors are present in both $\mathbf{x}$ and $\mathbf{w}$. One of them is continuous, the other a dummy.

Continuous variable, only in x

$$g_{ki} = \beta_k e^{\mathbf{x}_i'\boldsymbol{\beta} + (\rho\sigma)^2/2} \frac{\Phi(\rho\sigma + \mathbf{w}_i'\boldsymbol{\delta})}{\Phi(\mathbf{w}_i'\boldsymbol{\delta})}$$

Continuous variable, only in w

$$g_{ki} = \delta_k \frac{e^{\mathbf{x}_i'\boldsymbol{\beta} + (\rho\sigma)^2/2}}{\Phi(\mathbf{w}_i'\boldsymbol{\delta})} \left(\phi(\rho\sigma + \mathbf{w}_i'\boldsymbol{\delta}) - \phi(\mathbf{w}_i'\boldsymbol{\delta}) \frac{\Phi(\rho\sigma + \mathbf{w}_i'\boldsymbol{\delta})}{\Phi(\mathbf{w}_i'\boldsymbol{\delta})} \right)$$

Continuous variable, both in x and w

$$g_{ki} = \beta_k e^{\mathbf{x}_i'\boldsymbol{\beta} + (\rho\sigma)^2/2} \frac{\Phi(\rho\sigma + \mathbf{w}_i'\boldsymbol{\delta})}{\Phi(\mathbf{w}_i'\boldsymbol{\delta})}$$
$$+ \delta_k \frac{e^{\mathbf{x}_i'\boldsymbol{\beta} + (\rho\sigma)^2/2}}{\Phi(\mathbf{w}_i'\boldsymbol{\delta})} \left(\phi(\rho\sigma + \mathbf{w}_i'\boldsymbol{\delta}) - \phi(\mathbf{w}_i'\boldsymbol{\delta}) \frac{\Phi(\rho\sigma + \mathbf{w}_i'\boldsymbol{\delta})}{\Phi(\mathbf{w}_i'\boldsymbol{\delta})} \right)$$

Continuous variable, main effects both in x and w, interaction only in x

$$g_{ki} = (\beta_k + \beta_{lj}v_{ji})e^{\mathbf{x}_i'\boldsymbol{\beta} + (\rho\sigma)^2/2} \frac{\Phi(\rho\sigma + \mathbf{w}_i'\boldsymbol{\delta})}{\Phi(\mathbf{w}_i'\boldsymbol{\delta})}$$

$$+ \delta_k \frac{e^{\mathbf{x}_i'\boldsymbol{\beta} + (\rho\sigma)^2/2}}{\Phi(\mathbf{w}_i'\boldsymbol{\delta})} \left(\phi(\rho\sigma + \mathbf{w}_i'\boldsymbol{\delta}) - \phi(\mathbf{w}_i'\boldsymbol{\delta}) \frac{\Phi(\rho\sigma + \mathbf{w}_i'\boldsymbol{\delta})}{\Phi(\mathbf{w}_i'\boldsymbol{\delta})} \right),$$

where there is an interaction term $v_l v_j$ for $l = k$, β_{lj} is the parameter for the interaction term, and v_j is the dummy variable that v_k is interacting with.

Dummy variable, only in x

$$g_{ki} = e^{\mathbf{x}_i'\boldsymbol{\beta} - x_{ki}\beta_k + (\rho\sigma)^2/2}(e^{\beta_k} - 1) \frac{\Phi(\rho\sigma + \mathbf{w}_i'\boldsymbol{\delta})}{\Phi(\mathbf{w}_i'\boldsymbol{\delta})}$$

Dummy variable, only in w

$$g_{ki} = e^{\mathbf{x}_i'\boldsymbol{\beta} + (\rho\sigma)^2/2} \left(\frac{\Phi(\rho\sigma + \mathbf{w}_i'\boldsymbol{\delta} - (w_{ki} - 1)\delta_k)}{\Phi(\mathbf{w}_i'\boldsymbol{\delta} - (w_{ki} - 1)\delta_k)} - \frac{\Phi(\rho\sigma + \mathbf{w}_i'\boldsymbol{\delta} - w_{ki}\delta_k)}{\Phi(\mathbf{w}_i'\boldsymbol{\delta} - w_{ki}\delta_k)} \right)$$

Dummy variable, both in x and w

$$g_{ki} = e^{\mathbf{x}_i'\boldsymbol{\beta} - x_{ki}\beta_k + (\rho\sigma)^2/2}$$

$$\times \left(e^{\beta_k} \frac{\Phi(\rho\sigma + \mathbf{w}_i'\boldsymbol{\delta} - (w_{ki} - 1)\delta_k)}{\Phi(\mathbf{w}_i'\boldsymbol{\delta} - (w_{ki} - 1)\delta_k)} - \frac{\Phi(\rho\sigma + \mathbf{w}_i'\boldsymbol{\delta} - w_{ki}\delta_k)}{\Phi(\mathbf{w}_i'\boldsymbol{\delta} - w_{ki}\delta_k)} \right)$$

Dummy variable, main effects both in x and w, interaction only in x

$$g_{ki} = e^{\mathbf{x}_i'\boldsymbol{\beta} - x_{ki}\beta_k - v_{li}v_{ji}\beta_{lj} + (\rho\sigma)^2/2}$$

$$\times \left(e^{\beta_k + v_{li}\beta_{lj}} \frac{\Phi(\rho\sigma + \mathbf{w}_i'\boldsymbol{\delta} - (w_{ki} - 1)\delta_k)}{\Phi(\mathbf{w}_i'\boldsymbol{\delta} - (w_{ki} - 1)\delta_k)} - \frac{\Phi(\rho\sigma + \mathbf{w}_i'\boldsymbol{\delta} - w_{ki}\delta_k)}{\Phi(\mathbf{w}_i'\boldsymbol{\delta} - w_{ki}\delta_k)} \right),$$

where there is an interaction term $v_l v_j$ where $j = k$, β_{lj} the parameter for the interaction term, and v_l the continuous variable that v_k is interacting with.

Numerical consideration

Whenever the denominator, e.g., $\Phi(\mathbf{w}_i'\boldsymbol{\delta})$ gets near zero, the individual effect g_{ki} is set to zero, giving a conservative estimate.

Bootstrap procedure

The idea behind the bootstrap technique is to draw repeated random samples from the observed data and estimate the quantities of interest using each of these samples. These bootstrap estimates are expected to behave in the same way, compared to the original estimates, as the original estimates behave, compared to the underlying population. We can, hence, compute, e.g., bias, standard error, and confidence intervals for the original estimates, using the empirical distribution of the bootstrap estimates.

CHAPTER 6

Early Retirement

Kristian Bolin, Matias Eklöf, Daniel Hallberg*, Sören Höjgård
and Björn Lindgren

In this chapter, we present estimates and the implications of the retirement decisions in the SESIM simulation model. As with sickness absence, economists have analyzed early retirement mostly as a labor supply problem (see for instance Lumsdaine and Mitchell, 1999, for an overview). Generally, the theoretical framework applied does not separate retirement due to disability from retirement due to other causes. The individual is, hence, assumed to choose the age of retirement so that it maximizes lifetime utility, given the restrictions posed by public and/or private pension schemes and his or her personal characteristics.

Most studies have primarily analyzed the effects of economic incentives inherent in public pension schemes, since this is an instrument over which policy makers may exert some control. In most empirical models, some proxy for health status is included as an explanatory variable. This is because (a) several public pension schemes allow for retirement before statutory retirement age due to bad health, (b) health status may affect the individual's earnings possibilities (and thereby the accrual rate), (c) it may affect the individual's life expectancy (and, hence the period to be financed by "pension wealth"), and (d) health status may affect the utility of leisure versus that of income (a lower earnings' capacity because of poor health may increase the marginal utility of income, but poor health may also make work more stressful and increase the marginal utility of leisure for recuperative purposes).

Here, the decision to permanently withdraw from the labor market is separated into two models. The first model takes care of early retirement via disability insurance, while the second handles early retirement via old

---

* Corresponding author.

CONTRIBUTIONS TO ECONOMIC ANALYSIS
VOLUME 285   ISSN: 0573-8555
DOI:10.1016/S0573-8555(07)00006-5

age pension. While the first model deals with early-retirement decisions via disability insurance for all age groups, the second is naturally more focused on the elderly as it emphasizes the use of old age pension.

By assumption, entrance into the disability insurance scheme is considered health induced, whereas early retirement via old age pension is voluntary. However, just as with sickness absenteeism, there is no clear-cut borderline between retirement for health reasons and a voluntary choice to retire early, even though there is a formal requirement of work capacity reduction due to illness in the disability insurance. Also here, both individual preferences and the regulatory framework of the disability benefits scheme play their roles. Health problems, especially long-standing conditions, should, though, be a major explanatory factor in most cases. Nevertheless, retirement via disability and old age pension represent the two most common ways to permanently leave the labor force.[1]

An important feature of the model for disability retirement is the indicator of individual health, introduced in Chapter 4. Another important feature is that we control for labor market sector affiliation – for two reasons. In Sweden, practically every worker has complementary income insurance in case of disability via a collective agreement. There is also supplementary occupational pension through collective agreements. This latter may be used to finance early withdrawal.[2] The rules differ, however, depending on labor market sector affiliation. For blue-collar workers in the private sector in particular, the possibility to make an early withdrawal via occupational pension is limited. The model takes the sequential element in occupational pension and public old age pension into account by calculating economic incentive measures accordingly.

In addition, employees who are close to statutory retirement age have a non-negligible probability of getting a special economic incentive from their employer if they accept to retire early.[3] In Sweden, firms occasionally have incentives to set up early-retirement pensions of this kind, because the pension premiums the employers have to pay increase with increasing age of the employees. It is likely that such offers were quite common, in

---

[1] There are other important routes, especially among individuals over age 50 that frequently turn out to be a permanent labor market withdrawal; long-lasting unemployment or sickness absence, for instance. Unemployment and sickness absence are modeled in other modules of the SESIM simulation model (see Chapters 3 and 5 in this book).

[2] Under certain circumstances, the individual will be better off to claim pension benefits solely from the occupational pension system until normal retirement age and then start claiming benefits from the public old age pension system as well, and micro-evidence shows that many Swedes do use these two pension schemes sequentially (Eklöf and Hallberg, 2004).

[3] In the retirement literature such programs are often known as early-retirement windows (see, e.g., Brown, 2002), golden handshakes, buyouts, etc. Here we will use the term "early-retirement pension" for such special agreements.

particular, during the 1990s when there was substantial downsizing and restructuring of the Swedish economy. The empirical model takes such early-retirement pensions into account by simultaneously modeling early retirement via old age pension and the event of receiving an early-retirement pension offer.

Early retirement will be defined as retirement before the statutory age of 65.

The chapter is organized as follows. It first briefly presents the rules and legislations governing retirement via disability insurance and old age pension, respectively; makes an international comparison of empirical observations relevant for this chapter, along with some stylized facts for the Swedish case; presents the models of the early-retirement decision, describes the data sources used, presents the empirical specifications, and empirical results (Sections 1–7). Next (Section 8), the simulation results are reported.

There is a baseline scenario and two alternative scenarios. The first alternative scenario aims at illustrating a policy that counteracts a future shortage of manpower. In order to hold on to the current work force, the employers are assumed to remove the strong economic incentives for early retirement created by early-retirement pensions. This will have the effect that the economic incentives for an early retirement will weaken, which will potentially result in more individuals working until the statuary retirement age. Also, the second alternative scenario studies what happens when the average retirement age increases. In this scenario, there is an exogenous increase in the retirement age norm. We implement it as an arbitrary change of the age profile for old age retirement. In this scenario, individuals are allowed to work longer than the statuary retirement age. One interesting outcome is to see what happens to pension levels in the two scenarios. A higher retirement age on average will have consequences for the financial situation in the public sector.

Section 9 concludes the chapter.

1. Disability insurance in Sweden

In the 1990s, individuals aged 18–64 were eligible for disability insurance, if their work capacity was reduced by at least 25 percent (50 percent before 1993). In the beginning of the period, before 1991, disability insurance could also be granted for labor market reasons (i.e., if unemployed had been compensated long enough to exhaust their benefits – obtained benefits for 300 days). This possibility was gradually phased out after 1991. In 1995, the enforcement of the rules was tightened. When evaluating applications for disability pensions, local insurance offices now had to request a medical certificate and a work-related test of the applicant's degree of work capacity. Local offices also had to consult the applicant's employer, physician, or other qualified personnel, and even pay personal visits to the applicant. The possibilities for rehabilitating the applicant should also be investigated. From 1997, work incapacity should be evaluated in relation to all possible employment opportunities. Potential income changes resulting from changes in employment should not affect the evaluation[4] (National Social Insurance Board, 2005).

Until 2003, the disability pension scheme entailed the same rate of compensation as the old age pension scheme.[5] To compensate persons who retired early due to disability for the loss of years during which pension rights could have been earned, their benefits were calculated on the assumption that their income during the years lost would have been the same as during the better half of all their previous years in the labor force. It may be noted that, in combination with occupational pension agreements, the compensation under the disability pension scheme could in some cases exceed 100 percent of the income foregone (Edebalk and Wadensjö, 1989, 1990), while in most cases the compensation level was around 65 percent.

In 2003, both the disability pension scheme and the sickness allowance scheme were transferred from the Swedish pension system to the Swedish health insurance system, and renamed as *sickness compensation* (sjukersättning) and *activity compensation* (aktivitetsersättning), respectively. This had no effect on the eligibility conditions, although it did affect the compensation levels (National Social Insurance Board, 2005). The annual amount of compensation received under the two schemes is 64 percent of earned income, subject to an upper limit for earned income corresponding to 7.5 basic amounts (BA). The income base towards which the 64 percent are applied is not the same for the two programs. In the

---

[4] In addition to the disability pension scheme, there also existed another possibility of early retirement for disability reasons – the sickness allowance scheme (sjukbidrag) – with the same eligibility conditions as the disability pension scheme, but intended for persons with work incapacities of less permanent nature. That is, the incapacity should be expected to persist for at least 1 year, after which a re-evaluation was to take place. This was rarely done, however, and most sickness allowances were converted to disability pensions after some time. One may note that, disregarding compensation from occupational pension agreements, compensation from the health insurance system is more generous than compensation from the pension system (this was particularly the case during the period before 1991). Hence, an early exit from the labor force under the sickness allowance scheme (or by being long-term sickness-absent) may have seemed a better option than an early exit under the disability pension scheme.

[5] The compensation rates in DI and OAP used to be the same. Since July 1 1995, however, the level of the basic pension (FP) in DI has been reduced to 90 percent of the base amount for single pensioners and 72.5 percent for married pensioners, while it was 96 percent of the base amount for singles and 78.5 percent for married people in the OAP system. Since January 1 1996, disability pensioners receive the lower amount even if their spouse is not drawing a pension. The reduced levels have been partly offset by a raised pension supplement.

sickness compensation scheme it is age dependent. Persons who have low or no earned income are in both programs guarantied a compensation of about 50 percent of the maximum compensation.

Now, although eligibility for disability pension is to be determined on medical grounds, other factors have apparently had a substantial influence (particularly for older workers), too. This is reflected in the development of the annual inflow to early retirement (both disability pensions and sickness allowances) in Sweden over time (cf. the discussion in Wadensjö and Sjögren, 2000).

2. Old age pension in Sweden

In the empirical analysis, we are focusing on the pension systems in effect from 1992 through 2000. The old age pension system in Sweden consists of two main parts: the public old age pension covering essentially the whole population, and occupational pension plans which cover 90 percent of the labor force. The former was designed by the parliament, whereas the latter were designed in negotiations between the employers' associations and the unions. In addition, employees may receive early-retirement pension offers from their employers.

2.1. Public old age pension

In the 1990s, the Swedish public old age pension consisted of a basic part and a supplementary part. All Swedish citizens and all persons residing in Sweden were entitled to the basic pension. It provided roughly the same amount regardless of previous earnings, but was reduced if the individual had resided in Sweden for less than 40 years or had Swedish work history for less than 30 years. The supplementary part depended on earnings history. Pension benefits could be approximately calculated as 60 percent of average earnings up to the social-security ceiling (7.5 basic amounts, BA) during the individual's best 15 years.[6] Benefits could be claimed in advance of the statutory retirement age or postponed. Before 1988, public old age pensions could be withdrawn from the age of 60, after 1998 from 61; or postponed until the age of 70. Early withdrawal triggered an actuarial reduction of 0.5 percent per month.[7]

---

[6] The BA was until 1999 decided for 1 year at a time by the Swedish Parliament, following closely the consumer price index. In 1999 the BA was renamed the price base amount, and has since been completely linked to the CPI. In 1999 1 BA was 36 400 SEK, approximately 4040 €.

[7] Until 2000, it was also possible to claim an early part-time pension from the public pension system.

Ståhlberg (1995) argues that the old public pension system may have led to financial instability as a result of an increase in early retirement, along with increased longevity, low economic growth, and the retirement of large birth cohorts (such as those of the 1940s). During the 1990s, the average pension level rose, because there was a decrease in the share of retired individuals with just basic pension, and new pensioners consistently received higher supplementary benefits compared to older cohorts (National Social Insurance Board, http://www.rfv.se).

Approved in the parliament in 1998, Sweden implemented a new public old age pension system in January 2001. The main features of the new pension system include a more flexible retirement age, and a tighter link between contributions, benefits, and life expectancy. Sundén (2000) argues that since Sweden has accumulated reserves, the new system should be financially stable in the long run.

The new public old age pension consists of three parts: the income pension, the premium pension, and the guarantee pension. The new system uses the concept of notionally defined contributions, which creates a link between contributions and benefits. Hence, the income pension is a function of the individual's entire earnings history, not only the 15 best years as in the supplementary part of the old system. Pension rights are not only given for gainful employment, but are also extended to studies, military service, and care of small children. Moreover, the retirement age is not fixed. The income pension and the premium pension can be drawn starting at the age of 61, while the earliest age for receiving the guarantee pension is 65. There are actuarial adjustments to early pensions as well as postponed benefits. Pensions in the new system are indexed to labor earnings rather than to prices, as in the old system, and to changes in life expectancy.

Transition rules will apply for cohorts born between 1938 and 1953, whose pensions will be determined in part by the old system, in part by the new.

Like the old system, the new one is set up as a pay-as-you-go scheme. Only a small part, the premium pension, is funded. It might be argued, then, that potential financial problems associated with the retirement of the large birth cohorts of the 1940s have not really been solved. However, elements are in place to balance the system if the financial pressure becomes persistent. One of these is to reduce the income indexation of the pensions (commonly known as "the break").

2.2. Collectively agreed occupational pension

The Swedish labor market is highly unionized, and collective pension agreements between labor unions and employer organizations cover almost 95 percent of the labor force. There are basically four separate occupational pension plans, one for each of the main sectors of the labor market: blue-collar workers in the private sector, white-collar workers in the private sector, central government employees, and local government employees.[8] Although some important differences exist across sectors, the specific agreements are fairly similar in structure as to defined benefits, contribution rates, age eligibility, etc. The usual design is to define benefits as a function of previous sector-specific earnings, the number of years of service within a sector, and retirement age. The occupational pensions are partly designed to compensate income losses above the social-security ceiling not covered in the public old age pension plan. For that reason, the replacement ratio is fairly low (about 10 percent) below the social security ceiling but higher for certain income segments above it. With a few exceptions the stipulated normal retirement age is 65.[9]

Before 1996, the pension plan of *private-sector blue-collar workers* included a pension benefit of 10 percent of the earnings below 7.5 BA. Above that threshold, there were no pension rights. The benefits were based on average earnings 5 years prior to the retirement date. A worker did not have the option to withdraw occupational pension benefits before normal retirement age of 65. Full benefits were received if the individual had 30 years or more of employment; otherwise they were proportionally reduced. In 1996, the plan was renegotiated and became a defined contribution plan, with an earliest withdrawal age of 55. During a transition period this age is set to 60. The new pension is flexible with regards to period of payment. The recipient can choose between a lifelong annuity and an annuity for shorter period of at least 5 years. In estimating our retirement model we will make the simplifying assumption that all sample members follow the old agreement.

For *private-sector white-collar workers*, benefits are based on average earnings during last year of employment. Full benefits are received if the employee has 30 years or more of employment; otherwise the benefits are proportionally reduced. Benefits can be claimed from age 55 or postponed to age 70. After the normal retirement age of 65, benefits amount to 10 percent of qualifying earnings up to 7.5 BA, 65 percent between 7.5 and 20 BA, and 32.5 percent between 20 and 30 BA. If the employee retires before the normal retirement age, the replacement rate in the lower bracket is increased to 65 percent until the retiree becomes 65. This construction facilitates early retirement without claiming public old age pension. However, early benefits reduce lifelong benefits by approximately 6 percent per year. Postponed retirement is awarded with an actuarial increase.

---

[8] There are a number of minor pension schemes for smaller "sub-unions" across the labor market. However, these alternative pension plans are generally only minor modifications of the main agreements. In the analysis we focus on the four main agreements.

[9] All occupational schemes also have small contribution-defined benefits. In our study, we disregard this pension component.

For *central government employees,* benefits are based on average earnings during the five years prior to retirement. Full benefits are received if the individual has 30 years or more of employment; otherwise they are proportionally reduced. For most central government employees, who have the so called PA-91 agreement, the normal retirement age is 65, the lowest and highest ages are 60 and 70 respectively. Benefits amount to 10 percent of the qualifying wage up to 7.5 BA, 65 percent between 7.5 and 20 BA, and 32.5 percent between 20 and 30 BA. If retirement age is less than 65, the benefit level is 101 percent up to 1 BA, and 65 percent between 1 and 20 BA until age 65 is reached. Pension benefits are reduced in case of early retirement. If retirement age is less than 65, benefits after 65 are reduced by 2.6 percent per month for retirees who had earnings below 7.5 BA, and by 0.4 percent for those who had earnings above 7.5 BA. If claims are postponed after age 65, benefits are increased by 0.5 percent per month.

In 2003, a new agreement was introduced in the state sector, PA-03. The main features of this agreement are that all pension below the ceiling is contribution defined, that the benefit replacement levels above the ceiling are somewhat reduced compared to the old agreement, and that early withdrawal of pension are more on previous contributions. The setup of PA-3 is basically that the pension wealth can be used as an annuity and/or a "temporary pension" until normal retirement age.[10]

For *local government employees,* pension benefits are fully coordinated with the social-security system including the public old age pension plans. Full benefits are received, if the individual has more than 30 years of employment; otherwise benefits are proportionally reduced. Several subgroups have a lower mandatory retirement age than 65 and, subsequently, a lower earliest age of withdrawal (for instance, if normal retirement is at 65 (60), the earliest age for withdrawal is at 60 (57)). The benefits are based on the average income of the best 5 years of the 7 years predating retirement. The benefits amounts to 95 percent of earnings below 1 BA, 78.5 percent for earnings from 1 to 2.5 BA, 60 percent for 2.5–3.5 BA, 64 percent for 3.5–7.5 BA, 65 percent for 7.5–20 BA, and 32.5 percent for 20–30 BA. Early withdrawals imply a reduced pension but the reduction depends on the mandatory retirement age and the number of months of early claim. Withdrawal can be postponed after age 65, although not longer than to age 67, with a 0.1 percent increase in the benefit level per month of postponed withdrawal.

As of 2006 this group got a new pension agreement too. Like most new agreements it is more of the contribution-defined type than the earlier.

---

[10] There was also an introduction of a part-time pension scheme.

2.3. Early-retirement pension offers

Before September 2001, an employee lost her right to remain in employment after her 65th birthday. In September 2001, this rule was relaxed such that the employee now has the right to remain employed until her 67th birthday. This means that the employer cannot end the employment and force the employee into early retirement before 67 without the employee's approval.[11] If an employer would prefer to dismiss an employee before that age, the situation is more complicated. In Sweden, older employees have stronger employment protection than younger employees. Unless there are specific circumstances, the employer must lay off less senior employees first (the "last-in first-out" principle). However, some collectively agreed occupational pension plans give the employer and employee the option to agree on other retirement conditions than the ones given by the standard pension agreements. This can be used as a tool for the employer to persuade the employee to leave her employment thereby circumventing the "first-in last-out" principle. We refer to such individual agreements as early-retirement pension offers, which are not to be confused with the collectively agreed option to withdraw standard benefits before normal retirement age. After all, early-retirement pension offers aim at giving the employees stronger incentive to retire than the standard agreements.

Some collectively agreed occupational pension plans are designed such that employers contributions to the plan for employees close to their normal retirement age increase drastically. In these plans a wage increase at the end of a career will yield a lifelong stream of higher pension benefits. As the increase in future benefits needs to be financed by payments over an ever-shorter time span, the pension costs increase rapidly. This creates strong incentives for the employer to reduce costs by pushing an old employee into early retirement.[12]

The level of compensation in early-retirement offers is negotiable and varies across agreements. However, some guidance is given by the "complementary rule" regulating the employer's tax deductions. This complementary rule defines the maximum pension that admits tax deductions. The deduction level varies by income segment and age of the

---

[11] Conversely, the employee must have the employer's consent to retire early and use benefits from the occupational pension system.

[12] Also in the UK the disincentive effects of hiring elderly created by pension costs seem to be important. A 1995 survey of British firms (see Auer and Fortuny, 2000) concluded that 46 percent of the firms reported pension costs as being an important or very important reason for being reluctant to hire older people. Further, the majority (55 percent) of firms that had established a maximum hiring age responded that pension costs were important. Among those that found pension costs unimportant only 25 percent had established a maximum hiring age.

employee.[13] But for all sectors it is higher than the replacement rate in the standard pension scheme. Thus, the complementary rule opens up for the possibility of individual agreements about early retirement.[14]

3. Stylized facts

Compared to other OECD countries, Sweden has a comparatively favorable position with regards to labor force participation of the older population. Figures 1 and 2, which present historical labor force participation rates for a selection of OECD countries, show that Swedish women, in particular, have a leading position in terms of participation rates, even though increased female participation rates have been observed in the industrialized world for quite some time. In the beginning of the 1990s, however, labor force participation rates for Swedish women no longer increased, they even fell. For men in the age group 55+, one can observe internationally declining participation rates. Between 1968 and 1998, the participation rates for Swedish men in the age groups 55–59 and 60–64 fell from 93.6 to 84.5 percent and 83.7to 54.5 percent, respectively. Since the mid-1990s, however, these trends have been reversed for both genders. The latest data from the end of the 1990s until 2004 show increasing participation rates, in particular for the age group 60–64. In fact, the participation rate has never been higher in Sweden for women in this age group.

In 2000, the average retirement age in Sweden was about 62, which positioned Sweden in the upper third among the OECD countries (OECD, 2004).

Considering the disability insurance, Sweden is in a less favorable situation. In 1999, expenditures on disability insurance were 3.8 percent of GDP, compared to the EU 15 average 2.2 percent. The percentage of the population 20–64 with severe or moderate disabilities was 21 percent in Sweden compared to the EU average of 16 (OECD, 2003). The equivalized household income of a household with a disabled adult member was as high as about 97 percent of the average income of non-disabled households. Other EU countries average about 80–85 percent.

---

[13] If an employee retires before age 65, the employer can at most deduct 80 percent of pensionable income below 7.5 BA, 70 percent between 7.5 and 20 BA, and 40 percent between 20 and 30 BA. When the retiree reaches the age of 65 the maximum deduction is limited to 20 percent of pensionable income below 7.5 BA, 70 percent between 7.5 and 20 BA, and 40 percent between 20 and 30 BA.

[14] Presumably many early retirement offers do not only include a higher compensation rate than the standard agreement, but they also compensate for future losses in pension benefit levels after normal pension age due to early withdrawal.

Figure 1. Labor force participation rates, males 50–54 (NW), males 55–59 (SW), females 50–54 (NE), and females 55–59 (SE)

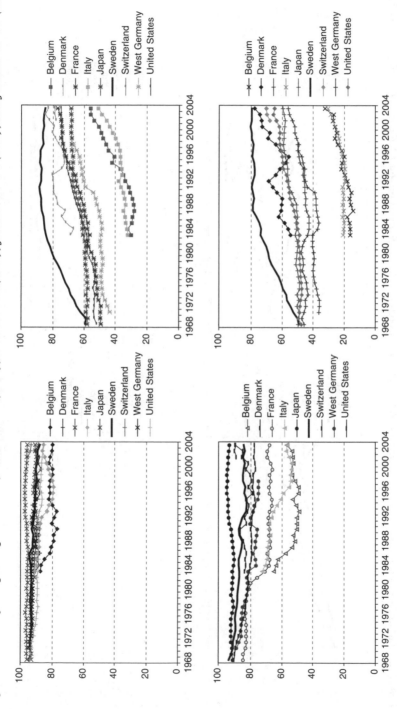

Figure 2.   Labor force participation rates, males 60–64 (NW), males 65–69 (SW), females 60–64 (NE), and females 65–69 (SE)

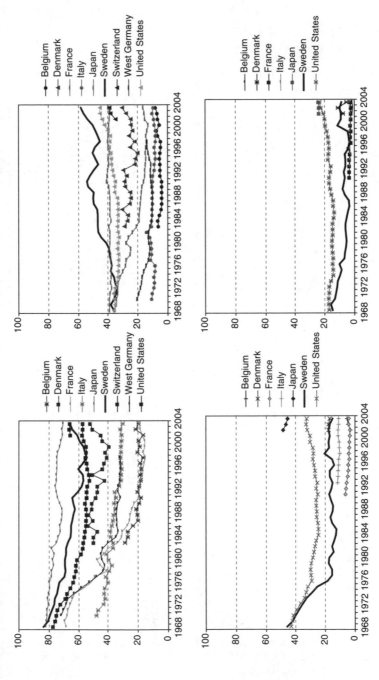

Source: OECD employment and labour market statistics

There are several potential sources of income in the transitions from employment to retirement. In Table 1, we present sample shares of individuals aged 55–59 and 60–64 (in 1992–2000) by main income source (more than 50 percent of total income). The most important sources (beside income from work) are disability insurance (both age groups), unemployment benefits (55–59), and occupational pension benefits (60–64). It is notable that the share of individuals having public old age pension as their main income is very low in all labor market sectors. Instead, disability insurance, occupational pension, and unemployment insurance seem to be more frequent sources of main income.

There are notable differences across the four labor market sectors. Only 2 percent of blue-collar workers in the 60–64 age group receive their main income from occupational pension, whereas the corresponding shares

Table 1. **Main source of income, by sector and age, in percent, 1992–2000**

	Blue-collar workers in the private sector	White-collar workers in the private sector	Central government employees	Local government employees	Total
Age 55–59					
Work	65.1	76.2	74.9	74.7	73.0
Disability insurance	16.2	8.6	10.0	10.7	11.2
Public old age pension	0.0	0.0	0.0	0.0	0.0
Occupational pension	0.2	0.9	2.7	0.5	0.9
Sickness insurance	2.9	2.7	2.1	2.7	2.7
Unemployment	5.9	4.8	3.8	3.5	4.5
Private pensions	0.5	0.6	0.3	0.3	0.4
Capital	2.9	2.0	1.4	2.1	2.1
Transfers	2.2	0.6	0.9	1.6	1.3
Inconclusive	4.1	3.6	3.8	3.9	3.8
Age 60–64					
Work	38.5	50.0	43.2	46.7	44.7
Disability insurance	33.1	16.9	19.3	21.6	23.5
Public old age pension	2.7	2.2	1.1	1.2	1.9
Occupational pension	2.1	9.5	21.6	11.7	9.6
Sickness insurance	2.2	1.9	1.2	2.2	2.0
Unemployment	7.3	6.1	3.6	2.8	5.1
Private pensions	0.8	1.5	0.5	0.7	0.9
Capital	3.4	2.6	1.8	3.2	2.9
Transfers	2.3	0.8	0.8	1.6	1.5
Inconclusive	7.7	8.5	6.9	8.2	8.0
Total	100.0	100.0	100.0	100.0	100.0

Note: "Inconclusive" category; those with no income or with no income above 50 percent of total income, and those with part-time pension as main source of income. "Work" includes income from active business, but not sickness insurance, parental leave, etc. "Transfers" include housing allowances and social assistance. Only the four major labor market sectors are included.

for white-collar and local government employees are about 10 percent and for central government employees over 20 percent. This is explained by the fact that blue-collar workers in the private sector, before the new agreement in 1996, generally could not collect occupational pension benefits before age 65. After 1996, early withdrawals can be made from age 55, but it is not likely that many will do so, since their occupational pension is too small to alone finance early retirement. Blue-collar workers are on the other hand more likely to collect disability insurance compared to the other groups. This is especially notable in the age group 60–64 where 33 percent of the blue-collar workers have their main income from disability insurance, whereas the shares of other groups range from 17 to 22 percent. It can also be noted that there is a smaller share among blue-collar workers than among the other groups that receives their main income from work. For people in the upper age groups in the labor market, unemployment is also a pathway to permanent retirement. As evidenced by the Labor Force Surveys (Statistics Sweden), unemployment spells are typically much longer for older than for younger workers. Few of the older workers, hence, find re-employment after an unemployment spell. The results in Table 1 also suggest that the share of unemployed is higher in the private sector (blue- and white-collar) than in the public sector (central and local government).

According to Figure 3, the total annual transition rate in 1992–2000 for transitions from having earned income as main source of income to another source ranges from 5.5 to 8.0 percent for the age group 55–59, and 17–22 percent for the age group 60–64. For these age groups most transitions go to occupational pension, unemployment benefits, and

*Figure 3. **Annual exit rate from work, by sector and age, in years 1992–2000***

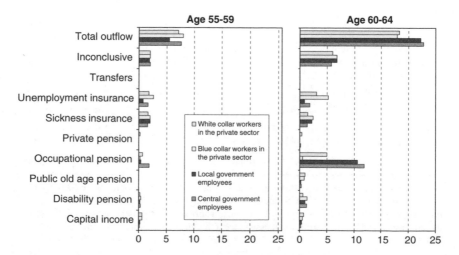

sickness insurance income. There are, however, notable differences across the labor market sectors. For local and central government employees, the annual outflow to occupational pension is less than 2 percent in the age group 55–59, but increases dramatically to about 12 percent in the age group 60–64. For white-collar employees in the private sector aged 60–64, the annual transition rate to occupational pension is about half of that of central government employees. For blue-collar workers, the transition from work to occupational pension is almost negligible.

Transitions to unemployment increase by age. There is a higher transition to unemployment in the private sector, inparticular for blue-collar workers, than in the public sector. For local government employees and blue-collar employees, we also detect a slightly higher rate for those who go from work to sickness insurance as their main source of income. Long-lasting periods of sickness insurance are usually an entrance to disability insurance. The periods of sickness insurance, which precede disability insurance, generally become shorter with increasing age (cf. Palme and Svensson, 2004). Hence, the observed transition from work directly to disability insurance is low, because people first go on sickness benefits.

Some of the sector differences in transition pattern may be explained by institutional differences. Before 1996, blue-collar workers did not have the possibility of an early withdrawal of occupational pension. Instead, there were many blue-collar workers with disability insurance. One interpretation of this finding is that blue-collar workers are more exposed to occupational hazards than other groups, but one cannot exclude that some use the health related sickness and disability insurances to become "early retired".

4. Models of early retirement

In this section, we present our models for predicting exit from the labor force. If exit takes place before normal retirement age, we denote this as early retirement. As transitions to sickness insurance and unemployment benefits do not represent permanent exits from the labor force, they are not considered as retirement and consequently included elsewhere in the simulation model. We consider only transitions into disability insurance and old age retirement, which both are assumed to be permanent exits from the labor force.

Retirement at normal retirement age is undisputedly the most common exit from the labor market. However, it is hard to find any economic motives for this behavior. Here, we consider retirement at normal retirement age as a social norm less influenced by economic incentives. On the other hand, individuals that do retire before normal retirement have potentially responded to economic incentives. Therefore, we do not set out to model retirement at normal retirement age, but focus on the decision to retire early.

The process of early retirement is separated into two parts: a health-induced early retirement via disability insurance, and a voluntary early retirement using the available old age pension plans. We consider these two routes to retirement to be distinct and mutually exclusive. However, this is not an obvious choice. For example, Palme and Svensson (2004) combine the two types of exits into a single model using Swedish data. Our main argument is that disability insurance is increasingly directed toward individuals with severe health issues that reduce their working capacity. Hence, this type of retirement should not be considered voluntary from the individual's perspective and the analysis calls for high-quality information about the individual's health status. Second, in order to account for early-retirement pensions, we need a more complex model, which would be difficult to combine with other routes into retirement. Hence, for the sake of simplicity, we have chosen to model the two routes into retirement (via disability insurance or old age pension) separately.

Considering the voluntary decision to retire via the collectively agreed occupational (or public) pension systems, there are three typical types of models in the economic literature. In the lifetime budget-constraint approach (Burtless and Hausman, 1978; Hausman and Wise, 1980; Burtless, 1986), the individual faces a discontinuous, or kinked, lifetime budget constraint. The lifetime budget constraint is analogous to the standard labor–leisure budget constraint, with annual hours replaced by years of labor force participation, and annual earnings replaced by cumulative lifetime compensation. The slope is interpreted as the "price" of retiring 1 year earlier and is a function of the accrual rate (i.e., the rise in retirement income entitlement caused by continuing to work for one more year). The kinks are produced by changes in the accrual rates caused by the conditions in the pension schemes. The optimal age of retirement is then determined by a utility function defined over years of work and cumulative compensation. The individual is assumed to know with certainty the opportunities that are available to her even in the distant future.

In the option value approach (Lazear and Moore, 1988; Stock and Wise, 1990; Börsch-Supan, 1999; Blundell *et al.*, 2002), the individual calculates, for each potential retirement year, the difference in expected lifetime utility from retiring that year and some other year – given the conditions of the pension schemes – in order to find the optimal age of retirement. The option value at age t (of postponing retirement to some later age) is the difference between expected lifetime utility from retiring at the optimal age of retirement and expected lifetime utility from retiring at age t. The individual is assumed to update the option value in the light of new information (such as unexpected changes in the pension schemes), which may result in changes in the accrual rate.

In the hazard-model approach (Diamond and Hausman, 1984; Hausman and Wise, 1985; Siddiqui, 1997; Röed and Haugen, 2003; Bütler *et al.*, 2004), the individual reacts to changes in current and one-period ahead social-security wealth. This is a reduced-form technique, which has been used to capture the net effects of changes in social-security wealth and other variables on retirement. The hazard-model approach is not as forward-looking as the lifetime budget-constraint approach. It does, however, allow for continuous updating of information as individuals grow older. That is, for an individual who is still active at age t, the probability of retiring at age $t+1$ is typically modeled in terms of annual wage earnings, private pension accruals, health status, etc., until age t as well as in terms of changes in these variables from t to $t+1$, while effects of changes occurring after $t+1$ are not considered.

In our final choice of models, we are constrained by the structure of the simulation model in which the early-retirement modules are to be implemented. We are limited by the available information in the model, and the intrinsic chronological structure of the simulations. Hence, the simulation model does not allow constructions of lifetime budget-constraints ex ante, and the computational burden must be kept as light as possible. As a consequence, we must rule out the lifetime budget-constraint models as well as the computationally intensive option value models. Instead, we use the third option and model both the exit to disability insurance and early retirement with old age pension as reduced forms similar to the hazard-model approach.

4.1. Early retirement via disability insurance

Early retirement via disability insurance is assumed to be influenced by individual characteristics, including health. The process is modeled as a discrete outcome such that

$$d_{it} = 1 \quad \text{if } d_{it}^* = z_{it}'\delta + \eta_{it} > 0$$
$$d_{it} = 0 \quad \text{otherwise.} \tag{1}$$

where $d_{it} = 1$ indicates the event of early retirement with disability insurance, given that no exit occurred in a period before, d_{it}^* is a latent variable, and z_{it} is a vector of observable individual characteristics with weights δ. The error term η_{it} reflects unobserved factor influencing the risk to retire early via disability insurance. The choice of variables reflects our viewpoint that the event of early retirement via disability insurance is involuntary from the individual's perspective. Hence, the individual characteristics that enter the model reflect health risks rather than economic incentives to retire via this route.

4.2. Early retirement via old age pension

In the old age retirement model, we focus on the relation between pension benefits and retirement behavior. The model includes, along with individual characteristics as controls, the discounted values of future net benefits and pension wealth accruals. These measures are standard in the literature but, for clarity, the definitions are given below. Let the net present value of the future pension benefits after tax (NPV) be defined as

$$
\text{NPV}_{it} = \sum_{s=t}^{T} (1 + \rho_{is})^{t-s} B_i(s,r), \tag{2}
$$

where $B(s,r)$ denotes the pension benefits after tax received in period s, if retiring in period r ($B(s,r)=0$ for $s<r$) and ρ_{it} the time-, age-, and gender-specific discount rate accounting for survival rates and an exogenous time preference discount component of 3 percent annually. In the analysis, we adopt a simplified tax system including only year-specific central and local taxes. The after-tax pension benefits for the public and the standard collective agreements, $B(s,r)$, are derived from the individual's income history and the conditions in the relevant pension contracts as discussed in Section 2.[15] The setup of early-retirement programs is discussed below.

The net present value accrual ACC_{it} measures the effects on NPV when postponing retirement 1 year,

$$
\text{ACC}_{it} = \frac{1}{1 + \rho_{it+1}} \text{NPV}_{i,t+1} - \text{NPV}_{it} \tag{3}
$$

Depending on the actuarial adjustments with respect to the timing of the claims, the accrual can be positive as well as negative. Delaying benefit claims generally increases the benefits during the payout periods, i.e., $B(t,r+1) \geq B(t,r)$ for $t \geq r+1$, but simultaneously reduces the number of years during which the benefits are received. The net effect on the accrual varies across individuals and time and can take positive as well as negative values.

As the net present value reflects an income effect, we would expect it to be positively correlated with the probability to retire. The accrual measures a relative price effect, so it should be associated with a negative correlation. However, both net present value and its accrual are functions of the wage

---

[15] The benefit level is defined as a function of qualifying wage, retirement age, present age (if retired), and the number of service years (entitlement years) within relevant occupational sector. From data we can observe neither the qualifying wage nor the number of service years perfectly, which means that they had to be estimated. We estimate the qualifying wage as the 5-year mean of individual taxable income prior to the year of the first occupational pension withdrawal. We have chosen to assign the maximum number of service years, which is 30 years for all sectors, to everyone in the sample.

rate via the earnings history; in general, both the NPV and the ACC are positively correlated (in absolute values) with the wage rate. Kreuger and Pischke (1992) and Coile and Gruber (2000), among others, note that social-security wealth (our net present value) and its accrual are a non-linear functions of past earnings, and unobserved retirement propensities may very well be correlated with earnings levels. This means that we may have an endogenous variable problem; if high wage rates signal strong preferences for work, we might see negative correlation between NPV and retirement probability. In order to control for the wage rate, we could include it as a control variable, or rescale the net present value and its accrual by the wage rate. Unfortunately, we do not have direct access to the wage rate. In this analysis we will adopt the latter approach and define

$$\text{NPV}_{it}^{Q} = \frac{\text{NPV}_{it}}{Q_{it}}$$

$$\text{ACC}_{it}^{Q} = \frac{\text{ACC}_{it}}{Q_{it}} \tag{4}$$

where Q_{it} denotes the average after-tax annual income over the 5 years predating retirement. An alternative rational behind this specification is that individuals relate after-tax pension wealth to after-tax annual earnings. The rescaled measures will have the interpretation of wealth in terms of annual earnings, i.e., $\text{NPV}_{it} = 10$ would mean that the individual has 10 after-tax annual earnings in after-tax pension wealth.

The individual's choice to retire is assumed to be given by the discrete choice model

$$y_{it} = 1 \quad \text{if} \quad y_{it}^{*} = \mathbf{x}_{it}'\beta + \varepsilon_{it} > 0$$

$$y_{it} = 0 \quad \text{otherwise} \tag{5}$$

where $y_{it} = 1$ indicates that the individual exit into retirement in period t, $\mathbf{x}_{it}$ is a vector of individual characteristics including rescaled net present values and accruals with weights β and ε_{it} reflects unobserved variables influencing the retirement decision.

Retirement via the old age pension model includes financial incentives, which are derived from the future stream of pension benefits. As discussed in Section 3, old age benefits are generally determined by the public old age pension and the collectively agreed occupational pension systems. However, we also indicated the incidence of individual contracts between the employer and the employee close to normal retirement age, denoted as early-retirement pension offers. This type of pension is not available to all individuals at all times, but it is the outcome of an unobserved negotiation process between the employee and the employer. Ideally, we would like to model the process by constructing a structural model including the main determinants of early-retirement pension offers and the level of early-retirement pension benefits. However, that is not possible with the data at hand and we are forced to retreat to a reduced form, capturing the main individual variables in the process. Here, we assume that the probability of receiving an early-retirement pension is determined as a discrete choice model such that

$$v_{it} = 1 \quad \text{if } v_{it}^* = \mathbf{w}_{it}'\delta + \xi_{it} > 0 \tag{6}$$

where $v_{it} = 1$ indicates that the individual has access to an early-retirement pension, $\mathbf{w}_{it}$ denotes a vector of individual characteristics with weights δ, and ξ_{it} unobserved variables reflecting the probability to receive an offer.[16] There are some econometric complications as the early-retirement pension is only indirectly observable for those who have retired. These problems and the proposed solutions are discussed in the next section.

5. Data

The theoretical models emphasize different issues, and hence we are forced to use different data sources for the analysis of early retirement via disability insurance and old age pension, respectively. The data set used for the disability insurance model originates from HILDA presented in Chapter 4, whereas the data set used for early retirement via old age pension originates from LINDA introduced in Chapter 3. In this section, we focus on the variables used in the empirical specification and refer the reader to these chapters for an introduction to the data sets.

5.1. Data for early retirement via disability insurance

In the empirical literature, there has been a debate focusing on what measure to use to account for differences in health. Early studies often used self-reported health or disability as proxies for health status.[17] In most cases, the variable was highly significant, with a substantial positive effect on the probability of retirement. On the other hand, the effect of economic incentives in the pension schemes turned out to be more modest (although in most cases statistically significant and with the expected signs).

---

[16] As the accrual value of social security wealth includes also its future value, there is an issue on the individual's expectation of future access to early-retirement programs. In this analysis we assume that an individual do not anticipate to receive an offer next year.

[17] See for instance Boskin and Hurd (1978), Quinn (1979), Gordon and Blinder (1980), Burkhauser and Quinn (1983), Hanoch and Honig (1983), Burtless and Moffitt (1984), Wadensjö (1985), Burtless (1986), Gustman and Steinmeier (1986), and lastly, Hogarth (1988).

However, there has been concern about self-reported health being endogenous, for instance, because there are incentives to report poor health to gain social acceptance for the decision to retire early (Anderson and Burkhauser, 1985; Stern, 1989; Kerkhofs and Lindeboom, 1995; Dwyer and Mitchell, 1999; McGarry, 2002), or to become eligible for disability pension (Stern, 1989; Bound, 1991; Kerkhofs and Lindeboom, 1995; Börsch-Supan, 1999; Kreider, 1999; Blundell *et al.*, 2002), or because both health status and labor force participation depend on some unobserved factor (Anderson and Burkhauser, 1985; Stern, 1989; Kerkhofs and Lindeboom, 1995). The potential endogeneity of health may, inter alia, result in an overestimation of the effects of health status and an underestimation of the effects of the economic incentives.

To address these problems, some authors have attempted to control for health differences by using "more objective" health indicators such as the number of sickness days (Berglind, 1977; Bratberg *et al.*, 2004), actual mortality experiences (Parsons, 1982; Anderson and Burkhauser, 1985), the existence of and the number of chronic conditions (Hedström, 1980; Siddiqui, 1997; Dwyer and Mitchell, 1999). Other authors have used the objective indicators to instrument health status (Stern, 1989; Dwyer and Mitchell, 1999). This has generally resulted in health status having smaller and economic incentives larger effects on the retirement probability.

Both these approaches have been questioned, though. The first on the grounds that the objective health indicator in question may not be a good indicator of work-related health (Bazzoli, 1985; Bound, 1991; Kreider, 1999), in which case the effect of health status may be underestimated. The second approach has been questioned because good instruments are hard to find and may not by itself solve the problem of endogeneity (Bound, 1991). Hence, which indicator to use in order to get an unbiased estimate of its effect on the retirement probability still is an unresolved issue.

In our analysis, we use pooled cross sections of HILDA for the years 1988–1997 to analyze early retirement via disability insurance. Each cross section includes register data of received disability pensions as well as other background variables.

As dependent variable we use an indicator that equals 1, if the respondent was granted early retirement via disability insurance the subsequent year, and 0 otherwise. Thus, for the year 1988 we checked whether the respondent was granted disability insurance in 1989, etc. As described in Section 1, an individual may be eligible for part-time retirement from the disability insurance system. Here, we abstract from this possibility and combine part- and full-time retirees in the same group.

The main independent variable is our health index, denoted by HI. This is a categorical variable discussed in detail in Chapter 4. The health index has four different levels ranging from 1 to 4, with 4 representing full health and 1 severe health conditions. This variable enters the model as a set of dummy variables reflecting the four categories – HI1 reflects full health, while HI2 reflects good health. As the health variable is an imperfect indicator of health, we also include a dummy variable, denoted by SICKL, with value 1 if the individual received more than 15 days of sickness benefits the year before the interview, and 0 otherwise.

Education has several potential influences on the probability of being early retired via the disability insurance system beside the direct health effect discussed in Chapter 4. First, educational achievements may influence the individual's opinion about early retirement via disability insurance. Second, it is plausible that different types of employments present different opportunities to remain at work given a reduced health condition, and these positions are probably related to the educational level of the individual. Hence, in the empirical specification we include the educational level achieved in 1996/1997 as an independent variable. The latter also suggests that the individual's labor market sector affiliation should enter the model. Here, we include dummy variables for private blue- and white-collar employees), local or central government employees, or self-employed.

Previous studies have indicated income is an important determinant. In order to avoid effects of nominal growth in income, we use the individual's relative position in the income distribution, here measured in terms of income quartiles. We thus include a set of dummy variables indicating the income quartile that the individual belongs to. Finally, we include the individual's age, an indicator if born in Sweden, and sex as independent variables.

5.2. Data for early retirement via old age pension

We used a panel data set from 1992 to 2000 originating from LINDA (described in Chapter 3) to estimate the early retirement via old age pension. Only a restricted subsample was used in the estimations of the parameters in Eqs. (5) and (6).

We limited the analysis to the age group 60–64. The argument for this is that very few actually start to claim their occupational pension before age 60, and not many continue work (without withdrawing pensions) after the age of 65 (see Section 3).[18] Hence, the large part of the early retirement via old age pension takes place among those who are 60–64 years old.

We define the risk group as those who were classified as working at least one preceding year (has work or active business incomes summing to at least 1 BA), and did not claim any public, private, or occupational old age

---

[18] The decision whether or not to retire is assumed to be taken and executed in the same calendar year.

pension, or disability insurance in that year.[19] Therefore, the preceding year serves as a qualifying period, meaning that the first claim can be observed in 1993.

The dependent variable indicates the individual's first year of retirement. The year of retirement is the first year with an occupational pension claim, which is defined as the year in which occupational pension is paid out given that none was received in the preceding year. To avoid the usual problems with annual data of the type we employ, we do not measure income with data from the transition year (to retirement) in our study.[20] Instead, incomes are measured in the first and the third year of a 3-year panel, centered on the transition year. This implies that the first year of occupational pension claim must be observed no later than the second to last year before the panel ends, i.e., in 1999.

In addition to the variables measuring the economic incentives discussed in Section 4, we control for educational level, sex, age, calendar year, if the individual was born in Sweden, the individual's marital status, and (if applicable) the spouse's labor market status. It is reasonable to believe that the subset of workers – mostly white-collar workers in the private sector – that continue working longer than others (Table 1) is a quite selective group in terms of health, productivity, and quality of work place. The included controls capture at least partly such heterogeneity. In the literature, there are results indicating that married couples tend to retire at the same time. In order to take full account of the household decision to retire, we would need a much more complex model than what is feasible here. Hence, we are forced to use the spouse's lagged labor market status in the individual's decision to retire so that we do not create complicating simultaneity problems. Here, we define the spouse's labor market status by checking the income from work. If this is less than 1 BA, the spouse is considered not working.

For the calculation of economic incentives, it is crucial that each person's labor market sector affiliation can be identified in order to correctly implement the relevant collectively agreed occupational pension plan. Sector affiliation is not coded for all groups, however, so it has to be estimated for parts of the sample. In this process, we use all individuals aged 50 years or more in the data set. After dropping a minor share of

---

[19] Data show that retirement is definitive; Hallberg (2003) showed that the transition rate back to work was 0.1 percent for disability insurance and 0.4 percent for occupational pension among male workers aged 60–64. One can note that conditioning on longer work history does not change the risk group, and therefore not the estimates very much.

[20] Since individuals may change status any time during the year there is a high possibility that, with the annual structure of the data, the registered income from the transition year is difficult to use. It may be difficult to differentiate work on a part-time basis from work part-of-the-year.

individuals with inconsistent income records, we observe 33 704 men and 41 383 women that are 50+ during 1992–2000. Sector affiliation is determined in a series of steps. For each retired individual with occupational pension benefits, we can observe the source of the pension payments. That is, we know from which collective agreement occupational pension the individual receives her benefits. This information is then used to classify the individuals into appropriate labor market sectors.[21] If the individual did not retire within the observed periods, we cannot observe directly her sector affiliation through the occupational pension payouts. In that case, we use additional information in the data on labor market affiliation. All employed individuals are coded in data as employed in the private, central government, or local government sector. For individuals in the central or local government sector who do not retire before the end of the panel, we use this register information directly to code sector affiliation.[22] For employed in the private sector, this is not possible, since these could be either white- or blue-collar workers. For this group, predictions from a logit equation are used to determine white- or blue-collar sector affiliation.[23]

In the available data, the same variable contains both "normal" occupational pension benefits originating from the collective agreements, and early-retirement pension offers accepted on an individual basis. Hence, there is no explicit information whether an individual has received an early-retirement pension offer or not. We must, therefore, make a few assumptions to identify this event. The strategy that we pursue here is to rely on how the observed pension-benefit level corresponds to standard conditions in the relevant occupational pension plan. The standard pension level (if retiring) is calculated using the qualifying wage, retirement age, and sector. We assume that benefits that exceed a certain threshold level constitute an accepted early-retirement pension offer. The threshold is given by the standard conditions in the relevant collective agreement occupational pension, excluding actuarial adjustment for early

---

[21] To avoid unnecessary complications, individuals that receive benefits from more than one occupational pension source are dropped.

[22] This code says in which sector most of the income was earned in a particular year. We backlag this value from the last year of the panel to every year in order to have only one value per individual.

[23] The prediction equation is estimated on those observed retired as either white-collar workers or blue-collar workers. Explanatory variables in that prediction model are taxable income, gender, education, and industry, and interactions. The reported measure of fit is high (given the particular uniform random draw, the ratio of "correct" predictions was about 75 percent). As a sensitivity check, we compared the register information on sector code with the actual pension source among those we observe as retired, and found a very good correspondence between these measures.

withdrawal.[24] We also consider if an early-retirement option exists in the collectively agreed occupational pension contract. If we observe an occupational pension withdrawal at an age earlier than what is stipulated in the agreement as early-retirement age, we code this as an early-retirement pension.[25,26]

In reality, early-retirement pension contracts are frequently individually designed and the exact conditions, including the benefit levels, are not known to us. They vary presumably with industry, company, age group, perhaps also gender. Yet, in this study we will, for simplicity, use a single construction for the early-retirement pension and assume that the replacement rates are given by the complementary rules as discussed in Section 2.

In the equation determining accessibility to early-retirement pensions, we also control for the pensionable income and sector affiliation. The motivation for this is that the pension cost for the employer, which we believe is an important driver behind these offers, varies with pensionable income and collectively agreed occupational pension plans. We also control for period and age effects.

In Table 2, we present some sample descriptions. In panel A, we present the sample exit rates by age and gender. The annual exit rate from work to early retirement is about 7 percent for males and 8.5 percent for females for age groups 61–63. At age 64, the rates increase to 10 percent for males and 30 percent for females. Panel B gives the share of early retirees with an early-retirement pension. This share is about 35 percent for males and 25 percent for females. Finally, in panel C we present the share of early retirees with an early-retirement pension by sector affiliation. The results indicate that the early-retirement pensions are more frequent in the private white-collar sector than in the central or local government sectors.

In Table 3, we present the sample averages of the net present values of future pension benefits with early-retirement pensions and standard collectively agreed occupational pensions. We also present the rescaled versions, where the net present values are scaled by the after-tax

---

[24] The classification of individuals with early-retirement pension is naturally sensitive to the threshold. We make a conservative estimate of the threshold by assuming maximum number of service years for everyone (which is not known from data), and excluding the actuarial adjustments due to early withdrawal.

[25] Fölster et al. (2001) also studies early-retirement pensions within the occupational pension system. It is, however, difficult to compare results since their definition differs from ours; it codes everyone with an early-occupational pension withdrawal but not an early public old age pension withdrawal as having an early-retirement pension.

[26] The early-retirement option in the occupational pension schemes should not be confused with the lower mandatory retirement age that some minor occupational groups have. The definition of early-retirement pension we use will probably include these minor groups.

Table 2. Exit rates and sample shares with early-retirement pensions

Age	Males		Females	
	Work	Retired	Work	Retired
A. Exit rates from work (in percent)				
60	97.4	2.6	97.3	2.7
61	91.1	8.9	90.9	9.1
62	92.5	7.5	91.4	8.6
63	93.8	6.2	90.8	9.2
64	89.6	10.4	70.5	29.5
Total	93.4	6.6	89.8	10.2
	Standard	Early-retirement pension	Standard	Early-retirement pension
B. Share of retirees with standard and early retirement pensions (in percent)				
60	61.8	38.2	71.2	28.8
61	65.7	34.3	67.9	32.1
62	67.9	32.1	73.8	26.2
63	61.1	38.9	74.2	25.8
64	65.4	34.6	80.2	19.8
Total	65.0	35.0	75.0	25.0
C. Share of retirees with early-retirement pension by sector				
Central	71.6	28.4	77.1	22.9
White-collar	53.9	46.1	64.2	35.8
Local government	71.3	28.7	76.3	23.7
Blue-collar	100.0	0.0	100.0	0.0

Table 3. Net present value of future pension benefits (NPV) with early retirement pension and standard agreement among the retired, by sector (sample means)

Sector	NPV, early-retirement pension (in SEK)	NPV, standard pension (in SEK)	Rescaled NPV, early-retirement pension	Rescaled NPV, standard pension
Central	1 644 000	1 441 000	11.0	9.6
White-collar	1 726 000	1 552 000	10.8	9.7
Local government	1 409 000	1 184 000	11.9	10.0
Blue-collar		935 000		8.3

Note: In 1999, 1 BA was 36 400 SEK.

pensionable income. Note that the net present values are based on after-tax benefits. The results indicate that, for central government employees, the average net present value of the early-retirement pension is about SEK 1 644 000 (in 1999 price level) compared to SEK 1 441 000 for the standard pension. In terms of pensionable income, this represents about 11 and 9.6 years of after-tax annual incomes, respectively.

6. Empirical specifications

Considering the early retirement via disability insurance, the only empirical specification needed is the distribution for the error terms. Here we assume that the error term is logistically distributed, yielding a standard logit model. The parameters are allowed to vary over age in that the parameters are estimated separately on three age groups, 16–29, 30–60, and 60–64. Furthermore, since the observed transition frequency from disability insurance back to work is negligible, we consider the state as early retired as an absorbing state.

For early retirement via the old age pension systems, the situation is more complicated. First, as the observed frequencies of transitions from retirement back to work are negligible in practice, we consider retirement via old age pension as an absorbing state too. Second, access to early-retirement pension is not observable for non-retirees. This complicates the situation as the dependent variable in Eq. (6) becomes only partially observable, and some of the independent variables in Eq. (5) become error prone and correlated to the error term. The proposed model (Eklöf and Hallberg, 2006) is similar to the bivariate probit models with partial observability proposed by Abowd and Farber (1982) and Poirier (1980), but in this case there is an additional problem, since the independent variables are also only partially observed.

In Eq. (5), the problem is that $\mathbf{x}_{it}$ is observed with error for non-retirees, i.e., when $\varepsilon_{it} < -\mathbf{x}'_{it}\beta$. This implies that we have an endogenous variable problem since the measurement error in $\mathbf{x}_{it}$ is related to the error term ε_{it}. Furthermore, since the accessibility of early-retirement program is observed for retirees only, this implies that the data is censored with respect to v_{it} and we have a sample selection problem in Eq. (6).

Assume that the utility parameters are not affected by the accessibility of an early-retirement pension. Let $\mathbf{x}_{it} = v_{it}\mathbf{x}_{it}^{ERP} + (1 - v_{it})\mathbf{x}_{it}^{STD}$ where the superscript ERP refers to variables relevant if the individual has access to an early-retirement pension and STD refers to the standard contracts. Then we can construct a system of simultaneous equations as

$$\begin{cases} y_{it}^* = (v_{it}\mathbf{x}_{it}^{ERP} + (1 - v_{it})\mathbf{x}_{it}^{STD})'\beta + \varepsilon_{it} \\ v_{it}^* = \mathbf{w}'_{it}\delta + \xi_{it} \end{cases} \tag{7}$$

where the simultaneity stems from that $\mathbf{x}_{it}$ is a function of v_{it} and v_{it} is only observed if $y_{it} = 1$, i.e., if $(v_{it}\mathbf{x}_{it}^{ERP} + (1 - v_{it})\mathbf{x}_{it}^{STD})'\beta + \varepsilon_{it} > 0$.

The probability to observe the event (y_{it}, v_{it}) is thus

$$\Pr(y_{it}, v_{it}) = \int_{\underline{\xi}_{it}}^{\bar{\xi}_{it}} \int_{\underline{\varepsilon}_{it}}^{\bar{\varepsilon}_{it}} f(\varepsilon, \xi) d\varepsilon d\xi \tag{8}$$

where $f(\varepsilon, \xi)$ denotes the joint density of $(\varepsilon_{it}, \xi_{it})$ and with integration limits defined as

$$\bar{\varepsilon}_{it} = \begin{cases} (v_{it}\mathbf{x}_{it}^{ERP} + (1 - v_{it})\mathbf{x}_{it}^{STD})'\beta & \text{if } y_{it} = 1 \\ \infty & \text{otherwise.} \end{cases}$$

$$\underline{\varepsilon}_{it} = \begin{cases} -\infty & \text{if } y_{it} = 1 \\ (v_{it}\mathbf{x}_{it}^{ERP} + (1 - v_{it})\mathbf{x}_{it}^{STD})'\beta & \text{otherwise.} \end{cases} \tag{9}$$

and

$$\bar{\xi}_{it} = \begin{cases} \mathbf{w}_{it}'\delta & \text{if } v_{it} = 1 \\ \infty & \text{otherwise.} \end{cases}$$

$$\underline{\xi}_{it} = \begin{cases} -\infty & \text{if } v_{it} = 1 \\ \mathbf{w}_{it}'\delta & \text{otherwise.} \end{cases} \tag{10}$$

Furthermore, as the propensity to retire is potentially related to unobserved individual characteristics, we control for individual-specific time invariant effects. Assuming that the unobserved time invariant individual effects are uncorrelated with the idiosyncratic random error and with the observable independent variables allows us to estimate a random-effect model. The probability to observe a sequence of outcomes $(\mathbf{y}_i, \mathbf{v}_i) = (y_{i1}, \ldots, y_{iT_i}, v_{i1}, \ldots, v_{iT_i})$ is

$$\Pr(\mathbf{y}_i, \mathbf{v}_i) = \int_{\underline{\xi}_{i1}}^{\bar{\xi}_{i1}} \cdots \int_{\underline{\xi}_{iT_i}}^{\bar{\xi}_{iT_i}} \int_{\underline{\varepsilon}_{i1}}^{\bar{\varepsilon}_{i1}} \cdots \int_{\underline{\varepsilon}_{iT_i}}^{\bar{\varepsilon}_{iT_i}} f(\varepsilon_{i1}, \ldots, \varepsilon_{iT_i}, \xi_{i1}, \ldots, \xi_{iT_i}) d\varepsilon_{iT_i} \cdots d\xi_{i1} \tag{11}$$

To simplify, we assume that the error term in the retirement decision model is independent of the error term in the early-retirement program equation. Let $\varepsilon_{it} = u_i + e_{it}$ where $u_i \sim iidN(0, \sigma_u^2)$ and $e_{it} \sim iidN(0, 1)$. This implies that ε_{it} is uncorrelated with ε_{is} for $t \neq s$ conditional on u_i. As $\mathbf{x}_{it}$ is observed only when $y_{it} = 1$ we join the outcomes $(y_{it}, v_{it}) = (0, 0)$ and $(y_{it}, v_{it}) = (0, 1)$.

The probability conditional on u_i can thus be written as

$$
\Pr(\mathbf{y}_i, \mathbf{v}_i | u_i) = \prod_{t=1}^{T_i} [\Phi(\mathbf{x}_{it}^{ERP'} \beta + u_i, \mathbf{w}_{it}'\delta, \rho)^{y_{it}v_{it}} \{\Phi(\mathbf{x}_{it}^{STD'} \beta + u_i, \infty, \rho)
$$
$$
- \Phi(\mathbf{x}_{it}^{STD'} \beta + u_i, \mathbf{w}_{it}'\delta, \rho)\}^{y_{it}(1-v_{it})}
$$
$$
\times \{1 - \Phi(\mathbf{x}_{it}^{ERP'} \beta + u_i, \mathbf{w}_{it}'\delta, \rho) - [\Phi(\mathbf{x}_{it}^{STD'} \beta + u_i, \infty, \rho)
$$
$$
- \Phi(\mathbf{x}_{it}^{STD'} \beta + u_i, \mathbf{w}_{it}'\delta, \rho)]\}^{1-y_{it}}] \tag{12}
$$

Integrating over u_i gives the unconditional probabilities as

$$
\Pr(\mathbf{y}_i, \mathbf{v}_i) = \int_{-\infty}^{\infty} \Pr(\mathbf{y}_i, \mathbf{v}_i | u) f_u(u) \mathrm{d}u \tag{13}
$$

which can be rewritten on a form suitable for numerical integration routines (e.g., Gauss–Hermite quadrature) as $\Pr(\mathbf{y}_i, \mathbf{v}_i) = \int_{-\infty}^{\infty} \exp(-r^2) g(r) \mathrm{d}r$ where $g(r) = (1/\sqrt{\pi})\Pr(\mathbf{y}_i, \mathbf{v}_i | \sqrt{2\sigma^2} r)$.

7. Results

In Table 4, we report on the results of our estimation of the logit specification of the event of early retirement via disability insurance. The table presents marginal effects evaluated at sample means. The p-values in brackets refer to estimated marginal effects. Note that this specification assumes that the event is non-voluntary, so financial incentives do not enter the model. We have explored several alternative specifications, resulting in the final specification indicated by the table. Variables that turned out highly insignificant were dropped from the model, here indicated by empty cells.

The results indicate that the effect of the health status on the probability of being granted disability insurance is negative, i.e., the higher the health status, the lower is the probability of being granted disability insurance. This effect is also stronger, the older the age group. Lagged sickness absenteeism increases the probability of being granted disability insurance for those 30–60 years of age, which is intuitive as this variable captures some unobserved health-related variables. Having a university degree significantly lowers the probability, which could reflect that higher education is associated with job descriptions with less health-related problems and more options in terms of job assignments. Belonging to the two lowest income quartiles increased the probability of being granted disability insurance pension for those in age group 30–60, while it decreased the probability for those 60–64 years of age. This is probably also related to the effects of job market sector affiliation. Being privately employed decreased the probability of being granted early-retirement pension for those aged 30–60, while it

Table 4. Logit estimates, marginal effects. Probability to exit labor force to early retirement via disability insurance

Variable	Age group		
	16–29	30–60	60–64
HI1 (FULL HEALTH)	−0.00256 (0.007)	−0.018 (0.000)	−0.0234 (0.000)
HI2 (GOOD HEALTH)		−0.380E−2 (0.000)	−0.785E−2 (0.002)
SICKL	0.000964 (0.165)	0.0128 (0.000)	
UNIV		−0.000988 (0.023)	−0.00659 (0.037)
QUARTILE1		0.000951 (0.059)	−0.0109 (0.001)
QUARTILE2		0.00115 (0.019)	−0.0000905 (0.980)
QUARTILE3			−0.000835 (0.804)
PRIVAT	−0.000565 (0.013)	−0.00127 (0.001)	0.0191 (0.003)
GOVERN		−0.000825 (0.134)	
COMMUN		−0.00163 (0.000)	0.00881 (0.204)
OWNEMPL		−0.00000275 (0.001)	0.0000126 (0.016)
AGE	−0.0000184 (0.374)	0.000197 (0.000)	−0.00417 (0.000)
SWED		−0.000936 (0.037)	
SEX (1 for male)		−0.000251 (0.462)	−0.00627 (0.031)
lnL	−130.0472	−1698.567	−309.3895
Observations	13 431	28 074	3246

Note: p-values within parenthesis.

increased the probability for those older than 60 years of age. This can be explained by the fact that blue-collar workers in the private sector do not have access to early retirement via occupational pension and, hence, to a larger extent use the disability insurance system to exit early from the labor market. This is also reflected by the age effect in the two oldest age groups. In age group 30–60, the probability of early retirement via disability insurance is increasing with age, whereas the probability is decreasing with age in age group 60–64. The negative relationship in age group 60–64 is probably caused by the fact that individuals who want to exit early do so as close as possible to their 60th birthday. Finally, Swedes are less prone to retire via the disability insurance in age group 30–60, and males are less likely than females to retire early via disability insurance.

In preliminary analysis, substantial behavioral differences in voluntary early retirement emerged between males and females. Hence, the voluntary early-retirement model is estimated separately for males and females. The results are presented in Table 5. There are two panels of estimates. In panel A, we present the estimates of the retirement equation and in panel B the estimates of the "access to early-retirement pension" equation. The marginal effects are evaluated at sample means of the independent variables. For the economic variables relating to pension benefits, we use the sample means of those given by the standard contracts. For a comprehensive set of estimates comparing different specifications with respect to definitions of early-retirement programs, etc., we refer to Eklöf and Hallberg (2006).

Considering the retirement decision (panel A), the results are mostly in line with intuition in that an increase in the net present value of future benefits in terms of qualifying wage implies a higher probability of retirement for females, but this is insignificant for males. However, these effects are small as an increase in net present value by one annual income increases the probability to retire by 1.1 percentage points for females and just 0.2 percentage points for males. This corresponds approximately to a 10 percent increase in retirement probability for females. A higher accrual value implies a lower probability of early retirement using the occupational pension for both females and males. Higher education increases the probability to retire early. Married or cohabiting individuals are less likely to retire early unless their spouse is not working. If the spouse is not working, the net effect is essentially the same as for the reference group of singles. The individual variation is substantial as indicated by the estimated standard deviation of the individual effects.

Turning to the access to early-retirement pension equation (panel B), the wage effect is small and positive, although significant only for males. Higher education is associated with a higher probability of having access to early-retirement pension, as is being born in Sweden. The results also indicate that female white-collar employees in the private sector and male employees in the local government sector are more likely to have access to early-retirement pensions than the reference group of central government employees. Note that our model precludes blue-collar workers in the private sector from having access to early-retirement pensions. Hence, for this group the dependent variable is deterministically equal to 0 and therefore not estimated.

8. Simulations

In this section, we present the implications of the estimated models in terms of simulated outcomes. We mainly focus on early-retirement behavior and closely related issues. The basic scenario, discussed in Chapter 3, defines

Table 5.   *Marginal effects, coefficients estimates of a model of old age retirement*

	Females			Males		
	Marginal effects[b]	Coefficients	Standard deviation	Marginal effects[b]	Coefficients	Standard deviation
A. Retired = 1						
Constant		−16.82***	(1.073)		−6.390***	(0.939)
NPV/Qualifying wage (after tax)	0.011	0.785***	(0.078)	0.002	0.087	(0.064)
Accrual/Qualifying wage (after tax)	−0.038	−2.834***	(0.383)	−0.080	−3.258***	(0.413)
College	0.013	0.966***	(0.133)	0.010	0.410***	(0.102)
University	0.012	0.917***	(0.153)	0.023	0.934***	(0.159)
Married/Cohabiting	−0.008	−0.625***	(0.135)	−0.005	−0.222**	(0.094)
Spouse not working	0.006	0.475***	(0.112)	0.006	0.254***	(0.088)
Born abroad	−0.003	−0.213	(0.288)	−0.009	−0.364**	(0.179)
If year = 1993 (reference)						
If year = 1994	0.010	0.757***	(0.154)	0.007	0.289**	(0.121)
If year = 1995	0.013	0.949***	(0.170)	0.002	0.098	(0.130)
If year = 1996	0.015	1.118***	(0.173)	0.004	0.175	(0.129)
If year = 1997	0.019	1.394***	(0.181)	0.010	0.420***	(0.140)
If year = 1998	0.014	1.037***	(0.179)	0.005	0.215	(0.138)
If year = 1999	0.017	1.299***	(0.175)	0.009	0.383***	(0.147)
If age = 60 (ref.)						
If age = 61	0.026	1.931***	(0.166)	0.030	1.207***	(0.163)
If age = 62	0.036	2.660***	(0.221)	0.033	1.332***	(0.214)
If age = 63	0.044	3.259***	(0.271)	0.032	1.290***	(0.243)
If age = 64	0.070	5.228***	(0.315)	0.044	1.796***	(0.277)
SE(u_i)		3.289***	(0.193)		1.706***	(0.242)

(Continued on next page)

B. Access to early-retirement pension = 1

Constant		−1.853*** (0.138)		−2.020*** (0.113)
Qualifying wage (before tax)	0.003	0.023 (0.015)	0.002	0.019** (0.008)
College	0.026	0.228*** (0.063)	0.014	0.127** (0.064)
University	0.033	0.296*** (0.076)	0.018	0.161** (0.073)
Born abroad	−0.005	−0.044 (0.140)	−0.015	−0.136 (0.138)
Central government (reference)				
White-collar	0.016	0.144* (0.082)	0.004	0.033 (0.062)
Local government	0.004	0.033 (0.071)	0.021	0.185** (0.077)
Blue-collar[a]				
If year = 1993 (ref.)				
If year = 1994	−0.063	−0.562*** (0.099)	−0.049	−0.438*** (0.099)
If year = 1995	−0.058	−0.520*** (0.095)	−0.034	−0.302*** (0.097)
If year = 1996	−0.071	−0.637*** (0.097)	−0.029	−0.254*** (0.092)
If year = 1997	−0.028	−0.248*** (0.084)	−0.026	−0.233*** (0.089)
If year = 1998	−0.041	−0.368*** (0.087)	−0.037	−0.326*** (0.090)
If year = 1999	−0.070	−0.620*** (0.091)	−0.036	−0.323*** (0.087)
If age = 60 (ref.)				
If age = 61	0.051	0.459*** (0.083)	0.054	0.476*** (0.070)
If age = 62	0.045	0.402*** (0.091)	0.055	0.491*** (0.079)
If age = 63	0.055	0.487*** (0.096)	0.082	0.726*** (0.092)
If age = 64	0.092	0.822*** (0.091)	0.125	1.107*** (0.093)
lnL		−6657.0		−5223.8
Individuals		8170		8381
Observations		20 425		20 579

Note: Significant on *** = 1%, ** = 5%, * = 10% percent. The estimates are based on Gauss–Hermite quadrature using 10 nodes.

[a]Blue-collar workers in the private sector are not allowed to receive early-retirement pensions.

[b]The marginal effects refer to an infinitesimal small change in the independent variable. Hence, for dummy variables, the marginal effect presented here does not refer to a discrete change from 0 to 1.

the point of departure. We also present simulations in two alternative scenarios, where we first remove the early-retirement pension option and then increase the normal retirement age to 70. The motives behind these alternative scenarios are that the labor force is expected to decrease in the near future, which would potentially reduce firms' incentives to offer early-retirement pensions. Furthermore, the age at which the employee loses her right to remain at employment is increasing, and this is expected to influence the normal retirement age. Here we assume that the normal retirement age will increase to 70.

In the simulations, we are forced to make some simplifying assumptions. The estimated model for early retirement using an early-retirement pension offer includes time dummies. Hence, we need to decide which combination of time dummies we want to use as we project behavior into the future. Here, we have used the level of the latest period available as our point of departure. In the simulations, we will use the level of the constant as given by the 1999 time dummy. Further, the estimated models focus on early retirement, that is, retirement before the normal retirement age at 65. Unfortunately, we have very few observations of individuals that postpone retirement beyond age 65, so we do not estimate a model for postponement. Thus, in the basic scenario, all individuals are forced to retire at age 65 at the latest. As discussed in Section 2, individuals with disability insurance, or any other social-security insurance, are transferred to retirement at age 65 automatically. Finally, one should also note that the models are estimated on data for the 1990s. Since then, the public old age pension scheme, and some collectively agreed occupational pensions have been reformed. We assume that the parameters estimated above are constant over time.

When calculating the net present values of future pension benefits, the simulation algorithm iterates over time periods for each individual separately and calls the relevant model functions defining the benefits. This produces a prediction of the sequence of future benefits that are discounted to a present value (including a 3 percent time preference) and summed up. However, as the simulation model is actually stepped forward, the outcomes of the benefits could differ from the predicted stream of benefits as these depend on stochastic variables that are not realized at the time of the net present value calculations.

8.1. Basic scenario

The baseline scenario involves mandatory retirement at age 65 at the latest. Individuals are allowed to retire early via the occupational pension or disability insurance systems according to the models described in Section 4. Blue-collar workers are the only ones allowed to retire early via the public pension system, as they lack early-retirement opportunities via the occupational pension system.

Figure 4. **Population and simulated shares in work, old age retirement, and disability insurance for the age group 60–64, by gender**

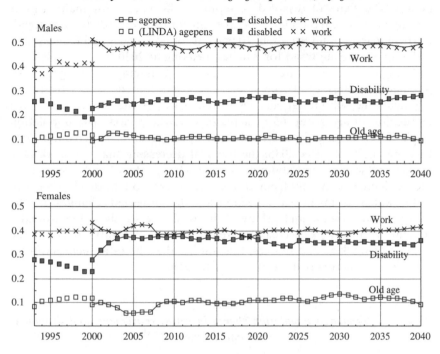

We start with a broad view of the simulated population shares in work, early retirement, and disability insurance for the interesting age group 60–64. We present both the simulated shares from 2000 through 2040 and the observed shares in the LINDA 1993–2000 database (Figure 4). However, one should note that the model for early retirement via disability insurance is not estimated on LINDA. The gap in the year 2000 between sample and simulated shares originates from the initialization procedure of SESIM, which defines the initial labor market status of an individual. Specifically, in the estimation sample, we define early retirees as individuals who collect either public or occupational pension benefits. SESIMs initial definition is more restrictive in that only individuals who collect public pension benefits are defined as retired. This implies that there is an under-representation of early retirees in the initial SESIM population compared to the estimation sample. This difference fades out in a few years, as the simulated population grows older and becomes exposed to the less restrictive retirement model.

The population share of male workers aged 60–64 (cross marked) is about 50 percent with minor fluctuations, whereas the share of female workers is about 40 percent. The initial decrease in the share of workers (both male and female) is due to the fact that individuals are exposed to the less restrictive early-retirement model, which induces more individuals to retire early. There are no strong trends in any shares over the studied period. The share of disabled is about 25–30 percent for males with a slightly increasing trend and 35–40 percent for females with no clear trend. Early retirees account for about 10 percent for both males and females with a slightly increasing trend for females, peaking at 2030.

In Figure 5, we illustrate the importance of demographic changes on the population shares of workers, disabled, and retired. This illustration highlights the substantial changes in the shares as the proportion of the population in age group 65+ increases over the period. The population share of workers steadily decreases from a peak of about 46 percent in 2005 to a low in 2035. After 2035, the trend of decreasing share of workers is broken and levels out at about 42 percent. On the other hand, the share of retirees increases sharply from 18 percent in 2005 to almost 25 percent in 2040, which is mainly a reflection of the projected changes in the demographic structure. The share of disabled is relatively stable around 4 percent with a weak decreasing trend. In terms of ratio between the number of workers and retirees, this implies that the ratio increases from 0.4 retirees per worker in 2000 to 0.57 in 2040.

Figure 5. *Simulated population shares in work, retirement, and disability, all age groups*

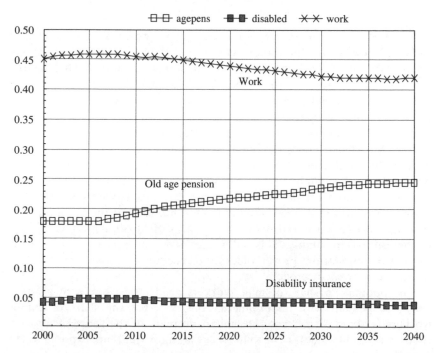

Figure 6. Simulated average age at transition into retirement from different status, by gender

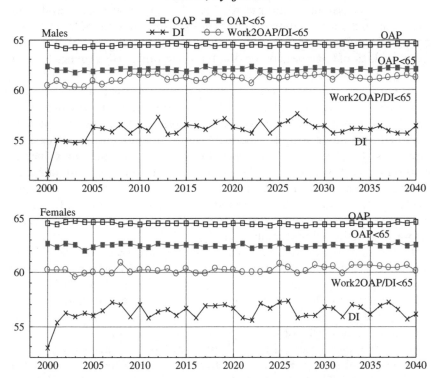

We turn next to the average age at transition to retirement via either old age pension or disability insurance. In Figure 6, we present four graphs representing various transition ages. First, we present the average age at transition into old age pension (OAP). Individuals who collect any type of social-security benefits, e.g., unemployment benefits and sickness or disability insurance, are automatically transferred to the old age pension at age 65. Hence, in order to separate these automatic transits to retirement, we also present the average age at transition for the subsample of individuals younger than 65 that transit from any source to old age pension (OAP<65). The transit to disability insurance (DI) is also given in the graph. Finally, we illustrate the average age of transition from work to either old age pension or disability insurance for individuals younger than 65 (WORK2OAP/DI<65). This is assumed to capture the general exit directly from work into the absorbing states of retirement.

The OAP-graph says that the average age of transition into old age retirement is very close to 65 for both males and females. However, there are large groups that are automatically transferred from other social-security insurance benefits to old age pension at age 65. Considering the subgroup that transfers before age 65 (OAP < 65), the average age is again quite stable and similar across males and females. Also, the average age at transition to disability insurance is stable, but at a lower level (about 56) than the age of transition to old age pension (about 62). The only observable difference between males and females is the age of transition from work to old age pension or disability insurance. Here, males have an average transition age around 61, females about 60.

In our basic scenario, the assumptions about returns to financial assets and growth in real wage rates imply that benefits from the new public old age pension system will be reduced as compared to the old system. Although one might expect some increase in private pension savings, the incentives to retire is likely to be reduced as the net present values of pension benefits will decrease. As a direct consequence, one would expect to observe an increase in the average retirement age. However, as indicated by the estimates of the retirement model presented in Section 8, the impact of financial incentives is quite weak, especially for men. Hence the observed response in retirement is small.

In the final set of analyses in this section, we focus on the relative economic situation of the retired compared to the working generation. The public old age pension system that was introduced in 2003 will be fully matured by 2022 in the sense that all individuals that retire at age 65 will get their benefits from the new system only. During the transition period, the observed pension benefits will consist to some part of the old system and to some part to the new system. The introduction of the new pension system will affect the economic outcomes of the retirees. There are several ways of representing the effects of retirement on economic outcomes. A commonly used measure is the replacement rate, which gives the ratio between the individual's annual earning during the working years close to retirement and the pension thereafter. However, this measure is less relevant if we want to analyze the positions of the retirees in the income distribution. In that case, it is more interesting to illustrate the incomes of the retirees relative to the working generation. In Figure 7, we present the ratio of retirees' pension benefits with respect to the earnings of the current workers. Here, we focus on the pure pension benefits and earned incomes before tax. (See Chapter 8 for a discussion of the distribution of disposable incomes.) Hence, if there are net transfers from workers to retirees, the ratios will increase. As the collectively agreed occupational pensions differ across sectors, we present the relative income by labor market sector affiliation. We present four graphs for each sector. The top graph presents the ratio of average pension benefits for current retirees by sector to earned income for current workers. Note that the ratio is calculated with respect to the same average of current workers earnings. The separate pension-benefit components contribution to the ratio is given by the remaining graphs.

Figure 7. Relative income of retirees compared to the earnings of current workers by pension source and sector affiliation

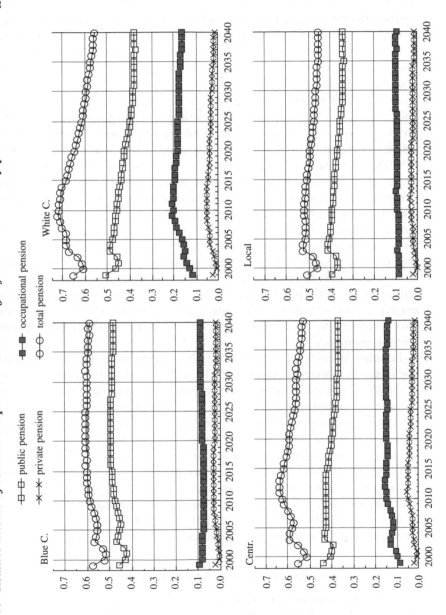

The graphs exhibit some unexpected and interesting features. First, the initial drop in the ratio of public pension with respect to earnings for all sectors originates from a strong growth in earnings, which is not transferred into an equally strong growth in public pension benefits. Second, the subsequent growth in public pension ratios is most likely due to the lagged effect of the previous growth in earnings. This is also reflected in the initial increase in the ratios of occupational pension for white-collar and central government employees, which respond much faster to the growth in earnings.

A third and more confusing feature is the shift in ranking between, e.g., blue-collar and white-collar employees regarding public pension levels. Initially, the public pension of blue-collar workers corresponds to about 45 percent of current workers' earnings, whereas the public pension of white-collar employees corresponds to 45–50 percent. However, as time passes, this ratio increases slightly to 50 percent for blue-collar employees, whereas it decreases to less than 40 percent for white-collar employees. As both ratios are based on the same current workers' earnings, this means that white-collar employees receive less and less public pension compared with blue-collar workers. This could potentially be explained by the fact that the new pension system is based on lifetime earnings and white-collar employees usually have longer periods in school with low earnings, and this implies lower public pension benefits in the new system. However, there are corresponding reductions in the public pension benefits of central and local government employees, and these reductions are not as easily explained by lifetime earnings.

Looking at the total effect, the relative income of retirees will decrease for all sector affiliations except for blue-collar workers. The total pension of local government employees will decrease from a top level of 52 percent of workers' earnings in the early 2000 to 45 percent in 2040. For white-collar and central government employees, the drop is even more drastic – from a top level in 2010 of 70 percent for white-collar and 65 percent for central government employees, respectively, to about 55 percent in 2040. This should be compared to blue-collar workers, who will receive about 60 percent in 2040. The decreased ratio between benefits and earnings indicate that the pensioners in the future will move downward in the income distribution, unless there is a strong re-distributional system that counteracts this movement (c.f. the discussion in Chapter 8).

8.2. Alternative scenario 1: no early-retirement offers

The projected demographic changes in the coming decades indicate that there might be a shortage of labor. The early-retirement model presented in Section 5 is estimated on a period where there was a recession in the economy and, consequently, an excess of labor. This was manifested by the frequent early-retirement pension buyouts, which was accounted for in our empirical model. In the simulations, there are reasons to believe that the number of early-retirement pensions will decrease. Therefore, our first alternative scenario in the early-retirement model is to remove the option of early-retirement pensions. The incentives to retire will then be reduced for individuals that in the basic scenario receive early-retirement pensions. Consequently, the average retirement age is expected to increase, although slightly. The postponed retirement will have further implications for the economic situation for the retirees, but the directions of these effects are ambiguous.

Here, we present only a selected set of results aiming to describe the main differences between the basic and this alternative scenario. First we discuss the effect on the simulated shares of population in work, early retirement, and disability insurance.

In Figure 8 we present the difference in simulated shares in the alternative and base scenario for the age group 60–64. The shares of early retirees generally decrease for both males and females. There are, nevertheless, some variations over time, some of which stem from pure simulation variation. However, on average the share of voluntary early retirees decreases (i.e., excluding disability insurance retirees) by 1.3 percentage points for males and 0.9 percentage points for females. Including disability retirees, the share decrease to 1.1 percentage points for males and increase to 1 percentage point for females. Finally, the share of workers in the age group increase on average by 1 percentage point for males and 0.8 point for females.

Figure 8. Difference between alternative and base scenario simulated shares in work, retirement, and disability insurance for age group 60–64

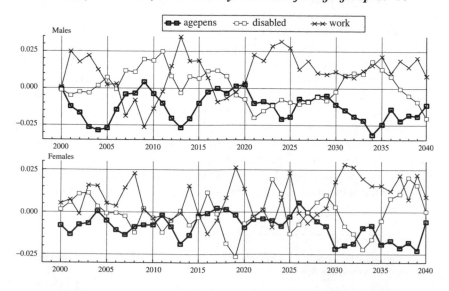

8.3. *Alternative scenario 2: delayed retirement*

The second alternative scenario studies what happens if there is an exogenous delay in the retirement age. This can be interpreted as a change in the retirement age norm. In particular, we are interested in what happens to pension levels in the two scenarios.

This alternative simulation is constructed as an arbitrary change of the estimated age profile in the old age retirement model presented above. (We make no alteration of the disability retirement model.) In this scenario, individuals are allowed to work until age 70, instead of, as in the base scenario, until the statuary retirement age of 65. However, as the estimation sample includes only ages 60–64 we have no empirical results that guide us as to how the age profile of the old age retirement hazard may look like beyond (or before) that age. The models we estimated for old age retirement include age-specific intercepts for age 60–64. The scenario is executed by "cloning" these age-specific intercept, so that the dummy for age 60 applies to age 60 and 61, that for age 61 applies to age 62 and 63, etc. At age 70, all remaining individuals are automatically forced to retirement.

Table 6 shows age profiles (the marginal effects) for the base and the second alternative scenarios. As can be seen, we decided to clone the intercept age 62 to apply for three age groups, 64, 65, and 66. Also, the latest age for the retirement decision is age 70, i.e., we changed the age criterion for the retirement decision from 60–64 to 60–69.[27] All remaining effects, e.g., of economic incentives, are unchanged in the simulation. We furthermore let all rules that concern, e.g., unemployment insurance, disability insurance, old age pension, etc., apply unaltered. Hence individuals on disability insurance will automatically transfer to old age pension at 65 without becoming eligible for work, and subsequently, for old age retirement at a later age.

Figure 9 shows the shares of workers, old age pensioners, and disability pensioners by age group using simulated data for the years 2010–2040. As a result of our exogenous age profile change, there is now a substantial share of elderly that remain workers beyond their 65th birthday. The figure shows that the share of employed workers falls from about 70 percent in age 60 to just fewer than 30 percent in age 64. Then the workers share fall gradually until age 70. As for old age pensioners 9 percent exit early between ages 60 and 64. At age 65, there is huge increase in the number of old age pensioners from 9 percent at age 64 to 72 percent for age 65. As mentioned most other social-security schemes are terminated at 65, which is the main explanation for this big increase. For instance one can note

---

[27] Corresponding age-specific intercepts in the model for getting an early-retirement pension are cloned in the same fashion.

Table 6. **Implementation of age-profile* in the base scenario and alternative scenario 2**

	Males		Females	
	Base scenario	Alternative scenario 2	Base scenario	Alternative scenario 2
60	0.000	0.000	0.000	0.000
61	0.030	0.000	0.026	0.000
62	0.033	0.030	0.036	0.026
63	0.032	0.030	0.044	0.026
64	0.044	0.033	0.070	0.036
65	1.000	0.033	1.000	0.036
66		0.033		0.036
67		0.032		0.044
68		0.032		0.044
69		0.044		0.070
70		1.000		1.000

Note: * Represents the marginal effect concerning the age-specific intercept in the probability of becoming retired.

Figure 9. **Shares in old age pension, disability pension, and work, by age; the alternative scenario 2; years 2010–2040**

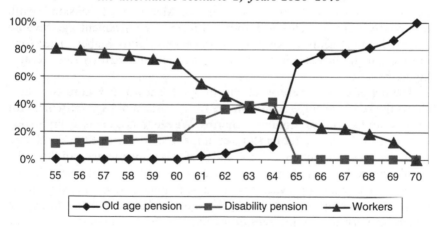

that all disability pensioners, which before age 65 are accumulated to a considerable group (two out of five 64-year olds), are transferred directly to old age pension.

A major difference in this scenario compared to the base scenario lies in the speed at which the group of old workers 60+ become old age pensioners. In this alternative scenario, the decline in this age group is much more gradual compared to the rapid decline in the base scenario. Remaining coefficients in the model for old age retirement is unaltered compared to the base scenario, e.g., the effect of economic incentives is unchanged, as is the process of how economic incentives are calculated.

Kristian Bolin et al.

Figure 10. Average transition age to old age retirement

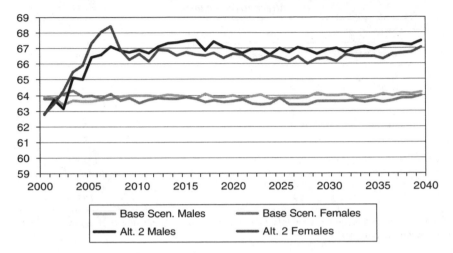

However, since a worker in this scenario has a chance to remain in work at an older age than before, it is likely that the economic incentives will be higher compared to the base scenario. Measures of pension wealth and accrual are, as mentioned above, affected by retirement age because actuarial adjustments make postponed benefit claims higher. Therefore, our mechanical increase in the age profile is counteracted by (on average) higher benefits.

The net effect on average retirement age is shown in Figure 10, which shows the yearly average transition age from work to old age retirement for the base and second alternative scenarios. We see that there is a very strong increase in the average retirement age in the first 10 years of the simulation when the exogenous change to the age profile is implemented, and that the simulation seems to stabilize at about 2010. We focus on the period after 2010 to avoid simulation years that include individuals who faced both the old and the new age profiles. The figure suggests that the average transition age from work to old age pension of males is 67.1 (females: 66.5) in the alternative scenario, compared to 63.9 (63.6) in the base scenario (ignoring the period until 2009). Changing the retirement age norm in the described way and allowing for the latest retirement to be at 70 instead of 65 hence result in an increase in the average retirement age from work to old age retirement by about 3 years.

What is the expected increase in employment for the whole population of this experiment? Figure 11 shows the percentage point difference in the shares of workers, old age pensioners, and disability pensioners in the population between the base scenario and the second alternative scenario. The graph indicates that we would expect a 1.5 percentage point increase in the share of workers in 2010 (from 45.5 to 47.0 percent in 2010) and even

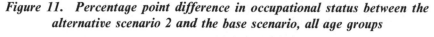

Figure 11. Percentage point difference in occupational status between the alternative scenario 2 and the base scenario, all age groups

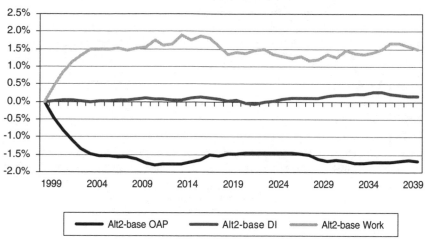

higher increases around 2015. This development is mirrored almost exactly by an equal decline in the share of old age pensioners. As the simulation progress the initial relative increase in the participation rates seem to be balanced by relative increases in share of old age pensioners. There is practically no difference in the share of disabled between the two scenarios, which is what we expect since we have not changed the process in which individuals become disability pensioners.

In the base scenario, the pension incomes of old age pensioners relative to the earnings of workers was expected to decline as a result of a strong growth in real earnings. In this scenario we saw that retirement was on average postponed by about 3 years. As we discussed above, later retirement is rewarded by (on average) higher benefits. In this scenario the situation for pensioners compared to workers should therefore be better.

In Figure 12, we present the relative incomes for pensioners compared to workers for this scenario and the base scenario. Again we focus on the period after 2010 as we want the simulations to be clean from individuals that faced both the old and the new age profile. The figure shows that in 2020 the pensioners' relative earnings in the population are expected to improve by as much as 5 percentage points as a result of the delayed retirement, from 54 percent to about 60 percent. After that the gap remains about as wide. However, the general tendency toward lower relative incomes of pensioners is present also in this alternative scenario.

A detailed inspection (in Figure 13) shows that after 2004 the relative increase in public pension income is responsible for the major part of the total relative income improvement of pensioners. Also, before 2014 the relative development of occupational pension income works in the

Figure 12. Relative incomes of old age pensioners and workers in the alternative scenario 2 and the base scenario

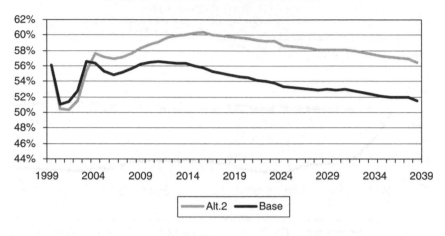

Figure 13. Percentage point difference in relative incomes of old age pensioners and workers between the alternative scenario 2 and the base scenario

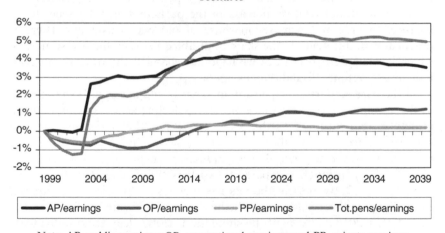

Note: AP, public pensions; OP, occupational pensions; and PP, private pensions

opposite direction as it actually is relatively lower in the alternative scenario compared to the base scenario. From 2015 and onwards, however, these types of incomes will also contribute to the improvement of pensioners' incomes.

It also seems like the delayed retirement improves the earnings of workers. Figure 14, shows that the average earnings in the worker population, as a whole, increase when retirement is postponed. This figure illustrates a relative increase in the mean earnings in the alternative

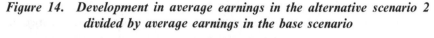

Figure 14. **Development in average earnings in the alternative scenario 2 divided by average earnings in the base scenario**

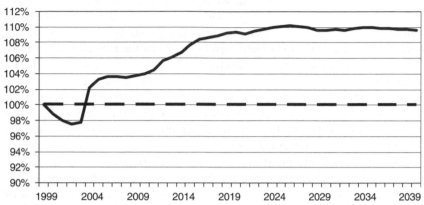

scenario relative that in the base scenario (= 100 percent). This relative increase continues until 2024. In that year, the average earnings in the second alternative scenario are about 10 percent higher than in the base scenario. One reasonable explanation for this is that, since older workers remain active longer, the composition with respect to workers has changed to consist of more high paid workers. A situation where highly paid are less prone to leave the labor market for retirement might naturally contribute to this development. However, one should be cautious in interpreting this result. Old workers' earnings may be difficult to predict considering that, in reality, few remain in work as long as is forecasted in this scenario.

9. Conclusions

This chapter presents the modeling of early exit from the labor force. We propose two separate and distinct models for early retirement via the old age pension or disability insurance systems. Retirement via the old age pension system is considered voluntary and driven by economic factors, whereas retirement with the disability insurance is considered involuntary and primarily driven by health factors. Regarding the early retirement via the old age pension system, we also emphasize the influence of early-retirement pension offers. These offers are occasionally given by employers to employees in order to retire older employees before their mandatory retirement age.

Individuals' responses to financial incentives when deciding on retirement are key factors when designing an efficient pension system. Previous studies have used the individual variation in financial incentives caused by the public and occupational pension systems to estimate the responsiveness. These previous studies have primarily used the information contained in the legislation and agreements to construct individual-specific financial incentives. For Sweden, we argue that this is not the full story. Empirical as well as anecdotal evidence indicate that, the group of individuals that is most likely to respond to financial incentives, i.e., potential early retires, may have significantly stronger incentives to retire than what is stipulated in the collectively agreed pension contracts. This is caused by individual agreements offered by the employer in order to persuade the employee to leave her employment and enter early retirement, here denoted as early-retirement pensions. Neglecting these early-retirement pensions may create bias in the estimated responses to financial incentives in the retirement decision.

The exit from work into disability insurance retirement is modeled using reduced forms and emphasizing the health's impact on the decision. The old age retirement decision is modeled using a simple reduced-form approach focusing on financial incentives such as net present values of future pension benefits and its' accruals. We propose an estimation strategy that handles the problems of partial observability of early-retirement pensions, in that they are only indirectly recorded for early retirees and not recorded for non-retirees. Our estimation strategy includes a system of equations determining the retirement and access to early-retirement pension probabilities simultaneously.

Our empirical results indicate that health has a strong impact on disability insurance probabilities. For old age early retirement, the estimated marginal effects on retirement probabilities are positive with respect to net present values of future pension benefits and negative with respect to accrual, all in line with previous studies and intuition.

The simulations include three different scenarios relevant for labor force participation decisions. The base scenario was described in Chapter 3. We also present two alternative scenarios representing various assumptions about future access to early-retirement pensions and prolonged work life. In the first alternative scenario we remove the option of early-retirement pensions. The second alternative scenario involves a prolonged work life until age 70.

The results from the base scenario indicate that the average retirement age does not change very much as a consequence of the maturing new public pension system. However, the sample population share of retirees increases rapidly from about 22 percent in 2000 to 30 percent in 2040. This is mostly driven by demographic changes. The projected relative income of retirees with respect to workers differs across sectors. Whereas the relative income of retired blue-collars in the private sector are predicted to increase, the retirees associated with the other sectors are predicted to first experience an increase in relative income and thereafter a decrease. The net effect over the next 40 years is slightly negative for white collars and local government employees.

The results from the scenario where early-retirement pensions are removed indicate that the share of retirees in the age group 60–64 will decrease by about 1–2 percentage points. Hence, in the base scenario about 10 percent of the age group 60–64 entered early retirement via the old age pension system. In the alternative scenario about 8 percent became early retirees.

The results from the scenario with a 5-year increase in mandatory retirement age indicate that the average retirement age increases by approximately 3 years to age 67. Furthermore, the share of workers will increase by 1.5 percentage points. Finally, the relative income of retirees with respect to workers will increase by about 4 percentage points.

References

Abowd, J. and H. Farber (1982), "Job queues and the union of status of workers", *Industrial and Labor Relations Review*, Vol. 35, pp. 354–367.

Anderson, K.H. and R.V. Burkhauser (1985), "The retirement-health nexus: a new measure of an old puzzle", *Journal of Human Resources*, Vol. 20, pp. 315–330.

Auer, P. and M. Fortuny (2000), "Ageing of the labour force in OECD countries: economic and social consequences", Employment Paper, 2000/2, ILO.

Bazzoli, G. (1985), "The early retirement decision: new empirical evidence on the influence of health", *Journal of Human Resources*, Vol. 20, pp. 214–234.

Berglind, H. (1977), "Förtidspensionering eller arbete? En studie av utveckling och regionala variationer", In SOU 1977:88, Förtidspensionering.

Blundell, R., C. Meghir and S. Smith (2002), "Pension incentives and the pattern of early retirement", *The Economic Journal*, Vol. 112, pp. 153–170.

Börsch-Supan, A. (1999), "Incentive effects of social security under an uncertain disability option", NBER Working Paper Series, (Working Paper 7339, http://www.nber.org/papers/w7339).

Boskin, M.H. and M.D. Hurd (1978), "The effect of social security on early retirement", *Journal of Public Economics*, Vol. 10, pp. 361–377.

Bound, J. (1991), "Self-reported versus objective measures of health in retirement models", *Journal of Human Resources*, Vol. 26, pp. 106–138.

Bound, J., M. Schoenbaum and T. Waidman (1995), "Race and education differences in disability status and labor force attachment in the health and retirement study", *Journal of Human Resources*, Vol. 30(Suppl.), pp. S227–S267.

Bratberg, E., T.H. Holmås and Ö. Thögersen (2004), "Assessing the effects of an early retirement program", *Journal of Population Economics*, Vol. 17, pp. 387–408.

Brown, C. (2002), "Early retirement windows", Working Paper 2002–028, Michigan Retirement Research Center, University of Michigan and National Bureau of Economic Research, Cambridge, USA.

Burkhauser, R.V. and J.F. Quinn (1983), "Is mandatory retirement overrated? Evidence from the 1970s", *Journal of Human Resources*, Vol. 18, pp. 337–358.

Burtless, G. (1986), "Social security, unanticipated benefit increases, and the timing of retirement", *The Review of Economic Studies*, Vol. 53, pp. 781–805.

Burtless, G. and J. Hausman (1978), "The effect of taxation on labor supply", *Journal of Political Economy*, Vol. 86, pp. 1103–1130.

Burtless, G. and R.A. Moffitt (1984), "The effect of social security benefits on the labor supply of the aged", in: H.J. Aaron and Burtless, editors, *Retirement and Economic Behavior*, Washington, DC: Brookings Institution.

Bütler, M., O. Hugueni and F. Teppa (2004), "What triggers early retirement? Results from Swiss pension funds", CEPR Discussion Paper Series (Discussion Paper 4394, http://www.cepr.org/pubs/dps/DP4394).

Coile, C. and J. Gruber (2000), "Social security and retirement", Working Paper 7830, National Bureau of Economic Research, Cambridge, USA.

Diamond, P. and J. Hausman (1984), "Individual retirement and saving behaviour", *Journal of Public Economics*, Vol. 23, pp. 81–114.

Dwyer, D.S. and O.S. Mitchell (1999), "Health problems as determinants of retirement: are self-rated measures endogenous?", *Journal of Health Economics*, Vol. 18, pp. 173–193.

Edebalk, P.G. and E. Wadensjö (1989), "Arbetsmarknadsförsäkringar", Rapport till Expertgruppenn för studier i Offentlig Ekonomi (EFO). Finansdepartementet, Ds 1989:68.

Edebalk, P.G. and E. Wadensjö (1990), "Det okända socialförsäkringssystemet", *Ekonomisk Debatt*, Vol. 3, pp. 263–270.

Eklöf, M. and D. Hallberg (2004), "Private alternatives and early retirement programs", Mimeo, Department of Economics, Uppsala University, Sweden.

Eklöf, M. and D. Hallberg (2006), "Estimating early retirement programs with special retirement offers", Mimeo, Department of Economics, Uppsala University, Sweden.

Fölster, S., S. Larsson, and J. Lund (2001), "Avtalspension -dagens ättestupa?", Rapport 5, Pensionsforum, Stockholm, Sweden.

Gordon, R.H. and A.S. Blinder (1980), "Market wages, reservation wages, and retirement decisions", *Journal of Public Economics*, Vol. 14, pp. 277–308.

Gustman, A.L. and T. Steinmeier (1986), "A structural retirement model", *Econometrica*, Vol. 54, pp. 555–584.

Hallberg, D. (2003), "A description of routes out of the labor force for workers in Sweden", Working Paper 23, Department of Economics, Uppsala.

Hanoch, G. and M. Honig (1983), "Retirement, wages and labor supply of the elderly", *Journal of Labor Economics*, Vol. 1, pp. 131–151.

Hausman, J. and D. Wise (1980), "Discontinuous budget constraints and estimation: the demand for housing", *Review of Economic Studies*, Vol. 47, pp. 75–96.

Hausman, J. and D. Wise (1985), "Social security, health status and retirement", in: D. Wise, editor, *Pensions, Labor and Individual Choice*, Chicago: University of Chicago Press.

Hedström, P. (1980), *Förtidspension – välfärd eller ofärd?* Stockholm: Institutet för social forskning.

Hogarth, J.M. (1988), "Accepting an early retirement bonus: an empirical study", *Journal of Human Resources*, Vol. 23, pp. 21–33.

Kerkhofs, M. and M. Lindeboom (1995), "Subjective health measures and state dependent reporting errors", *Health Economics*, Vol. 4, pp. 221–235.

Kreider, B. (1999), "Latent work disability and reporting bias", *Journal of Human Resources*, Vol. 34, pp. 734–769.

Kreuger, A. and J.-S. Pischke (1992), "The effect of social security on labor supply: a cohort analysis of the notch generation", *Journal of Labor Economics*, Vol. 10(4), pp. 412–437.

Lazear, E. and R. Moore (1988), "Pension and turnover", in: Z. Bodie, J. Shoven and D. Wise, editors, *Financial Aspects of the United States Pension System*, Chicago: University of Chicago Press.

Lumsdaine, R.L. and O.S. Mitchell (1999), "New developments in the economic analysis of retirement", in: O. Ashenfelter and D. Card, editors, *Handbook of Labor Economics*, Vol. 3C, Amsterdam: Elsevier Science Publishers.

McGarry, K. (2002), "Health and retirement: do changes in health affect retirement expectations?", NBER Working Paper Series (Working Paper 9317, http://www.nber.org/papers/w9317).

National Social Insurance Board (2005), See the following web address: http://www.forsakringskassan.se/omfk/socialforsakringen/historik/forandringar

OECD (2003), "Transforming disability to ability. Policies to promote work and income security for disabled people", OECD, Paris.

OECD (2004), "The labor force participation of older workers: the effects of pension and early retirement schemes", Manuscript, Economics Department, May.

Palme, M. and I. Svensson (2004), "Income security programs and retirement in Sweden", in: J. Gruber and D. Wise, editors, *Social Security and Retirement Around the World: Micro-estimates*, Chicago: Chicago University Press.

Parsons, D.O. (1982), "Male labor force participation decision: health, reported health and economic incentives", *Economica*, Vol. 49, pp. 81–91.

Poirier, D. (1980), "Partial observability in bivariate probit models", *Journal of Econometrics*, Vol. 12, pp. 209–217.

Quinn, J.F. (1979), "Microeconomic determinants of early retirement: a cross-sectional view of white married men", *Journal of Human Resources*, Vol. 12, pp. 329–346.

Röed, K. and F. Haugen (2003), "Early retirement and economic incentives: evidence from a quasi-natural experiment", *Labor*, Vol. 17, pp. 203–228.

Siddiqui, S. (1997), "The impact of health on retirement behaviour: empirical evidence from West Germany", *Health Economics*, Vol. 6, pp. 425–438.

Stern, S. (1989), "Measuring the effect of disability on labor force participation", *Journal of Human Resources*, Vol. 24, pp. 361–395.

Stock, J.H. and D.A. Wise (1990), "Pensions, the option value of work, and retirement", *Econometrica*, Vol. 58, pp. 1151–1180.

Ståhlberg, A.-C. (1995), "Pension reform in Sweden", *Scandinavian Journal of Social Welfare*, Vol. 4, pp. 267–273.

Sundén, A. (2000), "How will Sweden's new pension system work?", Center for Retirement Research at Boston College.

Wadensjö, E. (1985). "Disability pensioning of older workers in Sweden. A comparison of studies based on time-series and cross-section data", Meddelande 15/1985, Institutet för Social Forskning, Stockholm.

Wadensjö, E. and G. Sjögren (2000), Arbetslinjen för äldre i praktiken, En studie för Riksdagens Revisorer (The work policy for elderly in practice, a study for the parliamentary auditors). Institutet för Social Forskning (The Swedish Institute for Social Research, SOFI), Stockholm, Sweden.

Appendix

Table A.1. Examples of specifications used and variables included in empirical studies

Author	Dependent variable	Explanatory variables	Empirical specification
Berglind (1977) Swedish data; Cross-section, 1974	Percentage of disability pensioners in local community	*Demographic*: Percentage unmarried, percentage foreigners, percentage with low education *Labor market*: Percentage unemployed, percentage blue-collar workers *Health*: Number of sick-days, number participating in anti alcohol-abuse programs	OLS
Hedström (1980) Swedish data (Swedish Level of Living Survey); time-series, 1969–1972	Provision of disability pension	*Personal*: Gender and age *Labor market*: Regional unemployment rate, personal unemployment, employment security, work-environment *Health*: Mobility limitation, circulatory problem, pain in motorical system, psychosocial status	OLS
Wadensjö (1985) Swedish data (Swedish Level of Living Survey); cross-section, 1978	Disability pension (0/1)	*Personal*: Age, marital status, gender, nationality *Labor market*: Unemployment rate *Health*: Reduced work capacity	Logit

(Continued on next page)

Table A.1.　(*Continued*)

Author	Dependent variable	Explanatory variables	Empirical specification
Anderson and Burkhauser (1985) US data (Health and Retirement Study); cross-section, 1969	Working (0/1)	*Personal*: Age, marital status, number of children, race, wage rate, social-security and pension wealth, real estate wealth *Health*: Self-reported (estimated as a function of the personal characteristics), mortality (died within a specified time period, also estimated as a function of the personal characteristics) *Interaction terms*: Between working and bad health, and between working and mortality	Bivariate logit
Stern (1989) US data (Survey of Disability and Work); cross-section, 1978	Working (0/1)	*Personal*: Gender, age, marital status, education, race *Health*: Self-reported health, self-reported limitation, proxied by number of conditions, self-reported health as a function of personal characteristics and conditions, self-reported limitations as a function of personal characteristics and conditions	Probit

Study	Dependent variable	Independent variables	Method
Bound (1991) US data (Retirement History Survey); cross-section, 1969	Working (0/1)	*Personal*: ln(income from an extra year of work), ln(discounted lifetime earnings), age, marital status, education, race. *Health*: Self-reported, proxied by mortality, instrumented by personal characteristics, instrumented by mortality – which in turn is instrumented by personal characteristics	Probit, Bivariate probit, Trivariate probit
Bound *et al.* (1995) US data (Health and Retirement Study – alpha release); cross-section, 1992	Working (0/1)	*Personal*: Age, education, race. *Health*: Self-reported, proxied by ADL, chronic conditions, etc.	Logit
Kerkhofs and Lindeboom (1995) Dutch data (Centre for Economic Research on Retirement and Ageing); cross-section, 1993	Self-reported health (categorical variable); separate regressions for employed, unemployed, disabled, and early retired	*Personal*: Gender, age, marital status, education, regular church attendance. *Health*: A score constructed from the Hopkins Symptom Checklist	Ordered probit
Siddiqui (1997) German data (German Socio-economic Panel); period not stated	Time to retirement	*Personal*: Age, marital status, education, foreigner, employed in public sector. *Health*: Self-reported degree of disability, chronic condition. *Labor market*: Age-group and gender-specific unemployment rate	Survival analysis

(*Continued on next page*)

Table A.1. (*Continued*)

Author	Dependent variable	Explanatory variables	Empirical specification
Dwyer and Mitchell (1999) US data (Health and Retirement Study); cross-section, 1992	Self-reported expected age of retirement	*Personal*: Discounted lifetime income from working to 62, change in discounted lifetime income from working to 65, other assets (real estate, vehicles, businesses, savings, inheritances, trusts), health insurance *Health*: Self-reported, Proxied by objective measures (ADL, IADL, FL, chronic conditions), Instrumented by objective measures	OLS IV approach
McGarry (2002) US data (Health and Retirement Study); longitudinal, interviewed in 1992 and in 1994	Self-reported probability of working at the age of 62 Self-reported probability of working at the age of 65	*Personal*: Age, gender, race, marital status, education, self-reported probability to live to age 85, annual earnings, household wealth, occupational pension, pension wealth, health insurance at work, health insurance as retired, union at work, offered retirement incentive *Health*: Self-reported, proxied by chronic conditions, proxied by activity limitations	OLS

Röed and Haugen (2003) Noweigian data (Several administrative registers merged); monthly data, 1993–1997	Time to early retirement Time to ordinary retirement Time to long-term sickness absence	*Personal*: Gender, marital status, education, work experience, spouse working, age-difference between spouses, sickness-absence record, ln(income in continued work), ln(income in destination state), income trend last 5 years *Health*: None *Firm*: Number of employees, downsizing firm, turnover rate, type of industry	Survival analysis
Bütler *et al.* (2004) Swiss data (from 15 pension funds); time-series, 1990–2003	Time to retirement	*Personal*: Gender, marital status, age, accumulated retirement wealth *Health*: None	Survival analysis

CHAPTER 7

Geographical Mobility and Tenure Choice

Urban Fransson* and Matias Eklöf

For many elderly wealth in housing represents a large share of non-pension assets. It is an important part in the mix of various economic resources in a household. Residential mobility of a household living in ownership or in tenants-ownership housing involves, among other things, economic transitions. Real gains from home-ownership give, for instance, elderly a possibility to compensate for low retirement pensions or it constitutes means for potential expenditures for institutional care when becoming chronicly disabled. Housing is also an issue of future welfare for the elderly. Today, the real value of an owned dwelling varies between different regions in Sweden. Consequently, the assets of the households differ geographically. Will future migration increase or decrease this variation?

In this chapter, we will analyze the geographical mobility of young, middle-aged, and elderly households on a local as well as a regional level, in order to evaluate the impact of mobility on tenure choice and of migration on the regional distribution of the population in Sweden.

1. Urbanization and migration

Concerning migration on a national level, two phenomena emerge: people migrating from one region to another and people moving from the countryside to the cities. The geographical shift of the population between regions in a country is a slow process. In Sweden, only a few percent of the

---

* Corresponding author.

CONTRIBUTIONS TO ECONOMIC ANALYSIS
VOLUME 285   ISSN: 0573-8555
DOI:10.1016/S0573-8555(07)00007-7

population migrate yearly. Nevertheless, migration has caused and still causes considerable redistribution of the population toward the metropolitan regions in Sweden. This section will emphasize general trends in population concentration through urbanization and migration in Sweden and compare these trends with changes in other countries.

1.1. Regional redistribution of the population

Within the past 150 years, the distribution of the population across different parts of Sweden has changed considerably. After 1870, the Stockholm region has increasingly increased its share of the Swedish population. The economic boom in Sweden after the Second World War brought about an increased demand for labor, which led to labor force immigration. Most of these immigrants came from other Nordic countries. Later people from other parts of the world constituted the major share of the immigration. Besides the Stockholm region, the metropolitan regions of Göteborg and Malmö also grew at a rate higher than the country average. The process of migration is rather selective in the sense that some parts of the population are more migratory than others are (Clark, 1986). This differential can have both social and economic effects in the area of origin as well in the area of destination. Age-dependent migration rates have changed during the 1990s. Young people migrate to a much greater degree than before. It has been suggested that this is due to increased participation in higher education (Nygren and Persson, 2002; Abramsson and Fransson, 2004).

Traditionally, individual unemployment has been regarded as a "push factor" for regional migration (Öberg, 1997). Available jobs in the region of destination and few jobs in the region of origin have given unemployed persons an incentive to migrate. Today this relation is weaker, among other things due to social security programs for the unemployed (Öberg, 1997; Andersson, 2000). Improvements in communication infrastructure have made long-distance commuting an alternative to migration or unemployment.

Like in Sweden the migration pattern changed in Europe: firstly, toward an increased share of younger people migrating to the metropolitan regions; secondly, families migrating from the big cities in Europe. Large cities offer young individuals high education, the first occupation, and an urban life style. The attraction of large cities decreases, however, for families among others (Rees and Kupiszewski, 1999). In the United Kingdom, most large cities, with the exception of London, have decreased in population since 1980. There, population growth is now occurring in the countryside. Some scholars argue that, in the United States, urbanization is increasingly being replaced by counter-urbanization as the major course of migration pattern, that is population growth in locations beyond the boundary of the daily urban system of a larger city (Champion, 1989; Clark, 2003).

This is the case in, for instance, the United Kingdom and the Netherlands, but not in countries like Poland, Romania, and Estonia. The urbanization was still very high in these countries in 1980s. The metropolitan regions gained internal migrants as the rural areas made losses. During 1990s the urbanization continued, but the population growth in the big cities were slower (Rees and Kupiszewski, 1999). In most countries in Europe, internal migration is the main factor in population changes. Sweden, like some other countries in West Europe, increases its population by net of immigration and emigration as well as by natural population increase. Two well-known exceptions are Italy and Germany where the immigration net is the more important part of the increase of the population than the natural population increase. It is also notable that many countries in the east of Europe show a population decrease (Salt, 2005).

In regions from where people have been out-migrating to other parts of the country for a longer period, the average age of the remaining population increases. Frail elders often require more or less continuous support. Health care and assistance require a high service rate and large staffs, which may be difficult to achieve in municipalities with an aging population. The age dependency ratio in the Swedish municipalities gives an indication of where in the country problems could arise (Andersson, 2004). The age dependency ratio is high in most municipalities in the interior of Norrland, but also in municipalities in South-eastern Sweden.

1.2. Urban concentration

Today, Belgium, the United Kingdom, Germany, and Denmark are the most urbanized countries in Europe. In 2000, as many as 73 percent of Europeans lived in urban places[1] (United Nations, 2003). In Sweden, the rate of urbanization increased from 20 to 83 percent over a period of 100 years, from 1880 to 1980. After 1980, the urbanization rate has remained essentially the same. In 2000, 84 percent of the Swedish population lived in urban areas and the remaining 16 percent in the countryside (Statistics Sweden, 2001).

The urbanization process ended some 20 years ago in Sweden, in the sense that the proportion of the population living in urban areas has been almost constant since then. The process of urbanization has in many

---

[1] In the Nordic countries, an urban area is defined as a group of buildings not more than 200 m apart and with a population of at least 200 inhabitants (Statistics Sweden). Another definition of urban places will make Sweden less urbanized. If a criteria of 2000 inhabitants is used in the Swedish case, the percentage of the urban population will decrease to 73 per cent (calculations by the authors).

countries been replaced by ex-urbanization, which indicates a growth in population in rural areas and a decline in the urban population (Champion, 1989; Lindgren, 2003). In Sweden, the population is growing in some rural areas near or in metropolitan regions and close to other expanding city areas in Southern and Central Sweden, whereas the population in the countryside is still decreasing in most parts of the country (Amcoff, 2000; Statistics Sweden, 2001). The population outside urban areas in the Stockholm region has increased by 12 percent during the period 1990–2000. Through investments in infrastructure, it has been possible to geographically enlarge the regional labor market, mostly by making it possible for people to commute longer distances than before.

Eight of the 10 largest urban areas outside the metropolitan regions have had higher population growth rates than the country average, when looking at the period 1994–2004. Some of these cities – Uppsala, Umeå, Örebro, and Linköping – also host the largest universities in Sweden outside the metropolitan regions. The expansion of large cities outside the metropolitan regions has been connected with an increase in the proportion of the Swedish population attending institutions of higher education.

One argument is that there is a supply effect at the location of the university. Graduates stay in the region and thereby serve as human resources for the expansion of local economic life. Other supply effects noted in the literature are, for example, shared facilities and services as well as the fact that similar companies tend to cling together due to co-operation benefits. Another argument implying a relation between universities and regional growth is the demand effect. The idea is that well-educated labor is attracted to growing regions (Wikhall, 2001). These regions could also be regarded as escalator regions, in the sense that they are able to provide a context in which people can attain better incomes and housing careers than in other regions (Fielding, 1992). The advantage of an escalator region, however, is dependent on the profession of the individuals.

The other side of the coin of urban transition is that some urban areas lose their position in the national urban hierarchy. These areas are largely located in Northern Sweden. Another type of town that is losing its position in the urban system is the old and minor industrial town located in small local labor markets in middle Sweden (Bergslagen), far from expanding regions. The regions are very sparsely populated and lose young and middle-aged inhabitants through out-migration directed at expanding university regions such as Umeå and Luleå in the North and the Stockholm region in Central Sweden. Consequently, the proportion of elderly has become high in the northwestern part of the country.

The metropolitan regions of Stockholm, Göteborg, and Malmö have continued to increase their proportion of the Swedish population. In 2000, one-third of the population lived in these areas. The number of employment opportunities grew as information and communication technologies developed and as a result of the increased production of services. Banks, exchange dealers, brokers, and insurance companies expanded to facilitate the increasing international transactions in the economy. The large cities have increasingly become part of a growing international economy (Bäcklund, 2002; Clark, 2003).

The urban population hierarchy is not only a national phenomenon. In a world with increasingly globalized economic activities, an urban hierarchy is also observed on an international scale. Cities such as Tokyo, London, New York, and Paris are important cities in the world economy because of their capacity in the areas of communications, trade, finance, education, culture, and technology. Many of the transnational companies are located in these cities, close to governments and capital markets. They are also major transport nodes and important manufacturing centers. Stockholm is part of this world hierarchy of large cities, yet it holds a lower ranking (Beaverstock *et al.*, 1999). However, this pattern of urban hierarchy is under transformation. Today the average annual rate of change in the urban population in Europe is small. The urban population increased in 2000 by 0.1 percent (UN, 2003). Elsewhere, for example, in Canada and the United States, the growth rate was substantially higher, i.e., 1.5 percent.

2. Housing

Migration to another region has implications for housing. The real value of houses differs in various regions of Sweden. Moving to a metropolitan region may imply a change in wealth for the migrating household in the long run. The choice of housing is dependent on the expected period of stay, but also on the variation in supply of housing in different parts of the country. The share of rent-occupied housing in Sweden is high, together with Germany and the Netherlands it is the highest in Europe. One of the reasons, in the Swedish case, is the strong position of tenant organizations (Bengtsson, 1995). They were developed in response to the economic and political turmoil of the 1920s. In this section, we briefly discuss the main features of Swedish housing stock and policy. The discussion will cover housing in the ordinary housing market, but not housing for the frail elderly (see Chapter 11).

2.1. The housing market in Sweden

2.1.1. The stock

2.1.1.1. Types of houses and dwellings
There are 4.3 million dwellings in Sweden: 2 million detached houses and 2.3 million dwellings in multi-family houses. In this context, the term "detached houses" also refers to linked houses, terraced houses, and semi-detached houses. A large share of the multi-family housing stock was

constructed between 1965 and 1974; this extensive construction effort is known as the "Million Program." The ambition was to meet the increasing demand for housing as well as to raise the standard of the Swedish housing stock. The consequence was large-scale reconstruction work in most Swedish cities and towns. During the period 1965–1974, new construction amounted to 670 000 multi-family housing units and 340 000 detached and semi-detached houses (Figure 1). The program to build a large quantity of multi-family housing units was interrupted at the beginning of the 1970s, due to the rising demand for detached and semi-detached housing and the economic recession in the wake of the 1973 oil crisis (Söderström 1993). Those houses built at the beginning of the period have a reputation for poor quality due to the transition into industrial design and construction at the time (Vidén and Lundahl, 1992). With regard to heating and hygiene, however, the standard of the Swedish housing stock from the 1970s and on is good. The multi-family housing stock is currently being improved by installing elevators, paid for by allowances from the government, in order to increase access to ordinary housing for disabled elderly (Boverket, 2002). The economic recession of the early 1980s resulted in reduced demand for all types of housing. Over a period of 15 years, new construction decreased from 110 000 housing units in 1970 to 30 000 units in 1985. In the mid-1980s, most new units were built in the metropolitan regions, especially for tenant ownership in multi-family housing. The impact of a new housing policy, in the beginning of the 1990s, radically reduced the extent of new construction down to a very low level. The number of new units was back to the low figures of the 1910s.

Figure 1. New constructions in Sweden 1958–2004

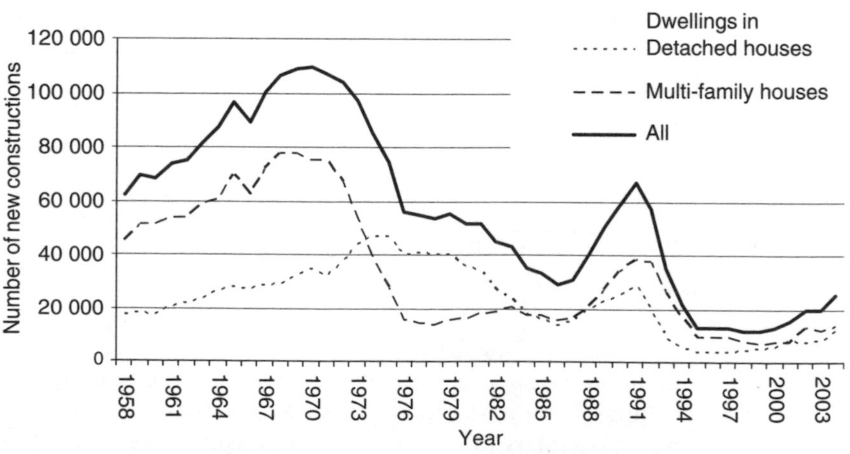

Source: Statistic Sweden

Most (98 percent) of the detached or semi-detached houses are owned by private persons. One-third of the multi-family housing units are owned by private persons, a full 20 percent by real estate companies, another 20 percent by co-operative building societies, and almost 20 percent by municipal housing companies.

Because most people in Sweden live in towns and cities, most dwellings are found there as well (Statistics Sweden, 1990). Nevertheless, 1.4 million persons live in the countryside (Statistics Sweden, 2001). The number of farms in the countryside has decreased for a long period. In 2003, there were 160 000 farms. Many of the residences on former farms have been converted into leisure homes. However, a major part of the farms has been converted into ordinary housing (Hjort, 2005).

The ratio of multi-family to detached or semi-detached housing varies considerably in different regions in the country. In the Stockholm area, multi-family housing dominates the housing market and detached or semi-detached houses are a minor part. As much as 73 percent of the market consists of multi-family housing. At the other end of the scale are the counties of Halland and Gotland in the South of Sweden, where the share of multi-family housing is very low, 32 and 35 percent, respectively. In this part of the country, with the exception of the Malmö area, detached or semi-detached housing dominates.

2.1.2. Tenure

New dwellings were constructed in the 1960s and 1970s all over Europe in large multi-family estates for renters (Priemus and Dieleman, 2002). Household from different social strata moved to these large multi-family complexes. However, as higher-income groups moved out, the estates became dominated by low-income households in the 1980s (Priemus and Dieleman, 2002). This was also the case in Sweden (Heinstedt, 1992).

In Europe, the rates of home-ownership have in general increased in 1990s and accordingly the rental sector has decreased (Priemus and Dieleman, 2002; Scanlon and Whitehead, 2004). For instances, in the Netherlands, the share of owner occupation rose from 45 to 52 percent; in the United Kingdom from 65 to 69 percent; in Belgium from 67 to 74 percent; and in Spain from 78 to 81 percent (Haffner and Dol, 2000). This has been achieved by new constructions, but also by privatization of social housing. In, for example, the United Kingdom the "Right to Buy" for council tenants were introduced in 1980 (Priemus and Dieleman, 2002). This trend is, however, not universally prevailing. In Finland and in Denmark the trend is the opposite. In those two countries, the share of owner occupation has decreased (Scanlon and Whitehead, 2004).

Owner occupation is today a common form of tenure in Europe. In many countries, this is a largest tenure form. Hungary, Lithuania, Greece, Spain, Ireland, Slovenia, and Iceland are countries with very high proportions (more than 75 percent) of owner occupation (Haffner and

Dol, 2000). Germany and the Czech Republic are, on the other hand, countries with <50 percent ownership (Scanlon and Whitehead, 2004). The rest of the EU nations have shares of owner occupation somewhere between 50 and 75 percent. This is also the case for Sweden if tenant ownership is regarded as owner occupation.

The most common tenures in Sweden are renting and owning. About 42 percent of households rent a dwelling, and 40 percent own their own house. An increasing share of the Swedish housing market consists of dwellings owned by co-operative building societies, later known as tenant ownership (Bengtsson, 1991). The possessor buys a share in the co-operative building society. This share entitles the possessor to a specific dwelling in the construction.

The correlation between tenure and type of housing is quite high. Most detached houses are owned by the households living in them. However, there is a small share of semi-detached houses in the rental sector (10 percent, 1990), mostly owned by municipal housing companies (Statistics Sweden, 1990). On the other hand, the most common tenures in multi-family housing are renting (68 percent) and tenant ownership (26 percent). There is also a clear relation between the size of the dwelling and tenure. Large dwellings are mostly to be found in owned detached houses and small dwellings in rental housing.

In the 1970s, the rent per square meter in municipal housing companies was quite stable in real terms. The rents increased dramatically, however, at the beginning of the 1990s as a consequence of reductions in subsidies and increases in real estate taxes (Englund *et al.*, 1995). This abrupt rent increase had an effect on affordability for low income households. Generally, the expenditures for housing has increased. For most household types, rent as a proportion of disposable income increased markedly during the 1990s. This increase was particularly sharp for single households, young as well as old (Turner and Whitehead, 2002). Prices of owner occupied housing have been instable in the past 20 years. The decrease at the beginning of the 1990s was caused by the economic recession together with earlier overproduction (Englund *et al.*, 1995). The prices regained their earlier level in 1997 and have been rising since then. Despite higher prices, new construction of detached houses was still low at the beginning of the 2000s. However, prices vary considerably across different parts of Sweden.

One general observation is that the price of detached houses in the metropolitan regions – Stockholm, Malmö, and Göteborg – has increased more than the country average. Prices in these regions have increased rather similarly between 1981 and 1997. After 1997, prices in the Stockholm and Malmö metropolitan regions have increased further. In Northern Sweden, the price development has been much slower. The rise in house prices in the mid-1990s did not fully reach the northern part of the country. On average, the northern regions have the lowest house prices in Sweden (Turner and Whitehead, 2002). These are also, with a few exceptions, areas with high unemployment rates, among the highest in Sweden (Statistics Sweden, 2004).

3. The Swedish housing policy

3.1. Subsidies and allowances

The origin of a housing policy came forward at the beginning of the twentieth century as a reaction to social problems associated with urbanization and the growth of industry. Later, municipal housing companies were established in several municipalities during the period between the First and Second World War. An important task was to manage newly constructed housing targeted for low-income families with children as well as for pensioners (Bengtsson, 1991; Söderström, 1993). Since then the companies have had a social housing responsibility.

The economic boom of the 1950s attracted more migrants to the cities. The housing shortage became severe. Available capital was seized by the growing industry, and production resources were directed away from the housing sector. The housing situation became a strain on the social democratic government in the 1960s. However, in 1965, at the initiative of the government, the Riksdag decided to produce 1 million housing units in a period of 10 years. Capital and labor were directed to the construction of new housing units. Newly established credit agencies placed long-term capital at construction firms' disposal (Söderström, 1993). A major part of the new and enormous housing stock was to be managed by the municipal housing companies as well as the co-operative building societies.

Both the national government and the local municipalities had a formal responsibility to provide housing. The government provided loans and interest subsidies for new construction as well as housing allowances. The municipalities, on the other hand, were responsible for physical planning and estimating housing needs at the local level (Anas *et al.*, 1985). Housing allowances is a type of intervention used in almost all European countries. This intervention is directed toward low-income families. Generally, the expenditure for this type of intervention later increased in 1990s.

3.2. Housing policy in the 1990s

It has lately been a rapid change in housing policy in many countries in Europe. The policy of general subsidies was designed in a period with large deficiencies of housing. This is not the case today. Generally, the housing policy has changed from general to directed subsidies. The Nordic countries together with other countries in Europe had for a long time directed the subsidies to investments in new construction. The subsidies were designed as interest support. One of the reasons was to create tenure neutrality (Turner and Whitehead, 2002). Other countries like the United Kingdom and Ireland chose another path. They directed the support to investments in social housing.

The housing policy in Sweden experienced a dramatic change in the 1990s. Sweden, like several other countries in Europe, shifted from a policy including general subsidies toward a targeted housing policy. In the Swedish case, however, the shift came from a more generous level of general subsidies (Turner and Whitehead, 2002).

One of the reasons to shrink the general subsidies was to reduce public expenditures and to deregulate the housing market (Turner and Whitehead, 2002). Today directed subsidies toward specific households or investments dominate in Europe. Another reason is the deregulation of the financial markets, which changed the prerequisites of financing investments in the housing market (ECB, 2003). Most European countries made use of tax deductions to increase new construction in the housing market. This type of intervention has, however, decreased (Andersson *et al.*, 2004).

In the political discussions of the 1980s, it was often stated that general subsidies were less urgent in the current housing market than they were a few decades earlier. One of the reasons put forward was that housing standards in Sweden were high and that households had good access to housing. Another argument against general subsidies was the concern that subsidies may have increased building costs. In 1993, interest subsidies were the major part of all subsidies and amounted to, on average, 8000 SEK per household (Turner and Whitehead, 2002). Subsidies such as interest rate guarantee levels and tax deductions became very expansive in the late 1980s. Irrespective of political party, most politicians agreed that something had to be done about the general subsidy system (Bengtsson, 1995).

The shift in housing policy in Sweden was accomplished at the beginning of the 1990s. The so-called Danell Commission suggested that the general interest subsidies should gradually decrease (Bengtsson and Kemeny, 1997). For new construction they began to phase out in 1992. The effect of the decision lagged behind, and not until 1995 and the years that followed did the overall housing subsidies begin to fall dramatically. Consequently, the new housing policy helped to reduce the amount of subsidies paid out. During the same period, the number of housing vacancies increased, which pressed the municipal housing companies to act more on market terms. Rents were gradually changed in the 1990s owing to the reduction in subsidies and the increase in real estate taxes (Englund *et al.*, 1995). Accordingly, housing expenditures for most households increased (Turner and Whitehead, 2002).

3.3. Current rent regulation

Another type of intervention in the housing market is rent regulation. It exists in almost all countries within the European Union. Rent regulations have been used for different reason. One reason is to make affordable housing available for low-income families and another to prevent segregation. Rent regulations have been criticized for among other things to increase the demand for renting, without giving incentive for new construction.

However, almost all countries within the European Union have in one way or the other adjusted their rent regulation policies since 1980. Sweden is one of the few that has not. In many countries, rent regulation has been adjusted, for example, to include rent indexation to the consumer price index. The only country in the European Union that has chosen to abolish rent regulation and allow the market to set the rents is Finland (ECB, 2003).

The current rent regulation system in Sweden, called the *use-value rent system* ("bruksvärdessystemet"), was introduced in 1969. The use-value rent system is based on the idea that comparable dwellings should have equal rents, whether they are owned privately or by municipal housing companies. The legislation states that rents in the municipal housing companies should be the reference for rent setting in the private sector. This system is based on the use-value of housing and the cost of construction and maintenance of the municipal housing companies. The rent is a result of negotiations between The Swedish Union of Tenants, the municipal housing companies, and the Swedish Property Federation. The Swedish Property Federation is an association of private landlords. The negotiations are carried out on a local level. This "soft" rent regulation system involves the whole rent sector in Sweden, not merely rental housing for low-income households (Svensson, 1998). By means of the use-value rent system, municipal housing companies have formally been given a vital position in pricing the rental housing market (Bengtsson, 1995).

Criticism has been aimed at this system over the years. Critics assert that the dwelling location is not given sufficient attention in rent setting (Turner, 1983; Lind, 1997). A study showed that year of construction was the dominant factor used as a proxy for dwelling quality. It had an even greater impact than did the location of the housing unit (Bergenstråhle, 1984).

4. Housing and mobility of the elderly

4.1. Introduction

For families with children, the size of the dwelling is highly associated with the size of the family and family type. Even though this relationship is weaker for elderly people, it still has an impact on the choice of housing.

Elderly people often live in large dwellings, despite the fact that their children have left the parental home. Many elderly bought and moved into newly constructed houses in end of the 1960s and the beginning of the 1970s. For this group the cost of owner occupation housing is now favorable, as inflation has undermined the real value of the mortgages. Elderly usually continue ageing in the same environment as before and mostly without any special care (Warnes and Ford, 1995). Several studies about the housing of the elderly have shown that most people stay in their dwelling, neighborhood, and municipality. Consequently, the mobility rate is generally low.

However, even if mobility is low, mobility is part of the process of adapting to changing needs and desires regarding housing and standard of living. For elderly households living in detached houses, maintenance could become strenuous. This might be a reason to move to another type of housing and change tenure. Another reason to move is that elderly who own their dwelling may sell it and become more liquid in order to compensate for low pensions.

In this section, we will describe the housing situation for elderly people in the ordinary housing market and their mobility, using data from Statistics Sweden. Elderly living in special housing accommodations is not discussed in this chapter.

4.2. Elderly housing and tenure

4.2.1. Housing

In the age range 65–74, most elderly people live as couples. With increasing age, single-family status becomes more frequent. The family status varies, however, as a function of sex. A majority of women older than 75 years of age live as singles, whereas older men live to a greater extent in couples. This is an effect of women's longer mean age span. Elderly individuals also live in other arrangements, such as together with adult children. However, this form of accommodation does not occur frequently.

Most elderly people live in regular housing for a long time. In 2000, 93 percent of elderly people 65 years and older lived in ordinary housing. The rest lived in different kinds of institutions for disabled elderly. With increasing age, fewer elderly live in ordinary housing. Still, 75 percent of elderly individuals 90 years and older live in regular housing (Lindgren and Lindström, 2004). About 55 percent of the younger elderly live in owner occupation housing. This kind of housing becomes less common with increasing age. Instead, the share of rental housing increase with increasing age (Figure 2). The share of dwellings owned by co-operative building societies (tenant ownership) does not vary much as a function of age. It depends, however, on family status. The proportion of elderly singles living in tenant ownership housing is higher than that of elderly couples.

Figure 2.   Elderly living in different tenures by age.   Share by age group in year 2000

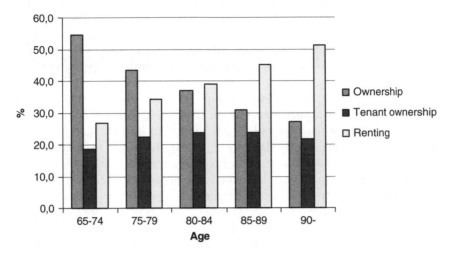

Couples, on the other hand, tend to live in owner occupation housing. About 60 percent occupy a house of their own. Besides living in tenant ownership housing, nearly half of all elderly singles inhabit rental flats.

Tenure also differs between men and women. Around 55 percent of elderly men live in owner occupation housing, while the corresponding figure for women is 40 percent. This difference reflects the variation in tenure among singles. Almost 50 percent of single women live in rental occupation housing, whereas men live in rental as well as owner occupation housing.

The regional differences in the housing stock constrain choices for the elderly. On average, 30 percent of the Swedish population live in rental housing. However, there is a large regional variation. For instance, 40 percent of the population in Stockholm live in rental housing, while the share in Gotland is just 20 percent.

Recently, other types of housing, designed to fulfill the different needs of the elderly, have been discussed. Public housing companies as well as other housing companies have reintroduced the concept of senior housing. This idea was first introduced in 1929. Nevertheless, it was not until the 1980s that senior housing becames popular. This kind of housing is adapted to less severe forms of disability. To have access to senior housing, people usually have to be 55 years or older. Senior housing is accessible through the ordinary local housing market. These properties usually contain some kind of common premises. Common kitchens and dining rooms occur. Such housing is managed in different ways, but the residents are usually responsible for managing these premises themselves (Lindgren and Lindström, 2004).

4.2.2. Neighborhood

People become established in places where they have lived for a long time –
where they have established social relationships and made friends. They
also have considerable knowledge of the local environment. Leaving
such a neighborhood is associated with strain, particularly when the near
future holds decreasing memory capacity and mobility (Björnsson and
Borgegård, 1989).

Elderly spend a great deal of time in their homes and in their
neighborhoods. This puts demands on these environments, especially in
recent decades, when the policy of "aging in place" has gained in
popularity (Marshall and McPherson, 1994). In order to maintain an
independent life and to cope, it is necessary for an aging individual to
find daily support in the neighborhood as well as other kinds of services;
these include friends, a nice environment, and a nearby day-care center for
elderly people (Paulsson, 1985; Herbert and Thomas, 1990; Boverket,
1995). In order to continue living in a familiar environment, poor
pensioners are able to get housing allowances from the government
(Försäkringskassan).

The health status of the elderly has a great impact on the kind of
support they need to manage living on their own. There are public services
to support elderly, for example, delivery of ready-to-eat food and taxi
service for the disabled. With increased disability, the dwelling needs to be
adapted to a life with handicap. The authorities provide economic support
for these types of adaptations (Arman and Lindahl, 2005).

4.2.3. Mobility and tenure choice

Most people stay and grow old in the place where they have already
lived for a long time and spent the last years of their working careers
(Warnes, 1986). The mobility rate is, accordingly, low for elderly people.
Few elderly people move in the local housing market. Only a small share
of elderly move over longer distances and to other regions. Experiences
from the United Kingdom and France show, however, that elderly who
have recently become pensioners, who are in good health, and have good
financial situations have a higher mobility rate than do others (Cribier and
Kych, 1993; Warnes, 1994). The mobility rate is also somewhat higher
among the oldest of the elderly. This is an effect of needing to move into
more appropriate housing, close to where they already live (Öberg *et al.*,
1993). The later may be caused by increasing disability, which implies a
move to a more suitable dwelling or close to an adult child. In case of
severe disability and when the help and support of family members and
relatives is not sufficient, elderly have to move into special housing
accommodation (Litwak and Longino, 1987).

Older people in detached and tenant ownership housing have a lower
mobility rate than do renters (Lundin, 1991). Most elderly persons in

owner occupation housing are aware that they will eventually have to move to a less demanding form of living. For example, elderly people in detached housing experience problems with maintenance and gardening with increasing age, and disabled elderly in multi-family housing may have to move because the current building lacks an elevator (Björnsson and Borgegård, 1989).

Strikingly, many elderly do not change tenure when they move to other housing. This observation is valid for renters as well as for owners and elderly living in tenant ownership housing (Lundin, 1988, 1991; Ekström and Danermark, 1993; Warnes and Ford, 1995). Households who own their home state that they prefer tenant ownership to rental occupation because ownership allows them to have an influence over their housing. However, the transition to rental occupation from owner occupation or tenant ownership housing increases with increasing age. The transition to tenant ownership and owner occupation housing decreases correspondingly (Andersson *et al.*, 1992; Borgegård and Fransson, 2002).

Younger singles have a higher migration rate than do other types of households. When it comes to the elderly, the situation is the opposite. Almost 33 percent of those who move to another municipality are couples (Borgegård and Fransson, 2002). Among the elderly migrating to another municipality, some return to the region of origin, others to places where they have a social network or to their leisure home (Lindström and Åhlund, 1982; Hjort, 2005). Today very few persons migrate to the distant countryside, but elderly is to some extent an exception (Hjort, 2005).

As part of their housing career in the cities, elderly households in owner occupation housing eventually move to tenant ownership or rental occupation. Elderly people migrating to distant regions or to the countryside make another type of career, due to the local structure of housing. They move largely into owner occupation housing, independent of their former tenure. This is because a privately owned detached house is one of the few options available in many rural areas (Borgegård and Fransson, 2002).

5. Modeling migration and tenure choice

5.1. Model overview

In order to create a transparent, yet flexible model, we partition the individual's decision to relocate into three consecutive steps. Each step focuses on a specific motive for relocation, for example, migration to get a job or to enter a school or university, changed demand for housing, life-cycle events, etc. In the first step, each individual in the population faces the decision to migrate to another region. The second step depends on the outcome of the first; individuals who decide not to leave the region now face the decision to move within the region, whereas individuals who migrate from the region of origin choose a destination region. In the third and final step, individuals who have relocated face the decision of tenure (rental or owner occupied). The choices in each step are specified as conditional logit models, but the determinants vary across models. In Figure 3, we present a graphical illustration of the model organization.

The regional migration (model A), intra-regional migration (model B), and tenure choice (model D) models are all dichotomous conditional logit models with a focus on life-cycle events, for example, adolescents moving from parents, and labor market experiences, such as unemployment. The regional destination (model C) is a conditional logit model emphasizing labor market macro-variables, such as regional unemployment rates, taxes, and average housing prices. Finally, for all individuals who are designated to relocate, the tenure choice model (model D) focuses on changes in housing demand. The tenure choice of a household is analyzed in two models: one for households moving within the current region (model D1) and another for households migrating to another region (model D2). The models are described in more detail in the following subsections.

The current partitioned model construction implies that the decision in one part of the model is not affected by variables entering in other parts.

Figure 3. Model overview

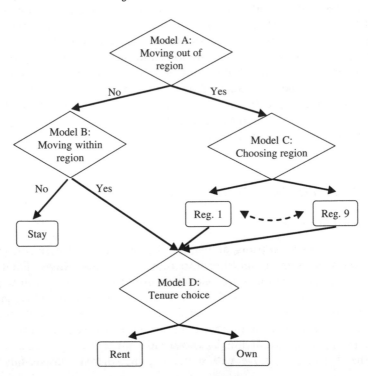

For example, the decision to move out of a region is independent of the attributes in any other region. Similarly, any change in the relative price between owner occupied and rented housing does not affect the probability to relocate. However, *conditional* on a regional emigration, the immigration patterns to the destination regions and to the available types of housing do depend on these attributes. We do acknowledge that a nested or multinomial model, in which all decisions are modeled simultaneously, in principle, could represent a better description of the "true process of relocation." For example, in such a model the attributes of any region would affect the emigration probability from any other region. However, the resulting large number of possible decisions in the choice set and the highly uneven distribution of actual choices would make the estimation process quite burdensome and potentially numerically unstable. Therefore, we have restricted the model such that the decisions are made according to the stepwise process described above.

5.2. Data

Data were collected from the GeoSwede database constructed by Statistics Sweden from databases maintained for the production of official statistics. It is a longitudinal database consisting of individual register data with an emphasis on demographic and housing data. The individual register data refer to the situation on December 31 of each year.[2] GeoSwede includes data for select variables for the period 1990–2002 for all 10 million plus individuals who at some point during the period resided in Sweden and were registered in the Swedish social security system. Three of the contributing databases are updated annually: education, income, and employment (Longitudinell databas för utbildning, sysselsättning och inkomst); personal details of all people registered with the tax authority (Register över totalbefolkningen); and geographic coordinates for all legally registered residents/dwelling combinations (Geografidatabasen). The individual's geographical position is measured down to an area of $100 \, \text{m}^2$ based on the real estate tax register. A fourth database, a property tax register (Fastighetstaxeringsregistret), contains data in 1990, 1995, 2000, and 2002.

For each individual, there is a unique identification code specific to this database. Within the database, it is possible to create "taxation households" through information on common children and marital status. Each individual has a household identification code equivalent to the individual identification code of the oldest member of the household. Unfortunately,

---

[2] The data from the real estate taxation register refer to January 1, 1991, 1996, 2001, and 2003, respectively.

we cannot construct households for unmarried couples without children. This implies that we underestimate the number of households without children and overestimate the number of single households. In total, we will overestimate the number of households.

The database also includes the "generation database" from Statistics Sweden. This database includes information on each individual's parents (except for the very old). This implies that it is possible to define which individual is parent(s) and child(ren) within a household. We can then observe changes in the household composition over time, for example, children moving away from the parental household.

The analyzed population is restricted to individuals residing in Sweden on December 31, 2001, and includes information on changes in 2002. There were originally 8.9 million individuals in the sample. We drop individuals who died, emigrated during 2001 and 2002, and individuals with missing household identification codes. Using the household identification code, household-specific data is created. The final data set consists of about 4.7 million households. Of these, about 720 000 households relocate to a new position (measured as xy-location down to $100 \, \text{m}^2$) during 2002.[3] The analyzed population for the models of tenure choice is defined differently from the migration models, because of lack of information concerning tenure in 2001. The database contains information on tenure in year 2000 and in 2002. For that reason the population is defined as households not moving during 2001, but moving respectively not-moving during 2002. We are then able to estimate models of tenure choice for the period December 31, 2001, to December 31, 2002.

In the analysis, Sweden is divided into nine regions. These regions are derived from H-region using the following geographical definitions: (1) Stockholm/Södertälje A-region, (2) Göteborg A-region, (3) Malmö/Lund/Trelleborg A-region, (4) urban areas (municipalities with population $> 90\,000$ within 30 km of the municipality center) in Götaland, (5) urban areas in Svealand, (6) urban areas in Norrland, (7) rural areas (municipalities with population $< 90\,000$ within 30 km of the municipality center) in Götaland, (8) rural areas in Svealand, and (9) rural areas in Norrland. H-regions consist of clusters of labor market areas (A-regions) in order to create homogenous regions.

The main dependent variable is an indicator of relocation. The variable is defined as equal to 1 if the xy-location of the individual on December 31, 2001, is not equal to the xy-location on December 31, 2002, and otherwise as equal to 0. This means that the variable includes three distinct

---

[3] Note that an individual could relocate to a new location within the same 100-m^2 area and still being coded as a non-mover.

groups: individuals who relocate locally, i.e., within the same municipality, individuals who relocate between municipalities within the same region, and individuals who relocate between regions.

Basically, we use three different types of independent variables: variables that describe the household and the changes in household composition, variables that describe individual's characteristics, and variables that describe region attributes.

The household is divided into four types in 2002: (1) couples (married) without children, (2) couples (married/unmarried) with children, (3) single parents with children, and (4) singles (unmarried couples without children). The household composition changes are defined as: (1) separating couples, (2) one partner dies, (3) a child leaves the parental home, (4) two singles create a household, (5) a child enters the household (generally a newborn), (6) the last remaining child leaves the parental home, and (7) no household composition changes. This variable is identified using the household compositions at two different dates (December 31, 2001 and 2002). The tenure form is constructed from the property tax register, where information on the estate's owner type and the type of houses (detached/semi-detached or multi-family) is used to create the tenure forms rental vs. owner occupied. Tenant ownership is regarded in this analysis as owner occupation. Individual characteristics such as age and place of birth (Sweden vs. other) are taken from registers. We also use household disposable income 2001 (sum of adults income) and the household position in the distribution of the population incomes as a dependent variable. The education level is defined as a category of years of education, following the Swedish Standard Classification of Education, which is adapted to the international standard. It is applied to the head of the household.

Finally, in the models, we also include region-specific variables reflecting the labor market status and housing costs. First, we include the municipal taxes of 2001. As a region consists of several municipalities, there is an issue of aggregating the taxes. We have chosen to use a population-weighted average across municipalities.

5.3. Analyzing migration behavior

5.3.1. Model A: regional migration

The regional migration model establishes the propensity for a household to leave the region of origin and to migrate to another region. The analysis is based on a population consisting of migrating and non-migrating households for a period from December 31, 2001, to December 31, 2002. The relocation of households into another region depends on the region of origin. Households in metropolitan regions may migrate of other reasons than households from rural areas. There is also a cause to believe that the decision to migrate depends on the type of household. Important to a migratory decision are also events like young individuals leaving the parental home, couples moving together, or splitting up (Clark and Dieleman, 1996). Such family events are triggers for moving to other places. Although mostly recognized in residential mobility studies, this has implications for migrating longer distances as well. For these reasons, the analysis of out-migration is conditioned on the region of origin and on the type of household.

The migration rate varies with age and sex and differs in a similar way in most countries in the developed world (Boyle *et al.*, 1998). However, the rate varies as a function of the scale of migration, from local to national. Young people move to a much greater extent than do other age groups, regardless of whether they move to another residence in the neighborhood or to another part of the country. The migration rate peaks around the age of 20 and gradually declines to the age of 64. Then it rises again at about the age of 75. Furthermore, there is also a difference in migration rate between the sexes. Young women have, at a certain age, a higher migration rate than young men do. The gender difference in mobility is a result of young women leaving the parental home earlier than young men do. But it is also an effect of women usually marrying or cohabiting with men who are around 3 years older. Age is a proxy for the position of the individual in the life career. Young people are less concerned about moving to family than are the elderly, but much more interested in moving to regions with career opportunities than are other age groups (Niedomysl, 2005). Regional migration rates are also high for persons with a higher level of education than for those with a lower level. These disparities are linked to the trade for which a person is qualified (Champion *et al.*, 1998). This is related to the type and the number of vacancies in the regional labor market. Given that the migration rate varies with age, it also differs between household types. The general pattern is that the mobility rate for a single household is always higher than for a family with child(ren) at a given age.

Unemployment of the individual is often referred to in the literature as a trigger to migrate from the region of origin (Öberg, 1997). We believe that households with at least one member unemployed are more likely to migrate to another region than are households with all members employed. A well-known phenomenon mentioned in migration research is that if a person has moved once, he/she will soon move again. This could be caused by absence of place attachment in the region of destination. If no place-bound social relation is established, earlier alterative destinations would be considered and the risk of migration will by that increase. In the analysis, we also include the disposable income of the households. Also, various ethnical and social factors influence the mobility rate. Results from the United Kingdom indicate that local and regional migration rates for ethnic minority groups are higher than the rate for the majority group (Champion *et al.*, 1998). Swedish data show that the migration rate for ethnic minority groups is about twice that for native Swedes (Andersson, 2000). In the literature on residential mobility, the relationship between the propensity to move to other housing and current housing tenure is often acknowledged. We assume that tenure also affect the decision to migrate longer distances.

The estimations of the propensity to migrate from the region of origin are divided into 36 models. There is one model for each combination of nine regions and four different household types. The estimates of the effects of household characteristics are presented in Table 1. Due to the many models we only present estimates for two regions and four household types. The entire table with all regions is published in Fransson and Eklöf (2007).

The analysis shows that factors like unemployment, level of education, and age of the head of the household co-vary with the migration of households. The propensity that young households migrate to another region varies by the region of origin. The estimate is low in the metropolitan regions, but high in sparsely populated regions. The regional variation in the propensity to migrate also depends on the country of birth. Native Swedes living in the metropolitan region of Stockholm are more likely to migrate to another region, than people born in other countries. However, the relation is the opposite in the Northern part of Sweden. In these parts of the country, foreign-born persons migrate to other regions in a much larger extent than do Swedish born. The results from the analysis also show that the migration risks for highly educated persons co-vary with region. The risk is considerably higher in sparsely populated regions than in metropolitan regions.

Demographic events like couples moving together also co-vary with migration to another region. Housing tenure also co-varies with regional migration. Families owning their dwelling migrate to a lesser extent than those who live in rental housing.

5.3.2. Model B: Intra-regional migration

Most intra-regional moves are short-distant. About 80 percent of all middle-aged singles move less than 10 km within the region of origin. Young singles move a bit further, 80 percent move less than 15 km (calculations by the authors). For couples, the intra-regional migration distance is even shorter. This shows that most intra-regional migration occurs locally. The demand for housing is an important determinant in the decision to relocate locally. We are then able to apply findings from the research of residential mobility. Results from this research demonstrate intra-regional migration as a function of certain household characteristics.

The population of our intra-regional migration model consists of those households that do not migrate to another region. They still live in the same region in 2002. The population amounts to 4 million households,

Table 1. Parameter estimates of model A – migration out of Stockholm (region 1) and rural Norrland (region 9), by household type[a]

Variable	Couples without children		Couples with children		Singles with children		Singles	
	Region 1	Region 9	Region 1	Region 9	Region 1	Region 9	Region 1	Region 9
Point estimates								
Intercept	−5.392**	−4.707**	−5.882**	−4.397**	−6.588***	−4.496**	−5.727**	−4.267**
Age								
0–24	1.417***	2.725**	1.008**	1.555**	1.373**	1.870**	1.678**	2.762**
25–39	0.740***	1.500***	0.963**	1.208**	0.925***	1.288***	1.155***	2.155**
40–64	0.398***	−0.103	0.092	0.684*	0.295	0.944**	0.596***	0.894**
65+	0.000	0.000	0.000	0.000	0.000	0.000	0.000	0.000
Country of birth								
Sweden	0.398**	−0.850**	0.866**	−1.288**	0.828**	−0.794**	0.423**	−0.807**
Other country	0.000	0.000	0.000	0.000	0.000	0.000	0.000	0.000
Education								
Post-gymnasium	0.120	1.322**	0.181**	0.818**	−0.144	0.286*	0.094**	1.159**
Gymnasium	0.178**	0.568**	0.036	0.210	0.032	0.004	0.141**	0.515**
Pre-gymnasium	0.000	0.000	0.000	0.000	0.000	0.000	0.000	0.000
Family changes								
Separation					1.027**	0.765**	1.766**	1.418***
Partner dies					0.704*	0.406	0.203	0.294
Nestleave							1.654**	2.177**
MoveTogether	1.099***	0.527*	1.122**	0.967**	1.339**	0.775*		
Birth of a child			1.551**	1.589**				

Youngest child leaves the parental home	0.769**	0.813**					1.242**	1.094**
	0.000	0.000					0.000	0.000
No change	0.000	0.000					0.000	0.000
Unemployment								
Unemployed	0.449**	0.370**	0.233**	0.252**	0.167*	0.137	0.279**	0.092**
	0.000	0.000	0.000	0.000	0.000	0.000	0.000	0.000
All employed	0.000	0.000	0.000	0.000	0.000	0.000	0.000	0.000
Previous migration								
Mover: previous year	1.384**	1.692**	1.420**	1.464**	2.301**	2.012**	1.265**	1.209**
	0.000	0.000	0.000	0.000	0.000	0.000	0.000	0.000
Stayer	0.000	0.000	0.000	0.000	0.000	0.000	0.000	0.000
Disposable income								
Quintile 1	0.282*	0.619*	0.863**	0.440	1.287**	0.404	0.485**	−0.269
Quintile 2	0.119	0.362	0.557**	0.295	1.159**	0.244	0.255**	−0.682**
Quintile 3	−0.009	0.082	0.374**	0.253	0.750**	−0.179	0.116*	−0.809**
Quintile 4	0.160**	−0.066	0.414**	0.108	0.508**	−0.087	0.001	−0.471**
Quintile 5[b]	0.000	0.000	0.000	0.000	0.000	0.000	0.000	0.000
Tenure								
Owner occupation	−0.067	−0.746**	−0.331**	−1.159**	0.085	−0.385**	0.130**	−0.165**
	0.000	0.000	0.000	0.000	0.000	0.000	0.000	0.000
Rental occupation	0.000	0.000	0.000	0.000	0.000	0.000	0.000	0.000
Sex								
Men	—	—			−0.291	−0.388	−0.028	−0.206
					0.000	0.000	0.000	0.000
Women	—	—			0.000	0.000	0.000	0.000
Number of households	128263	72534	191444	78946	89694	30792	558489	202365
McFadden R2	0.046	0.133	0.075	0.12	0.093	0.085	0.131	0.325

[a] For information about standard error, see Fransson and Eklöf (2007).
[b] Range of quintiles – 1026; 1027–1492; 1493–2093; 2094–3215; 3216 – in hundreds of SEK.

which constitute 85 percent of all households in the database. The prospect of the households for other housing, job, and education varies between different parts of Sweden. For that reason, we have chosen to analyze the intra-regional migration conditional on the region of living.

The work by Rossi (1955) and Clark and Dieleman (1996) emphasize the importance of housing size in a residential mobility decision. Unfortunately, we cannot observe the size of the dwelling for all forms of tenure. Housing tenure will in the analysis serve as a proxy for the size of dwellings. Ownership also implies that a household has some wealth. Previous studies have also demonstrated that they migrate less frequently then renters (Clark and Dieleman, 1996). The literature emphasizes that the position in the life course is important for the demand for housing. Age will serve as a proxy for the position in the life course. The life course of a household can also be characterized by different family constellations, housing, and income. In our analysis, we include disposable income expressed in quintiles. We also include demographic changes or life-course transitions, as the birth of a child, the last remaining child leaves the parental home, and a partner dies (Champion and Fielding, 1992; Clark and Dieleman, 1996). Residential mobility is sometimes the geographical outcome of social mobility. Education is in this analysis a proxy for social aspirations (Cadwallader, 1992). We also include gender in the models for singles.

The estimates of moving to new housing in the current region decrease as expected with age for all four household types. However, it is notable that the estimate for singles with children is also high in the upper middle-age range (Table 2). Here, moving to new housing may be caused by the separation of a couple or high housing costs in the rental sector for a household that decreases in size. The models in Table 2 also include tenure form for all four household types. The result shows that households in owner occupation housing are less likely to move than are households in rental occupation. There are, however, substantial differences among owners. Couples with children who own their dwelling are less likely to move than are singles with children. Single households with children living in metropolitan regions, have a higher probability of moving if they own their dwelling than if they rent. This result is probably related to divorces. For this type of households the effect of tenure on the mobility decision is generally weaker in the metropolitan regions than in rural areas.

Family events often generate a move to another residence. In our analysis, a family event may have a considerable effect on the propensity to move to new housing in the current region.

5.3.3. Model C: Inter-regional relocation

The inter-regional relocation model determines the destination region conditional on regional emigration. This implies that the choice set varies

Table 2. **Parameter estimates of a model for the probability to move to a new dwelling within the current region (model B), by household type and Stockholm (region 1) and rural Norrland (region 9).**

Variable	Couples without child		Couples with Children		Single with children		Singles	
	Point estimates							
	Region 1	Region 9	Region 1	Region 9	Region 1	Region 9	Region 1	Region 9
Intercept	−3.186**	−2.816**	−3.471**	−2.592**	−3.832**	−3.684**	−2.833**	−2.490**
Age								
0–24	2.301**	3.293**	2.413**	2.620**	2.610**	3.121**	1.814**	2.070**
25–39	1.548**	1.239**	1.570**	1.315**	1.640**	2.063**	1.363**	1.235**
40–64	0.311**	0.109*	0.668**	0.507*	1.100**	1.521**	0.341**	0.227**
65+	0.000	0.000	0.000	0.000	0.000	0.000	0.000	0.000
Family changes								
Separation					1.666**	1.738**	2.669**	2.896**
Partner dies					−0.130	−0.379	0.578**	0.575**
Nestleave							3.379**	3.366**
MoveTogether	0.979**	1.590**	1.635**	1.487**				
Birth of a child	0.593**	0.665**	1.191	1.478				
Youngest child leaves the parental home					1.738**	1.765**	1.253**	1.285**
No change	0.000	0.000	0.000	0.000	0.000	0.000	0.000	0.000
Disposable income								
Quintile 1	0.093*	0.291**	0.138**	0.419**	0.181**	0.671**	−0.169**	0.198**
Quintile 2	−0.073	0.048	0.188**	0.132*	0.136**	0.549**	−0.047**	0.056*
Quintile 3	0.028	−0.100	0.083**	−0.090	0.087*	0.440**	−0.107**	0.066*
Quintile 4	−0.113**	−0.145*	0.049*	−0.137	0.056	0.276**	−0.070**	0.048
Quintile 5	0.000	0.000	0.000	0.000	0.000	0.000	0.000	0.000

(Continued on next page)

Table 2. (Continued)

Variable	Couples without child		Couples with Children		Single with children		Singles	
	Point estimates							
	Region 1	Region 9	Region 1	Region 9	Region 1	Region 9	Region 1	Region 9
Tenure								
Owner occupation	−0.379**	−0.947**	−0.604**	−1.888**	0.142**	−0.680**	−0.085**	−0.563**
Rental occupation	0.000	0.000	0.000	0.000	0.000	0.000	0.000	0.000
Education								
Post-gymnasium	0.108**	0.000	0.208**	0.234**	0.049	0.064	0.075**	0.053*
Gymnasium	0.014	0.058	0.061*	0.086	0.085**	0.111	0.019	0.103**
Pre-gymnasium	0	0	0.000	0.000	0.000	0.000	0.000	0.000
Sex								
Men	—	—	—		−0.166**	−0.694**	−0.026**	−0.125**
Woman	—	—	—		0.000	0.000	0.000	0.000
Number of households	118521	68219	168542	71123	77335	24823	450052	160297
McFadden R2	0.076	0.048	0.094	0.156	0.09	0.159	0.181	0.23

across individuals as the individuals are not allowed to choose their original home region (intra-regional relocation is handled in model B). Furthermore, the migration patterns depend on the region from which the individuals migrate. For example, individuals migrating from the northern regions relocate to other regions than individuals migrating from the southern regions. To accommodate such differences, we estimate regional specific models. In contrast to the other migration models, this model makes use of a repeated cross-section of regional migrants from 2000 and 2002. For each region, we fit a conditional logit model with eight alternatives (excluding the home region).

The motives for regional relocation differ between individuals and consequently the individual-specific choice probabilities are influenced by a number of variables. Furthermore, region-specific variables also influence the relocation pattern. In the model, we include individual characteristics as well as region attributes. A potential reason for relocation is to attain education. However, demand for education is not observed in the data. Hence, we are forced to use age as a proxy for demand for education and other motives that might be age related. Age enters the index function as a linear spline with five segments with kinks at 20, 24, 40, and 65. The high density of kinks at younger ages is to accommodate the frequent regional relocation at younger ages. Furthermore, the household's position in the income distribution may affect the relocation pattern. We include the household income divided by the median income.

Regional unemployment is believed to affect the relocation pattern such that regions with high unemployment become less attractive than others. As we use region-specific constants in the analysis, we already control for all variables that are fixed within a region over time. However, as we use a repeated cross-section, we can identify the impact of the changes in the unemployment rate in the regions over time. Regional housing prices and local tax rates may also affect relocation patterns. However, while testing alternative specifications these variables turned out insignificant and were therefore dropped from the model.

A transition matrix is presented in Table 3. In the top panel, we present the transition matrix between regions with the original region in rows and the target region in columns. For example, 7.67 percent of the households that migrate from the Stockholm region move to the Gothenburg region.

For each region, we estimate seven alternative-specific constants, 5×7 age coefficients, 4×7 other individual characteristic coefficients, and two alternative attribute coefficients, in total 72 coefficients per region. To preserve on space we only present a selection of these estimates. We focus on three distinct regions namely Stockholm, urbane Götaland, and rural Norrland, representing three types of regions in Sweden.

In Table 4, we present the estimates of the individual characteristics for the three selected regions. The table is partitioned into three panels,

Table 3. Transition matrix between regions

To	Sthlm	Gbg	Mlm	UrbGtl	UrbSve	UrbNorr	RurGtl	RurSve	RurNorr
From Sthlm	0	0.0767	0.0707	0.177	0.237	0.0767	0.0943	0.181	0.086
Gbg	0.202	0	0.0733	0.347	0.0857	0.0355	0.185	0.0369	0.0347
Mlm	0.189	0.0882	0	0.496	0.0575	0.0249	0.103	0.0195	0.0229
UrbGtl	0.174	0.197	0.194	0	0.0923	0.0318	0.245	0.038	0.0268
UrbSve	0.332	0.0914	0.0382	0.151	0	0.0684	0.0575	0.212	0.05
UrbNorr	0.273	0.0801	0.0334	0.103	0.147	0	0.0339	0.0477	0.281
RurGtl	0.122	0.151	0.076	0.495	0.0796	0.0222	0	0.0325	0.0216
RurSve	0.224	0.0617	0.0195	0.128	0.408	0.0536	0.0617	0	0.0438
RurNorr	0.199	0.0612	0.0212	0.1	0.12	0.407	0.0394	0.0522	0

each one representing one original region. The columns give the estimates of the individual characteristics indicated by row label. As the original region is not included in the choice set, no coefficients are estimated for this region. The reference region, for which the utility is normalized to zero, is indicated by a column of zeros.

A positive estimate indicates that the individual characteristic will have a positive influence of the choice probability for that region compared to the choice probability of the reference region. For example, if income increases w.r.t. the median income for an individual migrating from Stockholm, the probabilities of relocating to urbane or rural Norrland decrease significantly compared to the probability to relocate to Göteborg. We will illustrate the implications of the estimates below as we discuss the simulation results.

Next, we present estimates relating to the alternative attributes (Table 5). The estimates refer to the individuals moving away from the region indicated by the column headers.[4] As we have only two repeated cross-sections, and region-specific intercepts, we have very few degrees of freedom to estimate the effects of region attributes. Here we present estimates for the unemployment rate and the regional average housing price. The regional unemployment rate is generally associated with a negative coefficient (except for Stockholm) as expected, whereas the price variable is mostly insignificant.

5.3.4. Model D: Tenure choice

The analysis of tenure is achieved for families moving to new housing within the current region as well as families migrating to another region.

---

[4] For example, consider the second column labeled "Gbg." For an individual moving away from the Gothenburg region, the price ratio and unemployment rate of the destination region are negatively correlated with the choice probabilities as expected.

Table 4. Estimates of a multinomial model for the probability to move to a specific region, effects of individual characteristics

		New region								
		Sthlm	Gbg	Mlm	UrbGtl	UrbSve	UrbNorr	RurGtl	RurSve	RurNorr
Sthml	sdink/median	0	0	0.017 (0.036)	0.023 (0.026)	−0.001 (0.027)	−0.101* (0.045)	−0.014 (0.030)	0.029 (0.025)	−0.090* (0.038)
	svenskf	0	0	−0.123 (0.119)	0.143 (0.100)	−0.066 (0.095)	0.040 (0.117)	0.464** (0.116)	0.308** (0.100)	0.318** (0.114)
	1(0<utbtdsim<1)	0	0	−0.474** (0.138)	−0.027 (0.112)	0.259* (0.106)	−0.026 (0.131)	0.665** (0.121)	0.967** (0.110)	0.781** (0.123)
	1(1<utbtdsim<2)	0	0	−0.245** (0.089)	0.223** (0.074)	0.307** (0.071)	0.233** (0.087)	0.593** (0.086)	0.840** (0.077)	0.683** (0.087)
Urb Gtl	sdink/median	0	−0.020 (0.021)	−0.098** (0.023)		−0.319** (0.047)	−0.417** (0.116)	−0.005 (0.009)	−0.253** (0.065)	−0.285** (0.077)
	svenskf	0	0.224** (0.064)	0.298** (0.065)		0.240** (0.082)	0.414** (0.136)	0.721** (0.063)	0.487** (0.108)	0.549** (0.139)
	1(0<utbtdsim<1)	0	0.292** (0.079)	0.179* (0.079)		−0.051 (0.099)	−0.052 (0.156)	1.442** (0.072)	1.116** (0.118)	0.896** (0.148)
	1(1<utbtdsim<2)	0	0.182** (0.048)	0.135** (0.048)		0.047 (0.061)	0.262** (0.090)	0.976** (0.048)	0.719** (0.086)	0.670** (0.101)
Rur Norr	sdink/median	0	−0.388*** (0.125)	−0.429* (0.175)	−0.026 (0.079)	−0.159* (0.075)	−0.091** (0.032)	−0.047 (0.108)	0.002 (0.049)	
	svenskf	0	−0.171 (0.150)	−0.575** (0.214)	−0.281* (0.118)	−0.071 (0.116)	0.496** (0.096)	−0.348* (0.151)	0.211 (0.154)	
	1(0<utbtdsim<1)	0	−0.146 (0.160)	−0.267 (0.251)	0.007 (0.128)	−0.328** (0.123)	−0.148 (0.094)	0.485** (0.177)	0.608** (0.152)	
	1(1<utbtdsim<2)	0	−0.038 (0.103)	−0.232 (0.153)	−0.025 (0.087)	−0.265** (0.080)	−0.088 (0.060)	0.292* (0.126)	0.278* (0.112)	

Note: + Age splines for age groups 16–20, 21–24, 25–39, 40–64, 65 + .

Table 5.   Estimates of alternative attributes

	Region of origin				
	Sthlm	Gbg	Mlm	UrbGtl	UrbSve
Price_ratio	1.32*	−1.18	−0.0428	−0.38	−0.683
	(0.688)	(1.07)	(1.76)	(0.547)	(1.26)
Unempl_rate	0.0348	−0.403**	−0.235*	−0.103**	−0.128*
	(0.0654)	(0.0737)	(0.123)	(0.0388)	(0.0706)

	UrbNorr	RurGtl	RurSve	RurNorr
Price_ratio	2.94*	2*	0.13	0.294
	(1.38)	(1.07)	(0.834)	(0.94)
Unempl_rate	−0.457**	−0.217**	−0.164**	−0.29**
	(0.0856)	(0.068)	(0.0586)	(0.0757)

Previous studies have shown that ownership rises with age and family formation. Forming and expanding a family require larger space (Rossi, 1955). In Sweden, as in other countries, the tenure of ownership is strongly associated with larger housing. Demographic changes in a household are usually related to up-market movement. This means that households in ownership do not move to a less spatial housing when the children have left the parental home. Most elderly couples in ownership continue to live as owners. Previous studies have also shown that owners migrate less frequently then renters, while those who do move from a house tend to move to another house (Clark and Dieleman, 1996).

However, the distribution of the housing stock is geographically uneven in cities. Different quality, tenure, and price lead to a spatial separation of households by type, income, and ethnical background (Clark and Dieleman, 1996). Some of these residential areas, mainly in metropolitan areas, have large concentrations of immigrants. These areas can be regarded as ports of entry to the rest of the local housing market for immigrants and other socio-economic weak households moving into the region (Bråmå, 2006). These neighborhoods consist to a large share of rental housing.

For owners as well as for renters, income is an important variable in the housing choice. Previous research has shown that low-income owners change to less expensive owned housing or stay within the rental sector. High-income earners, on the other hand, often move into larger ownership housing, due to larger economic resources. We include disposable income expressed in quintiles as explanatory variables. Housing consumption, besides age and income, also rise with education (Clark and Dieleman, 1996). The price of detached and semi-detached houses varies across regions. We thus include a region-specific variable in order to capture this variation.

5.3.4.1. *Households moving to new housing within the region*

The tenure choice model determines housing tenure for households moving to new housing within the current region. The population of households moving within a region amounts to nearly 340 000 households.

The analysis results in Table 6 show that the age of the head matters in the choice of housing. In the age range 25–39, there is a considerably higher propensity, as expected, to move into owner occupation than there is in any of the other age groups. However, this is not applicable to singles with children.

The estimates of the probability to move into ownership increase with increasing education for all four household types, although it is most obvious for families with children. As expected, the probability to choose ownership decreases with decreasing income. The estimate is considerably lower for low-income households than for high-income households. This is especially evident for couples.

Family events generate mobility. They also influence the choice of housing under certain circumstances. Couples that separate are likely to move to rental occupation, as a consequence of lower household disposable income or for temporary living (Clark and Dieleman, 1996). The result from our analysis confirms this relationship. Unexpectedly, our results also suggest that couples are more inclined to move into a rented flat than into an owned dwelling, when they have a new born child.

5.3.4.2. *Choice of tenure by in-migrants*

The population of this model includes households that migrate to another region. This is basically the same type of model as the former model. We assume that migrating to another region principally is as part of a job or educational career and the housing career comes second. We have also reason to believe that a migrant to a new region only has limited knowledge about the new local housing market. This will imply an increased risk that they move into temporary arrangements, before they make a more serious approach to the housing market (Clark and Dieleman, 1996). Previous research has demonstrated that long-distant mobility for job reasons often includes a move from owning into renting.

Our estimates of the logistic regression model suggest that the probability of ownership increases with income (Table 7). This is an expected effect, and the result is similar to that of the tenure choice of households moving within the region of origin. Another similar result is the effect of country of birth. The head's native country defines country of birth. The household is more likely to choose ownership if the country of birth is Sweden as opposed to another country.

The association between former tenure and the choice of new tenure is strong for all household types. This is the same kind of result as in the previous analysis of local residential mobility. But previous tenure has somewhat smaller effect now. The propensity to choose ownership is also

Table 6. Estimates of a logit model of tenure choice (if owner) for households moving intra-regionally (model D1), by household type

Variables	Couples without children		Couples with children		Singles with children		Singles	
	Estimate	SE	Estimate	SE	Estimate	SE	Estimate	SE
Intercept	−1.137	0.102**	−0.160	0.291	0.232	0.179	−1.175	0.039**
Age								
0–24	0.274	0.142*	0.374	0.292	−1.134	0.181**	0.677	0.029**
25–39	1.213	0.070**	1.230	0.283**	−0.590	0.169**	0.950	0.028**
40–64	0.878	0.057**	0.725	0.283*	−0.775	0.169**	0.899	0.028**
65–79	0.664	0.051**	0.418	0.301	−0.727	0.195**	0.687	0.030**
80 +	0.000	.	0.000	.	0.000	.	0.000	.
Family changes								
Separation	−0.588	0.030**	−0.417	0.023**				
Partner dies	0.464	0.208*	−0.089	0.053*				
Nestleave			−0.511	0.015**				
MoveTogether					−0.009	0.052.	−0.488	0.030**
MoreChildren	−0.727	0.074**	−0.622	0.040**				
Last remaining child leaves			−0.185	0.059**	−0.005	0.038		
No change	0.000		0.000		0.000		0.000	
Disposable income								
Quintile 1	−1.128	0.052**	−1.203	0.044**	−0.621	0.043**	−0.896	0.016**
Quintile 2	−0.803	0.051**	−0.595	0.046**	−0.343	0.042**	−0.928	0.017**
Quintile 3	−0.387	0.049**	−0.423	0.047**	−0.219	0.042**	−0.616	0.015**
Quintile 4	−0.193	0.048**	−0.305	0.048**	−0.158	0.043**	−0.342	0.014**
Quintile 5	0.000		0.000		0.000		0.000	

Previous tenure								
Owner occupation	1.668	0.033**	1.489	0.024**	1.130	0.025**	1.080	0.010**
Rental occupation	0.000	.	0.000	.	0.000	.	0.000	.
Country of birth								
Born in Sweden	0.333	0.043**	0.759	0.027**	0.542	0.033**	0.355	0.015**
Not born in Sweden	0.000	.	0.000	.	0.000	.	0.000	.
Education								
Pre-gymnasium	−0.238	0.046**	−0.579	0.035**	−0.590	0.036**	−0.216	0.015**
Gymnasium	−0.133	0.042**	−0.280	0.027**	−0.320	0.028**	−0.114	0.01165**
Post-gymnasium	0.000	.	0.000	.	0.000	.	0.000	.
Regions								
Stockholm	0.233	0.062**	−0.457	0.052**	0.038	0.047	0.088	0.019**
Göteborg	0.120	0.071*	−0.380	0.057**	−0.234	0.055**	−0.310	0.022**
Malmö	0.289	0.081**	−0.120	0.065*	0.133	0.061*	0.069	0.024**
Urban Götaland	0.061	0.059	−0.137	0.053**	−0.201	0.046**	−0.243	0.019**
Urban Svealand	0.183	0.069**	−0.163	0.059**	−0.080	0.052	0.004	0.022
Urban Norrland	0.087	0.086	−0.222	0.070**	−0.224	0.063**	−0.089	0.026**
Rural Götaland	0.324	0.063**	0.085	0.058	−0.072	0.052	−0.012	0.022
Rural Svealand	0.203	0.072**	−0.070	0.065	−0.007	0.054	0.243	0.024**
Rural Norrland	0.000	.	0.000	.	0.000	.	0.000	.
Sex								
Men					0.135	0.032**	−0.111	0.010**
Women					0.000		0.000	.
Number of households	30103		57659		41915		276094	
McFadden, R2	0.160		0.196		0.089		0.093	

Table 7.   *Estimates of a logit model of tenure choice (if owner) for households migrating to another region (model D2), by household type*

Variables	Couples without children		Couples with children		Singles with children		Singles	
	Estimate	SE	Estimate	SE	Estimate	SE	Estimate	SE
Intercept	0.516	0.255*	0.710	1.165	1.407	0.543**	−0.395	0.102**
Age								
0–24	−0.924	0.317**	−1.089	1.166	−1.069	0.523*	−0.099	0.084
25–39	0.027	0.186	−0.272	1.151	−0.699	0.503	0.250	0.083**
40–64	0.455	0.170**	−0.273	1.151	−0.772	0.503	0.745	0.083**
65–79	0.225	0.164	−0.286	1.184	−0.704	0.557	0.510	0.089**
80+	0	.	0	.	0	.	0	.
Family changes								
Separation	−0.099	0.095	−0.083	0.056				
Partner dies	−0.070	0.527	−0.002	0.143				
Nestleave			−0.530	0.028**				
MoveTogether	−0.443	0.163**			−0.303	0.100**	−0.439	0.076**
MoreChildren			−0.015	0.127	0.131	0.085		
Youngest child leaves the parental home			0.197	0.141				
No change	0	.	0	.	0	.	0	.
Disposable income								
Quintile 1	−1.441	0.119**	−1.316	0.104**	−0.744	0.128**	−0.756	0.033**
Quintile 2	−0.972	0.115**	−0.590	0.114**	−0.543	0.132**	−0.829	0.035**
Quintile 3	−0.661	0.110**	−0.439	0.117**	−0.449	0.136**	−0.613	0.034**
Quintile 4	−0.379	0.110**	−0.297	0.119**	−0.287	0.138*	−0.331	0.033**
Quintile 5	0	.	0	.	0	.	0	.

Previous tenure								
Owner occupation	1.000	0.075**	0.882	0.062**	0.733	0.072**	0.506	0.022**
Rent occupation	0	.	0	.	0	.	0	.
Country of birth								
Born in Sweden	0.315	0.098**	0.812	0.075**	0.509	0.092**	0.327	0.033**
Not born in Sweden	0	.	0	.	0	.	0	.
Education								
Pre-gymnasum	0.010	0.103	−0.155	0.094*	−0.610	0.105**	0.050	0.030*
Gymnasium	0.151	0.089*	0.098	0.066	−0.381	0.083**	−0.016	0.022
Post-gymnasium	0	.	0	.	0	.	0	.
Region of origin								
Stockholm	−0.330	0.171*	−0.228	0.145	−0.951	0.170**	0.199	0.046**
Göteborg	−0.737	0.185**	−0.502	0.154**	−1.034	0.187**	−0.510	0.050**
Malmö	−0.829	0.193**	−0.190	0.172	−0.757	0.202**	−0.263	0.052**
Urban Götaland	−0.462	0.145**	−0.152	0.126	−0.610	0.155**	−0.353	0.046**
Urban Svealand	−0.202	0.162	−0.052	0.135	−0.686	0.165**	−0.131	0.048**
Urban Norrland	−0.549	0.204**	−0.746	0.160**	−1.120	0.196**	−0.733	0.055**
Rural Götaland	−0.068	0.150	0.272	0.135*	−0.244	0.163	0.190	0.050**
Rural Svealand	0.270	0.162*	0.427	0.140**	−0.149	0.169	0.396	0.053**
Rural Norrland	0	.	0	.	0	.	0	.
Sex								
Men					−0.045	0.100	−0.172	0.019**
Women					0.000	.	0.000	.
Number of households	8342		12002		6497		90027	
McFadden R2	0.143		0.149		0.076		0.096	

influenced by whether or not the household has children. Households in the middle-age range and without children are more likely to choose ownership when they arrive as in-migrants to a new region, than other age groups and households with children. The choice of rental housing among singles without children is strengthened if the single person is a man and not a woman. According to our result, family events are most likely to have a negative effect on the probability to choose owner occupation. In summary, comparing tenure choices between households making regional moves and households moving locally shows that the effects of former tenure, household disposable income, and country of birth are the same while the effects of age, education, and family events differ across the models.

6. Results from simulations

Assumptions about regional unemployment and housing prices are the main macro-assumptions affecting your simulations of regional mobility. First, we discuss simulation results at the macro-level, presenting changes in regional population size, and secondly we move to interesting features at a more disaggregated level.

The metropolitan and urban regions increase their population during the simulated period, while the population in the rural regions decreases. In Figure 4, we present the model predictions of regional population shares. The regions exhibit different growth patterns. The large metropolitan regions Stockholm, Göteborg, and Malmö grow relatively the other

Figure 4. Population shares by region

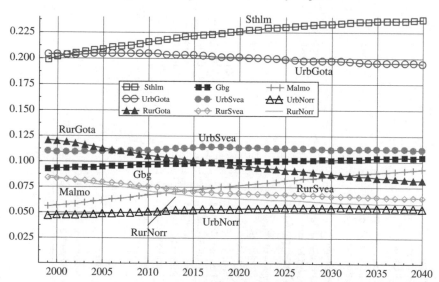

Table 8. *Average annual growth rates in percent by region*

Region	Annual growth rate in per cent
Stockhom	0.96
Göteborg	0.81
Malmö	1.76
Urban Götaland	0.41
Urban Svealand	0.56
Urban Norrland	0.87
Rural Götaland	−0.43
Rural Svealand	−0.12
Rural Norrland	−0.42

regions. According to the simulation, the largest rise in population will take place in the metropolitan region of Stockholm. It increases its share from 20 to 24 percent. Another expanding region is the Malmö metropolitan region. Its share increases from 5.5 to 9.5 percent. The Malmö region has the highest annual growth rate of all regions during the period of simulation (Table 8). The metropolitan region of Göteborg is expected to get only a modest increase in population size. The share of the other urban regions is quite stable. Urban Svealand and Norrland grow slightly, whereas urban Götaland decreases. The annual growth rate in urban Norrland is even higher than that for the metropolitan region of Göteborg. The rural regions decrease. The share of rural Götaland decreases about 4 percentage from 12 to 8 percent. The annual decline in growth rate is as high as in rural Norrland.

The regional population growth and age distribution are both affected by fertility, mortality, migration between regions, and international immigration as well as emigration. The migration model refers to the domestic migration pattern only, while national migration is fed into the simulation model exogenously. To facilitate an evaluation of all demographic components, we have simulated migration, fertility and mortality for selected regions. We find that the domestic net migration, as well as the natural population increase are negative in the long run in the Stockholm region (not shown). In the end of the simulated period, more people move from the region than into the region. At the same time, the natural population increase is almost zero. However, the total population increase in the region is an effect of positive net immigration from abroad.

The simulated development in the Stockholm region contrasts to the net effect of fertility and mortality in the Malmö metropolitan region (Figure 5). There is a natural population increase as well as a positive effect of net migration, although it decreases at the end of the simulated period. The natural population growth will become negative in Urban Götaland during almost the entire simulated period. This is an effect of an increasing number of deaths due to an aging population. The decline is only partly compensated by a positive net migration to the region. The population

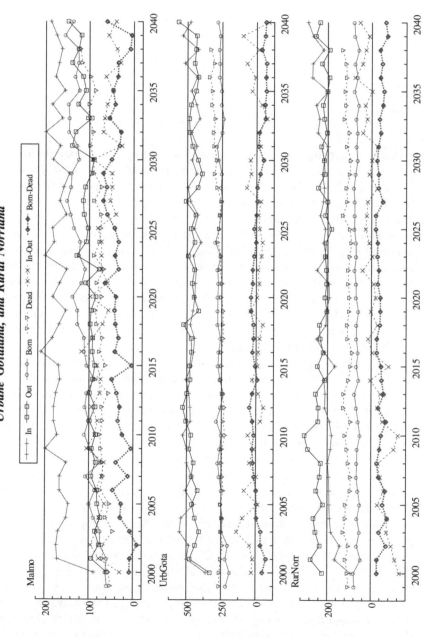

Figure 5. Population growth by migration, mortality, and fertility per region in the period 1999–2040 for regions Malmoe, Urbane Götaland, and Rural Norrland

share decreases. Despite a population decrease in rural Norrland, it is interesting to note that net migration to the region becomes positive in the end of period, as a result of a stable out-migration and an increasing migration to the region.

The inter-regional migration may enhance the natural changes in the age distribution within regions. The age distribution within regions is an important factor determining the demand and supply of health care and social care for the elderly. For this reason we have simulated and analyzed the regional age distributions.

Figure 6 shows that the age distribution in 2000 is stochastically dominated by the age distributions in 2040 for most regions. Malmö is an exception, its age distribution is more or less constant over time. The share of population aged 65 and above varies both over time and by region. For example, in Stockholm, the share of 65+ increases from about 12 to 20 percent. For rural Norrland there is an increase from 20 to 30 percent, whereas in Malmo the increase is much more moderate, just 3 percent. Figure 7 shows the distribution of age in 2040 for selected regions. The region to the right (Rural Norrland) will get a large share of elderly person, whereas the region to the left (Malmö) will get a younger population.

The difference in age structure across regions has implication for the support of elderly. The dependency ratio is calculated for each region over the period of simulation. We use two alternative definitions of the dependency ratio. The first part of Figure 8 shows the ratio of the total population to the number of gainfully employed, and the second part the ratio of number of individuals younger than 16 or older than 65 and the number of individuals aged 16–64. Bay and large both definitions give approximately the same picture. The dependency ratio of the three rural regions are much higher than for the rest of the country and the difference increases.

Earlier in this chapter, we have discussed tenure choice. We now turn to the corresponding simulation results.

The share of the total population living in ownership housing is simulated to increase considerably in the period 2000–2020. This is primarily an effect of population ageing. The age group 65+ increases. The share of each age group that owns a dwelling changes a little but with no clear trend (Figure 11). For the rest of the period the increase in ownership is not as strong (Figure 9). The number of renters aged 65–74 relative to the total population will also increase because the size of this age group increases (Figure 10). After 2020 it decreases while the relative number of older renters increase. The share of renters in the age group 65–74 also increases in the first twenty years (Figure 10). This is also the result of the increased size of this age group. After 2020 this share of renters decrease, while the shares of renters in the older age groups continue to increase. Even if the total share of people owning their dwelling increases, population ageing will not change the general relation between the share of owners and age. This share still decreases with increasing age (Figure 11).

Figure 6. Cumulative distribution of age by region in 2000 and 2040

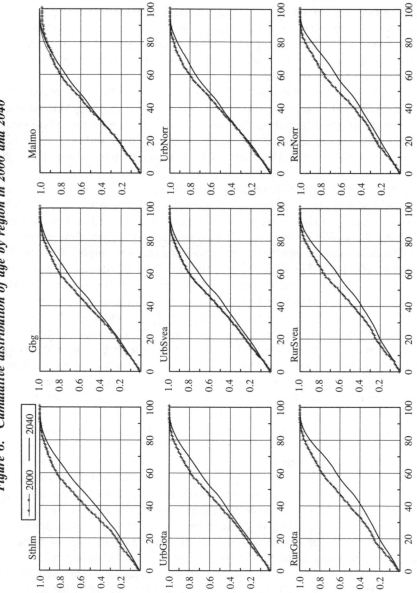

Figure 7. **Cumulative distribution of age in 2040 for regions Stockholm, Malmoe, and Rural Norrland**

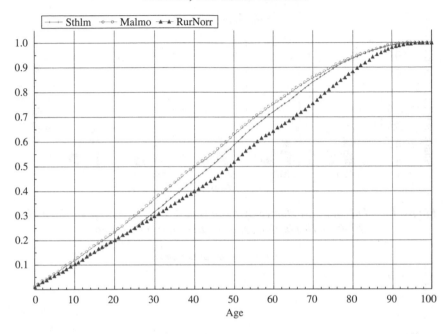

Figure 8. **Dependency ratio by region**

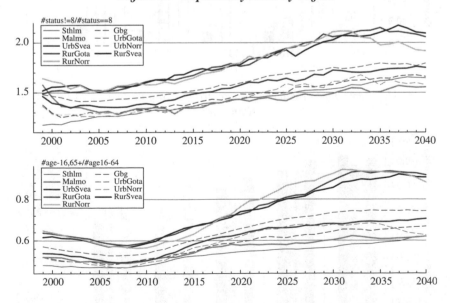

Figure 9. **The share of elderly living in ownership by age in the period 2000–2040 (in thousands of the total population)**

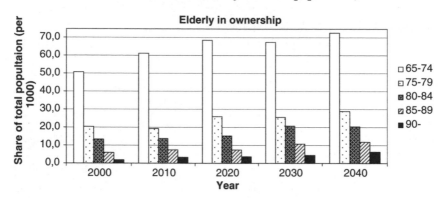

Figure 10. **The share of elderly living in rental housing by age in the period 2000–2040 (in thousands of the total population)**

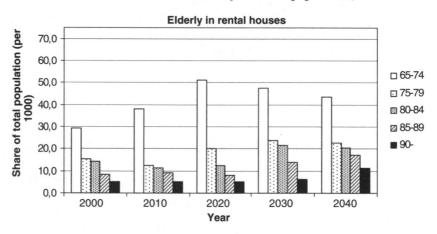

Figure 11. **The share of elderly per age group living in ownership by year of simulation**

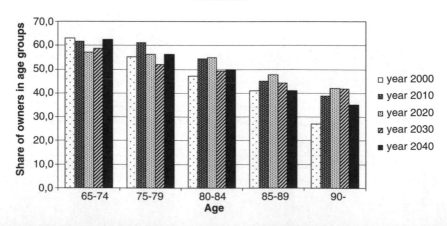

7. Conclusions

The results from the simulation show that the concentration of population toward large urban regions will continue in the next coming decades. The metropolitan regions of Stockholm, Göteborg, and Malmö have continued to increase their share of the Swedish population. The annual growth rates in the metropolitan regions differ substantially from the rest of Sweden. In year 2000, one-third of the population lived in these areas. Forty years later the proportion of the total population has risen to about 45 percent according to the simulation.

The redistribution of people between regions is a matter of consequence for the age distribution at the regional level. The result shows that the average age in the rural regions increases more than in the other regions during the period of simulation. The dependency ratio in the rural regions was higher already in year 2000 compared to the rest of the country. In the simulations it increases for all regions in Sweden. However, at the end of the simulation period, the dependency ratios for the rural regions have become considerably higher than for the rest of the country. This difference gives an indication of where in the country problems could arise concerning support and health care of frail elders. A high service rate may be difficult to achieve in municipalities in these regions.

Most elderly people live in regular housing, only a few lives in various forms of institutional care. Ownership is the most predominant tenure for elderly people. Tenant ownership is regarded as ownership in this analysis. However, housing tenure varies by the age of the elderly. In the age 65–79, ownership dominates as housing tenure. Among the eldest, renting is the most common form of tenure though.

Many elderly do not change tenure when they move to new housing. This holds for renters as well as for owners and elderly living in tenant ownership housing. But there are transition into renting from ownership and they increase with increasing age. According to our simulations these transitions preserve the general pattern of decreasing ownership with increasing age after the age of 65. But in all these age groups the share of owners increase somewhat.

References

Abramsson, M. and U. Fransson (2004), "The first years as independent actors in the housing market: young households in a Swedish municipality", *Journal of Housing and the Built Environment*, Vol. 19, pp. 145–168.

Amcoff, J. (2000), "Samtida bosättning på svensk landsbygd", Kulturgeografiska institutionen, Uppsala universitet.

Anas, A., U. Jirlow, J. Gustafsson, B. Hårsman and F. Snickars (1985), "The swedish housing market: structures, policy and issues", *Scandinavian Housing & Planning Research*, Vol. 2(3–4), pp. 169–187.

Andersson, E. (2004), Sveriges äldrelandskap. Äldrelandskapet. Äldres boende och flyttningar. U. Fransson, Institutet för bostads- och urbanforskning, Uppsala universitet. Forskningsrapport 2004:1.

Andersson, K., E. von Essen and B. Turner (2004), "Bostadspolitiska förändringar i Europa", Arbetsrapport nr 46. Institutet för bostads- och urbanforskning, Uppsala universitet.

Andersson, R. (2000), "Varför flyttar man?" Hemort Sverige. B. Ornbrant, Integrationsverket.

Andersson, S., L.E. Borgegård, et al. (1992), "Då kan jag springa ner på stan-Om medelålders småhusägarhushålls prioriteringar i framtida boende", Statens institut för byggnadsforskning, Gävle och Kulturgeografiska institutionen, Umeå universitet.

Arman, R. and L. Lindahl (2005), "Nyttan och värdet av bostadsanpassningar i olika perspektiv", Delrapport 1, FoU/Väst.

Beaverstock, J.V., P.J. Taylor, et al. (1999), "A roster of world cities", *Cities*, Vol. 16(6), pp. 445–458.

Bengtsson, B. (1991), *Att lägga marknaden till rätta-Bostadsfrågan under 1900-talet. Arkiv i nuet Om arkitektur och arkiv*, Arkitekturmuseet: Årsbok.

Bengtsson, B. (1995), *Bostaden-välfärdsstatens marknadsvara. Statsvetenskapliga institutionen*, Uppsala: Uppsala universitet.

Bengtsson, B. and J. Kemeny (1997), "Från en generell marknadspolitik till en bostadspolitik för dom andra", Bostadspolitik för tjugohundratalet. Återtåg och nya värden. B. Turner and E. Vedung. Gävle, Meyers Information & Förlag AB.

Bergenstråhle, S. (1984), *Bruksvärdering och hyressättning i Stockholm, Göteborg och Malmö*, Stockholm: Byggforskningsrådet.

Björnsson, L. and L.E. Borgegård (1989), "Intervjustudie av äldre och deras boende i Västerås kommun", Med inriktning på de serviceboende. Del II. SB:21, Statens institut för byggnadsforskning.

Borgegård, L.E. and U. Fransson (2002), "Lokala och regionala flyttningar och boendekarriärer bland äldre", Tillgänglighet och boende. Bilagedel D till Riv ålderstrappan! Livslopp i förändring (SOU 2002:29).

Boverket. (1995), *Boende för äldre-om vanliga bostäder och särskilda boendeformer*, Karlskrona: Boverket.

Boverket. (2002), *Hur bor morgondagens äldre? En nyckelfråga i kommunernas boendeplanering*, Karlskrona: Boverket.

Boyle, P., K. Halfacree and V. Robinson (1998), *Exploring Contemporary Migration*, Harlow: Longman.

Bråmå, Å. (2006), "Studies in the dynamics of residential segregation", Kulturgeografiska institutionen, Uppsala universitet.

Bäcklund, D. (2002), "Industrilokalisering under massproduktionens epok", Industrialisemens tid. Ekonomisk-historiska perspektiv på svensk industriell omvandling under 200 år. M. Isacson and M. Morell. Stockholm, SNS Förlag.

Cadwallader, M. (1992), *Migration and Residential Mobility, Macro and Micro Approaches*, London: The University of Wisconsin Press.

Champion, A.G. (1989), *Counterurbanization: the concept and methodological challenge. Counterurbanization. The changing pace and nature of population deconcentration*, London: Edward Arnold.

Champion, T. and T. Fielding (eds.) (1992), "Migration processes and patterns", *Research progress and prospects*, Vol. 1, London: Belhaven Press.

Champion, T., S. Fotheringham, P. Rees, P. Boyle and J. Stillwell (1998), "The determinants of migration flows in England: a review of existing data and evidence", Report, University of New Castle.

Clark, D. (2003), *Urban World/Global City*, London: Routledge.

Clark, W.A.V. (1986), *Human Migration*, Beverly Hills: SAGE.

Clark, W.A.V. and F. Dieleman (1996), *Households and Housing. Choice and Outcomes in the Housing Market*, New Brunswick, NJ: Center for Urban Policy Research.

Cribier, F. and A. Kych (1993), "A comparison of retirement migration from Paris and London", *Environment and Planning A*, Vol. 25, pp. 1399–1420.

ECB. (2003), *Structural Factors in the EU Housing Market*, Frankfurt am Main: European Central Bank.

Ekström, M. and B. Danermark (1993), "Migration patterns and migration motives among the elderly", *Scandinavian Housing & Planning Research*, Vol. 10(2), pp. 75–89.

Englund, P., P.H. Hendershott and B. Turner (1995), "The tax reform and the housing market", *Swedish Economic Policy Review*, Vol. 2, pp. 318–356.

Fielding, A.J. (1992), "Migration and social mobility: south east England as an escalator region", *Regional Studies*, Vol. 26(1), pp. 1–15.

Försäkringskassan. Online. Available: http://www.forsakringskassan.se/språk/eng/bobidrag/, 10 Jan 2008.

Fransson, U. and M. Eklöf (2007), "Estimate of geographic mobility in Sweden", Working paper. Institute for Housing Research, Uppsala University.

Haffner, M.E.A. and C. Dol (2000), *Housing statistics in the European Union 2000*. The Hague: Ministerie van Volkshuisvesting, Ruimtelijke Ordening en Milieubeheer.

Heinstedt, L. (1992), "Boendemönster som kunskapskälla" En studie av allmännyttan i Stockholms län, Statens institut för byggnadsforskning.

Herbert, D.T. and C.J. Thomas (1990), *Cities in space: city as place*, London: David Fulton Publishers.

Hjort, S. (2005), "Rural migration in Sweden: a new green wave or a blue ripple", Kulturgeografiska Institutionen, Umeå Universitet.

Lind, H. (1997), "Boendepolitik utan hyrespolitik", Kommentar till en lucka i den bostadspolitiska utredningen. Bostadspolitik för tjugohundratalet. Återtåg och nya värden. B. Turner and E. Vedung. Gävle, Meyers Information & förlag AB.

Lindgren, J. and I. Lindström (2004), *Aktuellt om äldreomsorgen*, Svenska: Kommunförbundet.

Lindgren, U. (2003), "Who is the counter-urban mover? Evidence from the Swedish urban system", *International Journal of Population Geography*, Vol. 9, pp. 399–418.

Lindström, B. and O. Åhlund (1982), Åldrande och boende. Att bo i det ordinära bostadsbeståndet, Arkitektursektionen, Lunds universitet.

Litwak, E. and C. Longino (1987), "Migration patterns among the elderly: a developmental perspective", *The Gerontologist*, Vol. 27, pp. 266–272.

Lundin, L. (1988), *Mobility and Housing of the Elderly. Housing, Policy, and Urban Innovation, ENHR, Amsterdam*, Gävle, Sweden: The National Swedish Institute for Building Research.

Lundin, L. (1991), "Movers and stayers on the housing market in the postparental stage: the Swedish case", *Scandinavian Housing & Planning Research*, Vol. 8(1), pp. 19–24.

Marshall, V. and B. McPherson (1994), *Aging*, Peterborough: Broadview Press.

Nygren, O. and L.-O. Persson (2002), Det enkelriktade Sverige. Tjänstesektorn och den framtida regionala befolkningsutvecklingen., TCO-rapport.

Öberg, S. (1997), "Theories on inter-regional migration: an overview", in: H.H. Blotevogel and A.J. Fielding, editors, *People, Jobs and Mobility in the New Europe*, Chichester: Wiley.

Öberg, S., S. Scheele, et al. (1993), "Migration among the elderly, the Stockholm case", *Espace, Population, Societes*, Vol. 3, pp. 503–551.

Paulsson, J. (1985), De äldre. Bostadsboken. S. Thiberg, Statens råd för byggnadsforskning. T8:1985.

Priemus, H. and F. Dieleman (2002), "Social housing policy in the European Union; past, present and perspectives", *Urban Studies*, Vol. 39(2), pp. 191–200.

Rees, P. and M. Kupiszewski (1999), *Internal migration and regional population dynamics in Europe: a synthesis*, Correction Demography, Strasbourg: Council of Europe.

Rossi, P.H. (1955), *Why Families Moves. A Study in the Social Psychology of Urban Residential Mobility*, Glencoe.

Salt, J. (2005), *Current trends in international migration in Europe*, Strasbourg: Council of Europé Publ.

Scanlon, K. and C.M.E. Whitehead (2004), *Housing Tenure and Mortgage Systems: A Survey of 19 Countries*, Cambridge: European Network for Housing Research Conference.

Söderström, B. (1993), Vem tar ansvar för bostadsförsörjningen? Göteborg, Svenska Kommunförbundet och Kommentus Förlag AB.

Statistics Sweden (2004), Bostads- och byggnadsstatistisk årsbok 2004. Statistiska centralbyrån.

Svensson, K.A.S. (1998), "Neither market nor command economy: Swedish negotiative rent setting in practice", *Scandinavian Housing & Planning Research*, Vol. 15, pp. 79–94.

Turner, B. (1983). Hyror och hyrespolitik, Statens institut för byggnadsforskning.

Turner, B. and C.M.E. Whitehead (2002), "Reducing housing subsidy: Swedish Housing Policy in an International Context", *Urban Studies*, Vol. 39(2), pp. 201–217.

United_Nations. (2003), *Demographic Yearbook*, New York: United Nations.

Vidén, S. and G. Lundahl (1992), Miljonprogrammets bostäder. Bevara-förnya- förbättra. Stockholm, Statens råd för byggnadsforskning.

Warnes, A.M. (1986), "The residential mobility histories of parents and children, and relationships to present proximity and social integration", *Environment and Planning A*, Vol. 18, pp. 1581–1594.

Warnes, A.M. (1994), "Cities and eldery people: recent population and distributional trends", *Urban Studies*, Vol. 31(4/5), pp. 799–816.

Warnes, A.M. and R. Ford (1995), "Housing aspirations and migration in later life: developments during the 1980s", *Papers in Regional science*, Vol. 74(4), pp. 361–387.

Wikhall, M. (2001), *Universiteten och kompetenslandskapet. Effekter av den högre utbildningens tillväxt och regionala spridning i Sverige. Institutionen för kulturgeografi och ekonomisk geografi*, Lund: Lunds universitet.

CHAPTER 8

The Income of the Baby Boomers

Lennart Flood*, Anders Klevmarken and Andreea Mitrut

1. Introduction

While several studies have examined the fiscal consequences of the aging problem, there has been less focus on the level or on the distribution of income.[1] The main objective of this chapter is thus to analyze the distribution of income of the baby-boom generation in comparison with earlier and later generations. Data from the Luxemburg Income Study (LIS) are used for the international comparison, data from the panel study HEK and the LINDA panel for historical income earning profiles, and finally SESIM to forecast future income. Future income for the baby-boom generation is predominantly income from pension. To better understand the relative income position of the retired, we will focus on replacement rates and similar measures that relate the income of the retired to their own previous income or, respectively, to the incomes of the working generations. We intend to address the following topics:

- Incomes and pensions in Sweden compared to a few OECD countries.
- Income and labor force participation in the period 1992–2003.
- Future incomes under different scenarios; effects of alternative assumptions about the return on financial assets and about the age of retirement.

---

* Corresponding author.

[1] Recent exceptions are Mantovani et al. (2005) who use the micro-simulation model EUROMOD to study pension income for the EU-15. The SHARE project reports income for 55+ in Börsch-Supan et al. (2005). Income and income distribution for older households in Sweden is also discussed in Andersson et al. (2001).

CONTRIBUTIONS TO ECONOMIC ANALYSIS
VOLUME 285   ISSN: 0573-8555
DOI:10.1016/S0573-8555(07)00008-9

- The relative importance of the three pillars in the pension system – the public pensions, the occupational pensions, and the private pensions – and income from capital.
- A comparison of different definitions of replacement rates.
- Income of the pensioners in relation to the active population.
- Distribution of income and incidence of poverty.

Since SESIM is of a fundamental importance for this analysis, we also give a short presentation of the income-generating mechanisms in the model, focusing on earnings and income from capital.

2. Sweden in an international comparison

According to Statistical Sweden (2003), the level of equalized disposable income in Sweden is below the average level for the EU-15 countries and the income distribution is more compressed than in most other countries. Figure 1 presents the level of disposable income for households aged 55–90 in a sample of OECD countries. Data come from the LIS and include single as well as non-single households.[2] As expected the Scandinavian countries have the most compressed income distribution. The relation between the top and bottom deciles is lowest for Norway (2,6) followed by Finland and Sweden (2,7). The US has the highest ratio (5,3), followed by Spain (4,6), Italy (4,1), and the UK (3,9). The high value for the US is due to a high level of income in the ninth decile (about $57 000), and not from a low first decile. The income in the first decile is approximately at the same level for several countries, the exceptions being lower incomes in Spain, only about $5500, and Italy $7200 and higher in Canada and Norway $12 700 and $11 600, respectively. The median value is highest in the US, almost $25 000, which is more than twice the median level in Spain ($11 500). Sweden with a median income of $17 400 is ranked in the middle.

Finland, Sweden, and Norway have the smallest difference between the lowest and the highest decile and the income dispersion is highest in the United States, Canada, Austria, Italy, and Germany due to a very skewed right tail. According to Whitehouse (2003), these are all countries with a relative small maximum benefit from the public pension schemes. Thus, private pension plans are more important and since these plans lack a ceiling a higher income distribution can be expected. While in countries like

---

[2] The household size is controlled for by dividing household income by the square root of number of household members. Conversion to US dollars uses OECD purchasing power parities (PPP).

Figure 1. The income distribution of households aged 55–90 in a few selected OECD countries

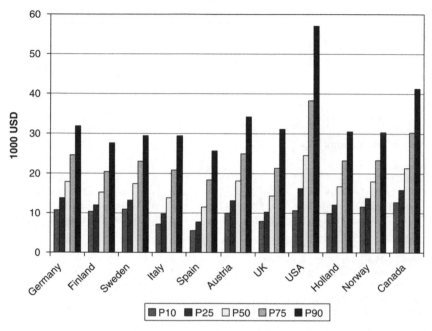

Note: Net income divided by square root of family members in households aged 55–90.
The income year is 1999 for the UK and Holland and 2000 for all others. P10 income
at first decile, P25 at first quartile, P50 at median, P75 at third quartile, and P90
at upper decile
Source: Luxemburg Income Studies (LIS)

Sweden, Norway, Finland, and Holland public pensions and transfers dominate and make the income distribution more equal.

A large component of the 55–90 years old retiree's income is income from pension, the size of this component depends to a large extent on previous market work and on labor force participation rates. In Table 1 LIS data have been used to classify individuals into pensioners or employed.[3] There are substantial differences in cross-country retirement behavior. In the youngest age interval (51–55), Italian men stand out with almost 35 percent pensioners and an employment rate of only 65 percent. For all other countries the corresponding retirement rate is between 4 and

---

[3] It should be noted that this classification is not without problem and that there are country differences in definitions and categories, and also that the sample size is small for some countries.

Table 1.   Shares of pensioners and workers by age for selected OECD countries

Age	Status	Germany	Finland	Sweden	Italy	Spain	Austria	UK	USA	Norway
Male										
51–55	Pensioner	3.8	7.3	6.8	34.8	0	–	9.0	4.6	4.9
	Market work	84.6	85.5	89.8	65.2	87.5	–	85.1	92.3	91.8
56–60	Pensioner	16.3	24.1	9.7	57.7	7.6	54.8	14.5	10.7	12.1
	Market work	59.9	64.3	87.9	38.2	61.1	37.9	66.0	80.8	85.0
61–65	Pensioner	69.8	69.7	38.2	79.2	48.4	94.7	42.1	33.7	38.3
	Market work	24.7	28.1	58.6	18.2	27.6	4.6	35.8	58.7	58.2
66–70	Pensioner	93.0	95.5	87.6	94.0	96.2	100.0	87.5	59.0	80.4
	Market work	6.4	4.5	12.4	5.3	2.2	0	12.5	33.7	18.1
Female										
51–55	Pensioner	9.3	6.1	10.3	11.8	0	3.8	–	7.3	13.9
	Market work	60.0	80.8	83.9	29.0	23.3	46.2	66.7	70.9	74.0
56–60	Pensioner	13.5	21.8	12.2	26.3	0	34.3	14.8	15.7	20.3
	Market work	45.9	59.6	80.6	17.5	18.9	19.8	48.4	61.9	65.4
61–65	Pensioner	68.7	70.7	49.3	50.9	8.3	59.6	81.3	41.0	38.1
	Market work	9.9	24.22	42.4	4.5	7.4	2.2	18.7	39.8	44.6
66–70	Pensioner	91.6	98.1	93.6	61.5	31.5	52.1	93.5	66.5	77.8
	Market work	2.5	1.9	6.4	1.1	1.4	2.1	6.5	18.8	15.3

Source: Luxemburg Income Studies (LIS).
Note: No information available for Holland or Canada.

9 percent. The highest employment rate for young males is in the United States (92 percent), followed by Norway and Sweden. In most countries there is a strong increase in retirement after age 55. The highest share for the males in the age bracket 56–60 is in Italy (58 percent) closely followed by Austria (55 percent), and Finland (24 percent). The lowest share is in Spain, less than 8 percent, and for the other countries the share is somewhere between 9 and 16 percent. For males aged 61–65 there is a clear division into two groups of countries; a high share of retired, 70–95 percent – Germany, Finland, Italy, and Austria – and the rest with a much lower share 34–48 percent. Also in the oldest age group there are large differences in retirement, from the highest in Austria (100 percent), Spain (96 percent), and Finland (95 percent) to the lowest in the United States (59 percent), Norway (80 percent), and Sweden (88 percent).

For both males and females there are large categories not included in Table 1 namely unemployed and housewives. For the youngest ages three countries have a female employment share below 50 percent – Spain (23 percent), Italy (29 percent), and Austria (46 percent) – in Germany and the UK the share is between 60 and 70 percent and for the rest above 70 percent (highest in Sweden 84 percent). The cross-country differences in female employment rate are substantial for the age bracket 56–60.

Two groups of countries can be identified: low rates ranging from 17 to 48 percent in Italy, Spain, Austria, Germany, and the UK; and high rates ranging from 60 to 81 percent with the highest in Sweden. For the oldest, the highest employment rate is found in the United States (19 percent) followed by Norway, the UK, and Sweden. In some countries, it is possible to distinguish the self-employed as a separate category and this group stands out in terms of late retirement.

The female employment share plays a crucial role for the standard of living of elderly households. Countries characterized by the "male bread winner model" are all ranked low in household disposable income. Income below the first quartile is lowest in countries with the lowest female employment rates. Thus, Spain, Italy, UK, and Austria have a disposable income below $10 000 in the first quartile.

Comparing pension and pension system across countries is complicated. However, a recent OECD report, Whitehouse (2003), compares the values of pension entitlements in nine OECD countries. The paper includes both public and private pensions. An important distinction in this study is the difference between countries with a low or high ceiling in the pension system. Countries like Canada, Germany, Japan, the United Kingdom, and the United States have ceilings for contributions and/or benefits in the mandatory system. Finland and the Netherlands have no ceilings, while Sweden and Italy have a high ceiling. At low level of earnings, the benefits are similar in all the countries, but at higher levels, benefits do not increase in countries with ceiling and increase if there is no ceiling. Countries with high ceilings provide income insurance through the mandatory retirement system. The replacement rate in those systems can be high even for high-income earners. In countries with low ceilings the mandatory systems are focused more on redistribution, only ensuring that all pensioners meet a reasonable minimum income standard.

It is also important to remember the role played by the tax and benefits system. In most countries older people pay less income tax compared to people of working age. Some treat pension income more favorably than earnings, and most do not levy social security contributions on older people. These policies mean that the tax burden of older people is lower than for people of working age. Whitehouse (2003) reports that at an average income the average tax burden (in the nine countries studied) is 10 percentage points lower for pensioners than it is for workers. Therefore, differences in taxes between pensioners and workers are an important means of governments to support people during their retirement. The so-called net replacement rate – the value of pension benefits for a full-career worker relative to earnings when working, is a measure that captures this kind of compensation. Again according to Whitehouse, on average, one-fifth of the net replacement rate for a worker is due to tax differentials rather than to the pension system.

Figure 2.   Equalized disposable income 1975–2003 (means per family unit in thousands of SEK, 2003 price level)

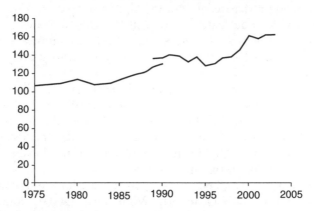

Note: Disposable income includes realized capital gains
Source: Statistical Sweden (2003, p. 11)

3. The Swedish experience

3.1. Changes in income 1975–2003

In the period 1975–2003 mean disposable income per household, adjusted by an equivalence scale, on average increased by a modest 1.5 percent annually in fixed prices.[4] Figure 2 details these changes with the recession in the first half of the 1990s and the subsequent recovery. The discontinuity in the beginning of the 1990s is explained by changes in the definition of income concepts at the time of a major tax reform in 1991–1992. Similar to many other countries the inequality of income has increased, in particular in the 1990s, influenced by the boom in the stock market at the end of this period (Figure 3). We find, for instance, that elderly and married or cohabiting partners gained more in income than young and singles. Families with children also experienced a rather low growth in income.

3.1.1. Income and labor force participation of the baby-boom generation in 1992–2003

In the sequel, we will not focus on cross-sectional distributions but rather on cohort differences.[5] Because we are interested in the baby-boom

---

[4] The household concept "family unit" does not include adult children living with their parents. They are considered singles.

[5] The data used in this section comes from the Swedish register-based LINDA and consists of a large panel of individuals and their household members, from 1992 to 2003. All figures in this section are based on a balanced panel from LINDA.

Figure 3. *Gini coefficients for equalized disposable income per family unit*

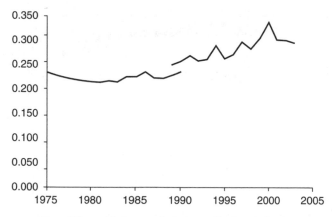

Note: Disposable income includes realized capital gains
Source: Statistical Sweden (2003, p. 12)

generation we follow closely the economic status of those born in 1940–1949. Also, as a comparison, we consider two older cohorts (born in 1934 and 1937) as well as two younger cohorts (born in 1952 and 1955).

For most people income from market work is the most important income source. To study changes in labor force participation as people age and across generations are thus important in order to understand differences in income. Figures 4 and 5 show the labor force participation rates for men and women belonging to the birth cohorts mentioned. Participation is here defined as having income from employment or business.

In 1992, the cohort born in 1934 was 58-year-old and those born in 1955 were 37. As expected these cohorts start out with a high participation rate, males with a rate close to 95 percent and women with one close to 90 percent. Due to the recession in 1992–1993 there was a decrease for all cohorts, but the long-run effect was quite different across cohorts. The youngest cohorts recovered immediately, while the participation rates among men and women aged 52 and 58 in 1992 never recover but dropped monotonically down to almost 50 percent for men and 40 percent for women in 1999 (when they were 65 years old). There was an asymmetry in the effect of the recession, young workers returned to work after the recession, while many of the older workers never returned. However, we should perhaps not overemphasize the effect of the 1992 recession on labor force participation. Even without a recession we should have seen a withdrawal from the labor market among these cohorts, in particular after the age of 60. At the age of 64, one year before the typical retirement age, the labor force participation rate was low: 55 percent for men and only 42 percent for women. These differences in labor force participation explain

Figure 4.   Male Labor force participation rates

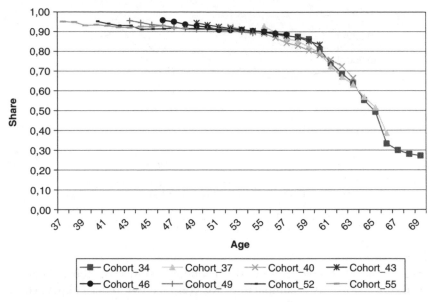

Source: LINDA data 1992–2003

Figure 5.   Female Labor force participation rates

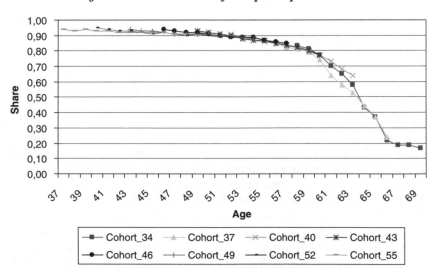

Source: LINDA data 1992–2003

Figure 6. ***Male incomes from employment and business in year 2000 prices***

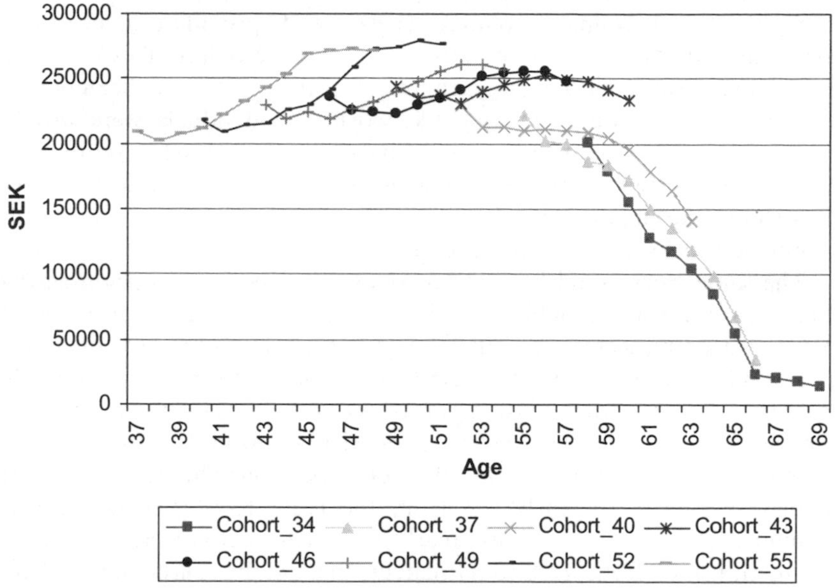

Source: LINDA data 1992–2003

much of the income differences with increasing age as well as cohort differences in income.

Figure 6 shows the income from employment and business.[6] These income estimates include all individuals regardless of working status. Compared to the corresponding graphs for labor force participation, this graph illustrates once more how the 1992s recession influences labor incomes for the cohorts considered. There is a decrease in mean income in 1992, but also a recovery for all cohorts except the oldest ones (cohorts 1934,1937, and 1940). The drop for these old cohorts reflects the decrease in participation. We also observe that the youngest cohorts (1955, 1952) recover faster compared to the middle ones (1949, 1946, 1943). Apart from a lower level of earnings the corresponding profiles for females are similar.

Note that the earnings profiles discussed above include income for workers as well as non-workers. If we only consider income for those who work the recovery trend is more evident for all cohorts, including the oldest ones. Females born in 1937, have an almost constant income from work

---

[6] In reality income from employment is the all dominant source. We use income at fixed year 2000 prices.

from age 55 to age 62, followed by a sharp decrease. Compared to the two oldest cohorts, the 1940 cohort recovers faster but, also, much slower if compared to the youngest cohorts. These trends provide evidence of an increasing number of part-time retirees among the oldest. This raises the interesting question of the long-term effect of the crisis in the beginning of the nineties. Because many old age working individuals were offered attractive occupational pensions (see Chapter 7) they chose to retire early. Since we intend to forecast the income of the elderly this is important and it also shows the importance of allowing for differences in outcome of an economic shocks across birth cohorts.

The same story could be told based on incomes from pensions. Male incomes from pension, public as well as private, are presented in Figure 7. Again, we see an increase for all cohorts but much stronger for the oldest as a result of a significant decrease in the labor force participation. The increase in income from pension is starting with age 58–59 and continues through age 65. Then we observe a relatively constant income because people start to collect old age social security pension. This relatively sharp increase is due to the early exit from the labor force, which was very common among the old cohorts (early retirement). It is usually the case, during transition from work to retirement, that people collect benefits from the public sector such as disability pension or unemployment compensation,

Figure 7. Male incomes from pensions in year 2000 prices

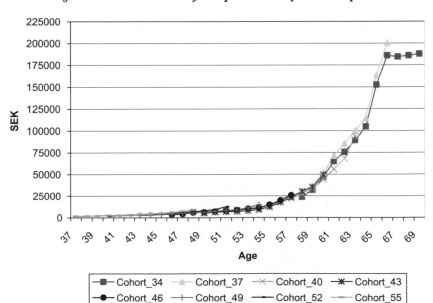

Source: LINDA data 1992–2003

Figure 8. Male incomes from capital in year 2000 prices

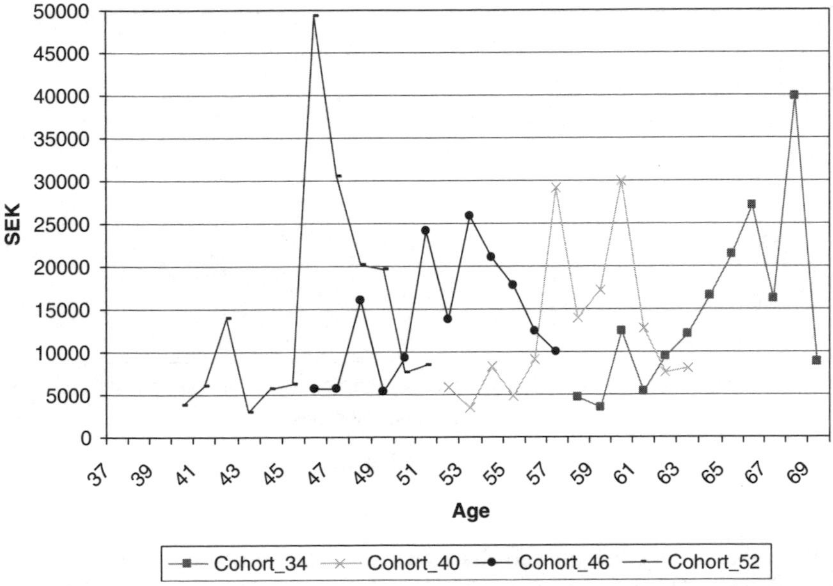

Source: LINDA data 1992–2003

while only after 65 they start to claim old age social security pension. For females the change in income with increasing age shows about the same pattern, but they reach a lower pension at the age of 70, about 125 000 SEK compared to 185 000 SEK for the males.

Because income from capital is an important income source for at least some retirees, we also analyze the cohort profiles of capital income (see Figure 8 for males only). The level, compared to income from employment or pensions, is lower and the profiles much more erratic. The distribution of income from capital is highly skewed to the right and in fact the median income for all cohorts and all years is zero. Still there is an increasing trend with increasing age, but it is to a large degree explained by the increase in the price of shares and by the fact that elderly hold a higher share of stocks in their portfolio. Both 1999 and 2000 represent periods of an unprecedented high level of the Stockholm Stock Exchange general index (see Figure 9).[7]

The subsequent dramatic decrease in stock prices moved the income distribution in the opposite direction, but the effect on average income was not that great. According to Statistical Sweden (2003) 67 percent of the

---

[7] The corresponding profiles for females have a similar variability but a lower level.

Figure 9.   The Stockholm exchange general index 1987–2003

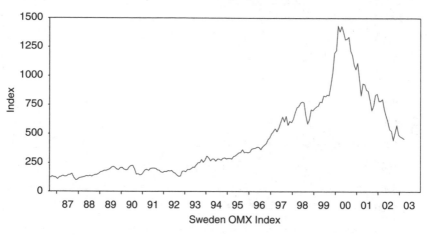

Source: EcoWin

total value of Swedish quoted shares was in 2000 owned by 1 percent of the population. Households for which shares represent both a substantial value as well as a substantial part of the portfolio are rather few. On the other hand, the decreased return on financial wealth have a broader and more general effect on other assets, like pension savings, including PPM, mutual funds, etc.[8] The unequal distribution of financial wealth explains why the boom and bust of the Stockholm Stock Exchange did not have a more dramatic effect on household average incomes.

In order to finally arrive to an analysis of cohort changes in economic standard Figure 10 shows disposable income. We see similar patterns for all cohorts except the oldest ones. Disposable income starts to decrease around the age 57–58 when workers start to withdraw from the labor market. The decline continues until age 64, one year before they start to collect old age pension, then it starts to increase. However, after 65–66 disposable income declines again. Comparing disposable income in the years immediately after retirement to that in the years prior to retirement (at age 65) we will get a rather high replacement rate but it declines as people age.

Section 5 below provides a closer look at the replacement rates based on SESIM simulations. In order to better understand these, a presentation of the models used to simulate income is given in the next section below.

---

[8] PPM (Premiepensionssystemet) administers a funded part of the social security pension system. Within PPM people invest in mutual funds.

Figure 10. Equalized disposable income (means per family unit in year 1999 prices)

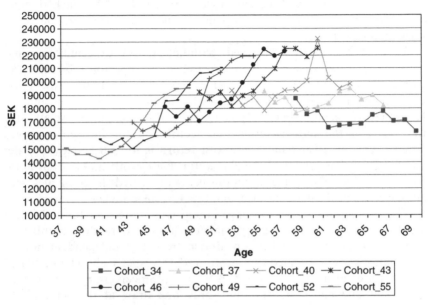

Source: LINDA data 1992–2003

4. Income generation in SESIM

4.1. Income from earnings

Due to the importance of earnings a detailed description of this process is provided. It is well known that using information from a cross section only in general produce incorrect predictions of individual earning profiles. As a consequence, it also produces incorrect predictions for a given cohort. For this reason, the estimated earnings model in SESIM is a random parameter model estimated on panel data, i.e., the same individual is observed repeatedly in the data. The model is given as:

$$Y_{it} = \mathbf{X}_{it}\boldsymbol{\beta} + \gamma_i + \varepsilon_{it}, \text{ where } \gamma_i \sim N(0, \tau^2) \text{ and } \varepsilon_{it} \sim N(0, \sigma^2)$$

The error components γ_i and ε_{it} are assumed to be independent. The random intercept γ_i is designed to represent unobserved heterogeneity (typically interpreted as ability). The implication is that earnings for a given individual are not independent over time, but independent across individuals.[9]

---

[9] For a presentation of statistical models for panel data see, for example, Baltagai (2001).

The earnings equation is estimated on a 4-year panel and includes in the X-vector variables such as; experience, highest level of education, marital status, and nationality. Separate models are estimated for each occupational sector as well as for each gender. The dependent variable is the logarithm of earnings.

Table 2 shows the estimated parameters. As expected, earnings increase at a decreasing rate in experience. Except for self-employed, women have a lower return on experience as well as a flatter experience-earning profile. There is an educational premium in all sectors and the largest return on a university degree (compared to compulsory level) is for the males in the state governmental sector and for the self-employed females. On the other hand, the lowest return is for self-employed males and females in the private blue-collar sector. Nationality and marital status have only minor effects, the exceptions being that Swedish born males, self-employed or in the state governmental sector, have higher earnings.

The simulations of the earnings equation is based on the individual attributes in X_{it}, the estimated parameters $\hat{\boldsymbol{\beta}}$ and the random numbers $\tilde{\gamma}_i$ and $\tilde{\varepsilon}_{ij}$. The random numbers are drawn from two independent normal distributions with estimated variance $\hat{\tau}^2$ and $\hat{\sigma}^2$, respectively. The simulated earnings are calculated as $\tilde{Y}_{it} = \mathbf{X}_{it}\hat{\boldsymbol{\beta}} + \tilde{\gamma}_i + \tilde{\varepsilon}_{it}$. Since $\tilde{\gamma}_i$ is specific for each individual and constant over time, only one draw at the start of the simulation is needed, but draws for $\tilde{\varepsilon}_{it}$ have to be repeated for each year (and new individual). As follows from Table 2, the individual variation, $\hat{\tau}^2$, is larger than the variation of the purely random component, $\hat{\sigma}^2$, in all sectors. However, there are large cross-sector differences in these estimates. The self-employed have the largest individual variation, indicating the large heterogeneity in this sector. Self-employed includes people in low-skilled and low-paid jobs as well as highly paid consultants. The lowest individual variation is found among blue-collar males and among females employed by local governments.

Note, that the model described only generates income from market work, i.e., for individuals with status = market work. For other individuals incomes are generated conditional on their status.

4.2. Pension income and other benefits

Social security pensions are computed using the rules that apply each year jointly with simulated income histories and eligibility status. Each worker is simulated to belong to one of the four major contract areas and will then receive occupational pensions accordingly, following the rules of each contract. The details of benefits from disability pension and early retirement have already been explained in Chapter 6.

How the stock of private pension annuities has been estimated is explained in Chapter 9. The income generated from these stocks can optionally be obtained for a limited period of time or for life. In all the

Table 2. **Estimates of a random effect model for earnings**

		Male		Female	
		Estimate	Standard error	Estimate	Standard error
Private blue-collar					
Intercept		11.7355	0.0387	11.7136	0.0595
Experience	Log(experience)	0.2630	0.0126	0.1790	0.0193
	Experience^2/100	−0.0224	0.0014	−0.0158	0.0020
Education	Compulsory	−0.2028	0.0204	−0.1907	0.0289
	Upper secondary	−0.1581	0.0190	−0.1228	0.0266
	University	1.0000	−	1.0000	−
Nationality	Swedish born	0.0791	0.0148	0.0187	0.0213
Marital status	Single	−0.0021	0.0084	0.0714	0.0135
Individual variance $\hat{\tau}^2$		0.0732		0.0947	
Random variance $\hat{\sigma}^2$		0.0202		0.0214	
Private white-collar					
Intercept		11.7791	0.0718	11.7506	0.0869
Experience	Log(experience)	0.3845	0.0257	0.2817	0.0316
	Experience^2/100	−0.0220	0.0028	−0.0231	0.0037
Education	Compulsory	−0.3588	0.0289	−0.2306	0.0387
	Upper secondary	−0.2384	0.0172	−0.1861	0.0220
	University	1.0000	−	1.0000	−
Nationality	Swedish born	0.0205	0.0278	0.0309	0.0324
Marital status	Single	−0.0436	0.0147	0.0605	0.0180
Individual variance $\hat{\tau}^2$		0.1547		0.1329	
Random variance $\hat{\sigma}^2$		0.0268		0.0199	
State Governmental					
Intercept		11.6771	0.0950	11.6030	0.1059
Experience	Log(experience)	0.3327	0.0337	0.2937	0.0373
	Experience^2/100	−0.0248	0.0034	−0.0203	0.0036
Education	Compulsory	−0.4261	0.0314	−0.3831	0.0347
	Upper secondary	−0.2804	0.0206	−0.3113	0.0245
	University	1.0000	−	1.0000	−
Nationality	Swedish born	0.1532	0.0378	0.0553	0.0367
Marital status	Single	−0.0936	0.0175	0.0336	0.0195
Individual variance $\hat{\tau}^2$		0.1044		0.0875	
Random variance $\hat{\sigma}^2$		0.0177		0.0142	
Local Governmental					
Intercept		11.6227	0.0994	11.7522	0.0471
Experience	Log(experience)	0.3320	0.0349	0.1800	0.0163
	Experience^2/100	−0.0195	0.0033	−0.0092	0.0016

(*Continued on next page*)

Table 2.   (Continued)

		Male		Female	
		Estimate	Standard error	Estimate	Standard error
Education	Compulsory	−0.3687	0.0295	−0.4134	0.0158
	Upper secondary	−0.2468	0.0209	−0.3097	0.0096
	University	1.0000	–	1.0000	–
Nationality	Swedish born	0.0410	0.0304	0.0058	0.0158
Marital status	Single	−0.0780	0.0164	0.0544	0.0086
Individual variance $\hat{\tau}^2$		0.1056		0.0684	
Random variance $\hat{\sigma}^2$		0.0150		0.0143	
Self–employed					
Intercept		11.4644	0.2864	11.3812	0.3396
Experience	Log(experience)	0.1630	0.1010	0.2887	0.1181
	Experience^2/100	−0.0078	0.0074	−0.0232	0.0102
Education	Compulsory	−0.1595	0.0641	−0.4337	0.0983
	Upper secondary	−0.1771	0.0594	−0.4408	0.0811
	University	1.0000	–	1.0000	–
Nationality	Swedish born	0.1154	0.0653	−0.0690	0.0879
Marital status	Single	−0.0290	0.0401	0.1881	0.0678
Individual variance $\hat{\tau}^2$		0.1722		0.1332	
Random variance $\hat{\sigma}^2$		0.0734		0.0560	

simulations reported here a 5-year period after retirement has been used. Table 5 of Chapter 9 includes information about the share of individuals with incomes from private pension savings, column (4), and the mean values for people with an income, column (5). These incomes are relatively small. The reason is that this kind of savings is a new phenomenon and the generated stock is still relatively small. However, the average amount for the 4.8 percent who had an income in year 2000 was as much as 32 196 SEK.

Benefits other than pensions such as housing allowances, child allowances, and social relief are computed using the rules of these benefit systems (see Chapter 3).

4.3. Income from capital

The structure of the set of models specified to simulate incomes from capital is partly determined by the income tax legislation. Incomes from capital in the form of interest, dividends, and capital gains are taxed by a flat rate tax of 30 percent. The tax base is net of interest paid and capital losses according to certain rules. The tax on capital gains on own home can under certain conditions be postponed if a new replacement home is acquired.

SESIM now includes one model that simulates interest and dividend incomes, a set of rules that determines the capital gain on an own home and any postponement of taxation, a model that simulates the capital gains from other assets and finally one that simulates interest paid on debts.

4.3.1. Interest and dividend incomes

It is natural to model interest and dividend incomes as a rate of return on financial assets. In order to do this the mean of the assets at the end of 1999 and 2000 was computed for every household in our LINDA sample and related to the sum of all interest and dividends earned in 2000. The first quartile of the mean asset variable was just 3121 SEK and most households in the first quartile had no financial assets at all. To avoid excessively high return rate estimates, all households with less than 1000 SEK were dropped from the sample. As a result 22 percent was dropped and of these only 2 percent had any interest or dividend incomes and they were small. The mean was only 889 SEK. The quartiles of the resulting distribution of the rates of return were 0.6, 1.1, and 1.7 percent, respectively. There were, however, a few unrealistically high values, most likely caused by too small mean asset estimates. It is possible that a few households owned an asset part of the year and collected a return, while their financial assets were small both in the beginning and in the end of the year. For this reason, we truncated the right tail of the rate of return distribution at 5 percent and thus dropped another 4 percent of the sample. The resulting distribution is censored from the left because between 5 and 10 percent of the households had no return on their financial assets. A tobit model was estimated using schooling, age, a dummy variable for marital status, and the mean value of the assets as explanatory variables. The results are found in Table 3.

Interpreting these results we find that the less schooling the smaller return. Schooling does not only increase the return in the labor market but also in the financial markets. There is a clear relation with age. People in middle age have a higher return than both young and old. One explanation is that they have a higher share of shares and stocks in their portfolios compared to those who are younger and older. Couples on average get a higher return than singles. The relation with the amount of assets owned is reversed U-shaped. Wealthy people have more investment opportunities and find it easier to get a good return. They might also be in a better position to diversify than less wealthy. Why the very wealthy earn relatively less is more difficult to explain.

Although the interpretation of the model parameter estimates is interesting the model explains relatively little of the variability in returns.

Table 3.   Estimates of a tobit model for the rates of return on financial assets

Explanatory variable	Slope estimate	Standard error	t-score
If only basic schooling	−0.0030	0.0002	−12.10
If secondary schooling	−0.0017	0.0002	−8.75
If a couple	0.0036	0.0002	20.27
Age 30–44	0.0019	0.0003	5.59
Age 45–59	0.0034	0.0003	9.86
Age 60–74	0.0028	0.0004	7.62
Age 75 or above	−0.0005	0.0004	−1.38
Mean assets $\times 10^3$	0.0358	0.0029	12.11
Mean assets $\times 10^3$ squared	−0.0065	0.0007	−8.90
Intercept	0.0123	0.0003	39.26
Standard error of residual	0.0346	0.0001	
Number of observations	198 900		
Pseudo R^2	−0.0016		

Note: The dependent variable was a ratio in the range 0–0.5.

Table 4.   Deciles of the distribution of rates of returns on financial assets

1	0.0012	6	0.0132
2	0.0045	7	0.0157
3	0.0068	8	0.0197
4	0.0089	9	0.0306
5	0.0109	Maximum (after truncation)	0.5

Most of the simulation variability will come from the residual that has a rather large variance. For this reason, we found that we could as well simulate the rate of return by drawing randomly from the empirical distribution, the deciles of which are displayed in Table 4. In the simulations, we have interpolated linearly between the percentiles and also imposed a maximum of 0.3. The motive is that the high rates of return observed in data probably resulted from measurement errors. This distribution applies to the year 2000. If the average return in the financial markets changes cyclically or trend wise these estimates have to change accordingly. When simulating we thus multiply the rate of return drawn from this distribution by the ratio of a market rate for the current year and the year 2000.

4.3.2. Capital gains on own home

In SESIM we simulate both purchases and sales of owner-occupied homes and record the price at which a transaction takes place (see Chapters 7 and 9). The difference between the sales price and the purchase price of a given property is the capital gain, 80 percent of which is added to the taxable income of capital.[10] If there is more than one owner of the property the capital gain is divided according to the shares owned. If a household sells their home and then buys another one within one year, and the gain exceeds a threshold, adding 80 percent of the capital gain to the taxable income of capital is partly or completely deferred. If the new house is more expensive than the old the whole amount is deferred, if it is less expensive a share of the amount is deferred equal to the ratio of the market value of the new house to that of the old. This procedure is repeated for every new sale and purchase until the owner moves to a rented home or dies. In this way it is, in principle, possible to defer the tax on the capital gains of own homes until the owners die. Then the survivors have to pay the tax out of the deceased's estate. For each homeowner who has previously sold a house or an apartment and used the opportunity to defer tax there is a cumulated deferred capital gain registered with the tax authorities. SESIM also keeps track of these amounts and applies the rules of deferred taxation.[11]

4.3.3. Capital gains from other assets than own home

Capital gains taxation also applies to gains from other properties and from financial assets. Register data only include information about total capital gains (losses) and it is not possible to distinguish gains by source. This makes it difficult to estimate a model for the gains accruing from other assets than own home. Register data, however, include information about the tax-assessed value and an estimated market value of own homes. We used these data to eliminate from the sample all households that had reduced their investments in own homes in order to get a cleaner sample of households with capital gains from other sources. A potential source of error is the fact that we cannot eliminate those who sold their property and bought a replacement at the same or a higher market value. But this group is likely to defer the taxation of their capital gains from their old home, and the corresponding amount will not be included in the reported capital gain figure.

The distribution of net capital gains (the sum of gains and losses) is rather strange. The center of the distribution is essentially zero, while there is a left tail with large negative values and a right tail with even larger (positive) values. The distribution thus has a high kurtosis and is positively skewed. The median is zero and the mean is 28 467 SEK. It became difficult

---

[10] This applies symmetrically to losses.

[11] There is one simplification. If sales and purchases are not done in the same year then the household is assumed to move to a rented home and no deferral is allowed. In SESIM we thus do not strictly apply the one-year rule.

to find a model that could reproduce this distribution. Instead we have opted in favor of separate models for capital gains and losses. We first estimated a probit for the probability of having a non-zero gain, then a probit for having a loss conditional on no gain, and finally a model explaining the size of the gain (loss) if the household had one.

Table 5 exhibits the estimates for the first probit model. Except for age and marital status we use changes in the investments in property and financial assets, and gross wealth to explain the probability to have a capital gain. The change variables take the form of dummy variables, one for each quartile of the distribution of the change variable. For instance, the first of these dummy variables in Table 5 takes the value one if the household belongs to the first quartile of the distribution of decreases in real estate investments. The default is no decrease. Households which have decreased their assets are expected to have capital gains with a higher

Table 5.   A probit model for the probability of having a capital gain

Explanatory variable	Slope estimate	Standard error	t-score
Age 30–44	−0.1440	0.0114	−12.60
Age 45–59	−0.1989	0.0119	−16.78
Age 60–74	−0.3067	0.0127	−24.08
Age 75 or above	−0.6225	0.0135	−46.05
If couple	0.1808	0.0068	26.54
Reduction in real estate value			
Q1	0.0901	0.0223	4.04
Q2	0.1890	0.0215	8.78
Q3	0.2887	0.0208	13.86
Q4	0.2735	0.0213	12.86
Increase in real estate value			
Q1	0.1367	0.0098	13.95
Q2	0.1779	0.0099	18.03
Q3	0.2154	0.0100	21.58
Q4	0.1978	0.0106	18.63
Reduction in financial wealth			
Q1	1.6891	0.0169	99.71
Q2	1.8980	0.0170	111.87
Q3	2.0762	0.0171	121.69
Q4	2.3603	0.0174	135.01
Increase in financial wealth			
Q1	1.1840	0.0165	71.75
Q2	1.3864	0.0163	84.79
Q3	1.5853	0.0163	97.23
Q4	2.0414	0.0166	123.26
Gross wealth relative to median gross wealth	0.0390	0.0010	38.03
Intercept	−2.1202	0.0156	−135.95
Number of observations	245166		
Pseudo R^2	0.2053		

probability than households that have not changed or increased their assets and the more they have decreased their assets the higher probability they should have for a capital gain. The estimates of Table 5 confirm to this pattern. Sales of financial assets give a capital gain with a higher probability than sales of real estate. The effect of an increase in assets on capital gains is not as obvious. We only observe the net change that could hide a combination of sales and purchases. Because increases in net holdings result in capital gains, according to the estimates of Table 5, most investors must have sold and reinvested. The estimate for the last variable, gross wealth, suggests that large players have a higher probability of making a capital gain. The probability to make a gain is also higher for young people than for old and for couples compared to singles.

The results for the probit model of having a realized capital loss given that the household had no realized gains are rather similar to the previous results (Table 6). The probability that young people will make a loss given that they made no gain is higher than the probability of a loss for old people. Couples have a higher probability than singles. Households that have no gains but have still reduced their investments in property have a higher probability to realize a loss than households that have a net increase in property investments. A net reduction of one's financial investments also gives a higher probability to loose than a net increase, but the difference is only marginal. People who have high transactions without having gained have a relatively high probability of loosing. If wealthy people do not gain they have a higher probability of loosing.

The robust regression of the size of the capital gain on the same explanatory variables, given that the household had a realized gain, shows that old people make somewhat larger gains than young people and that couples on average have somewhat larger gains than singles (Table 7). The change in investment variables shows that it is the size of the transaction that matters more than if the household makes a net investment or disinvestment. This is, in particular, clear for changes in financial holdings. Large increases or decreases in holdings result in large gains, while small changes only give small gains. As one might expect wealthy houscholds gain more than less wealthy.

We were not very successful in formulating and estimating a model for the size of capital losses. Instead we have chosen to draw randomly from the empirical distribution of the variable as such, the deciles of which are displayed in Table 8. Random draws are obtained from a distribution with linear interpolation between percentiles. Capital gains and losses are indexed by the CPI to capture changes in the general price level.

4.3.4. Interest paid and deducted

Almost 25 percent of all households had deductions for interest paid on mortgages and loans. The median deduction was just above 14 000 SEK,

Table 6. **The probability to have a capital loss conditional on no capital gain**

Explanatory variable	Slope estimate	Standard error	*t*-score
Age 30–44	−0.0551	0.0173	−3.18
Age 45–59	−0.2075	0.0184	−11.22
Age 60–74	−0.4457	0.0212	−21.01
Age 75 or above	−0.7958	0.0245	−32.45
If couple	0.0373	0.0114	3.26
Reduction in real estate value			
Q1	0.2157	0.0354	6.09
Q2	0.2825	0.0350	8.07
Q3	0.3245	0.0351	9.25
Q4	0.1722	0.0388	4.44
Increase in real estate value			
Q1	0.0546	0.0168	3.25
Q2	0.0641	0.0171	3.74
Q3	0.0993	0.0174	5.72
Q4	0.1574	0.0182	8.62
Reduction in financial wealth			
Q1	0.7042	0.0238	29.56
Q2	0.8525	0.0242	35.20
Q3	0.9660	0.0247	39.04
Q4	1.4261	0.0249	57.17
Increase in financial wealth			
Q1	0.6879	0.0204	33.79
Q2	0.7232	0.0209	34.61
Q3	0.8048	0.0213	37.83
Q4	1.0439	0.0225	46.32
Gross wealth relative to median gross wealth	0.0185	0.0019	9.50
Intercept	−2.1309	0.0190	−112.39
Number of observations	165 856		
Pseudo R^2	0.0977		

while the mean was close to 26 000 SEK. The distribution is positively skewed and the largest deductions amount to a few millions.

It might be natural to relate the interest deducted to the total debt and simulate the corresponding rate. The problem with this approach is that about 25 percent of all households have deducted interest although they did not have any debt at the end of the same year and about 10 percent of all households have deductions without having any debt neither in the beginning of the year nor in the end. It is, of course, possible to pay interest on a debt that was repaid before the end of the year, and it is also possible to take a loan after the beginning of a year and repay it before the end and still have interest to pay. Similarly we find households in the data set with large deductions but rather small debts.

Table 7. **Robust regression of the size of the capital gains, if the household gained**

Explanatory variable	Slope estimate	Standard error	*t*-score
Age 30–44	−238.45	189.34	−1.26
Age 45–59	392.11	194.31	2.02
Age 60–74	1648.06	206.40	7.98
Age 75 or above	2251.64	228.78	9.84
If couple	333.40	109.94	3.03
Reduction in real estate value			
Q1	868.96	363.57	2.39
Q2	964.64	329.68	2.93
Q3	1645.86	299.60	5.49
Q4	950.99	285.07	3.34
Increase in real estate value			
Q1	822.74	160.89	5.11
Q2	949.60	157.90	6.01
Q3	1109.31	155.39	7.14
Q4	1228.79	153.51	8.00
Reduction in financial wealth			
Q1	−5040.23	450.99	−11.18
Q2	−1262.73	447.12	−2.82
Q3	4183.65	444.92	9.40
Q4	8891.11	442.78	20.08
Increase in financial wealth			
Q1	−4805.44	456.48	−10.53
Q2	−3336.77	449.32	−7.43
Q3	−1394.29	444.97	−3.13
Q4	1935.80	440.21	4.40
Gross wealth relative to median gross wealth	0.0003	8.68e–06	38.29
Intercept	7577.54	439.41	17.24
Number of observations	79 308		

Table 8. **Deciles of the empirical distribution of capital losses in year 2000 (SEK)**

Deciles	Deciles value
1	59
2	188
3	460
4	1060
5	2197
6	4266
7	8519
8	17 929
9	42 775
Maximum	10.6×10^6

In spite of these difficulties the advantages of modeling a rate rather than an amount are so great that we preferred this approach even if we will not be able to simulate a positive amount for households with no debt at the end of a year. The interest rate on debts was defined as the ratio of the interest paid by the household to the sum of all debts at the end of the year if this sum exceeded 1000 SEK. This truncation floor was used to avoid excessively high rates. Households with a debt less than 1000 but still had paid interest were dropped from the sample. With this definition 83 percent of all households had a positive rate. The median was 5.6 percent and the mean 7.8 percent. The 95th percentile was 14.1 percent and there were a few observations exceeding 1.

The sample was split into two groups, one that did not pay any interest in the previous year and one that did pay. For each group a two-phase model was estimated: a random effects probit model for the probability to have paid interest and a model for the amount. Note that in the probit models the alternative to paying interest is to have no debt or to have a debt but still not pay interest (in the current year).

The estimates of the probit models are given in Tables 9 and 10. The probability to start to pay interest on debts is highest among young people, while the probability to continue to pay is highest among middle aged. People with secondary schooling have higher probability than people with

Table 9. *Random effects probit model for the probability of paying interest on debts, if the household did not pay interest in the previous year*

Explanatory variables	Slope estimates	Standard error	*t*-score
Age 30–44	0.0372	0.1065	0.35
Age 45–59	−0.0261	0.1119	−0.23
Age 60–74	−0.3885	0.1241	−3.13
Age 75 or above	−0.4258	0.1317	−3.23
If only basic schooling	0.1067	0.0968	1.10
If secondary schooling	0.2089	0.0794	2.63
Debt ratio	2.4557	0.2500	9.82
If debts > assets	−1.6039	0.2263	−7.09
Real assets relative to median	0.0682	0.0354	1.93
Sum of all taxable labor incomes relative to median	0.5124	0.0698	7.35
Intercept	−1.4091	0.1229	−11.46
Sigma of household variance component *u*	0.4550	0.0971	
Fraction of residual variance due to *u*	0.1715	0.0607	
Number of observations	2795		
Number of households	1230		

Note 1: The debt ratio is the ratio of all household debts to gross assets if gross assets > 0. This ratio was top-coded to 1. If gross assets = 0 and debts = 0 then the ratio = 0. If gross assets = 0 but debts > 0 then the ratio = 1.

Note 2: Real assets were divided by the median 970 805 SEK and the sum of all taxable labor incomes by the median 367 624 SEK.

Table 10. Random effects probit model for the probability of paying interest on debts, if the household paid interest in the previous year

Explanatory variables	Slope estimates	Standard error	*t*-score
Age 30–44	0.6342	0.1071	5.92
Age 45–59	0.7635	0.1122	6.81
Age 60–74	0.4857	0.1192	4.07
Age 75 or above	0.0002	0.1458	0.00
If only basic schooling	0.0816	0.0928	0.88
If secondary schooling	0.4402	0.0733	6.00
If a couple	−0.2035	0.0762	−2.67
Debt ratio	5.5443	0.2566	21.60
If debts > assets	−3.8855	0.2279	−17.05
Real assets relative to median	0.4245	0.0407	10.42
Financial assets relative to median	−0.0032	0.0008	−4.12
Sum of all taxable labor incomes relative to median	0.9827	0.0766	12.82
Intercept	−0.9965	0.1453	−6.86
Sigma of household variance component *u*	1.2364	0.0626	
Fraction of residual variance due to *u*	0.6045	0.0242	
Number of observations	18 520		
Number of households	5329		

Note: The financial assets of the household were divided by the median 146 020 SEK. See also the note of Table 9 of Chapter 9.

less or more schooling. Couples have a lower probability to continue paying interest than singles, while this variable has no significant effect on the behavior of those who start to pay interest. The higher the debt ratio is the higher is the probability to pay interest, while if debts exceed gross assets this probability is reduced. One possible explanation is that those who have debts exceeding their gross assets have borrowed from parents and relatives and do not have to pay interest or postpone any payments on these loans. The more real assets the household owns the higher is their probability to pay interest. The amount of financial assets owned only influences the probability for those who already pay interest and the effect is negative. This variable probably captures those households that do not need to borrow because they have financial assets. The estimates for the income variable shows that the probability to pay interest increases with increasing income. People with good incomes can afford to pay interest.

The estimates of the regression models explaining the amount of interest paid conditional on paying can be found in Tables 11 and 12. In both cases the dependent variable is the log of the interest rate paid in order to pull in the right tail of the distribution and avoid simulating negative rates. The number of panel observations is too small to estimate a panel model for the group that did not pay interest in the previous year, so in this case a simple OLS regression was used (Table 11). For the other group of households, we used a random effects GLS regression (Table 12).

Table 11.   *Robust regression model for the log (interest paid on debts/sum of debts), if the household did not pay interest in the previous year but does so in the current year*

Explanatory variables	Slope estimates	Standard error	*t*-score
Age 30–44	0.4001	0.4078	0.98
Age 45–59	0.6203	0.4512	1.37
Age 60–74	0.9068	0.6302	1.44
Age 75 or above	1.9524	0.8818	2.21
If only basic schooling	1.7520	0.4769	3.67
If secondary schooling	1.0819	0.3296	3.28
Debt ratio	−1.3488	0.4553	−2.96
Real assets relative to median	0.1487	0.1984	0.75
Financial assets relative to median	−0.0483	0.0223	−2.16
Sum of tax assessed income from work relative to median	0.3009	0.3151	0.95
Change in investments in property elative to the median investments in property	0.3075	0.4548	0.68
Intercept	−5.6367	0.5564	−10.13
Number of observations	408		

Note: Only households with a debt exceeding 1000 SEK have contributed to this regression.

Table 12.   *Random effects GLS model for the log amount of interest paid on debts, if the household paid interest in the previous year and continues to do so in the current year*

Explanatory variables	Slope estimates	Standard error	*t*-score
Age 30–44	0.3622	0.0500	7.25
Age 45–59	0.3439	0.0514	6.68
Age 60–74	0.4021	0.0567	7.08
Age 75 or above	0.4276	0.0844	5.07
Debt ratio	−0.5122	0.0470	−10.89
If debts > assets	−0.1043	0.0372	−2.81
Real assets relative to median	−0.0406	0.0082	−4.97
Change in investments in property relative to the median investments in property	−0.1239	0.0136	−9.09
Log(debt rate)$_{t-1}$	0.3666	0.0075	49.03
Intercept	−1.8714	0.0604	−30.98
Sigma of household variance component u	0.5807		
Sigma of white noise variance component	0.5530		
Fraction of residual variance due to u	0.5244		
Number of observations	11 954		
Number of households	4247		

Of those who take up a loan and start to pay interest old people pay higher rates than young, probably because they have smaller incomes and perhaps less to offer in collateral. The less schooling the higher rates people tend to pay. The relation with age is less clear for those who already pay interest and the schooling variables came out insignificant. The higher debt ratio the smaller interest rate which might appear counter intuitive, but most households with high debt ratios probably have high mortgages on their homes, and interest rates on mortgages are usually lower than the rates on consumer credits and other loans. Support for this interpretation is found in the negative estimate for the amount invested in property for those who already had debts. The corresponding estimate for those who take up new debt is insignificantly different form zero. For this group, we also find that the larger financial assets owned the less in interest they pay. The dummy variable indicating that debts exceed gross assets has no effect on the interest paid by new payers; they would probably never get a loan, while it has a counter intuitively negative effect for those who already pay.

5. Retirement income of the baby boomers

5.1. Concepts and measures

One of the most common indicators used in pension policy analysis is the replacement rate. It provides information regarding the income in retirement relative to the income while working. There is an issue about the choice of the most appropriate benchmark for pre- and post-retirement incomes. For pre-retirement incomes there are typically two main approaches. One is to use the incomes of the last year prior to retirement, the average income in the last 5 years prior to retirement; or to include the peak income defined as the average of the highest 3 or 5 years out of the last 10 years prior to retirement, or the income at age 55 (Smith, 2003). The alternative approach preferred by some scholars is to use average income for all working years (Boskin and Shoven, 1987). Their argument is that all labor incomes build up retirement income, not just the incomes of the peak years. They also note that in the last years before retirement some individuals are forced to career breaks, part-time work, or not to work at all due to sickness or other problems independent of their choice, which cause a substantially decrease in their earnings. The sensitivity analysis in Appendix, Table A.2 illustrates the effects of using different pre-retirement incomes when computing replacement rates.

We believe that people usually form their expectations about retirement at the end of their work life, say 5–10 years before retirement, and that they want to maintain the standard of living they have reached at that age. For this reason, we prefer to compare pensions to the incomes at the end of work life. If we should consider the average of a 10-year period, the average of the highest income of 3 or 5 years during this period or just at one specific age (such as 55) is a matter of debate, and the purpose of the sensitivity analyses in the Appendix is to evaluate the effects of these choices.

Apart from comparing income after with that before retirement, one should also consider pensions relative to contemporary incomes, that is, incomes of the working population.

5.2. Replacement rates for the baby boomers

SESIM is used to simulate incomes for a number of birth cohorts in the period 1999–2041. The pensions of these cohorts come both from the old and the new pension system. The transition from the old to the new system occurs gradually. The cohorts included in our analysis are those born in 1937 (completely in the old system), 1940 (6/20 in the new system), 1943 (9/20 in the new system), 1946 (12/20 in the new system), 1949 (15/20 in the new system), 1952 (18/20 in the new system), and 1955 (completely in the new system).

Table 13 shows replacement rates by birth cohort based on household disposable incomes (divided by the number of household members). These replacement rates have been computed for individuals who have worked at least 5 years before retirement, and then survived at least 10 years after retirement. In order to analyze the replacement rates for different level of income, we group the mean of disposable income for the 5 years before retirement into quartiles. Our simulations are based on the following assumptions: a yearly inflation rate of 2 percent, a real growth rate of 2 percent, and a return on financial assets of 5 percent (relevant for all funded pension systems, including the PPM and private pensions).

The overall impression, starting with the baseline results (retirement at 65) in columns (1) and (2), is that the baby-boom generation will not get a dramatic reduction in income, at least not immediately after retirement. For the average income earner, the replacement rate is highest for the oldest cohort (97 percent) and varies between 83 and 87 percent for the younger cohorts. Apart from the high rate for the 1937 cohort, there is no evidence that the new pension system reduces the replacement rate. Table 13 also shows that the replacement rate drops with increasing age. Compare, for instance, columns (1) and (2). For many cohorts the drop is around 10 percentage points. The main reason for this drop in income is our assumption that both private pension savings and some funded parts of the occupational pensions are only paid out during a few years after retirement. The funded components are more important for the younger cohorts.[12]

---

[12] Indexation also matters and this will be discussed further below.

Table 13.   Disposable income in 1999 prices before and after retirement for different birth cohorts, income levels, and retirement ages

Cohort	Income class	Age of retirement 65		Age of retirement 67		Age of retirement 63	
		Age 65–69 (1)	Age 70–74 (2)	Age 67–71 (3)	Age 72–76 (4)	Age 63–67 (5)	Age 68–72 (6)
1937	<P25	109	119	129	116	98	100
	P25–P75	97	90	99	91	82	77
	>P75	70	64	73	68	64	53
1940	<P25	102	99	111	103	96	98
	P25–P75	84	78	89	84	77	72
	>P75	71	59	77	68	67	56
1943	<P25	107	94	112	97	93	93
	P25–P75	84	74	89	84	78	74
	>P75	67	57	74	66	71	58
1946	<P25	101	96	108	100	96	99
	P25–P75	87	74	92	84	80	75
	>P75	72	57	77	64	67	55
1949	<P25	105	97	109	102	92	94
	P25–P75	84	75	90	78	77	71
	>P75	71	58	70	59	66	55
1952	<P25	96	93	99	94	88	85
	P25–P75	83	72	88	76	78	67
	>P75	70	58	73	60	67	54
1955	<P25	102	95	108	103	98	100
	P25–P75	83	72	89	75	82	77
	>P75	72	56	71	63	64	53

Note: SESIM generated 1999–2041. All individuals have worked at least 5 years preceding the retirement and survived at least until 10 years thereafter. Inflation ≈2 percent per year, real wage ≈2 percent per year, and long interest rate is 5 percent per year.

As expected, replacement rates vary with the level of income, from about 70 percent in the highest income quartile to more than 100 percent in the lowest quartile. These estimates are quite stable across both cohorts and age groups. There is only a small drop in the age group 70–74 compared to 65–69, about 4 percentage points in the first quartile and about 10 in the fourth. The ceiling in the pension system explains the lower levels among high-income households.

The new pension system (based on lifetime earnings) compared to the old (based on the best 15 years) is designed to give a higher penalty for early retirement and a better reward for late retirement. In order to estimate this effect, Table 13 shows replacement rates by retirement age. In columns (3) and (4) there are results assuming that everyone retires at age 67 and in columns (5) and (6) at age 63. For the average income household the cost of an early retirement, column (5) compared to the baseline in column (1), is 5–7 percent for all cohorts except the oldest (15 percent) and the youngest (1 percent), which does not agree with expectations.

One explanation for the large effect for the oldest is that with monotonically increasing earnings, the 2 last years with highest earnings will not be included in the 15 best years.

A retirement postponed to the age of 67, produces a replacement rate between 88 and 92 percent for the average income household and all cohorts except the oldest (99 percent). The result of delaying retirement with 2 years is an increase in the replacement rate by about 5 percent. But late retirees are not always rewarded, see the richest quartile for cohorts 1949 and 1955. On average low-income people get a higher reward for retiring late than anyone else (about 8 percent).

Next, the effect of alternative returns on financial assets is considered. Table 14 presents results based on a high return of 7 percent (columns (1) and (2)) and a low return of 3 percent (columns (3) and (4)). These should be compared to the baseline in Table 13 of 5 percent (columns (1) and (2)). As expected the replacement rates for the older cohorts are not affected much by the return on financial assets. The main reason is that time until retirement from our baseline year 1999 is too short, and also that the old

Table 14. *Disposable income before and after retirement for different birth cohorts in 1999 year prices*

Cohort	Income class	High return 7 percent		Low return 3 percent	
		Age 65–69 (1)	Age 70–74 (2)	Age 65–69 (3)	Age 70–74 (4)
1937	<P25	108	124	109	123
	P25–P75	97	91	97	90
	>P75	69	62	69	63
1940	<P25	102	98	104	96
	P25–P75	84	78	83	76
	>P75	71	61	70	59
1943	<P25	101	91	100	88
	P25–P75	83	73	82	74
	>P75	67	59	69	57
1946	<P25	98	99	103	95
	P25–P75	88	77	87	76
	>P75	77	62	71	58
1949	<P25	101	94	103	93
	P25–P75	85	76	83	73
	>P75	71	60	68	58
1952	<P25	101	95	92	88
	P25–P75	84	73	80	70
	>P75	70	60	68	57
1955	<P25	108	94	92	84
	P25–P75	86	75	82	70
	>P75	75	61	69	57

Note: SESIM generated 1999–2041. All individuals have worked at least 5 years preceding the retirement at 65 and survived at least until 75. Inflation ≈2 percent per year, real wage ≈2 percent per year, and long interest rate is 5 percent per year.

pension system had fewer components for which financial returns matter. However, there is no big effect for the younger either. For instance, for the 1955 cohort the household in the average income category have a replacement rate between 82 and 86 percent depending on the rate of return. We find the largest effect of differences in financial return for low-income earners in the youngest cohort. For example, the replacement rate for the 1955 cohort increases from 92 to 108 percent when the rate of return increases from 3 percent to 7 percent.

The conclusion is that if we base our estimates on disposable income, most rates for all scenarios are reasonably high. In fact, with only one exception, all replacement rates for low and average income earners are above or equal to 70 percent. The low rates are found among the high-income households and for the second 5-year period after retirement. For instance, high-income households with an early retirement, column (6) in Table 13, only get a rate between 52 and 58 percent.

In evaluating these results, it is important to remember that we study a "homogenous" sample of individuals that have worked before retirement. Thus, the sample members had high incomes. If the comparison had also included other groups such as unemployed, disabled pensioners, etc., then the replacement rates would have been even higher.

Disposable income is a household concept which includes other income components than labor incomes and pensions and it is net of taxes. In order to better understand the relative importance of the three pillars of the pension system, we next turn to an analysis of replacement rates based on taxable incomes. With only minor deviations taxable income before retirement is derived from labor incomes, and after retirement from pensions.

As presented in Table 15, the importance of the three pillars varies by income level, age, and birth cohort. For individuals born in 1940 with an income in the midrange, the average taxable income during the first 5 years after retirement is 78 percent of the average taxable income during the 5 years period before retirement. The major component is public pensions (57 percent of taxable income before retirement). Occupational and private pensions have about equal relative importance (10 percent of taxable income before retirement).[13] The replacement ratio in the second 5-year period drops to 69 percent and the main reason is the decrease in the private pensions. The occupational pension drops only slightly, because for this cohort most systems are based on defined benefits paid for life.

Private pensions are more important for older cohorts. This might be a result of under estimation of private savings for younger cohorts.

---

[13] Note that the components do not add up exactly to taxable income, this is because taxable income can also include income from other sources, for instance, income from capital.

Table 15. Replacement rates for different birth cohorts and income levels

Cohort	Income class	Age 65–69				Age 70–74			
		Taxable income (percent)	Public pension (percent)	Occupational pension (percent)	Private pension (percent)	Taxable income (percent)	Public pension (percent)	Occupational pension (percent)	Private pension (percent)
1937	<P25	111	88	9	12	106	90	8	4
	P25–P75	80	60	8	9	74	61	7	2
	>P75	67	43	13	9	62	44	12	4
1940	<P25	96	73	8	12	86	75	7	1
	P25–P75	78	57	10	10	69	58	8	1
	>P75	68	39	18	10	58	40	14	2
1943	<P25	91	68	11	10	83	70	8	1
	P25–P75	79	54	13	10	68	56	9	1
	>P75	66	35	19	11	55	36	13	3
1946	<P25	94	66	14	12	84	68	11	2
	P25–P75	78	52	14	10	66	53	10	1
	>P75	64	34	20	9	52	35	14	2
1949	<P25	93	66	14	12	80	67	11	1
	P25–P75	75	50	15	9	65	51	11	1
	>P75	63	32	21	9	50	33	14	2
1952	<P25	89	62	16	11	76	62	11	1
	P25–P75	75	48	16	9	62	49	11	1
	>P75	60	31	20	7	47	31	13	1
1955	<P25	93	65	17	9	81	65	13	1
	P25–P75	77	51	16	9	64	51	11	1
	>P75	64	33	22	7	50	33	15	1

Average income in age 65–69 and 70–74 related to average taxable income in age 60–64.

Note: SESIM generated 1999–2041. All individuals have worked at least 5 years preceding the retirement at 65 and survived at least until 75. Inflation ≈ 2 percent per year, real wage ≈ 2 percent per year, and long interest rate is 5 percent per year.

Remember that individuals born in 1940 were 59 years old when the simulation started, and thus most of their savings were known from data, while most of the savings of younger cohorts have been imputed during the simulation. An interesting finding is that private pensions are quite important for low-income earners.

For young high-income earners, the public pension component covers just a little more than 30 percent of pre-pension taxable income. The reason is that many are not fully compensated because they have incomes above the ceiling. What is not obtained from the public system is, however, partly recovered from the occupational pensions.

A more complete picture of the economic situation of the retired would not only include incomes but also wealth that can be made liquid for consumption. This issue is discussed in the next chapter.

5.3. Relative income of the baby boomers

The replacement rate is a measure relevant both for evaluating the need for private savings as well as the effects of changes in the pension and benefit rules. This rate reflects the expected changes in income after retirement; however, it is not informative about the income of a pensioner relative to that of the working population. A supplementary measure – called relative income – relates the income of the retired to the incomes of the working population. An OECD (2005) report uses such a measure, and according to the results Sweden has a strong link between pension entitlements and pre-retirement earnings, along with countries like Finland, Austria, Luxembourg, Germany, or Spain.

This relative income measure has been simulated for seven different cohorts in the age bracket 65–90 (see Figure 11). Relative income has been defined as average taxable income for each cohort and age divided by the average taxable income for all individuals aged 20–64 in the same year. At 65 years of age the average income of the pensioners is 74–79 percent of the average income for those aged 20–64. After 65, this ratio drops to 69–74 percent at age 69, and then sharply down to 56–65 percent at age 70. This first drop in the relative income reflects our assumption that the funded parts of the pension system are only paid out during the first 5 years. Because older cohorts, to a large extent, follow the old social security system they have no or just a small funded share, and the drop is thus considerably smaller for older cohorts compared to younger. After age 70, the relative income of the retired continues to drop and at age 90 the ratio becomes as low as 42–49 percent.

The main reason for the steady drop is the design of the price and income indexation of the old and new pension systems. The details of the income indexation are given in the Annual Report (2004) of the National Swedish Social Insurance Office (NSIO). In short the pensions are calculated as follows. The income pension is calculated by dividing the

Figure 11. *Average taxable incomes for pensioners relative to the average taxable income of the working cohorts (age 20–64)*

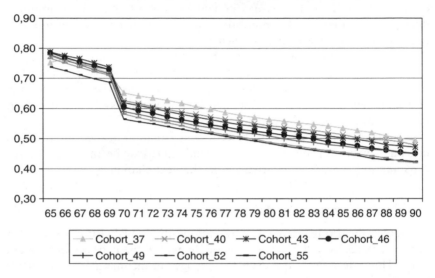

pension balance (the notional pension wealth) by an annuity divisor. There is a specific divisor for each birth cohort, and this divisor reflects the expected life length at the time of retirement but also an interest rate of 1.6 percent. The income pension is revalued annually by the change in an income index less the interest rate of 1.6 percentage points credited in the divisor. This means that pensions will only be unchanged in real terms if incomes increase by exactly 1.6 percent more than inflation. Applied to the assumptions used here – incomes increase by 2 percent more than inflation – this implies that pensions increase by 0.4 percent in real term. Thus, our assumptions and the indexation described above imply a higher relative income at age 65 than at higher ages. This is sometimes referred to as a front-loaded system.

It is important to remember that this is a result based on a simulation extended for 25 years and as always forecasted values must be interpreted with some care. One attempt to assess the realism in these seemingly low relative incomes for the very old is presented below. In Figure 12, we compare age–income profiles for the year 2003 from observed data in LINDA to simulated profiles from SESIM. The simulated data are close to the observed up to the age of 50, and then SESIM produces lower levels until they converge again at about age 70. Why does SESIM underestimate the income ratio in the age interval 50–70? The earnings model of SESIM was estimated using data from 1999 and earlier and major changes in earnings thereafter are not "in the estimates." A comparison with LINDA data from 1999 shows that a major change in relative income occurred

Figure 12. Average taxable incomes by age relative to average taxable income for everyone 20+; a comparison of LINDA and SESIM for the income year 2003

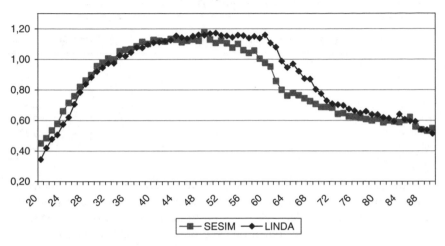

1999–2003 for those aged 55–60. For instance, at age 60 the relative income was about 116 percent in 2003 compared to only 106 percent in 1999. Thus, relative income for individuals in the age of 55–60 has gone up since 1999 and this increase is not reflected in SESIM, and as a consequence the simulated income in this age bracket is underestimated. Obviously it is difficult to base information on future relative incomes on only one cross section in 2003. It is difficult to tell if the change from 1999 to 2003 reflects a permanent change or if it reflects a cohort or business cycle effect. Inspection of Figure 4 in Section 3 above shows an interesting cohort effect for females. Those born in 1940 had a considerably higher labor force participation rate in 2003 compared to the 1937 cohort. If the same will be the case also for younger cohorts is an open question. Even if the income rate might be underestimated a little in the age bracket 55–70, the downward trend seems robust. The conclusion is that the pension system is not able to maintain the relative income standard of the elderly. There is no major difference in this respect between the old and the new pension system, but according to our simulations the new system actually gives somewhat lower income rates.

The low levels of average relative income for pensioners raise the important issue of the inequality of income. If the average income for a pensioner at age 80 is only 50 percent of the contemporaneous income of workers, how small is the income at the lowest quartile?

Table 16 shows the result for three cohorts and for three levels of relative income; at the first quartile, the second and third quartiles, and the fourth quartile. At age 65 the average relative income within the first

Table 16.   Taxable income of pensioners relative to taxable income of everyone aged 20–64, by birth cohort, age, and relative income quartile of the pensioners

Age	Cohort 1937			Cohort 1946			Cohort 1955		
	<Q25	Q25–Q75	>Q75	<Q25	Q25–Q75	>Q75	<Q25	Q25–Q75	>Q75
65	0.52	0.72	0.93	0.55	0.72	0.92	0.56	0.71	0.89
69	0.49	0.68	0.87	0.51	0.67	0.85	0.53	0.66	0.84
70	0.48	0.63	0.78	0.47	0.57	0.69	0.46	0.56	0.67
75	0.44	0.59	0.73	0.43	0.53	0.63	0.42	0.51	0.61
80	0.42	0.55	0.67	0.41	0.49	0.59	0.39	0.47	0.56
85	0.40	0.52	0.63	0.38	0.46	0.55	0.36	0.44	0.52
90	0.38	0.48	0.59	0.35	0.42	0.52	0.33	0.40	0.48

quartile is about 0.5 while it is about 0.9 in the fourth quartile. There are only small differences across cohorts. Relative income decreases with increasing age and the decrease is largest in the fourth quartile. Depending on cohort, people in the fourth quartile only get a relative pension of 50 percent at the age of 90 and in the first quartile it is as low as 35 percent. Thus, both the average and the inequality of the relative distribution of pensions decrease.

5.4. Income distribution and poverty

The discussion above has been focused on replacement rates and average pensions in relation to average incomes. It is also of importance to discuss the distribution of income for the ageing population. In Figure 13, the distribution of disposable income is presented for the cohort born in 1949 as it ages. In contrast to the previous section these results are based on an unbalanced panel. We simulate future income for all individuals in the 1949 cohort from age 50 (start year 1999) up to age 90. Everyone is assumed to retire no later than at age 65. For each simulated year the first decile, first quartile, median, third quartile, and ninth decile of the income distribution is calculated and presented in the figure. The general trend is a reduction in income inequality as this cohort ages. At the lower end of the income distribution this is due to an increase in income after retirement. Because this graph is drawn using all individuals, without any pre-retirement work condition, we include many low-income earners who do not work just before retirement. For these individuals, income goes up at retirement because both accumulated pension rights and the guarantee pension give a higher pension income. On the other hand, at higher income levels, retirement results in an income reduction. This is in line with the results discussed above, due to the ceiling in the pension system, high-income earners have lower replacement rates. The compression in the income distribution is further accelerated at the age of 70 when income

Figure 13. **The income distribution of the cohorts born in 1949; equalized**
disposable income (1999 prices)

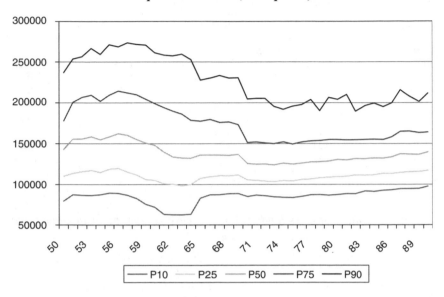

from private pension and funded occupational pensions are exhausted. To summarize, the ratio of decile 9 over decile 1 is about 4 shortly before pension, drops to 2.7 shortly thereafter and is then further reduced after age 70 to slightly above 2. The increasing trend in income after retirement comes from the assumption of a 2 percent real wage increase, which through the indexation of pensions as discussed above, gives an yearly real increase of 0.4 percent in public pensions. Similar results apply to other cohorts; income dispersion is reduced after retirement.

There are alternative measures of income inequality that might give a slightly different picture. One natural candidate is the Gini coefficient, which is more sensitive toward changes in the center of the distribution. Table 17 presents the average Gini measure for age intervals of 5 years and a number of birth cohorts. For the younger cohorts for which it is possible to compute the Gini before retirement, we find that inequality increases up to age 60–64, while there is no clear trend after retirement. There is no trend for the older cohorts either and no clear differences between cohorts. Thus, the pension system affect the income distribution mostly by reducing the highest and increasing the lowest incomes, but does not have any large impact on the distributions of intermediate incomes.

In the discussion of the effects of the pension system on the income distribution, it is natural to focus on the low-income households. The identification of poverty among pensioners is an old research and policy issue, and public pensions are – at least in theory – designed to keep most of

Table 17.   Gini coefficients by birth cohort and age

Age	Cohort			
	1937	1943	1949	1955
45–49				0.23
50–54			0.26	0.27
55–59		0.28	0.28	0.30
60–64	0.32	0.31	0.37	0.35
65–69	0.23	0.34	0.33	0.35
70–74	0.26	0.30	0.31	0.34
75–79	0.28	0.31	0.37	0.30
80–84	0.33	0.31	0.37	0.31
85–89	0.32	0.28	0.30	0.33

Figure 14.   Share of households below the poverty line, by birth cohort and age

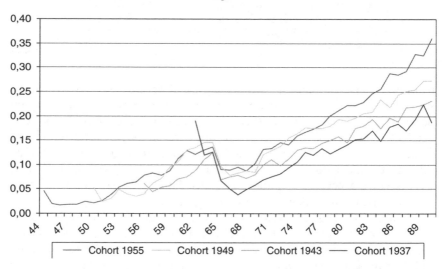

the elderly out of poverty. An attempt to identify the incidence of future poverty among the Swedish baby-boom generation is given in Figure 13. Thus, the median disposable income for the adult population has been calculated each year from 1999 to 2040, and then for the individuals belonging to the baby-boom cohorts the share with an income below half the median is recorded. For four of these cohorts the results are summarized in Figure 14. Due to falling labor force participation shortly before retirement, poverty increases before age 65. Because everyone is included in these calculations regardless of working status, many households have a low income before retirement. The poverty rate drops directly after 65, because the pension system offers a better low-income guarantee than other social insurance benefits. However, shortly after retirement the poverty ratio starts to increase again and at faster rate for the younger cohorts than for the older. For instance, at age 80 the poverty rate for the 1955 cohort is above 20 percent compared to about 15 percent for the two oldest cohorts and at age 90 this difference has increased. The poverty rate of the 1937 cohort is about 20 percent and that of the 1955 cohort as high as 35 percent. The rates at this high age should, however, be interpreted with care because the number of individuals is rather few at this age.

The fast increase in poverty is consistent with the drop in relative earnings reported in Figure 11. As time passes the indexation of the pension system erode the purchasing power of public pensions, resulting in a lower relative earnings as well as a higher incidence of poverty among the old.

6. Conclusions

The findings in this chapter highlight the importance of a longitudinal analysis and provide a strong argument for the dynamic micro-simulation approach. A major result is that the income standard of the young–old will become much higher than that of the very old. If our simulations bear the stamp of realism they suggest that we will see new and large poverty in Sweden among the very old in the future. The pension system contributes to this result. The "front-loaded" design gives with its reduced wage indexation a higher income immediately after retirement, but a much lower income at older age. From this perspective, it is unfortunate that so much attention is given to the discussion of replacement rates. The replacement rate, although interesting in itself, completely miss the long-run effect and just provides a comparison of incomes shortly after with incomes before retirement. If we instead focus on the relative income of older pensioners the results become quite different, as evident from Figures 11 and 14.

Our results challenge the conception of a sustainable pension system. If the relative income of older pensioners drops and at the same time expenditures for health and care increase, one might wonder how the old in our society will make both ends meet. If pensions become too small to meet "minimum standards," the requirement of financial sustainability of the pension system results in an increased financial burden on other parts of the general social protection system.

References

Andersson, B., L. Berg and A. Klevmarken (2001), "Inkomst-och Förmögenhetsfördelningen för dagens och morgondagens äldre" www.nek.uu.se/faculty/klevmark/reswork.html

Baltagai, B.H. (2001), *Econometric Analysis of Panel Data*, Wiley.

Börsch-Supan, A., A. Brugiavini, H. Jürges, J. Mackenbaach, J. Siegrist and G. Weber (eds.) (2005), *Health, Ageing and Retirement in Europe*, Mannheim: MEA.

Boskin, M. and J. Shoven (1987), "Concepts and measures of earnings replacement rates during retirement", in: Z. Bodie, J. Shoven and D. Wise, editors, *Issues in Pension Economics*, Chicago: University of Chicago Press.

Mantovani, D., F. Papadopoulos, H. Sutherland and P. Tsakloglou (2005), "Pension incomes in the European Union: policy reform strategies in comparative perspective", Iza Discussion Paper No. 1537.

OECD (2005), "Pensions at a glance. Public policies across OECD countries". OECD, Paris.

Smith, J.P. (2003), "Trends and projections in income replacement during retirement", *Journal of Labour Economics*, Vol. 21(4), pp. 755–781.

Statistical Sweden (2003), Income distribution survey 2003, Statistiska Meddelanden HE 21 SM 0501.

Swedish National Social Insurance Office, Annual Report (2004).

Whitehouse, E. (2003), "The value of pension entitlements: a model of nine OECD countries", OECD, DELSA/ELSA/WD/SEM (2003) 9.

Appendix A. Comparing different measures of replacement rates

Following the broad discussion from Section 5.1, the purpose of this appendix is to evaluate different measures of the replacement rate. The importance of the definition of pre-retirement income as well as the sample used for the calculations has been considered. For the sake of simplicity all calculations are based on the cohort born in 1950 and involve only the income from the public pension. The following five definitions on pre-retirement income has been used: average income in last 5, 10, 15 years before retirement; income at age 64; and finally at age 55. These definitions correspond to columns 1–5 in Table A.1. The following samples has also been used: (1) all individuals regardless of working status before retirement; (2) only individuals that have worked at least 5 years before retirement; (3) same as (2) but with an alternative earnings equation; and finally (4) only individuals with more than 30 years of pension rights and income below the ceiling. These four different samples are included in the rows of Table A.1 as well as in Figure A.1.

From Figure A.1 it follows that, as expected, the sample of individuals working prior to retirement had the highest level of earnings. As discussed in Section 4.1 above, the estimated earnings equations had a peak before the retirement age, however, the reason for the monotonically increase

Table A.1. *Sensitivity analyses of replacement rates for the cohort born in 1950*

Selections and definitions of income before 65	Different definitions of income before retirement at age 65				
	Average earnings for age 60–64 (1)	Average earnings for age 55–64 (2)	Average earnings for age 49–64 (3)	Earnings at age 55 (4)	Earnings at age 64 (5)
All	61	58	57	55	66
Worked before 65	45	46	48	48	45
Worked before 65 and adjusted earnings equation	50	48	49	48	56
At least 30 years of pension rights and only income below the ceiling.	66	64	64	62	71

Note: We assume that all individuals have retired at 65; inflation ≈2 percent per year, real wage rate ≈2 percent per year, nominal return on financial assets 5 percent per year. Average income at age 65–69 in relation to income prior to 65.

Figure A.1. *Taxable income for different samples of the cohort born in 1950*

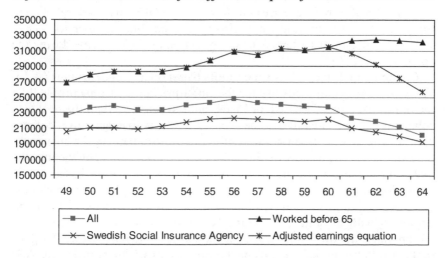

until age 64, in Figure A.1, is the assumed real wage increase of 2 percent per year. In order to test the sensitivity of the earnings profile an alternative profile is constructed by forcing earnings to decline the last 4 years prior to retirement. Thus, the alternative earnings equation does not have any support in the data but should only be considered as a test of the sensitivity of earnings profile prior to retirement. Figure A.1 also includes the earnings profile based on all individuals, regardless of working history.

This produces a considerable lower life earning profile. At any age from 49 and up, a large share of individuals is not working, as expected; this share becomes larger at older ages and therefore the average earnings decline from age 56 and at an accelerating pace from age 60. Thus, prior to retirement a large share is not working and the replacement rate based on this sample thus includes all kinds of transitions such as from unemployment and disability pension. Even if we argue that the most relevant calculation of replacement rates are for the transition from work to retirement, it is nonetheless interesting to evaluate the effect of including other transitions. The final sample included in Figure A.1 is based on individuals who have worked at least 30 years (30 years of pension rights) and with an income below the ceiling. The reason why this definition is of interest is because this is used by the Swedish National Social Insurance Office (NSIO), see Annual Report (2004). Thus, this definition has a special importance since this is the one used for calculations of the "official" replacement rates in Sweden; it is noteworthy that this measure produces the lowest level of the earning profile.

For the cohort born 1950, Table A.1 reports all the 20 replacement rates according to the definitions discussed above. Even if Table A.1 includes many entries, note that only two dimensions are considered; the sample used in the calculations which determines the level of the earnings profile and which period before retirement to consider. Of course, several choices for post-retirement income could also been used, but in order to keep it simple all calculations after age 65 are based on average income during the age interval 65–69.

Column 1 in Table A.1 lists the results based on average earnings 60–64. This definition is more sensitive for the curvature in the income profile than the results in column 2, based on 55–64, but less sensitive than the results in column 5, income at 64. If income is based on the whole age range, column 3, or a peak year, column 4, the result is not dependent on the curvature, only the level. Regardless of the definition of pre-retirement income the highest replacement rate are always produced for the sample based on the NSIO definition (row 4). The second highest is obtained if the calculations are based on all individuals (row 1), followed by individuals that worked before 65 with an adjusted earnings equation (row 3). The lowest rate are obtained in row 2 and based on individuals working before 65. This ranking follows immediately from the ranking of earnings in Figure A.1, a lower earning before retirement implies a higher replacement rate.

Even if the ranking of the results are trivial, the levels are not. For instance, if income before retirement is evaluated at 64, the rate varies from 45 to 71 percent. The reason for this huge difference is, of course, the declining income before retirement. For this reason it should be avoided to base before pension earnings on 1 year only. Another extreme is to use the full age range, as demonstrated in column 3, this produces a smaller variation (from 48–64 percent), but it implies that the individual base his

Table A.2.   An evaluation of the NSIO replacement rate

Selections and definitions of income before 65	Public pension (percent)
Working 60–64	44
Average income 60–64	
Number of year with pension rights ≥ 30	57
Average income 49–64	
Same as above and:	63
Only income < 8.07 income base amount	

Note: SESIM-simulated data 1999–2041. All individuals have retired at 65. Income for the cohorts born in 1950 at age 65 in relation to income before 65. Inflation ≈ 2 percent per year, real wage rate ≈ 2 percent per year, nominal return on financial assets 5 percent per year.

expected income as a pensioner on his full life earning profile. We argue that it is more realistic to base the comparison on income toward the end of the working carrier, last 5 or 10. The benefit of using the average income over several years is also that it reduces the sensitivity of declining earnings. Column 1 (60–64) reports a replacement rate of 45 percent based on the working criteria (row 2), given strongly declining earnings (row 3) the rate goes up to 50 percent. The corresponding results for column 2 based on a 10-year period are from 46 to 48 percent. This is an argument for using a 10-year period for pre-retirement income.

As mentioned above, the calculations done by NSIO can be considered as the official rates and hence have a certain importance. It is worth noting that these calculations are based on a definition (column 1 and row 4) that produces the third-highest rate, namely 64 percent. Due to the importance of the NSIO result, Table A.2 tries to give some further insights into the design of these high rates.

In order to follow the standard used by NSIO, the post-retirement income in Table A.2 is evaluated at age 65. In the first row the results are calculated using almost the same principles as in Table A.1 (column 1 and row 2), the only difference is that the in the numerator income is now defined at age 65 instead of average income at 65–69. According to Table A.2, public pension at age 65 covers 44 percent of the average taxable income at age 60–64 (based on a sample who has worked 5 years before 65). In the next row the first move toward the NSIO definition is presented; the sample is now based on all individuals with pension right more than 30 years and the income before pension is defined as the average value at age 49–64. Based on these definitions the replacement rate increase to 57 percent, thus an increase by almost 30 percent. Finally the definition above is extended by only including income below the ceiling. Of course this results in a further reduction of earnings before retirement and hence results in an even higher replacement arte. In Table A.2 the resulting replacement rate is 63 percent and this corresponds quite well to the one reported in Annual Report (2004).

To summarize, the NSIO standard produce a high replacement rate because of low pre-retirement income. This low income is obtained by including non-working individuals as well as by only considering income below the ceiling. Furthermore, the income used after retirement is income at age 65, given the discussion above regarding the design of the indexation of pension income, this produce the highest post-retirement income. The conclusion is that the numbers by NSIO cannot be considered as a guide for the individual who needs a measure of the income that he can expect as a pensioner.

CHAPTER 9

The Distribution of Wealth

Lennart Flood and Anders Klevmarken[*]

Standard economic theory suggests that most people try to keep their consumption standard approximately constant over the life-cycle and thus accumulate resources in active years and use them after retirement. Although this behavior is modified by changes in consumption needs over the life-cycle, the need to insure oneself against more or less unexpected expenditures and by a desire to leave bequests and inter vivo gifts to ones children, planning for a period of retirement with no labor incomes but with a need for resources to meet the potential expenditures for care at the end of life is basic to almost every household and individual. The accumulation of resources can take collective and private forms. In Sweden, like in most Western countries, public and occupational retirement schemes provide the basic resources to most households, but most of us also supplement with private savings in the form of an owned home, financial assets, or private pension annuities. In forecasting and evaluating the living standard of the elderly, it is thus not enough to look at the income stream from public and occupational pensions, one also has to evaluate the magnitude and portfolio composition of the private wealth of the elderly.

In simulating the future living standard of the elderly, we thus have to simulate their distribution of wealth. A particular issue of relevance to policy is if the baby-boom cohorts will have resources to cover the costs of their anticipated need of health care and social care. Will they have assets that can be liquidized and used to pay for these kinds of services?

---

[*] Corresponding author.

CONTRIBUTIONS TO ECONOMIC ANALYSIS
VOLUME 285   ISSN: 0573-8555
DOI:10.1016/S0573-8555(07)00009-0

Such payments could take the form of taxes, private insurance fees, or user cost fees.

The major asset of many households is their home. Statistics show that the share of home owners among the very old is smaller than among younger people. This could be the result of older people leaving their house for a smaller rented apartment or special housing for elderly or of older cohorts never having had as much invested in an owned home compared to younger cohorts. In the former case, some of the funds tied up in an own home are liquidized and thus become more readily available for consumption. In principle, a household that stays in its home might liquidize its asset too by increasing its mortgage, but in practice there is no good market solution to this problem that accommodates both the requirements of the lenders and the increase in the risk of the household portfolio when the mortgage is increased.[1] It is thus of great interest to simulate the share of financial assets of the portfolio of the elderly and to what extent they sell their owned home and move to a smaller owned or rented apartment.

1. The Swedish distribution of wealth in an international comparison

It is not easy to get a long perspective on the distribution of wealth in Sweden because there is no single data source that gives a consistent view for a long period of time. The early estimates of the distribution of wealth were based on the concept of tax-assessed wealth which is the basis of the wealth tax. This definition has the disadvantage of not including assets that were not taxed, and no or very unreliable data were given for the majority of the tax payers who were below the taxation threshold. Furthermore, this variable was defined for individuals and for jointly taxed individuals, but no economically meaningful household concept was available. Register data have since then improved, in particular after the late 1990s when data became available directly from banks, brokers, and insurance companies without the filtering of the tax payers. The problem with the household definition remains, but in SESIM we have made corrections to get a useful definition (see Chapter 3). A relatively large survey (HEK) run by Statistics Sweden which combines survey information about the household with register data on assets estimates the median household wealth to 156 000 SEK in 1999 and 197 000 SEK in 2003.[2] The latter estimate is in the 1999

---

[1] Only very recently Swedish financial institutes have started to offer elderly loans, either in the form of an annuity or a lump sum against their home, such that the principal and the accumulated interest need not be paid back until the house is sold or the owner dies.

[2] The exchange rate between the Euro and the Swedish Crown is about 9.3 SEK per Euro.

Table 1. Real and financial assets and debts per household in 1999 by age (medians)

Age	Real assets	Financial assets	Debts
25–35	52	16	143
36–45	359	37	247
46–55	483	70	196
56–60	455	134	104
61–65	424	158	36
66–75	240	183	0
76–85	36	164	0
86+	0	90	0

Note: Self-employed and farmers not included.
Source: Andersson *et al.* (2002), Table 3.5.

price level.[3] These estimates apply to all households independent of age. As will be shown below, the level of wealth depends very much on age.

According to a study by Spånt (1987), the inequality of wealth in Sweden declined from the beginning of the previous century to the middle of the 1970s. Jansson and Johansson (1988) claim that the decline came to a halt in the 1970s. Statistics Sweden estimated the Gini coefficient of household net worth to 0.78 in 1978. It then increased to 0.84 in the beginning of the 1990s and remained at about 0.85 with only small variations until 2003, the latest year of observation.[4]

The cross-sectional relation with age is typically reversed U-shaped with a peak in the age bracket 50–60. Table 1 shows the relation with age for real and financial assets and debts for the non-self-employed Swedish household population in 1999. While household members are in their 20s or 30s, they buy a home and finance it to a large extent with mortgages while their financial assets are small. The value of their real estate continues to increase until they are around 50 years old while they invest in larger homes and secondary homes. Debts do not increase, however, but are gradually reduced to zero as people become older. Financial assets increase and reach a peak around the age of 70. The increase after retirement age might be a result of households moving to smaller homes and thus liquidizing part of their assets tied up in real estate. Older households tend

---

[3] These estimates include real estate and financial assets less debts but not durables with the exception of automobiles, which are included. Real and financial assets abroad are included to the extent they have been reported to the Swedish tax authorities, but they are most likely underreported. The (notional) wealth accumulated in social security and occupational pensions is not included.

[4] Statistics Sweden (2000), Table 16, and Statistics Sweden (2005), Table 15.

to sell their homes and other properties and after the age of 75 many households have no real property at all.

This interpretation of the estimates in Table 1 follows that of the text book rather closely. The results in the table originate, however, from a single cross-section and could hide age differences that are not the result of ageing but rather come from the different experiences of these age cohorts. For instance, the small net wealth of the very old might not be a result of life-cycle decrease in assets for consumption purposes but rather reflecting that these cohorts never had any large wealth. The anatomy of age–wealth profiles were analyzed in Andersson *et al.* (2002) and Klevmarken (2004) and an attempt was made to separate cohort effects from age effects. They observed that the peak of the age–wealth profile gradually moved to higher ages, a change that cannot be explained by the life-cycle hypothesis. Their analysis showed that there were substantial cohort effects with those born in the 1940s and 1950s having the highest wealth and those born earlier the smallest. The age–wealth profile purged of these cohort effects showed almost no peak at all, mainly a trending increase, which suggested that the text book type of life-cycle savings had been rather weak in Sweden. If this interpretation of these results holds up, Swedes have to a large extent saved for other purposes than to maintain their consumption level after the age of retirement.

Inherited wealth and inter vivo gifts from parents contribute to the shape of the cross-sectional age–wealth profile. Klevmarken (2004) found that the median age of inheritance was 46 years while the median age of receiving a gift was 39 years. Most transfers were relatively small. The median amount inherited was only 76 000 SEK, but the mean was 270 000 suggesting a positively skewed distribution of bequests. If the wealthy cohorts born in the 1940s and 1950s will not consume up most of their currently large wealth, one would expect that intergenerational transfers will become even more important as these cohorts age.

One explanation to the relative success of the baby-boom cohorts is that they have been able to take advantage of the increase in real estate prices and in the booms of the stock market. We have observed rather sharp differences in the price increases of one family houses and condominiums in the three big city areas Stockholm, Gothenburg, and Malmö compared to the rest of the country. In particular in the greater Stockholm area, price increases have been much faster than elsewhere. Those who moved to these areas and invested in a house or condominium in the 1960s or 1970s have found that their property increased in value much more than in small cities and rural areas. A consequence is that we now observe large differences in wealth between those who own their home in these areas and those who rent it (see Andersson *et al.* (2002), Table 3.2).

How does the net wealth of Swedish households compare to that of households in other countries? Using roughly comparable data from the Swedish HUS surveys and the US PSID Klevmarken *et al.* (2003) found

Table 2.   *50+ household net wealth and financial assets in 2003 by country*

Country	Median net wealth (PPP adjusted)	Median financial assets (PPP adjusted)
Sweden	86.7	21.3
Denmark	110.6	31.9
Germany	99.1	16.5
The Netherlands	135.3	16.7
France	136.3	8.7
Switzerland	201.3	42.2
Austria	103.9	6.0
Italy	159.3	2.6
Spain	149.5	2.4
Greece	109.5	2.4
Australia	172.5	16.3

Medians, 1000 euros. Table applies to households with at least one member born in 1954 or earlier.
Note: All entries were adjusted by purchasing power parities to standardize for national differences in price levels. No PPP adjusted estimates can be found in Hesselius *et al.* (2005). Source: Hesselius *et al.* (2005), Table 6.1, based on data from the Survey of Health, Ageing and Retirement in Europe (SHARE). The Australian data that originate from the HILDA survey do not include superannuation.

that the median household net wealth was about the same in the two countries while the mean was much higher in the US distribution. A closer examination of the two distributions showed that every percentile to the left of the median was smaller in the United States than in Sweden, while the percentiles to the right of the median was smaller in Sweden than in the United States. Thus, poor households were less poor in Sweden than in the United States while rich households were much richer in the United States than in Sweden. This result held whether the Swedish distribution of wealth was compared to that of the whole US population or just that of the white population.

Table 2 offers a comparison across 10 European countries and Australia. The European estimates were obtained from the Survey of Health Ageing and Retirement in Europe (SHARE) that used the same harmonized set of interview questions in all 10 countries. The Australian estimates come from the HILDA survey of the Melbourne Institute of Applied Economic and Social Research.[5] The household population surveyed only included households with at least one member born in 1954 or earlier, i.e., people who were at least 50 years old. To compensate for the differences in the price levels of these countries median household wealth, net wealth, and financial wealth, respectively, were adjusted by purchasing

---

[5] www.melbourneinstitite.com

power parities. The results show that median net wealth per household is smallest in Sweden among the surveyed countries. It is 28 percent higher in our neighboring country Denmark, more than 70 percent higher in Italy and Spain and 132 percent higher in Switzerland!

The second column of the table gives Sweden a very different ranking by the median of financial assets. The Swedish median is the third largest, while households in the Mediterranean countries have very little of financial assets. This implies that Swedish households have relatively small values in real estate and/or high mortgages. Compared to most of the other countries, the share of households that rent their home rather than to own it is relatively high in Sweden, but there are also differences in real estate prices. Only the prices in the Stockholm area come in the neighborhood of those that apply in the more densely populated areas in Europe. Finally, there are differences in mortgage shares too. While Swedish banks often give loans and mortgages up to 90 percent of the market value of a property, banks in southern Europe are more cautious.

The same survey shows that Swedish households hold much more of their financial assets in the form of mutual funds and stocks than households in the other European countries. They are thus more exposed to market risks than households in the other countries.

We have thus found that Swedish households on average have less accumulated wealth than households in comparable European countries and that life-cycle savings are week. Can a common explanation be found? As demonstrated in Andersson *et al.* (2002), Swedes have a considerable notional wealth in the form of future claims on the public and occupational pension systems. On average the private wealth of blue collar workers is only about 15 percent of their notional wealth while the private wealth of white collar workers is a little less than 40 percent of their notional pension wealth. Considering this dominating importance of the public and occupational pension systems, that health care is publicly provided at low cost and that the tax burden is rather high, it is perhaps not so strange that Swedes have accumulated relatively less private wealth.

If we see private wealth as a potential source to finance the future costs of health care and social care, Swedish households have in total less to contribute compared to households in other European countries, but they have rather much in liquid form that more easily could be exchanged for services than an owner-occupied home.

2. The structure of the wealth module in SESIM

In SESIM, we have chosen to model financial wealth, savings in private pension annuities, the market value of owner-occupied homes, wealth invested in other real estate, and debts. Financial wealth includes a number of different assets such as bank accounts, bonds, mutual funds, stocks and shares, and life insurances, but not private pension annuities. The latter asset is modeled separately for two reasons, first because these kind of savings are designated life-cycle savings with the purpose of complementing public and occupational pensions, and second because investments in this asset are deductible from income at income taxation. We thus need this deduction to compute the income tax. A further break down of financial wealth by risk level would have been of interest, but it had required a completely different set of models and we also would have to model – (within or outside SESIM) the returns to each of these assets, a major task well outside our project.

Investments in real estate have been divided into two components, owner-occupied homes and other real estate, because the major asset of many Swedish households is just their home. This component includes both one and two family houses as well as condominiums. In 2002, about 43 percent of Swedish households owned a house and 14 percent a condominium.[6] Condominiums are most common in major cities. There are no direct data on market values of owner-occupied houses and condominiums in the registers of Statistics Sweden, but they have been estimated using the product of the tax-assessed value of each property and so-called purchase coefficients. These coefficients are the annual mean ratios of the price to the tax-assessed value of each sold unit in a relatively small area. Comparisons with self-reported survey data show that these estimates give good mean levels. They might though underestimate the dispersion of house values a little. These estimated market values form the dependent variable in our model for market values, see below.

Other real estate is a mixture of different assets. One large component is secondary homes. About 13 percent of Swedish households had a secondary home in 2002, some of which represented a major investment. Included in the aggregate, other real estate are also commercial apartment complexes, farm land and forests and other property owned by private households. There are rather few owners of these properties, but they represent large values for the owners. The corresponding distribution is thus strongly positively skewed.

Debts are modeled as a single category and it includes all kinds of debts such as mortgages on homes and other real estate, regular bank loans, and consumer credit. It might have been of interest to separate these different types of debts, but such detailed information is not available in the register data of Statistics Sweden, and it is not obvious that a separation is analytically meaningful. A household can increase the mortgages on their house not only to invest more in the house but also, for instance, to buy a

---

[6] These estimates are based on Linda using the family concept of this source.

car, a boat, or to go on a holiday trip. Thus, the legal form a loan takes does not necessarily say much about the uses of the borrowed money. Register data on mortgages and loans originate from banks and other credit institutes, which have to supply this information to the tax authorities for taxation purposes. Tax payers also have an interest to declare their loans because interest paid is deductible from incomes. Register data on mortgages and loans are thus considered being of good quality.

Figure 1 gives a view of the model structure and simulation path of the wealth model. The simulation starts with financial wealth. Different models are used depending on if the household had financial wealth or not in the previous year. Then follows the simulation of other real wealth, again the choice of model depends on the household having other real wealth or not in the previous year. In the third major step, private pension wealth is simulated, and in the fourth the value of any owner-occupied home. Ownership might change if the household moves and decides to buy a (new) house after the move. SESIM thus simulates geographical mobility and tenure choice (see Chapter 7) before the market value of a house is determined. Finally, the debt of each household is updated and the cost of housing is simulated. The latter entity is of interest in its own right, but also needed for the computations of housing benefits.

3. Modeling financial wealth

As mentioned, there are two components of financial wealth: private pension annuities and other financial wealth. The latter component includes stocks and shares, bonds, mutual funds, and bank accounts, and it will in the sequel for short be called just "financial wealth."[7] In modeling financial wealth, we have chosen to work with separate models for households, which previously respectively had and did not have these kinds of assets. In the first case, we use a dynamic panel model and in the second the combination of a logit model which simulates the transition from not having to having financial assets, and a regression model which simulates the amount. All three have been estimated using the Linda panel data. One might note that the period for which data are available (1999–2003) is a period of exceptional changes in the stock market, which might have resulted in estimates that are not typical for other periods. Furthermore, our short panel does not allow any elaborated dynamic specification,

---

[7] Financial assets abroad are included to the extent Swedish tax payers and tax authorities in other countries have reported them.

Figure 1. *Financial and real wealth and cost of housing in SESIM*

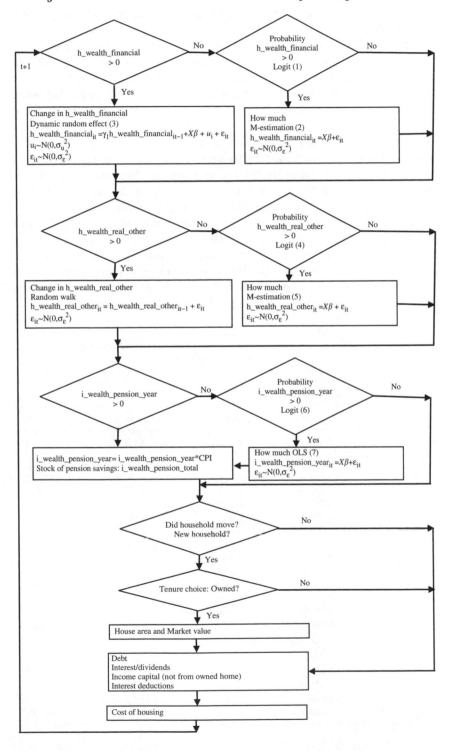

nor is it possible to identify and estimate cohort effects separately from period effects.

The model for those who did not have any financial wealth previously is a so-called two-part model. That is, the model for the probability to acquire financial wealth was estimated independently of the model that determines the amount of financial assets acquired. The reason for using the two-part model compared to, for instance, a generalized tobit model or a Heckit type of approach is that we focus on obtaining good robust predictions rather than on explaining selectivity. Manning *et al.* (1987) showed that the two-part model performs at least as well as the tobit type 2 model. Flood and Gråsjö (2001) demonstrated the sensitivity of the generalized tobit model to errors in the specification of the selection equation, which produce bias in all the estimated parameters.

Model specifications and estimates are exhibited in Table 3. For households that did not have any financial wealth, the probability to acquire some increases with increasing age. This could be the result of increased financial saving in middle age when mortgages have been reduced and children have left home, and of decreased investments in own home and other real estate after retirement. The relative position in the income

Table 3.   Estimates of models for financial wealth

Variable	If no financial wealth in the previous year			
	Logit model		Robust regression	
	Estimate	SD	Estimate	SD
Intercept	0.60048	0.0238	4.11968	0.0740
Age				
24	−0.88498	0.0165	−0.38918	0.0593
25–29	−0.69736	0.0143	−0.23525	0.0517
30–34	−0.81919	0.0148	−0.09806	0.0527
35–39	−0.93684	0.0153	−0.11248	0.0544
40–44	−1.04328	0.0157	−0.08929	0.0565
45–49	−1.16899	0.0160	−0.13599	0.0572
50–54	−1.14642	0.0160	−0.1094	0.0565
55–59	−1.08049	0.0165	0.10601	0.0588
60–64	−0.90114	0.0178	0.01721	0.0631
65–69	−0.733	0.0189	0.1681	0.0672
70–74	−0.65676	0.0189	0.05592	0.0675
75–79	−0.43381	0.0183	0.05422	0.0647
Taxable income				
P25	−2.60493	0.0216	−0.57373	0.0653
P25–P50	−2.13505	0.0212	−0.55061	0.0632
P50–P75	−1.57561	0.0212	−0.57211	0.0627
P75–P90	−1.04016	0.0219	−0.5316	0.0653
P90–P95	−0.61007	0.0262	−0.31861	0.0788

distribution also determines the probability to acquire financial assets. The higher the income the higher the probability.[8]

Although not uniformly and with the exception of the very old, the amount acquired increases with increasing age. The differences due to age are though relatively small. Those who are in the top right tail of the income distribution acquire more financial wealth than most people, about 25 percent more than those who have incomes below the 90th percentile.

In the dynamic random effects model, the estimated effect of the lagged stock of financial assets (Table 4) shows that there is a strong persistence in the investments of households. It is a little smaller among young people than among old, and among rich people compared to poor. The relative position in the income distribution has the expected effect, high-income households invest more. Price changes in the stock market have a strong influence on the stock of assets held by households. Finally, we might note that the variance of the purely random component is much larger than that of the unexplained household specific effects.

3.1. Tax-deferred pension savings

Because there are no register data on tax-deferred pension savings, we first need estimates of these stocks as of 1999, then a model which forwards these stocks after 1999.

Because register data include information about how much each individual has paid into pension policies and claimed deduction from income each year, the simple idea is to construct accumulated savings by using Linda panels. Individual savings are summed up over years and the resulting stock is increased each year by applying the average return given by life insurance companies. In order to reduce the starting value problem, we started as early as 1980, at which time private tax-deferred pension savings were rather unusual.

Table 5 summarizes the main characteristics of pension savings during the period 1980–2000. Column (2) gives the share of all individuals with pension savings; note, this is the share of the whole population, regardless of age. Thus, during this period there has been an increase from about 4 to 21 percent. The share with a positive accumulated savings, i.e., private pension wealth, is given in column (6). In year 2000, more than 30 percent had a positive accumulated savings, the mean value, column (7), was 110 863 SEK and the corresponding mean of yearly savings, column (3),

---

[8] We have here used a relative measure of income, i.e., the percentile of the income distribution, rather than income as such in order to avoid that a general increase in income level will drive the probability toward 1 as income increases over long periods. This is a general problem in simulation models such as SESIM.

Lennart Flood and Anders Klevmarken

Table 4. Estimates of a dynamic model for financial wealth

Variable	Estimate	SD
Intercept	0.95	–
Lag stock × age		
24	−0.0177	0.00171
25–29	−0.0152	0.00106
30–34	−0.0183	0.00092
35–39	−0.0169	0.00081
40–44	−0.0163	0.00077
45–49	−0.0151	0.00074
50–54	−0.0115	0.00072
55–59	−0.0066	0.00069
60–64	−0.0051	0.00070
65–69	−0.0032	0.00069
70–74	−0.0018	0.00066
75–79	0.0003	0.00063
Lag stock × taxable income		
P25	0.0429	0.00740
P25–P50	0.0304	0.00733
P50–P75	0.0177	0.00736
P75–P90	0.0114	0.00763
P90–P95	0.0029	0.00906
Taxable income		
P25	−0.4743	0.01292
P25–P50	−0.3560	0.01282
P50–P75	−0.2524	0.01286
P75–P90	−0.1863	0.01327
P90–P95	−0.0984	0.01565
Index Sthlm Stock Exchange	0.0040	0.00001
Lagged stock of financial assets	0.8832	0.00710
Sigma u	0.0197	
Sigma e	0.3732	

was 6591 SEK. Even if the share of pension savers has increased, the yearly amounts have not. The yearly savings reached the highest value in 1989 and since then it has gone down. The reason for this is that changes in the tax rules after 1989 made deductions of savings from income less generous, and that the return on these savings has been quite low in more recent years.

The accumulated pension savings are given in column (8). The low value in 1980 indicates that the starting value problem is quite small. Pension savings were unusual before 1980. The total pension wealth has increased to some 315 billion SEK in year 2000.[9]

---

[9] Compared to a few survey estimates from the Swedish Household Panel Survey (HUS), these estimates compare relatively well, see Klevmarken (2006).

Table 5. Tax-deferred pension savings 1980–2000

	Share with pension savings (percent)	Mean value given savings (tkr)	Share with income from pension savings (percent)	Mean value given income (tkr)	Share with pension wealth (percent)	Mean value given pension wealth (tkr)	Sum of pension wealth (mkr)	Assumed return on savings (percent)
1980	4.60	3529	0.00	936	4.10	3882	1396	10
1981	4.70	3962	0.00	1416	4.40	8086	3137	10
1982	4.90	4748	0.00	981	4.70	13 136	5449	10
1983	3.80	6968	0.00	2127	4.80	19 728	8411	12
1984	4.40	7846	0.00	1469	5.00	28 427	12 550	13
1985	8.20	8321	0.00	1427	5.40	39 080	18 828	15
1986	8.50	9229	0.70	11 621	6.90	43 074	26 553	14
1987	9.70	9969	0.80	14 074	8.70	46 748	36 056	12
1988	11.90	11 170	0.70	7676	11.00	51 523	50 285	14
1989	14.40	12 955	0.70	8027	13.60	62 291	74 903	21
1990	14.50	8138	0.70	8319	15.50	69 798	95 710	16
1991	12.50	9656	2.60	21 013	17.20	73 414	111 944	10
1992	12.80	8339	2.90	22 175	18.50	76 117	125 012	7
1993	13.30	8465	3.30	23 476	19.50	79 001	136 367	5
1994	15.00	8762	3.50	23 572	21.40	80 551	152 702	7
1995	16.20	6861	4.10	22 528	23.00	82 478	168 393	7
1996	17.30	6764	4.10	23 608	24.60	85 822	187 482	8
1997	18.20	6705	4.20	25 272	26.10	92 546	214 326	11
1998	19.20	6659	4.30	27 870	27.80	100 973	248 870	13
1999	20.50	6785	4.50	30 540	29.70	104 530	275 265	8
2000	21.90	6591	4.80	32 598	32.00	110 863	315 101	12

Note: Own calculations based on the Linda panel 1980–2000. Information on average returns, in column (9), comes from The Swedish Insurance Federation 〈www.forsakringsforbundet. com〉; these returns are returns before tax and administrative costs.

Given the accumulated stock of pension savings in 1999, we assume that those who claimed deductions in 1999 continue to do so in the following years until the age of 64 by the same amount increased by the CPI. For those who did not save anything in 1999 and were in the age range 18–64, we applied a two-part model estimated from Linda data (Table 6). The simulated amount saved in 2000 was then also applied to later years but increased by the CPI. For each year, the probability of pension saving is simulated. If an individual is predicted to be a pension saver, the amount is also predicted. Again it is assumed that the individual continues to save this amount (adjusted by CPI) until he retires. Thus, for those individuals who do not save, the probability of saving is simulated every year. Note, that the yearly amount saved is indexed by the CPI, but the stock of pension savings is increased by an interest rate for long-term bonds.

The estimates in Table 6 show that the probability to invest in private pension policies has a reversed U-shaped relation with age. As detailed in Figure 2, it peaks at about 30 years of age and stops just before the typical pension age of 65. The symbols in this figure denote the average share of pension savers for each year of age (a plus indicates observed and a

Table 6. Tax-deferred pension savings, logit for the probability of investing if no stock in previous year, and OLS for amount invested

	Logit model			Odds ratio	OLS model		
	Parameter estimate	SE	Probability value		Parameter estimate	SE	Probability value
Intercept	-2.465	0.033	<0.0001		3.35064	0.4657	<0.0001
0=male, 1=female	0.4726	0.00475	<0.0001	1.604	-0.36754	0.13405	0.0061
Age	0.0345	0.0015	<0.0001	1.035	0.20477	0.00584	<0.0001
Age squared	-0.0837	0.00182	<0.0001	0.92			
Basic education	-0.4867	0.00732	<0.0001	0.615	-1.3361	0.20714	<0.0001
Medium education	-0.1925	0.00506	<0.0001	0.825	-1.03162	0.1413	<0.0001
University reference	-			-	-		-
Marital status 1=married	0.0555	0.00475	<0.0001	1.057			
Taxable income <=P25	-1.6142	0.0117	<0.0001	0.199	-4.95757	0.31969	<0.0001
P25<taxable income<=P50	-0.689	0.0107	<0.0001	0.502	-5.63135	0.29677	<0.0001
P50<taxable income<=P75	-0.3699	0.01	<0.0001	0.691	-6.05472	0.27749	<0.0001
P75<taxable income<=P90	-0.2423	0.0102	<0.0001	0.785	-5.32838	0.28191	<0.0001
P90<taxable income<=P95	-0.1153	0.0122	<0.0001	0.891	-4.34155	0.33838	<0.0001
>P95 reference	-			-	-		-
Nationality: Swedish=1	0.5569	0.0111	<0.0001	1.745	-0.53785	0.31648	0.0893

Note: Models estimated using LINDA 1999/2000. The population was restricted to those who did not have any accumulated tax-deferred pension savings in 1999. The unit of observation is the individual.

Figure 2. Probability to save in a private pension policy in 2000 if no accumulated savings in 1999, predicted and observed values

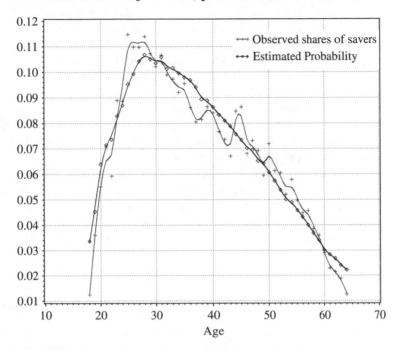

rectangle predicted). The curves give a polynomial approximation to the average values and from the figure it follows that the fitted and observed values are closely related. The estimates also show that the higher the education and the higher the income, the higher the probability to invest, and that immigrants have a smaller probability to invest than Swedes. The amount invested increases with increasing age. The relation is close to linear. Females have a higher probability to invest than males, but if they invest the amount is smaller than that invested by males. Schooling and income also determine the amount invested in the expected direction. The higher the education and income, the more is the investment. Among those who invest Swedes do not invest significantly more than immigrants.

4. Household real wealth

Household real wealth is decomposed into two components: own home and other real wealth. Since the probability of owning a home is modeled in the regional mobility module (Chapter 7), only the model that determines the market value of a home and the model that simulates other real wealth is discussed here.

The market value of a home is primarily determined by its location, size, and qualities. Changes in values depend on factors that influence demand

and supply, such as changes in income and wealth and in the cost of borrowing. We do not try to formulate and estimate a model of the market value in this sense. We need a model that predicts the market value of the home of a particular family. In addition to some of the variables mentioned, we will thus also use properties of the family as predictors.

The estimation of the market value model for own homes is based on both Linda and HEK data. Since information about house area is missing in Linda, HEK data from 1999 have been used to estimate a model of floor area (area in $m^2/100$) in order to impute this variable. The results are not reported here but the most important findings are that the age of the owner matters and that the size reaches a maximum in the age bracket 45–49. Marital status and number of children have strong effects. Income also has a strong effect. Those who belong to the first quartile have a house area $46\,m^2$ smaller than those in the highest income quartile. There is a large negative Stockholm effect, dwellings are $12\,m^2$ smaller compared to areas outside Stockholm, Gothenburg, and Malmö for otherwise comparable houses and families.

Using the imputed value of floor area, jointly with the other covariates reported in Table 7, a model was estimated on data from 1999. The sample was limited to house owners and owners of condominiums having a property

Table 7. **Estimates of a model of the market value of single family houses in 2000**

	Parameter estimate	SE	Probability value
Intercept	0.21501	0.04760	<0.0001
Age	0.02748	0.00162	<0.0001
Age squared	−0.02881	0.00131	<0.0001
Marital status 1 = married	0.22295	0.01371	<0.0001
Number children <18	−0.000493	0.00549	0.9284
Taxable income < = P25	0.16705	0.02972	<0.0001
P25 < taxable income < = P50	0.00117	0.02434	0.9618
P50 < taxable income < = P75	−0.03867	0.01929	0.0450
P75 < taxable income < = P90	−0.01329	0.01607	0.4080
P90 < taxable income < = P95	−0.03896	0.01074	0.0003
> P95 (reference)	–	–	–
Stockholm	0.88275	0.01085	<0.0001
Gothenburg, Malmo	0.73231	0.00862	<0.0001
Larger cities	0.40752	0.00707	<0.0001
Southern medium urban	0.30120	0.00742	<0.0001
Northern urban	0.15413	0.00929	<0.0001
Rural (reference)	–	–	–
House area square meters	0.81052	0.06021	<0.0001
Financial wealth < = P50	−0.58996	0.00739	<0.0001
P50 < financial wealth < = P75	−0.41537	0.00719	<0.0001
P75 < financial wealth < = P90	−0.27278	0.00729	<0.0001
P90 < financial wealth < = P95	−0.15499	0.00879	<0.0001
> P95 (reference)	–	–	–
R^2	0.40		

value between 50 tkr and 10 mkr. There is a clear age effect and again an inverted-U relation, the maximum value is about 1.1 mkr for households in their mid-40s to mid-50s. There are strong and significant effects of marital status, region, house area, financial wealth, and nationality. The market value of a house in the Stockholm region is $(e^{0.88}-1)100 = 141$ percent higher than a house in the reference region (rural region). The market value for a household with a financial wealth below the median is 42 percent of the value for a household in the highest wealth group.

The mixture of large and rather small properties in the aggregate other real wealth makes it difficult to estimate good models. The distribution is heavily skewed. In the simulations, we distinguish between households that have this asset and those who do not have it. In the first case, we use a simple random walk. In the second case, a logit model was estimated for the probability to buy property in the next year and a robust regression to simulate the amount.

The estimates of Table 8 show that the probability to invest in other properties reaches a peak at middle age. Couples have a higher probability

Table 8. *Estimates of a two-part model to explain new investments in other properties*

Variable	Logit model		Robust regression model	
	Estimate	SD	Estimate	SD
Intercept	−4.21229	0.0552	6.070	0.1364
Age				
24	−1.25596	0.0987		
25–29	−0.06498	0.0513		
30–34	0.52977	0.0443		
35–39	0.55369	0.0442		
40–44	0.68137	0.0441		
45–49	0.72257	0.0439		
50–54	0.75253	0.0435		
55–59	0.73157	0.0443		
60–64	0.69633	0.0463		
65–69	0.83386	0.0472		
70–74	0.57541	0.0498		
75–79	0.33514	0.0526		
80	0.0000			
Maximum age in household			−0.009	0.0017
If couple	0.24162	0.0206		
Taxable income				
P25	−2.0716	0.0420	−0.775	0.1222
P25–P50	−1.58002	0.0381	−0.733	0.1172
P50–P75	−1.16858	0.0355	−0.604	0.1175
P75–P90	−0.74813	0.0367	−0.501	0.1226
P90–P95	−0.50311	0.0449	−0.249	0.1505
P95	0.0000	0.0420	0.000	
Number of observations	170 673		1402	

to invest than singles and there is a rather strong income effect. High-income people have a much higher probability to invest than low-income people. Income also determines the amount invested.

5. Models of debts

In SESIM, we distinguish between study debts and other debts. Other debts include all debts, but the loans that are offered to the college and university students by the government. It is assumed that the take up rate is 100 percent and that students borrow as much as they are allowed to. Study debts are increased by an interest rate determined by the government. Repayments of principal and accumulated interest are proportional to the taxable income of the borrower according to certain rules, which are followed in SESIM. The reminder of this section deals with other debts than study loans.

Assuming that most households do not decrease or increase their debts much from one year to another, we need models that simulate debts at the end of next year conditional on current debts. We also need to account for any major investment of a household that might influence its decisions to take up new loans, such as buying a new home.

The analysis of the distribution of debts and the dynamics of debts was limited to stable households in the period 1999–2002. New households that have been formed through marriages, separations, and deaths will have their assets updated by adding the wealth of new household members, by following standard rules for bequests, and in the case of separation by dividing the assets between the newly formed households using common rules. Within stable households, 77 percent have debts. The median debt in this period was 156 000 SEK while the mean debt was 355 000 SEK. The distribution is thus positively skewed. The largest registered debt was 176 millions SEK.

A few households show major changes in debts in a year. The largest observed increase was 77 millions and the largest decrease was 97 millions. The changes observed for the majority of the households are, however, much smaller. The mean change was an increase of 13 600 and the median change was 0. Of those who had no debt in a year, 11 percent had one the following year. Of those who had a debt in a year, about 92 percent also had one the following year.

The purchase of a house or other property is usually partly financed by a mortgage or loan. One might thus expect that households that buy or sell property would increase and decrease their debts respectively unless they owned property before or bought new property after having sold their old property. Data show that households that had no real estate or real estate at a value of less than 10 000 SEK in a year but owned more than 10 000

SEK worth of real estate in the following year in the mean increase their debts by 450 000 SEK while the median change was a decrease of 6000!

A similar pattern emerges if one selects out households that owned real estate at a value of at least 10 000 in year, but had no such assets or at least less than a value of 10 000 in the following year. This group of households decreased their mean debts by 669 000 while the median decrease was only 15 000. There were, however, also households that increased their debts with large amounts.

We do find that changes in real estate investments influence the amount of debt a household has, but also that there is much heterogeneity in behavior suggesting that other factors than investments in real estate might sometimes have a dominating influence on the decisions to take up loans.

Lets first consider the group of households with no debts at the end of a given year $t-1$. We have first estimated a random effects probit model for the event of having debt at the end of the following year t. Explanatory variables were the age of the oldest household member, if single, the change in real estate investments, and, in financial assets, the change in the sum of taxable income from work for all household members and last years disposable income. The current value of disposable income cannot be used in this equation because it will become simulated after the debt variables in SESIM. For this reason, taxable income from work had to be used.[10] The cost of borrowing is captured by a real rate of interest on short assets. Table 9 gives the estimates.

The probability to go into debt decreases with increasing age. Singles have a smaller probability to take up loans than couples, while those who have increased their investments in real estate during the year have a higher probability. If financial assets have increased since last year, the probability to take a loan is smaller, but this effect is relatively weak. The higher the income, the easier the household has to pay interest and reduce the principle, and thus also easier to get into debt.

The model estimated to simulate the size of any loan is a random effect panel data model. The observations were conditioned to households with no debt in the previous year. The explanatory variables were the same as in the probit equation except for the variable change in taxable income from work, which was dropped, and the change in the real rate of interest, which was added. The results are displayed in Table 10.

The results show that not only does the probability to take up a loan decrease with increasing age, but so does the size of the loan taken. Singles borrow less than couples. The larger the increase in real estate investments, the larger will be the loan, and the higher the disposable income the larger

---

[10] If we had been able to use the change in disposable income, the estimates could have been interpreted in the following way: $bx_{t-1} + c(x_t - x_{t-1}) = (b-c)x_{t-1} + cx_t$.

Table 9. **Estimates of a random effects probit model for the probability of taking up a loan if the household had no loan previously**

Explanatory variable	Estimate	SE	z-score	Mean of explanatory variables
Age 30–45	−0.2522	0.0237	−10.63	0.1101
Age 45–60	−0.6428	0.0236	−27.19	0.1632
Age 60–75	−1.2922	0.0240	−53.71	0.2905
Age 70+	−2.0298	0.0263	−77.07	0.3828
If single	−0.3758	0.0130	−28.89	0.6170
Change in real assets	0.0003	0.0000	16.75	21.0871
Change in financial assets	−0.0000	0.0000	−2.53	−21.3270
Lagged disposable income	0.0001	0.0000	7.96	173.179
Sum of change in taxable income from work	−0.0001	0.0000	−1.13	3.2775
Real rate of interest	−0.2742	0.0102	−26.81	3.7600
Intercept	0.9049	0.0469	19.30	
SD of individual random effect component	0.8159	0.0098		
Number of observations	188 536			
Number of individuals	59 976			

Note: Explanatory variables in values are used in the unit 1000 SEK. The interest rate is in per cent.

Table 10. **Random effects GLS regression of the logarithm of new debts given that the household had no debt in the previous year**

Explanatory variable	Slope estimate	SE	z-score
Age 30–45	−0.3195	0.0650	−4.92
Age 45–60	−0.6601	0.0660	−10.00
Age 60–75	−1.2589	0.0686	−18.34
Age 75+	−1.8486	0.0816	−22.66
If single	−0.3047	0.0426	−7.16
Change in real assets	0.0010	0.0001	18.88
Lagged disposable income	0.0004	0.0001	7.88
Real rate of interest	−0.6098	0.0900	−6.77
Change in real rate of interest	0.0721	0.0600	1.20
Intercept	5.1921	0.3468	14.97
Sigma u	1.5711		
Sigma e	2.2520		
Number of observations	21 583		
Number of households	20 120		

loan can the household afford. The real rate of interest influences the size of the loan strongly, the higher the rate the smaller the loan. We might finally note that unmeasured heterogeneity among the households amounts to a little more than 30 percent of the total residual variation. The properties of the estimated residuals u and e suggest that a normal

Table 11. **Random effects probit estimates for the probability to stay in debt**

Explanatory variables	Slope estimates	SE	z-score
Age 30–45	−0.0773	0.0315	−2.45
Age 45–60	−0.1884	0.0309	−6.10
Age 60–75	−0.5062	0.0315	−16.08
Age 75+	−0.5784	0.0347	−16.65
Interactions			
(Age 16–29)*lagged log (debt)	0.3472	0.0075	46.35
(Age 30–45)*lagged log (debt)	0.3685	0.0044	83.44
(Age 45–60)*lagged log (debt)	0.3595	0.0039	91.64
(Age 60–75)*lagged log (debt)	0.3434	0.0041	83.73
(Age 75+)*lagged log (debt)	0.2921	0.0056	51.77
If single	−0.0885	0.0096	−9.24
Change in real assets	0.0001	0.0000	22.86
Change in financial assets	−0.0000	0.0000	−1.58
Lagged disposable income	−0.0000	0.0000	−3.30
Real rate of interest	−0.3282	0.0201	16.32
Change in real rate of interest	0.1649	0.0137	12.03
Intercept	2.1368	0.0826	25.86
Sigma u	0.5117		
Number of observations	633 616		
Number of households	170 037		

approximation is not too bad. It implies that normal random numbers can be drawn when the amount of debt is simulated.

Let us now turn to the larger group of households who already are in debt and analyze how their debt changes. Also in this case a two-part model was estimated. The results from a random effects probit model for the probability to stay in debt can be found in Table 11, and the results from the random effects regression model for the amount borrowed in Table 12.

The probability to stay in debt decreases with increasing age independently of the size of the debt. Independently of age the probability to remain in debt increases with increasing debt. This relation is almost the same through the whole age range, possibly with a somewhat smaller factor of proportionality above the age of 75. Singles have a smaller probability to stay in debt than couples, and households that have increased their investments in real estate have a higher probability. The effect of changes in the stock of financial assets is negligible. A high disposable income decreases the probability somewhat, but this effect is small. The cost of borrowing is important though, the higher the cost the smaller the probability to stay in debt.

It was not easy to find a satisfactory model for the size of the debt given that the household remained in debt. We have finally selected a random

Table 12.   Random effects GLS regression estimates of a model explaining the logarithm of debts for households who continue to have debts

Explanatory variables	Slope estimates	SE	z-score
Age 30–45	−0.3538	0.0214	−16.51
Age 45–60	−0.5651	0.0216	−26.18
Age 60–75	−0.9721	0.0234	−41.57
Age 75+	−1.1224	0.0319	−35.21
Interactions			
(Age 16–29)*lagged log (debt)	−0.2209	0.0041	−54.11
(Age 30–45)*lagged log (debt)	−0.1430	0.0015	−94.11
(Age 45–60)*lagged log (debt)	−0.1140	0.0014	−78.88
(Age 60–75)*lagged log (debt)	−0.0610	0.0023	−26.94
(Age 75+)*lagged log (debt)	−0.0442	0.0050	−8.81
Change in real assets	0.00006	0.000001	55.14
Lagged disposable income	0.000005	0.0000008	6.57
Change in taxable income from work	0.000008	0.000004	2.00
Real rate of interest	−0.0938	0.0033	−28.11
Change in real rate of interest	0.0414	0.0023	18.38
Intercept	1.5233	0.0235	64.69
Sigma u	0.3822		
Sigma e	0.4917		
Number of observations	583 688		
Number of households	157 016		

effects regression model that was estimated using a sample constrained to households with a lagged debt exceeding 10 000 SEK. Without this constraint, i.e., using all observations with a debt, the right tail of the distribution of the residuals became very thick. In the simulations, this resulted in a few households having excessively large debts. Although the sample was restricted to households with at least 10 000 in debts, the model will in SESIM be applied to all households with a debt.[11] The parameter estimates are displayed in Table 12.

Lagged debt is an important variable explaining current debt. The more indebted a household is the more will it reduces its debts. The estimates imply elasticities that vary from −0.2 among the youngest households to −0.04 among the oldest. So young people with high debts tend to decrease their debts more than elderly with high debts do, but independently of the size of the debt elderly generally reduce their debts more. Households that have increased their investments in real estate accumulate more debts than other households do, and the higher income a household has the more debts will it get. The cost of borrowing does not only influence the

---

[11] The restriction of the sample reduced its size by about 5 percent.

probability to stay in debt but also the size of the debt. The higher the cost the less borrowed.

Examination of the residuals, both the household unique component u and the general residual e, shows that both distributions are negatively skewed and have a rather high kurtosis. It is thus not advisable to simulate using random draws from normal distributions. Instead we have drawn random numbers from the empirical distributions.

6. Simulating the future of the distribution of wealth

When the model is run, the values of assets have been indexed by appropriate indices, the most important of which have been displayed in the second to fifth columns of Table 13. In all cases, we have used observed values up to and including 2005, which, for instance, implies that the down turn in the stock market around year 2000 is reflected in the stock market index. All series have been given "a steady state" value around 2010 with an adjustment period in between 2005 and 2010. The CPI is assumed to increase by 2 percent annually, the long interest rate is assumed to be 5 percent and the short 4 percent, while the stock market index increases by 3.75 percent. Dividends are supposed to yield 2.5 percent, and the total return on stocks thus becomes 6.25 percent. The market value of single family houses is assumed to increase by 3.5 percent annually after 2010. The resulting average annual increase in respective index is given at the bottom of the table. We find, for instance, that house values on average increase faster than stock values.

To get an idea of the sensitivity of our results to the assumptions detailed in Table 13, a simulation was also run with assumed less growth in the market value of real estate and in the long interest rate, while the change in stock market values remained the same. On average, the market

Table 13. Indices of wealth growth and financial markets (1999=100)

Year	CPI	Long bonds	Stock market	Market value of single family house	Mean net wealth in 1999 prices	Median net wealth in 1999 prices
1999	100	100.0	100.0	100.0	100.0	100.0
2000	101.0	105.1	95.6	111.0	107.2	152.0
2010	120.4	164.1	121.0	177.0	165.1	518.2
2020	146.7	267.3	174.9	249.6	221.7	798.3
2030	178.9	435.4	252.7	352.1	254.4	954.2
2040	218.0	709.2	365.1	496.8	267.8	1048.9
Average annual growth	1.9 percent	4.9 percent	3.2 percent	3.9 percent	2.4 percent	5.7 percent

value of real estate was assumed to increase by 2.7 percent annually compared to 3.9 percent in the main alternative and the long interest rate was on average 4.0 percent instead of 4.9 percent.

The last two columns of Table 13 show that the model in its basic scenario simulates a very strong increase in median net wealth, and it is about twice that of the mean. This is consistent with the assumed high increase in house values compared to stock values, and the implication is that the inequality of wealth decreases as verified in Table 14. In the alternative scenario, the growth in wealth is smaller and the inequality of the distribution increases, primarily because the left tail of the distribution is pulled out.

In the beginning of the period, net wealth shows the conventional reversed U-shaped relation with age, as demonstrated by the solid curve in Figure 3. But as the simulations proceed, the down turn of the curve at

Table 14.   Measures of central tendency and wealth inequality in 1999, 2000, 2020, and 2040 (household net wealth, thousands of Swedish crowns in 1999 prices)

Measure	1999	2000	2020	2040
P10	−187	−199	−170	−162
P25	−18	−10	171	217
P50	126	191	1002	1316
P75	666	794	2041	2552
P90	1648	1780	3460	3937
Mean	549	587	1217	1468
CV	2.54	2.62	2.24	1.80
Gini	0.93	0.96	0.90	0.80

Figure 3.   Mean net wealth by period and the age of oldest in the household (SEK in 1999 prices)

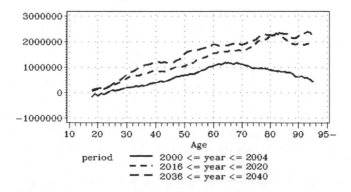

higher ages disappears and the retired cohorts become more wealthy relative to the working cohorts. This is further detailed in Table 15. In 1999 and 2000, those who were 80 or older had only about 40 percent of the wealth of those in the age bracket 60–69. In 2020, the oldest will, according to the simulations, have about 6 percent more than the 60–69 years old and 20 years later they will all have about the same median net wealth. Young cohorts will also improve their position relative to middle aged. In the alternative scenario, the relative position of the elderly increases even more, while the increase of the relative position of the young cohorts becomes much smaller.

Table 16 shows the change in the average portfolio composition as the simulations proceed. The share of single family homes increases from 43 percent of gross wealth to 55 percent, while both financial wealth other than tax-deferred pension savings and this kind of pension savings decrease from 41 to 33 percent and from 8 to 2 percent, respectively. Investments in other real estate decrease as well. The debt ratio decreases marginally. These shares behave differently in the alternative scenario. The share of financial wealth now increases, while the share of owned homes increases only very marginally. The share of debts also shows a considerable

Table 15.   *Median net wealth by age relative to median net wealth at the age of 60–69 in 1999–2040*

Year/ age	18–29	30–39	40–49	50–59	60–69	70–79	80+	Median net wealth at the age of 60–69 in 1999 prices
1999	0.000	0.068	0.177	0.568	1.000	0.767	0.393	534400
2000	0.027	0.010	0.208	0.582	1.000	0.777	0.417	626910
2010	0.238	0.407	0.457	0.699	1.000	1.188	0.973	1095857
2020	0.358	0.483	0.557	0.771	1.000	1.060	1.068	1517378
2030	0.352	0.496	0.611	0.828	1.000	1.060	1.054	1746015
2040	0.324	0.522	0.603	0.810	1.000	1.023	1.006	1954759

Table 16.   *Average portfolio shares of gross wealth in 1999–2040*

Year	Financial wealth	Private pension policies	Own home	Other real estate	Mean gross wealth	Debts other than	Study debts
	Shares of gross wealth				1000 SEK 1999 prices	Shares of gross wealth	
1999	0.412	0.080	0.434	0.154	798	0.281	0.032
2000	0.377	0.078	0.462	0.161	866	0.285	0.032
2020	0.423	0.038	0.459	0.118	2604	0.295	0.021
2040	0.333	0.022	0.553	0.115	4430	0.257	0.022

increase. It is thus in this scenario the relatively weak growth in real estate prices and the growth in debts that both explain the smaller growth in total net wealth and the increased inequality.

When the portfolio composition is also detailed by age (Table 17), we find for the basic scenario that in 1999 the share of financial assets increased with increasing age, the share of tax-deferred pension savings was highest immediately before retirement while the share of investments in real estate decreased with increasing age. The share of debts also decreased with increasing age. Compared to 1999, the share of owned homes and other real estate increases for the retired generations while the share of financial assets decreases. The increase in wealth for the elderly is thus to a large extent an increase in illiquid property. Some of this property will remain mortgaged as the share of debts also increases among the elderly.

Table 17. *Average portfolio shares of gross wealth by age in 1999, 2020, and 2040*

Age	Shares of gross wealth						Gross wealth in 1999 prices
	Financial wealth	Private pension	Home	Other real estate	Debts	Study debate	
1999							
18–29	0.2623	0.0399	0.5878	0.1498	0.5439	0.0904	581 996
30–39	0.3363	0.0894	0.4938	0.1698	0.3853	0.0554	752 923
40–49	0.3715	0.1163	0.4392	0.1893	0.3170	0.0260	853 028
50–59	0.3976	0.1504	0.4251	0.1773	0.2432	0.0053	1 003 715
60–69	0.4917	0.1062	0.3463	0.1619	0.1110	0.0004	1 199 119
70–79	0.5904	0.0259	0.2967	0.1128	0.0535	0.0001	887 262
80+	0.6793	0.0031	0.2461	0.0746	0.0207	0.0000	638 390
2020							
18–29	0.3025	0.0162	0.6553	0.0420	0.3501	0.0635	1 631 245
30–39	0.3467	0.0388	0.5766	0.0766	0.3656	0.0473	2 122 839
40–49	0.3791	0.0540	0.5085	0.1124	0.3990	0.0348	2 411 547
50–59	0.3882	0.0755	0.4905	0.1213	0.3551	0.0136	2 819 517
60–69	0.4395	0.0661	0.4135	0.1471	0.2782	0.0017	3 425 264
70–79	0.4972	0.0183	0.3364	0.1663	0.2437	0.0000	3 585 135
80+	0.5953	0.0085	0.2557	0.1489	0.1205	0.0000	3 517 927
2040							
18–29	0.2112	0.0118	0.7403	0.0483	0.2898	0.0717	2 837 113
30–39	0.2565	0.0243	0.6646	0.0788	0.3179	0.0496	3 801 998
40–49	0.2875	0.0342	0.6161	0.0962	0.3373	0.0319	4 118 182
50–59	0.2897	0.0440	0.6023	0.1079	0.2959	0.0119	4 875 397
60–69	0.3509	0.0437	0.5335	0.1155	0.2653	0.0010	5 662 461
70–79	0.4009	0.0105	0.4532	0.1458	0.2121	0.0000	5 684 748
80+	0.4718	0.0008	0.3368	0.1914	0.1555	0.0000	5 754 335

Table 18. **Mean net household wealth by region and year (1999 prices)**

Region	1999		2000		2020		2040	
	Mkr	Index	Mkr	Index	Mkr	Index	Mkr	Index
Stockholm	0.63	100	0.66	100	1.60	100	2.72	100
Gothenburg	0.50	83	0.45	68	1.40	87	2.48	91
Malmö	0.43	68	0.41	62	1.44	90	2.72	100
Urban Götaland	0.45	71	0.42	64	1.29	81	2.20	81
Urban Svealand	0.45	65	0.42	64	1.22	76	2.21	81
Urban Norrland	0.43	68	0.39	59	1.20	75	1.99	73
Rural Götaland	0.48	76	0.45	68	1.36	85	2.31	85
Rural Svealand	0.39	62	0.35	53	1.34	84	2.29	84
Rural Norrland	0.36	57	0.33	50	1.12	70	1.83	67

Wealth is unevenly distributed across the country. In 1999, mean net household wealth in the rural north was only 57 percent of mean net wealth in Stockholm (Table 18). Also the two other major urban areas – Gothenburg and Malmö – lagged behind Stockholm by 17 and 32 percent, respectively. At least partly the differences in real estate prices explain these differences. By 2040, most of the differences between the three big cities have disappeared in the basic scenario. In particular, the wealth of households in the Malmö area is simulated to increase much.[12] The household wealth in both urban and rural Götaland and Svealand other than in the three big cities also increase strongly, while the northern part of the country continues to lag behind. In the alternative scenario, the growth in relative wealth of Malmö and also Gothenburg remains, while the slower growth in real estate prices makes the rest of the country continue to lag behind the three major cities.

When analyzing the portfolio composition by region and year, we find that owned homes make a large share of gross wealth in the southern part of the country while other real estate (forests) makes a larger share in the northern part. There are no major regional differences in regular debt ratios, but study debts are relatively less important in the north. The most remarkable change in the simulations is the increase in the value share of own homes in particular in Stockholm and Malmö. The former increases from 49 to 62 percent and the latter from 45 to 61 (Table 19).

There is usually a positive correlation between disposable income and net wealth, as also evidenced in Table 20. This table compares the wealth distribution of households with a disposable income that is smaller than

---

[12] Malmö is located opposite to Copenhagen at Öresund and economically partly integrated in the greater Copenhagen area.

Table 19. *Portfolio shares of gross wealth by year and region*

Year/region	Financial assets	Private pension wealth	Own home	Other real estate	Debts	Study debts
1999						
Stockholm	0.404	0.070	0.487	0.108	0.248	0.035
Gothenburg	0.378	0.086	0.511	0.110	0.306	0.042
Malmö	0.431	0.081	0.454	0.114	0.320	0.056
Urban Götaland	0.422	0.082	0.404	0.173	0.288	0.028
Urban Svealand.	0.430	0.091	0.441	0.128	0.297	0.039
Urban Norrland	0.441	0.096	0.405	0.153	0.313	0.039
Rural Götaland	0.389	0.073	0.370	0.240	0.268	0.017
Rural Svealand	0.399	0.083	0.390	0.209	0.292	0.018
Rural Norrland	0.452	0.090	0.340	0.206	0.295	0.025
2020						
Stockholm	0.361	0.035	0.544	0.094	0.278	0.023
Gothenburg	0.398	0.038	0.501	0.099	0.294	0.023
Malmö	0.379	0.034	0.532	0.088	0.280	0.027
Urban Götaland	0.448	0.038	0.416	0.134	0.307	0.020
Urban Svealand	0.443	0.040	0.446	0.109	0.318	0.023
Urban Norrland	0.457	0.037	0.434	0.108	0.329	0.025
Rural Götaland	0.444	0.039	0.387	0.167	0.275	0.015
Rural Svealand	0.471	0.039	0.392	0.135	0.274	0.014
Rural Norrland	0.515	0.043	0.336	0.148	0.334	0.016
2040						
Stockholm	0.280	0.021	0.622	0.097	0.240	0.023
Gothenburg	0.310	0.021	0.584	0.105	0.252	0.024
Malmö	0.296	0.021	0.612	0.091	0.235	0.023
Urban Götaland	0.358	0.023	0.513	0.128	0.263	0.023
Urban Svealand	0.356	0.023	0.532	0.111	0.266	0.024
Urban Norrland	0.353	0.023	0.537	0.108	0.305	0.027
Rural Götaland	0.368	0.021	0.478	0.153	0.238	0.016
Rural Svealand	0.386	0.021	0.484	0.129	0.270	0.016
Rural Norrland	0.419	0.022	0.431	0.149	0.313	0.019

the first quartile of the income distribution to that for all households to investigate if there are any income poor but wealth rich. In 1999, poor households, as defined by the first quartile, have wealth at about 50 percent of the wealth level of all households. This share is simulated to increase to about 70–75 percent in 2020 and 75–80 percent in 2040 in the basic scenario. The wealth of the income poor is thus simulated to increase, not only in an absolute sense but also relative to all households.

It is also of interest to see to what extent the income poor have their wealth in a form that can easily be liquidized. Table 20 shows that the share of real property to gross wealth is about the same for income poor as for all households, approximately 40 percent. It increases over time as we have already seen above.

Table 20. *The distribution of net household wealth and the share of real properties in 1999, 2020, and 2040, if disposable income belongs to the first quartile of the income distribution as compared to all households*

Statistics	If disposble income<Q1	All households	Ratio of columns 2–3
1999			
Net household wealth, thousands of SEK in 1999 prices			
Q1	22	61	0.36
Q2	157	310	0.51
Q3	455	903	0.50
Mean	386	751	0.51
Share of real properties			
Q1	0.00	0.00	
Q2	0.09	0.21	
Q3	0.73	0.68	
Mean	0.34	0.34	
2020			
Net household wealth, thousands of SEK in 1999 prices			
Q1	388	680	0.57
Q2	1143	1614	0.71
Q3	2212	2966	0.75
Mean	1294	1944	0.67
Share of real properties			
Q1	0.00	0.00	
Q2	0.40	0.43	
Q3	0.73	0.70	
Mean	0.40	0.41	
2040			
Net household wealth, thousands of SEK in 1999 prices			
Q1	560	801	0.70
Q2	1565	1985	0.79
Q3	2796	3339	0.84
Mean	1607	2134	0.75
Share of real properties			
Q1	0.00	0.01	
Q2	0.50	0.54	
Q3	0.78	0.78	
Mean	0.45	0.47	

The relation between health and wealth in 1999 after holding age constant is rather weak but positive. It becomes stronger as the simulations proceed but the relation is reversed U-shaped. People with full health have smaller wealth than those who only have good or fair health! There is no direct causal link between health and wealth in the model, and apparently it does not build up any strong and believable indirect relation either. We experience a similar problem with the relation between ADL-score and wealth. This relation is even weaker in the simulated data.

Table 21. *House-ownership before and after retirement, and total realized wealth relative to disposable income at the age of 65 by birth-cohort and income-quartile*

Cohort	Income class	Share home-owners 60–64	Share home-owners 65–69	Wealth at 65 relative to average disposable income at age 60–64
1940	<P25	0.72	0.71	10.7
	P25–P75	0.70	0.69	8.1
	>P75	0.83	0.80	8.2
1952	<P25	0.67	0.68	8.8
	P25–P75	0.72	0.70	8.7
	>P75	0.76	0.73	7.7

Source: SESIM-generated, 1999–2041. Assumptions: all individuals worked 60–64, retired at age 65, survived at least until 75; inflation ≈ 2 percent/year, real wage growth ≈ 3 percent/year and long interest rate 5 percent.

In order to demonstrate the importance of wealth as a potential income buffer, total wealth at age 65 (the age of retirement) was calculated for two birth cohorts, 1940 and 1952. In these calculations, it was assumed that all real wealth was sold upon retirement, and the value net of debt and taxes added to financial wealth net of taxes. Thus, all real and financial wealth was capitalized and the value net of debt and taxes calculated at age 65. This value represents the potential value that can be used as a buffer in order to supplement pension income. The last column in Table 21 gives this total value in relation to average disposable income in the last five pre-retirement years. In the center and right tail of the income distribution, people have wealth corresponding to about eight annual incomes. For each birth cohort, the lowest income-quartile has the largest potential buffer relative to disposable income. For instance, on average for the lowest income quartile of the cohort born in 1940, total net wealth is almost 11 times higher than average pre-retirement income. As we have already found above much of this wealth comes from an owned home. Table 21 shows that about 70 percent of Swedish households have an owned home and that almost everyone keeps it at least in the first few years after retirement.

7. Conclusions

The simulation exercises of this chapter have demonstrated that the future of the wealth distribution depends very much on the growth in the real estate prices and the prices on financial assets. In our main scenario, real estate prices grew relatively much with the result that the differences between poor and rich decreased. The left tail of the wealth distribution increased much faster than the right tail in this scenario. The assets of both young and old increase more than those of middle age, and after the 2020s retired will on average become wealthier than middle aged. In 1999, income poor households only had about half as much wealth as an average household, but their relative position improves. In 2040, their average wealth is simulated to become about 75 percent of the general average. If real estate prices are assumed to increase less (relative to stock market prices) the inequality of the wealth distribution increases however, in particular because poor households will not improve their relative position.

In the main scenario, owner-occupied houses is the asset that increases most. This is also true for the elderly. A larger share of their increased wealth will thus consist of rather illiquid property. This tendency is particularly strong in the Stockholm and Malmö areas. Malmö is the area with the fastest growing wealth. The rural areas improve their position a little relative to the rest of the country, in particular in Götaland and Svealand, but the relatively low wealth in the north persists. Also in the alternative scenario, Malmö and, to some extent, Gothenburg improve their average wealth relative to Stockholm, but the rural areas show no improvement. They continue to lag behind the three big cities.

Already today the baby-boom cohorts are relatively wealthy and independently of scenario they will continue to be wealthy. Contrary to most life-cycle–based economic thinking, our model does not simulate a decrease in the wealth of the elderly. At the time of retirement, the baby-boom cohorts will have wealth amounting to about eight annual incomes. This might not be seen as much in an international perspective, but relative to lower pensions their wealth is an important buffer. Except for the very rich much of it is however tied up in an owner-occupied home and not so easy to liquidize. It is also interesting to note that the wealth buffer is relatively more important for the income poor than for those who have high incomes.

References

Andersson, B., L. Berg and A. Klevmarken (2002), "Inkomst- och förmögenhetsfördelningen för dagens och morgondagens äldre", in: SOU 2002:29, Bilagedel B, *Riv ålderstrappan! Livslopp i förändring*, Erlanders Gotab AB, Stockholm: Fritzes Offentliga Publikationer.

Flood, L. and U. Gråsjö (2001), "A Monte Carlo simulation study of tobit models", *Applied Economics Letters*, Vol. 8, pp. 581–584.

Hesselius, P., F. Johansson and A. Klevmarken (2005), "Inkomster, förmögenhet, konsumtion och fattigdom", in: A. Börsch-Supan and A. Klevmarken, editors, *50 + i Europa. En åldrande befolknings hälsa och ekonomi*, Chapter 6, Department of Economics, Uppsala University, Uppsala: Universitetstryckeriet.

Jansson, K. and S. Johansson (1988), *Förmögenhetsfördelningen* 1975–1987, Stockholm: Statistics Sweden.

Klevmarken, N.A. (2004), "On the wealth dynamics of Swedish families 1984–98", *The Review of Income and Wealth*, Vol. 50(4), pp. 469–492.

Klevmarken, N.A. (2006), "On household wealth trends in Sweden over the 1990s", in: E. Wolff, editor, *International Perspectives on Household Wealth*, Edward Elgar Publishing Ltd.

Klevmarken, N.A., J. Lupton and F. Stafford (2003), "Wealth dynamics in the 1980s and 1990s: Sweden and the United States", *The Journal of Human Resources*, Vol. 38(2), pp. 322–353.

Manning, W.G., N. Duan and W.H. Rogers (1987), "Monte Carlo evidence on the choice between sample selection and two-part models", *Journal of Econometrics*, Vol. 35, pp. 59–82.

Spånt, R. (1987), "The wealth distribution in Sweden 1920–1983", in: E.N. Wolff, editor, *International Comparison of the Distribution of Wealth*, Oxford: Clarendon Press.

Statistics Sweden (2000), "Förmögenhetsgfördelningen i Sverige 1997 med en tillbakablick till 1975", Rapport 2000:1, Örebro ISSN 1400-3147.

Statistics Sweden (2005), "Förmögenhetsstatistik 2003, Sammansättning och fördelning", Statistics Sweden, Örebro 2005.

CHAPTER 10

Utilization of Inpatient Care

Kristian Bolin, Sören Höjgård and Björn Lindgren[*]

The purpose of this chapter is to estimate the utilization of inpatient care; more specifically, the number of bed-days spent in hospital. We will provide a background on inpatient health care in Sweden, describe the data employed, estimate the empirical model, interpret the estimates, and discuss the simulations obtained from SESIM of the total number of days of inpatient care.

1. The Swedish health care system

1.1. General characteristics

The Swedish health care system is commonly characterized as a national health-service (or Beveridge) model (Freeman, 2000; Blank and Burau, 2004). It is certainly both financed by taxes and organized as a government responsibility, but it has developed over time as a decentralized rather than a national system (Lindgren, 1995). In Europe, only Finland seems to have a more decentralized system (Häkkinen, 2005). Most political decisions on health and health care in Sweden are made at the level of its presently 20 county councils and 290 local municipalities, which are empowered to put proportional income taxes on their citizens in order to finance their activities. Central government has a more passive role. Apart from supervising the fulfilment of the overall objectives of the health care

---

[*] Corresponding author.

CONTRIBUTIONS TO ECONOMIC ANALYSIS
VOLUME 285   ISSN: 0573-8555
DOI:10.1016/S0573-8555(07)00010-7

legislation, which has a strong emphasis on equity,[1] its influence is primarily manifested through indirect measures such as general and targeted subsidies. It can also impose ceilings on county council and municipality taxes.

Through the National Board of Health and Welfare, central government supervises health care personnel and performs evaluations of Swedish health care and related social issues. Finally, through the National Social Insurance Board, it administers the Swedish health insurance system. Although being compulsory and financed through proportional payroll taxes, health insurance plays a minor role in the financing of health care in Sweden. Its primary purpose is to compensate patients for income losses during ill health and, until the early 2000s, subsidize outpatients' expenditures on (prescription) pharmaceuticals. Anell (2005) provides an updated account of the main characteristics of the Swedish health care system and its possible future direction.

Out-of-pocket payments for patients are usually slightly higher in Sweden than in other European countries (Oliver *et al.*, 2005), and, since decisions on fees are made at the local level, they vary among the counties and municipalities. For an ordinary primary-care visit, the lowest fee in 2005 was SEK 100 (the county of Dalarna) and the highest SEK 150 (the county of Skåne). The fee for a visit to a specialist may vary between SEK 200 and SEK 300, depending on where the patient lives in the country. Patient fees are subject to a cap, though, implying that the maximum amount of out-of-pocket payments for services during a 12-month period is limited to SEK 900. The maximum fee for inpatient care was SEK 80 per bed-day. It should be observed that, in contrast to many other countries, a referral from a primary-care physician is not needed for a visit to a specialist at the hospital; the patient may have to pay a higher fee without a referral, though.

As to pharmaceuticals, patients pay the full amount for over-the-counter drugs, while pharmaceuticals prescribed to outpatients are subsidized at an increasing rate after the first 900 SEK.[2] They are also subject to a cap, implying that the maximum amount of out-of-pocket payments for prescription drugs during a 12-month period is limited to SEK 1800. Pharmaceuticals consumed during inpatient care are free of charge. For dental care, patients pay the major part of treatment costs out of pocket.

---

[1] The objective of the Swedish health care system is to "provide good health and health care on equal terms for the entire population regardless of where a person lives, and regardless of his or her income" (SFS, 1982).

[2] Patients pay the whole amount for prescriptions up to SEK 900. In the interval SEK 901–1700, the subsidy is 50 percent (i.e., patients pay a maximum of SEK 400 out of pocket). In the interval SEK 1701–3300, the subsidy is 75 percent (implying a maximum of SEK 400 out of pocket). In the interval SEK 3301–4300, the subsidy is 90 percent (implying a maximum of SEK 100 out of pocket). For amounts above SEK 4300, finally, the subsidy is 100 percent. For more details, see the web address: www.apoteket.se

Patients aged 65 and above pay lower fees at hospital in most counties and lower fees for dental care in all counties. They also pay considerably lower fees for primary care and specialist visits in one county (Dalarna).

In the 1990s, a few county councils tried paying providers according to predetermined rates based on the diagnosis-related groups (DRG) system. There were also attempts to introduce capitation payment systems in a family-doctor based primary-care system. Such systems are still used for paying private providers, but less so for public providers, the exception being public providers of family doctor services. County council block grants are nowadays the most common way of financing both inpatient and outpatient care. Publicly employed physicians and other personnel get monthly salaries, irrespective of performance. Performance-related remuneration is presently tested, however, in order to improve performance in the county of Stockholm. The share of privately provided health care varies among counties from 2 percent in Västernorrland to 23 percent in Stockholm (with 10 percent in average for Sweden as a whole). It consists mostly of primary care; there were only three privately operated hospitals: one in Stockholm with 204 beds, one in Simrishamn with 57 beds, and one in Gothenburg with 8 beds.

The political responsibilities for financing and delivering health care are divided between the county councils and the municipalities. Whereas the municipalities have had all the responsibilities for old age social care and assistance for centuries, they now, since 1992, also have the responsibility for taking care of elderly people with long-standing illness, both in long-term care and, for instance, in short-term recovery after an elderly patient has been considered to be medically "discharge-ready" from hospital. Municipalities are then supposed to deliver the care and assistance that the discharge-ready patient may need. If a municipality cannot provide a bed for a patient to recover in a nursing home, however, the prolonged stay at hospital would have to be paid for by the municipality. Since bed-days at hospital are much more expensive than in nursing homes, there certainly are incentives for municipalities to plan for a sufficient capacity of nursing-home care.

Total national expenditures for health care are politically determined in Europe, either directly through closed budgets or through the legislation and rules governing health care (Zweifel and Breyer, 1997). In Sweden, total budgets for health care are, to a very large degree, directly determined by political decisions; the exceptions are expenditures for dental care and for eyeglasses, etc., which are open systems. In 2002, total expenditures on health accounted for 9.2 percent of the Swedish GDP, which is slightly above the OECD average of 8.9 percent. That total spending on health is dependent on what a country can afford rather than what it may need, was concluded already in 1949 by the late Swedish economist, Sven Rydenfelt (Rydenfelt, 1949). Moreover, health care also seems to be a luxury good. So, there is a long-term trend that countries with a higher GDP per capita also have a higher share spent on health. Thus, the USA has by far the largest share; Sweden has a share, which roughly might be expected, judging from its GDP level. Public funding is dominant in all OECD countries, the exceptions being the USA and Mexico. In Sweden, 85 percent of health spending was funded by public sources, somewhat above the OECD average of 73 percent. About 70 percent of total Swedish health care expenditures is financed by county council and municipality taxes, about 15 percent by central government taxes (general and targeted subsidies), and about 15 percent by patients' out-of-pocket payments (National Board of Health and Welfare, 2002).

Several laws regulate the organization and financing of Swedish health care. The most important, though, is the Swedish Health Care Act (SFS, 1982). It should be observed that the Act does not give patients many rights. Instead, county councils and municipalities are legally and mandatorily responsible for providing the health care, which the residents of Sweden need. There are no sanctions stated in the Act against county councils or municipalities, which do not follow the Health Care Act, so there are few, if any, possibilities for individual patients or for central government to force county councils and municipalities to act in accordance with the Act. Evaluations made by the National Board of Health and Welfare show that county councils and municipalities often act against the Act and other central government regulations.

1.2. Inpatient care

Inpatient care, as opposed to outpatient care, requires at least one bed-day at hospital. With the exception of severe accidents, the utilization of inpatient care is determined in a rather complex process, sometimes short, but often long. The patient, of course, usually takes the first initiative, seeking a primary-care physician or a specialist after having felt some symptoms. The doctor may immediately come to the conclusion that there is no reason to worry, but in most cases only after some tests. The doctor may also consult colleagues, and, if judged necessary, refer to a hospital doctor who may suggest a treatment that requires inpatient care. Thus, the influence of the providers is substantial, and only if all providers were perfect agents of the patient, will the utilization be in accordance with individual preferences. The problem is that providers are also agents of the county councils and municipalities, and that they also act according to their own self-interests; neither may always coincide with the interests of the patients. So, the consumer demand element in inpatient-care utilization may sometimes be very weak, indeed, a fact that should be kept in mind when interpreting utilization figures as well as our estimations and simulations.

Thus, the supply of health care is rationed. Need is supposed to be the condition for access, but the concept of need has not been operationalized until recently. Since a few years, the Swedish National Board of Health and Welfare publishes guidelines for making vertical priorities within a specific therapeutic area. There has been no evaluation yet, so there is no information available on to which extent the county councils follow the guidelines. There are also guidelines for the maximum allowable waiting times for a number of specific tests and treatments. County councils have received extra money from national government to facilitate the reduction of waiting times, but according to evaluations made by the Swedish National Board of Health and Welfare, there is no evidence that waiting times have been reduced accordingly.

Key data on inpatient-care utilization and expenditure in Sweden 1992–2005 is reported in Table 1. The number of available hospital beds decreased by 60 percent between 1992 and 2005. Also hospital stays and the number of bed-days decreased, the latter more than the former, due to a 39 percent reduction in mean length of stay, during the same time period. It should be observed, however, that this trend might have come to an end. For the first time in many years, the number of hospital stays – and

Table 1.   Key data on inpatient care in Sweden, 1992–2005

	1992	1994	1996	1998	2000	2002	2004	2005
Number of available hospital beds	66 045	57 167	49 468	33 234	31 765	27 969	27 088	26 540
Number of hospital stays (thousands)	1 700	1 638	1 604	1 537	1 477	1 445	1 454	1 477
Number of bed-days (thousands)	17 355	13 882	11 536	10 351	9 663	9 211	9 005	9 105
Mean length of stay (days)	10.2	8.5	7.2	6.7	6.5	6.4	6.2	6.2
Expenditures in million SEK, current prices	51 103	48 044	53 005	55 171	58 280	54 770	60 331	n.a.
Expenditures as a share of total health care expenditures (percent)	43.3	40.3	39.9	38.4	36.1	28.9	29.5	n.a.
Cost per bed-day, SEK, current prices	2 945	3 461	4 595	5 330	6 031	5 946	6 700	n.a.
Cost per hospital stay, SEK, current prices	30 061	29 331	33 046	35 895	39 458	37 903	41 493	n.a.

Source: Statistics Sweden (various years).

the number of bed-days – increased in 2004–2005. From 1994 to 2004, inpatient expenditures increased by 1.3 percent and total health care expenditures by 5.6 percent per year, both in current prices, leading to a substantial decrease in the inpatient share of total health care expenditures from 40 to 30 percent, reflecting both the development of new health technologies and a political ambition to increase the standing of primary health care. During the same time period, GDP increased annually by 4.4 percent in current prices, the consumer price index by 1.2 percent per year, and the implicit GDP deflator by 1.5 percent.

Patients aged 65 and above account for 45 percent of all hospital stays. They have more stays per person than other age groups, and they have somewhat longer stays in average. It might also be observed that the number of beds per 1000 inhabitants and the mean length of a hospital stay are lower in Sweden than in most other OECD countries for which data is available.

2. Theoretical framework, previous empirical studies, and our choice of explanatory variables

The theoretical framework for our empirical work is the demand-for-health model; see Grossman (2000) and Chapter 4 for presentations of the model and its recent extensions. Inpatient care is one input in the individual's production of health investment. The most important predictions of the original model regarding health investments are that, under some plausible conditions, health investment should be positively correlated with age and wage rate but negatively correlated with education.

Recent extensions of the model to include the family as the producer of health suggest that health investment should be negatively correlated with divorce, widowhood, and the presence of children, and undetermined for marriage or cohabitation.

Inpatient care, however, is but one of several inputs into the individual's production of health investment, along with health-promoting behavior such as non-smoking, moderate drinking, and physical exercise. Whereas the latter type of inputs is used precautionary to reduce the risk of ill health, the former type is used to restore health when the individual has been struck by disease. In the original Grossman model, uncertainty is precluded; so all health investments are in a way precautionary. (One knows in advance if and when a disease will strike you, so why not counteract that fact already now.) We will, however, for the purpose of this chapter, treat health care activities that are meant to restore health in the same manner as health-promoting or disease-preventive activities, as, in fact, many authors have done in the past. The transformation of the demand for health investment to a demand for the inputs in the health-investment production function, including the inputs of time from the individual him- or herself and his or her family, may not be straightforward, though. It depends on substitution and complementary conditions among the inputs. Assuming here, for simplicity, that there are no incentives to change the relative size of any input (input factor neutrality), there would be a one-to-one correspondence between the demand for health investment and the demand for inpatient care. We also abstract here from the fact that the physician always will have a great influence on decisions that imply the admission to a hospital inpatient ward.

Empirical studies on the utilization of inpatient care have been done for a number of reasons. Research issues include equity in health care, impact of private insurance, and needs-based capitation formulae. Results on the determinants of inpatient-care utilization then come more or less as a by-product to the main objective of the study. The evidence is summarized in Table 2; statistically significant results on the determinants are reported for variables that are available in our micro-simulation model. The dependent variable varies between studies, due to differences in available data. Some studies used the probability of at least one hospital stay in 1 year as the only indicator of inpatient-care utilization, others added the number of bed-days (or weeks at hospital), given at least one hospital stay. *Ill health* was a strong positive, and the most important, determinant in all studies. The impact of *age* and of *female* was positive in most, but not all, studies. There was some evidence that *income* had a weak negative impact, but one study reported a weak positive effect. There were also single studies, indicating a negative effect of living *single*, a positive effect of being *married*, and a negative effect on utilization of *education*.

We chose the number of bed-days per year as the indicator of inpatient-care utilization in our model, since it corresponds more closely to resource use than other available indicators, i.e., number of hospital stays or the probability of having at least one stay in 1 year. Our choice of explanatory variables was governed partly by the theoretical framework and partly by the empirical evidence reported in Table 2. Thus, we included measures of health, age, education, income, sex, civil status (divorced), and foreign country of birth. In addition, we included indicators for geographical residence, since this reflects the cost of visiting a hospital; lagged utilization of inpatient care, since this is likely to be positively correlated with current rate of hospital utilization; and an indicator for the presence of a newborn child, since this explains hospitalization for reasons other than illness.

3. Data

HILDA data was used to estimate the utilization of inpatient care. More specifically, we used the HILDA cross section for the years 1996/1997, complemented with data on inpatient care for the year 1995. Thus, the

Table 2. *Empirical evidence on the determinants of inpatient-care utilization*

Source, country, year	Research issue	Data	Dependent variable	Results
Cameron *et al.* (1988), Australia, 1977/1978	Whether insurance-induced distortions lead to significant overconsumption of health care services	Individual utilization data from the 1977–1978 Australian Health Survey $n = 6539$ Ages: 18+	Number of bed-days in one year	Age, strong positive; female, strong negative; income, weak negative; ill health, strong positive; chronic disease, strong positive
Nolan (1993), Ireland, 1987	Impact on utilization of differential public entitlements to free health care services	Individual utilization data from the 1987 Irish household survey $n = 6350$ Ages: 15+	(a) Probability of at least one hospital stay in one year (b) Number of bed-days, given at least one stay, in 1 year	(a) Female, weak positive; ill health, strong positive (b) Age, strong positive; ill health, strong positive
Gerdtham (1997), Sweden, 1991	Equity in health care	Individual utilization data from the 1991 Swedish Level of Living Survey $n = 5011$ Ages: 18–76	(a) Probability of at least one hospital stay in 1 year (b) Number of weeks spent in hospital, given at least one stay in 1 year	(a) Ill health, strong positive (b) Ill health, strong positive
Holly *et al.* (1998), Switzerland, 1992/1993	Impact on utilization of different alternative health-insurance plans	Individual utilization data from the 1992/1993 Swiss Health Survey $n = 15288$ Ages: 15+	Probability of at least one hospital stay in 1 year	Age, positive; female, positive; income, negative; ill health, strong positive
Harmon and Nolan (2001), Ireland, 1994	Determinants of the demand for private insurance and the relationship between insurance and inpatient care utilization	Individual utilization data from the 1994 Irish household survey $n = 7393$ Ages: 16+	Probability of at least one hospital stay in 1 year	Age, weak negative; female, strong positive; single, strong negative; income, weak positive; ill health, strong positive
Gravelle *et al.* (2003), England, 2000	Implications for deriving a needs-based capitation formula of supply and demand influences on health care utilization	Small area (ward) data $n = 8414$	Number of admissions to acute (short-term) hospitals in 1 year	Income, negative; education, negative; ill health, strong positive
Iversen and Kopperud (2003), Norway, 1998	Impact of an individual's health status relative to the impact of access on specialist-care utilization	Individual data from the 1994–2000 waves of the Health Survey for England $n = 121746$		
		Individual utilization data from the 1998 Norwegian Survey of Living Conditions $n = 3449$ Ages: 16+	Probability of at least one hospital stay in one year	Ill health, strong positive
Lindström *et al.* (2003), Sweden, 2000	The influence of rates of GP visits on rates of hospitalization	Small area (primary health care center area) data $n = 50$	Number of hospital stays per 1000 inhabitants in 1 year	Age, strong positive; foreign-born, positive
Höfter (2006), Chile, 2000	Determinants of the demand for private insurance and the relationship between insurance and health care utilization	Individual utilization data from the Casen 2000 national household survey in Chile $n = 28797$	(a) Probability of at least one hospital stay in 1 year (b) Number of bed-days, given at least one stay, in 1 year	(a) Not reported (b) Age, positive; female, strong positive; married, strong positive; ill health, strong positive

number of individuals comprised in the analyses in this chapter is 11 604.[3] Chosen dependent variables are defined below.

3.1. Dependent variables

- INPAT is a count variable for the number of days in hospital the respondent had in 1996/1997.

3.2. Explanatory variables

- Variables HI962, HI963, and HI964 are dummy variables, which take the value 1, if the health status as measured by the health index described in Chapter 4 was 3, 2, and 1, respectively, in 1996/1997 and 0 otherwise. Comparison category: health index equal to 4.
- INPATL is a count variable for the number of days of inpatient care which the respondent consumed in 1995.
- AGE96 is a discrete variable indicating the age of the respondent.
- SPLINE is defined as AGEDUM (AGE96–30), AGEDUM is a dummy variable, which takes the value 1 if the respondent is older than 30 years of age.
- COLLEGE is a dummy variable, which takes the value 1 if the respondent's attained educational level is college level in 1996/1997 and 0 otherwise (corresponds to levels 31, 32, and 40 in Statistics Sweden's educational measure, SUN86).
- UNIV is a dummy variable, which takes the value 1 if the respondent's attained educational level is university level in 1996/1997 and 0 otherwise (corresponds to levels 50, 60, and 70 in Statistics Sweden's educational measure, SUN86).
- DIVORCED is a dummy variable, which takes the value 1 if the respondent was divorced in 1996/1997 and 0 otherwise.
- RELINC is a continuous variable for the ratio between the respondent's taxable income and the mean taxable income in the sample.
- GOTH is a dummy variable, which takes the value 1 if the respondent was residing in Gothenburg in 1996/1997 and 0 otherwise.
- MALLU is a dummy variable, which takes the value 1 if the respondent was residing in Malmo in 1996/1997 and 0 otherwise.
- SOUTHU is a dummy variable, which takes the value 1 if the respondent was residing in a large city area in the south of Sweden and 0 otherwise.

---

[3] One observation with more than 365 lagged hospital days was excluded.

- MIDSTU is a dummy variable, which takes the value 1 if the respondent was residing in a large city area in the midst of Sweden and 0 otherwise.
- NORTHU is a dummy variable, which takes the value 1 if the respondent was residing in a large city area in the north of Sweden and 0 otherwise.
- MIDTHR is a dummy variable, which takes the value 1 if the respondent was residing in a rural area in the midst of Sweden and 0 otherwise.
- NORTHR is a dummy variable, which takes the value 1 if the respondent was residing in a rural area in the north of Sweden and 0 otherwise.
- SWED is a dummy variable, which takes the value 1 if the respondent was born in Sweden and 0 otherwise.
- SEX reflects sex: 0 corresponds to the respondent being a female and 1 corresponds to the respondent being a male.
- SEX_RELINK is defined as SEX × RELINC.
- NEWBORN is a dummy variable, which takes the value 1 if the respondent is female and has a child less than 1 year of age.

4. Models

We estimated two different models of the utilization of inpatient care: (a) an imputation model and (b) a dynamic model for updating. These models were estimated separately for two different age groups: those older than 49 years of age, and those younger than 50 years of age. The reason for this is that we expected that the health-related behavior, and in particular the utilization of inpatient care, to differ between older and younger individuals. The same two models were used for estimating the utilization of inpatient care as for sickness absence in Chapter 5.

5. Results

The estimated marginal effects are reported in Table 3. The qualitative content of the results obtained from the estimated marginal effects are almost identical between the imputation equation and the dynamic year-to-year equation. The younger age group had opposite signs for DIVORCED, though. However, the marginal effect was not significant in the imputation equation. The effect of health status – as measured by the health index described in Chapter 4 – is in all cases positive and significant, i.e., people in bad health utilize more inpatient days. For instance, in the age group 50+ a person with bad health is expected to stay in hospital about two more days compared to someone with full health. The general average was 1.5 days in hospital.

The year-to-year equations contained the utilization of inpatient care in the previous year as an explanatory variable. The corresponding estimated

Table 3. **Estimates of zero-inflated negative binomial models for the utilization of inpatient care. Marginal effects (p-values within parentheses)**

Variable	≥ 50		< 50	
	Year-to-year	Imputation	Year-to-year	Imputation
HI962	0.423	0.512	0.042	0.191
	(0.000)	(0.000)	(0.000)	(0.000)
HI963	0.933	1.055	0.096	0.493
	(0.000)	(0.000)	(0.000)	(0.000)
HI964	1.793	2.015	1.944	2.445
	(0.000)	(0.000)	(0.000)	(0.000)
INPATL	0.038	–	0.036	–
	(0.000)		(0.000)	
AGE96	0.033	0.037	0.004	0.009
	(0.000)	(0.000)	(0.000)	(0.001)
SPLINE	–	–	−0.004	−0.011
			(0.001)	(0.002)
COLLEGE	−0.039	–	–	–
	(0.259)			
UNIV	–	0.082	–	–
		(0.094)		
DIVORCED	0.129	0.112	−0.025	0.019
	(0.024)	(0.074)	(0.024)	(0.600)
RELINC	−0.038	−0.077	−0.017	–
	(0.383)	(0.106)	(0.001)	
GOTH	0.142	–	−0.016	−0.051
	(0.030)		(0.021)	(0.038)
MALLU	–	–	−0.019	–
			(0.056)	
SOUTHU	−0.070	−0.110	0.009	0.036
	(0.112)	(0.019)	(0.072)	(0.036)
NORHTU	−0.099	−0.154	–	–
	(0.190)	(0.062)		
MIDTHU	–	−0.099	–	–
		(0.136)		
MIDTHR	−0.267	−0.277	–	−0.026
	(0.000)	(0.000)		(0.229)
NORTHR	−0.152	−0.232	–	0.036
	(0.003)	(0.000)		(0.111)
SWED	−0.068	−0.088	0.017	0.081
	(0.203)	(0.131)	(0.012)	(0.004)
SEX	0.124	0.107	−0.063	−0.256
	(0.025)	(0.070)	(0.000)	(0.000)
NEWBORN	–	–	0.252	0.715
			(0.000)	(0.000)
SEX_RELINK	0.033	0.066	–	–
	(0.489)	(0.198)		
N = 11 604				

marginal effect was positive and significant in both cases. Thus, the more inpatient care that was utilized in the previous year, the more inpatient care the respondent was expected to use in the current year. The effect of being divorced differs between the young and the old age groups. In the old age group being divorced increases the expected number of days of inpatient care, while in the young age group being divorced decreases the expected number of days of inpatient care. The relative income was found to affect the expected number of days of inpatient care negatively – the higher relative income the lower the expected number of days of inpatient care. Being born in Sweden significantly increases the expected number of days of inpatient care. Being a male increases the expected number of days of inpatient care for the older age group and decreases the expected number of days of inpatient care for the younger age group.

6. Simulations

In this section, we present the results of our simulations for the baseline scenario described at length in Chapter 3. The simulations are based on a 100% sample in SESIM. We follow the same structure of presentation as for health status in Chapter 4, and we also present our simulation results separately for men and women.

6.1. Cross-sectional age profiles of average number of days of inpatient care

Figure 1 reproduces simulated cross-sectional age profiles of the average number of days of inpatient care in 2000 (average for 1999–2001), 2020 (2019–2021), and 2040 (2039–2041) for men and women, respectively. The general shapes of the graphs are similar for men and women and very typical for inpatient care: the average number of days remains fairly the same from 20 to 70–75 years of age and rises exponentially thereafter. Over time, the cross-sectional age profiles do not seem to change. The simulated developments for the oldest old are based on so few observations that they are difficult to interpret as reflecting realities. Women seem in average to spend fewer days in inpatient care than men of the same age.

6.2. Cohort age profiles of average number of days of inpatient care

The age profiles above are cross-sectional representations and, hence, results of both cohort-specific effects and time effects. So, next, in Figure 2, we present simulated age profiles for the 50–100 years old of the three birth cohorts of 1930, 1940, and 1950 for men and women, respectively. Again, we cannot really distinguish any clear cohort-specific effect, or any time effect that might have reduced the cohort-specific effect. The age-specific average utilization of inpatient care does not seem to change over time

Figure 1. Simulated average days of inpatient care by age 0–100 for cross-sectional populations of 2000, 2020, and 2040 (men and women, respectively)

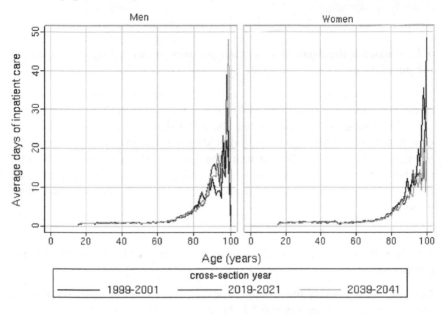

Figure 2. Simulated average days of inpatient care by age 50–100 for the birth cohorts of 1930, 1940, and 1950 (men and women, respectively)

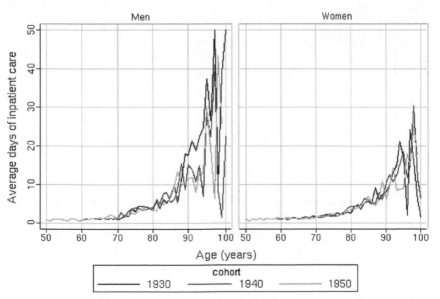

according to our simulations. The observation above that is, women on average spend fewer days in inpatient care than men of the same age seems reinforced, though.

6.3. Simulated development of average number of days of inpatient care for the population

Figures 3 and 4 reproduce the simulated development of average number of days of inpatient care 2000–2040 for the populations of 50–74 years old and 75+, respectively. As expected, the difference between the very old age group and the middle-aged and old is striking, roughly 1 day on average for the 50–74 years old for all years during the whole period 2000–2040, and between 4.5 and 6 days per year in average for the 75+. For most of the years, elderly men on average spend more days in inpatient care than women.

6.4. Simulated development of total number of days of inpatient care for the population

Figures 5 and 6 show the simulated development of the total number of days of inpatient care for the 50–74 and 75+ populations, respectively.

Figure 3. Simulated development of average number of days of inpatient care for the 50–74 population, 2000–2040 (men and women, respectively)

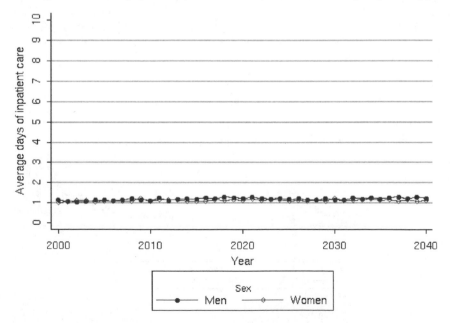

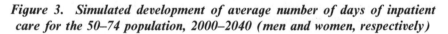

Figure 4. **Simulated development of average number of days of inpatient care for the 75+ population, 2000–2040 (men and women, respectively)**

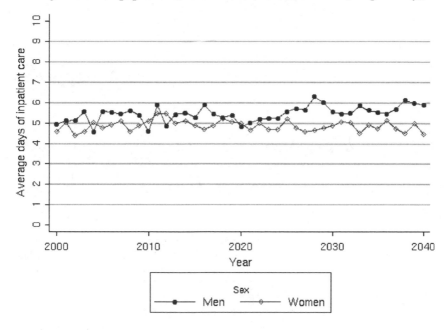

Figure 5. **Simulated development of total number of days of inpatient care for the 50–74 population (men and women, respectively)**

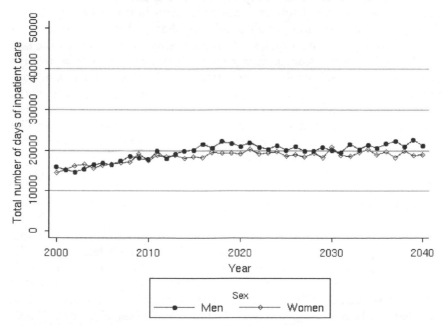

Figure 6.   **Simulated development of total number of days of inpatient care for the 75+ population (men and women, respectively)**

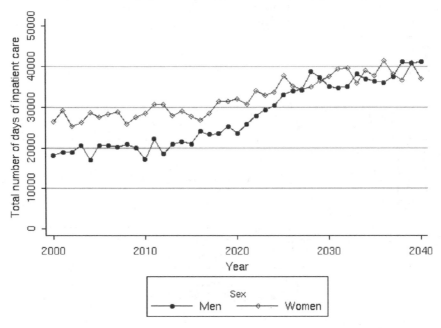

The increase in the total number of days for both men and women in the 50–74 populations is mainly due to increase in population size (Figure 5). That the female 75+ population has more days in inpatient care during 2000–2030 than the corresponding male population, despite the fact that a man on average spend more days in inpatient care, is explained by the fact that there are more women than men in these age groups. The relative increase in the total number of men explains why they seem to catch up toward 2040. Figure 7, finally, shows the simulated development of the total number of days of inpatient care for the total population 0–100 years of age between 2000 and 2040 for men and women, respectively. The increase over time in the total number of days of inpatient care is obviously determined by an increase in the number of 75+ in the population.

7. Conclusion

We have developed a module, which simulates the utilization of days spent in inpatient care. Determining factors are health status (simulated by the health module of Chapter 4), age, gender, education, relative income, civil status, the presence of children, geographical residence, and nationality (born in Sweden or not). According to our simulations, there are no clear changes in the age- or gender-specific utilization of inpatient care. Thus,

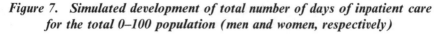

Figure 7. **Simulated development of total number of days of inpatient care for the total 0–100 population (men and women, respectively)**

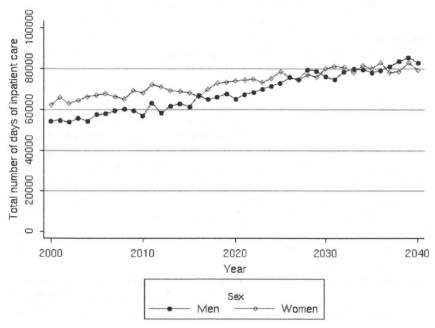

the increase in the utilization of days of inpatient care by more than 30 percent, simulated by this module, is certainly dependent mainly on the mere size of the 75 + population. To some degree, however, it is also due to the over time deteriorating health states of the elderly.

References

Anell, A. (2005), "Swedish healthcare under pressure", *Health Economics*, Vol. 14, pp. S237–S254.

Blank, R.H. and V. Burau (2004), *Comparative Health Policy*, Houndmills, Basingstoke: Palgrave Macmillan.

Cameron, A.C., P.K. Trivedi, F. Milne and J. Piggott (1988), "A micro-econometric model of the demand for health care and health insurance in Australia", *Review of Economic Studies*, Vol. 55, pp. 85–106.

Freeman, R. (2000), *The Politics of Health in Europe*, Manchester: Manchester University Press.

Gerdtham, U.G. (1997), "Equity in health care utilization: further tests based on hurdle models and Swedish micro data", *Health Economics*, Vol. 6, pp. 303–319.

Gravelle, H., M. Sutton, S. Morris, F. Windmeijer, A. Leyland, C. Dibben and M. Muirhead (2003), "Modelling supply and demand influences on the use of health care: implications for deriving a needs-based capitation formula", *Health Economics*, Vol. 12, pp. 985–1004.

Grossman, M. (2000), "The human capital model of the demand for health", in: A.J. Culyer and J.P. Newhouse, editors, *Handbook of Health Economics*, Amsterdam: Elsevier.

Häkkinen, U. (2005), "The impact of changes in Finland's health care system", *Health Economics*, Vol. 14, pp. S101–S118.

Harmon, C. and B. Nolan (2001), "Health insurance and health services utilization in Ireland", *Health Economics*, Vol. 10, pp. 135–145.

Höfter, R.H. (2006), "Private health insurance and utilization of health services in Chile", *Applied Economics*, Vol. 38, pp. 423–439.

Holly, A., L. Gardiol, G. Domenighetti and B. Bisig (1998), "An econometric model of health care utilization and health insurance in Switzerland", *European Economic Review*, Vol. 42, pp. 513–522.

Iversen, T. and G.S. Kopperud (2003), "The impact of accessibility on the use of specialist health care in Norway", *Health Care Management Science*, Vol. 6, pp. 249–261.

Lindgren, B. (1995), "Health care organisation and finance in Sweden", pp. 245–283 in: A. Alban and T. Christiansen, editors, *The Nordic Lights: New Initiatives in Health Care Systems*, Odense: Odense University Press.

Lindström, K., S. Engström, C. Bengtsson and L. Borgquist (2003), "Determinants of hospitalisation rates: does primary health care play a role?", *Scandinavian Journal of Primary Health Care*, Vol. 21, pp. 15–20.

National Board of Health and Welfare (2002). *Yearbook of Health and Medical Care*. www.socialstyrelsen.se

Nolan, B. (1993), "Economic incentives, health status and health services utilisation", *Journal of Health Economics*, Vol. 12, pp. 151–169.

Oliver, A., E. Mossialos and A. Maynard (eds.) (2005), "Analysing the impact of health system changes in the EU member states", Published with the support of funds provided by the European Observatory on Health Systems and Policies, Special issue of Health Economics, Vol. 14, pp. S1–S263.

Rydenfelt, S. (1949), "Sjukdomarnas samhällsekonomiska aspekt", PhLic Thesis, Lund, Department of Economics.

Statistics Sweden (various years), *Statistical Yearbook of Sweden*, Stockholm: Statistics Sweden.

Swedish Health Care Act (1982), (SFS, 1982, p. 763). See the web address www.riksdagen.se/lagar_forardningar.asp

Zweifel, P. and F. Breyer (1997), *Health Economics*, Oxford: Oxford University Press.

CHAPTER 11

The Demand for Old Age Care

Urban Fransson, Daniel Hallberg* and Mårten Lagergren

1. Care for elderly persons in Sweden

1.1. The Swedish system of public elderly care

In Sweden, responsibility for the public care of the frail elderly rests with three authorities acting at different levels. At national level, the Riksdag and the Government realize policy goals through legislation and financial control measures. At regional level, 18 county councils and two regions are responsible for the provision of health and medical care. At local level, Sweden's 290 municipalities have a statutory duty to meet the social service and housing needs of the elderly. Sweden's municipalities and county council have a high level of autonomy by international standards. Activities in caring services are ultimately controlled by politicians appointed to policy-making assemblies in municipalities and county councils through general elections. The decentralization of responsibility for elderly care makes it possible for local and regional conditions to be taken into account when policies for the elderly are formulated. The national authorities – the National Board of Health and Welfare and the 20 county/region administrative boards – are responsible for supervision, follow-up, and evaluation of municipal and county council caring services.

The so-called Ädel Reform, which came into force on January 1, 1992, made the municipalities comprehensively responsible for long-term service and care for the elderly and people with disabilities. Among other things, it became the duty of municipalities to provide health care in special forms

---

* Corresponding author.

CONTRIBUTIONS TO ECONOMIC ANALYSIS
VOLUME 285   ISSN: 0573-8555
DOI:10.1016/S0573-8555(07)00011-9

of housing accommodation and in daytime activities. One of the reform's important components was the transfer of financial responsibility for patients in county council hospitals and geriatric departments, whose medical treatment had been completed, from the county councils to the municipalities. This had the effect of greatly reducing the number of elderly "bed-blockers" in county council institutions, simultaneously with an expansion of municipal housing capacity for elderly in need of care and social services.

1.2. Range of services for elderly persons

Municipality care for the elderly in Sweden is provided in the form of home help services, daytime activities, or special housing accommodation. During the 1990s, it became increasingly common for persons in need of extensive care and attention to be looked after in their own homes. Home help service tasks include, for example, cleaning and doing laundry, help with shopping, post office and bank errands, and preparation of meals. Personal care can include assistance with eating and drinking, getting dressed, personal hygiene, and moving about. For those in need, municipal security alarms are available, which are usually linked to the nearest special housing.

In 2004, around 8 percent of persons aged 65 and older were entitled to home help services in ordinary housing. The proportion increases rapidly with age. The corresponding figure in the age group 80–84 years was 14 percent and among those over 85 years more than one in four (27 percent) received home help services. This means 132 300 recipients, of which 59 000 were over 85 years. The number has increased by 5 percent the last 6 years after a rapid decrease in the 1980s and the beginning of the 1990s. A higher proportion of women than of men are given help services in their homes. This reflects the fact that a higher proportion of women than men are single-living. Women's state of health – given age – is also on average worse than that of men.

Many municipalities have introduced a purchaser/provider split and though financing still is a public responsibility (cf. below) there are many private providers – especially in the big cities. Freedom of choice of provider is also being introduced, but still limited in most cases. Allocation of services is done after an assessment by municipality officials. It is possible to appeal in court against the decision. There are, in principle, no queues and services are seldom denied. Thus, supply and (expressed) demand tend to follow.

Those elderly receiving care services in their homes got on average 30 h of services per month. The variation, however, was great. Around 40 percent received less than 10 h per month and 3 percent more than 120 h. Those receiving home help services get more help today than earlier. The average amount of service hours awarded per person has increased by

6 percent compared to 5 years ago. The cost per hour of help is calculated to be between 350 and 450 SEK.

Long-term health care needs are provided for by home nursing. Today this can mean both qualified care and highly specialised medical care several times a day, as well as terminal care. About one-fourth of the persons that receive home help services also receive home nursing care. In about half of Sweden's municipalities responsibility for home nursing has been taken over from the county councils.

Daytime activities in the form of treatment and rehabilitation during daytime for persons suffering, for example, from senile dementia, persons with mental functional impairment, etc. are provided for around 13 000 persons aged 65 and older – less than 1 percent. In 2004 around 9000 persons were given short-term care in the form of temporary housing combined with treatment, rehabilitation, and care, partly for purposes of relief and alternate care.

Special housing accommodation is taken to include housing that in earlier legislation was classed as service blocks, old people's homes, group housing, and nursing homes. A place or apartment in special housing accommodation is granted as assistance under the Social Services Act. In most municipalities today, in order for older persons to qualify for special housing accommodation they must be in very extensive need of care and attention.

In 2004, roughly 7 percent of those aged 65 years and older were living permanently in special forms of housing accommodation. Also the proportion of elderly persons in special housing increases rapidly with age. In the age group 80–84 years 9 percent lived in this form of housing and among those 85 years and older 27 percent. In 2004, totally around 105 000 places were provided for the elderly in special housing accommodation. The number has decreased somewhat during the last 5 years – mainly because improved ordinary housing and better opportunities to receive home help services. Special housing accommodation is like home help services more common among women than men and for the same reasons.

1.3. Total expenditure and funding

The expenditures of the municipalities in Sweden are mainly funded by taxes levied on the population living in the municipality. Almost 70 percent is financed in this way. The municipality has the right to decide its taxation level – usually around 30 percent of income. In addition, there are state subsidies and income from user charges for different types of services. An elaborate equalization scheme ensures that the municipalities are given equitable resources for providing services.

The total expenditure for elderly care services amounted in 2004 to around SEK 79 billions. More than two-thirds of the expenditures,

SEK 53 billions, concerned caring services in special housing accommodation. Expenditure on caring services in ordinary housing totaled some SEK 24 billion. The rest – around SEK 2 billions – went to daytime activities. The cost per recipient of care was SEK 440 000 in special housing accommodation and 215 000 in home help services. There are fairly huge differences between different municipalities – in 2004, 10 percent of the municipalities had a cost lower than 140 300 SEK per recipient of care in home help services and 10 percent higher than 301 500 SEK. For special housing accommodations the corresponding variation was from 348 000 to 529 000. This may reflect differences in standard, quality of care, or efficiency in delivering the care.

The elderly care is heavily subsidized, with the recipient usually paying only a few percent of the actual cost. Thus, user charges amount to only around 4 percent of the total municipality expenditure on caring services for the elderly. Each municipality decides its own charges for elderly care and charges vary according to income and the amount of services given. However, there is a nationally set maximum charge – at present 1576 SEK per month. Around a third of the care recipients with low incomes do not pay any charges at all.

1.4. Non-public and informal care of the elderly

Formal care for the elderly in Sweden is almost entirely public as described above. The private sector, meaning privately organized services paid entirely by the elderly themselves, is very small – less than 1 percent of the total amount of services provided. However, there exists a fairly large amount of private entrepreneurs – especially in the larger cities – that provide elderly care services, but their operations are funded by the municipalities in the same way as the services organized by the municipality itself.

Informal care by family, relatives, friends, and neighbors still has a very important role in Sweden as in other countries. It is common that persons who receive formal municipal care also receive a substantial amount of informal care. Thus, the two forms of care are seen more as compliments than substitutes. However, married or cohabiting persons are less likely to receive formal care than single-living persons.

Access to informal care depends much on the family situation. In Sweden today, only a small proportion of elderly live with their adult children. Thus, informal help in Sweden – other than help from a partner – is more often *between* households than *within* a household. Table 1 shows the sources of care depending on family situation according to the HPÄD survey (Johansson et al., 2003). In this table "children" include sons/daughters-in-law. As seen from the table partners are the most important source of support for those who have a partner, whereas children are most important for those single-living persons (mostly women) that

Table 1. **Sources of care for elderly persons in need of support for daily living depending on family situation (percent)**

	Living with partner		Single-living	
	Children (*n* = 313)	No children (*n* = 37)	Children (*n* = 320)	No children (*n* = 100)
Help only by				
Partner	70	70	–	–
Children	3	–	30	–
Other relatives	–	3	4	13
Other household members	–	–	2	–
Friends/neighbors	1	3	6	14
Public home help	5	3	21	34
Combinations of help from				
Partner and children	6	–	–	–
Partner and home help	5	11	–	–
Partner and others	1	5	–	–
Children and home help	1	–	19	–
Children and others	1	–	4	–
Home help and others	–	–	3	19
No help	6	5	12	19
Total	100	100	100	100

have children. Other informal sources of help are quite infrequent – except for single-living persons without children. Voluntary services did not show up at all in this survey. The table also shows that combinations of formal and informal care are quite common, especially for single-living persons.

The HPÄD survey was quite small – in total only 770 persons – but other studies, such as the Kungsholmen and SNAC studies (see Section 3 below) have come up with essentially the same results. The conclusion remains: Informal care stills plays an important role in Sweden, but it is complimentary to formal care rather than substituting it.

Partners, children, and other relatives or friends also play an important role acting as "advocates" on behalf of the elderly dependent persons when it comes to applying for help, assisting in the choice of help, and monitoring quality of care.

2. Closeness to kin

Physical help from children requires of course that the children live nearby. As will be shown in this section a high percentage of elderly persons have children living in the same area. The development of this proportion is an important factor when it comes to estimate the future demand for formal care.

In order to bring some light to this important question, we have analyzed adult children's proximity to their parents with respect to characteristics of the aging parents. To analyze older people's proximity to their adult children, a statistical model has been set up that calculates the likelihood that adult children and their parents live in the same local labor market.

In the 20th century, Sweden went through transition from a predominantly agricultural society to an industrialized country. This entailed, for instance, that certain functions traditionally associated with the family have changed. One example of changed functions for the family is care of the older generation. Studies from the 1950s indicate that slightly more than 70 percent of retirees lived in the same municipality as the adult child living closest to them (Swedish Government Official Reports, 1956, p. 1; Teeland, 1978). Older women's proximity to their relatives has a socioeconomic dimension, such that the distance is significantly less among working-class than among white-collar women (Gaunt, 1987). This result is in accordance with similar findings from research in other countries (e.g., Lin and Rogerson, 1995).

Incomes and private wealth have increased for a growing proportion of retirees (Chapters 8 and 9). This implies that they can maintain their living and lifestyle habits even as they become older (Warnes, 1986; Bornefalk and Yndeheim, 2003). Parents' proximity to their adult children determines the type of relationships they can have as well as the frequency of mutual visits (Lin and Rogerson, 1995). The physical distance varies, for example, between countries. In southern Europe, it is common to live in the same household or the same building as the grown-up children (Figure 1). This is not the case in the northern part of Europe, where the distance is longer on average (Hallberg, 2005).

2.1. Relocation among children and parents, and the proximity of parents to adult children

As shown above adult children constitute an important source of help for elderly persons. Geographical separation between the elderly and their relatives prevent the provision of assistance and support. If children live far away there might thus be a wish to relocate in order to come closer and vice versa (Warnes, 1986; Silverstein, 1995; Rogerson et al., 1997). A Swedish study from 1989 show that slightly less than one-fifth of the elderly moved to a new residence in order to be closer to relatives (Ekström and Danermark, 1993).

Parents' relocation frequency decreases as they approach retirement age. At the same time, their adult children are in the beginning phase of their occupational and family careers. Thus, the likelihood that adult children will relocate is still high. Because adult children are more geographically mobile than are their parents, the adult children's

Figure 1. Proximity to nearest child (share of parents within distance)

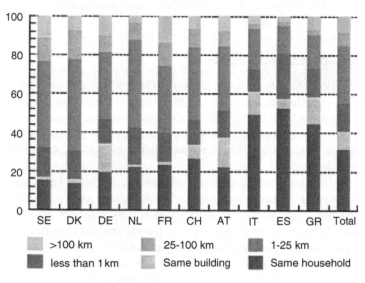

Source: Kohli *et al.* (2005), Figure 3

education, occupational careers, and socioeconomic affiliation are of importance for their proximity to their parents. Also the parents' socioeconomic status is of importance, due to the higher mobility rate among elderly with high socioeconomic status (Clark and Wolf, 1992; Lin and Rogerson, 1995).

If parents live in a metropolitan area with a multifaceted labor supply it is likely that their adult children live there as well. However, if parents live in areas with a less multifaceted labor supply the distance between well-educated adult children and parents will on average be greater, because the searchable labor market is geographically greater for an adult child with a high level of education than for one with a low level (Öberg, 1997).

Previous research has shown that the likelihood that elderly individuals will move closer to their adult children increases:

• with decreasing parental income,
• if parents live in a large city,
• if they have lived in their present residence for a long time, and
• if their physical health has worsened (Litwak and Longino, 1987; Silverstein, 1995).

It should be pointed out that causality might be working in the opposite direction. For instance, career-oriented adult children may need help from their parents with, for example, childcare. The number of grandchildren thus determines if older people will to take up residence near their children.

The more grandchildren they have, the greater the likelihood that this will happen. If the adult child is unmarried, the likelihood is even greater (Clark and Wolf, 1992).

2.2. Methods, data, and variables

The GEOSWEDE database contains information on all individuals living in Sweden, including, among other things, their demographic and socioeconomic situation as well as their housing. It is also possible to link records across generations, because included in the information for every person born after 1932 is that person's mother's and father's specific identity code.

The study population consist of retired individuals 65 years and older. The analysis of distance between adult children and their parents is separated into three parts: (1) analysis of elderly mothers who are living alone, (2) elderly fathers who are living alone, and (3) elderly couples. In the last case, the couple is represented by the older of the two. All together, the study population comprises 1 204 333 individuals for the year 2000. Slightly more than 20 percent of them have no children.

Even if it is possible to link records across generations in GEOSWEDE, this is not possible in the start data set of SESIM. Thus, we do not know if a person in the SESIM sample is living close to a child or not. For this reason a model of the probability that an elderly single or couple would live close to a child was estimated from GEOSWEDE and used to impute proximity in the start data set. A similar model using the panel information in GEOSWEDE was then used to simulate changes in proximity. If an older person had several adult children living in that person's own region, proximity was defined by the child living closest. Distance was computed using coordinate information of the dwellings of the parents and the adult children. Coordinate information consists of the middle point of a $100 \, \text{m}^2$ in which the individual's dwelling is situated.

To determine which factors affect older parents' proximity to their adult children we relied on previous studies. As pointed out above, the size and content of the local labor market are of great importance for adult children's ability to make an occupational career in their own home district. For this reason the dependent variable is a dummy variable indicating if an adult child lives in the same local labor market as its ageing parent. We use the official definition of local labor markets. Sweden is divided into 103 local labor markets, defined by the commuting flows between municipalities (Statistics Sweden, 2005).

Previous studies show that the relative relocation frequency is low among elderly people and that it varies with age. Thus, in an analysis of aging parents and adult children, the parents' age ($1 = 65$–74 years; $2 = 75$–79 years; $3 = 80$–84 years; $4 = 85$–89 years; $5 = 90+$ years) should be included.

The literature provides sufficient evidence of differences in the proportion of relocations for people living in different forms of tenures, given factors such as sex and age. For many people, personal identity is tied to their house (Almqvist, 2004). It is reasonable to assume that, for an older person living in his/her own house, it is more difficult to leave and take residence in another environment than it is for a person who is renting his/her dwelling. There is, therefore, reason to test whether tenure (1 = ownership or tenants ownership; 2 = rental occupation) has any influence on proximity to adult children.

Well-educated older people with high incomes are more likely to move to another place upon retirement than are retirees with a lower socioeconomic status (Warnes and Ford, 1995). Thus, we may expect that well-educated parents (0 = pre-gymnasium; 1 = gymnasium; 2 = post-gymnasium) with good retirement incomes will be less likely than other elderly to live in close proximity to their adult children. Disposable income is divided into quintiles for each study population, i.e., for elderly men living alone, elderly women living alone, and elderly couples.

Swedish municipalities vary in terms of population density and geographical position. We expect to find geographical variations in the proximity of adult children to elderly parents. In the analysis, we use the same type of region as in Chapter 7.

Previous studies have shown that elderly couples live farther from their adult children than do widows/widowers. Because elderly living as couples receive help and support from each other, they are less dependent on their children. This line of reasoning rests on the notion that both parents are in good health. Yet in many instances this is not the case. The woman is often a few years younger than her husband and, therefore, in better health. Thus, it is often the woman who gives her husband the care he requires. If we based our reasoning on the theory of Litwak and Longino (1987) that older people's health affects their decision to relocate, then there are probably incentives to move closer to an adult child, even if one spouse cares for the other spouse. We thus expect that elderly couples want to live in close proximity to their children too. The analysis of the distance between adult children and aging parents should, for this reason, include information on the marital status of the parents.

Table 2 shows the univariate distribution of the share of individuals who have adult children by region, age group, educational level, tenancy, income, gender, and family constellation. There are great differences between older men who live alone and older women who live alone. Older men are much less likely to have adult children than are older women. There are also great differences within the group of men, such that those with high disposable incomes are more likely to have adult children than are those with low incomes.

A corresponding pattern can also be seen among older women who live alone, although differences within the group are not as great as for men.

Table 2. *Number of elderly parents in study population and proportion having adult children by region, age, education, tenancy, income, gender, and family constellation, 2000*

	No children	Have adult children	Number of elderly		No children	Have adult children	Number of elderly
Region				**Disposable income**			
				Couples (quintiles)			
Stockholm	24.5	75.5	200 017	1	16.1	83.9	87 442
Göteborg	22.9	77.1	100 831	2	11.1	88.9	86 253
Malmö	23.5	76.5	66 603	3	10.5	89.5	87 403
Urban Götaland	21.4	78.6	258 949	4	9.3	90.7	86 579
Urban Svealand	19.9	80.1	121 449	5	8.0	92.0	87 040
Urban Norrland	18.3	81.7	53 013	All couples	11.0	89.0	434 717
Rural Götaland	22.0	78.0	164 785	Men (quintiles)			
Rural Svealand	20.3	79.7	117 540	1	58.6	41.4	45 267
Rural Norrland	19.9	80.1	121 146	2	43.3	56.7	45 426
Age				3	34.0	66.0	45 550
65–74	19.7	80.3	527 058	4	28.2	71.8	45 162
75–79	21.5	78.5	266 587	5	22.8	77.2	45 286
80–84	21.5	78.5	215 205	All men living alone	37.4	62.6	226 691
85–89	24.3	75.7	131 320	Women (quintiles)			
90+	34.4	65.6	64 163	1	31.9	68.1	107 818
Education				2	24.1	75.9	107 565
Pre-gymnasium	22.8	77.2	964 539	3	20.9	79.1	112 017
Gymnasium	16.6	83.4	164 948	4	21.1	78.9	106 743
Post-gymnasium	18.2	81.8	74 846	5	20.7	79.3	108 782
Tenure				All women living alone	23.7	76.3	542 925
Owner	18.5	81.5	704 379				
Rent	26.2	73.8	499 954				
Total	21.7	78.3	1 204 333				

Another interesting difference is that across regions. In metropolitan areas, the proportion of elderly who do not have children is higher than in most of the country. There are also many among the oldest elderly who do not have adult children. One explanation is – for parents in that age group – that adult children might have died. Another explanation is that the likelihood of never having had a child is higher among the oldest generations. There is also a correlation between tenure and whether or not older people have children. It is apparent that elderly who rent their dwelling are less likely to have children than are those who own it. This observation might, however, result from a correlation between age and tenure. It is common that the oldest of the elderly live in rented apartments.

All individuals in the study population are included in the analysis. Table 3, however, only shows the elderly who have adult children and displays the share of parents with adult children in the same local labor market by age, education, tenure, disposable income, and region type.[1]

There is considerable spread in Sweden regarding how common it is for elderly to have grown-up children within the same local labor market. Among elderly living in the Stockholm region, 95 percent have an adult child living there. This is in sharp contrast to the situation in rural Norrland, where only about 75 percent have adult children living in the same local labor market. There is also a variation among elderly with different education levels. The higher the older person's education level, the less likely it is to have children in the same local labor market. The differences across age groups and type of tenure are, however, quite small.

Single men are less likely to live in the same local labor market as their adult children compared to couples and single women. For singles but not for couples income differences are important for the likelihood of them living close to children.

2.3. Results of regression analysis

The above analysis shows how certain individual-level factors co-vary with proximity to the children, and serves as a guide as to which explanatory variables to use in our model. These variables mainly comprise individual-level characteristics, but we also include region. The latter variable reflects structural conditions on the labor market and, thereby, also differences in urban and rural characteristics.

---

[1] In 4 percent of the cases, there is no information on the municipality in which the person is registered, making it impossible to determine whether parents and children live in the same region.

Table 3. *Share of parents with at least one adult child in the same local labour market by socioeconomic characteristics of the parents*

	In same local labor market	Not in same local labor market	Number of elderly	Disposable income	In same local labor market	Not in same local labor market	Number of elderly
Region				Couples (quintiles)			
Stockholm	94.6	5.4	144 871	1	84.3	15.7	72 022
Göteborg	91.6	8.4	74 833	2	83.8	16.2	75 850
Malmö	89.7	10.3	48 835	3	82.9	17.1	77 295
Urban Götaland	80.6	19.4	195 282	4	82.0	18.0	77 626
Urban Svealand	83.7	16.3	93 993	5	82.6	17.4	79 492
Urban Norrland	83.0	17.0	41 855	All couples	83.1	16.9	382 285
Rural Götaland	76.2	23.8	124 492	Single men (quintiles)			
Rural Svealand	75.3	24.7	90 582	1	74.3	25.7	18 723
Rural Norrland	73.8	26.2	92 760	2	76.1	23.9	25 738
Age				3	76.8	23.2	30 047
65–74	83.3	16.7	410 873	4	76.3	23.7	32 437
75–79	83.1	16.9	201 971	5	79.4	20.6	34 950
80–84	82.4	17.6	161 445	All men	76.9	23.1	141 895
85–89	82.1	17.9	93 741	Single women (quintiles)			
90–	80.0	20.0	39 473	1	82.8	17.2	67 746
Education				2	83.7	16.3	75 423
Pre-gymnasium	83.5	16.5	714 692	3	85.4	14.6	81 871
Gymnasium	82.6	17.4	133 606	4	85.5	14.5	78 146
Post-gymnasium	75.6	24.4	59 205	5	86.2	13.8	80 137
Tenure				All women	84.8	15.2	383 323
Owner	82.3	17.7	556 733				
Rent	83.7	16.3	350 770				
All	82.8	17.2	907 503				

Note: Missing data on the localization in a specific local labor market of adult children, 35 437 cases.

Parameter estimates for three logistic regressions – one for each of the groups: elderly women living alone, elderly men living alone, and elderly couples – are reported in Table 4. As mentioned earlier the analysis includes all older individuals in the study population, regardless of

Table 4. ***Results from logistic regressions of aging parents' proximity to the closest adult child***

	Women living alone		Men living alone		Couples	
	B	Standard error	B	Standard error	B	Standard error
Intercept	−4.441	0.117	−1.887	0.085	−2.361	0.081
Same local labor market as an adult child in 1999						
Yes	10.090	0.039	7.700	0.038	7.379	0.027
No	0.000		0.000		0.000	
Region type						
1	−0.275	0.067	0.714	0.049	0.957	0.036
2	−0.126	0.079	0.584	0.056	0.905	0.040
3	−0.201	0.088	0.602	0.064	0.667	0.045
4	−0.022	0.063	0.273	0.047	0.204	0.033
5	0.243	0.071	0.383	0.055	0.403	0.039
6	0.161	0.094	0.403	0.069	0.266	0.050
7	−0.032	0.069	0.032	0.052	0.015	0.036
8	−0.060	0.075	0.061	0.055	−0.038	0.040
9	0.000		0.000		0.000	
Age						
65–74	0.553	0.070	−0.827	0.056	0.290	0.069
75–79	0.543	0.069	−0.626	0.057	0.096	0.070
80–84	0.487	0.069	−0.466	0.058	0.026	0.071
85–89	0.368	0.072	−0.182	0.061	0.012	0.075
90 +	0.000	.	0.000	.	0.000	.
Disposable income (quintiles)						
1	−0.656	0.054	−1.067	0.041	−0.558	0.028
2	−0.438	0.054	−0.680	0.039	−0.429	0.029
3	−0.349	0.054	−0.481	0.038	−0.467	0.027
4	−0.257	0.052	−0.335	0.037	−0.383	0.026
5	0.000	.	0.000	.	0.000	.
Education						
Pre-gymnasium	0.227	0.085	−0.220	0.055	0.059	0.031
Gymnasium	0.256	0.089	−0.029	0.057	0.005	0.032
Post-gymnasium	0.000	.	0.000	.	0.000	.
Tenure						
Own	−0.101	0.035	−0.015	0.025	0.080	0.020
Rent	0.000	.	0.000	.	0.000	.
McFadden R2	0.938		0.813		0.790	
Number of observations	542 925		226 691		434 717	

whether they have adult children or not. The estimates are to be interpreted such that high positive values increase the likelihood that an aging parent will have an adult child living in the same local labor market region.

The logistic regression model includes as an explanatory variable the lagged dependent variable, i.e., if there was an adult child in the same local labor market the preceding year. This variable picks up a strong persistence in people's choice of living close to their children. The most striking result from the analysis is the difference between single elderly men and the other two groups. The analysis shows that the older men are, the greater the likelihood that they live in the same local labor market as one of their adult children, while the opposite holds for elderly single women and elderly couples. This result may be a consequence of elderly men having greater difficulties than elderly women to manage on their own. They are thus more likely to move closer to their adult children than are elderly women. The age gradient is smaller for couples than for singles. The probability to live close to a child is somewhat higher for middle-aged couples compared to old couples. A possible explanation is that middle-aged couples might help caring for their grandchildren. Their adult children are still in the ages of having young children of their own, and proximity to their elderly parents could be an advantage for young couples.

There is yet another difference between single elderly men and the other two groups. More educated men have a higher probability to live close to a child than less educated men, while the reverse relation holds in particular for single women.

For all three groups, the likelihood of parents and adult children living in the same local labor market increases with increasing disposable income. The income gradient is particularly strong among single men. Region has the same effect for single women as for couples. The probability to live close to a child is higher in the metropolitan areas than in rural and northern Sweden. For single women, however, it is more likely to have an adult child close, if they live in a small city or in the countryside rather than in metropolitan areas. We might finally note that the persistence in living close to a child is somewhat higher for single women than for single men and couples.

2.4. Simulation results

A version of the estimated proximity model, which does not include the lagged dependent variable, was used to impute closeness to own children in the first simulation year (1999). The explanatory variables of this model were region, age of the elderly, income, education, and tenure. Most of the slope estimates are close to those exhibited in Table 4, but without the

Figure 2. Share of elderly living close to adult children

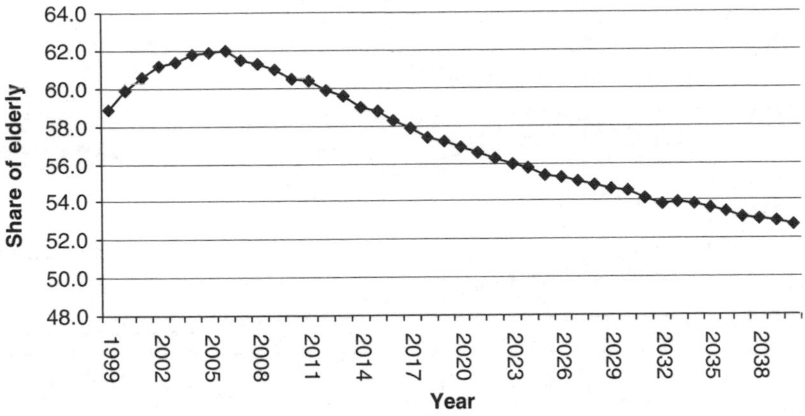

lagged dependent variable the fit to data is not as good.[2] In the subsequent simulations until year 2040, we use the estimates shown in Table 4.

The basic scenario suggests that the share of elderly (65 +) living close to at least one adult child increases to a peak at about 62 percent in 2006. It then decreases consecutively to 53 percent in 2040 (Figure 2). An increase in the share of the very old, in particular women, and their relatively low income explain the decrease after 2006. It is also likely that the continued migration of predominantly young people to the metropolitan regions contributes to the decrease in proximity.

Figure 3 illustrates the differences in proximity due to age and marital status. The share of couples that live close to a child is higher than that of singles and there is no decreasing trend. Although the path toward a share of almost 70 percent in 2040 for 65–79 years old and 80 + differs, the end result of 70 percent is an increase compared to the initial shares. For singles the picture is rather different. The share of the age group 65–79 declines all the time to reach 43 percent by 2040. For the oldest, 80 +, the share living close to a child first increases to a maximum of 66 percent in 2015, but then steadily declines to 53 percent. The shape of the curve is similar to that of couples 80 +, but at a lower level.

Figure 4 details by region the national curve of Figure 2. All regions show the same general pattern – first an increase for a few years and then a decrease – but there are significant regional differences. In the beginning the regional differences are rather small, but the decline in the frequency of proximity goes faster in the metropolitan than in the rural regions.

---

[2] The estimates are obtainable from the authors on request.

Figure 3.   Share of elderly living close to an adult child by family type and age over the simulated period

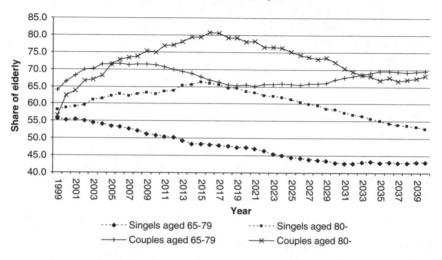

Figure 4.   Share of elderly living close to an adult child by region and year

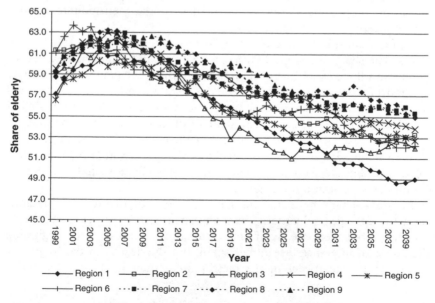

Note: Stockholm region = region 1; Göteborg region = region 2; Malmö region = region 3;
Urban Götaland = region 4; Urban Svealand = region 5; Urban Norrland = region 6; Rural
Götaland = region 7; Rural Svealand = region 8; Rural Norrland = region 9

For instance, in Stockholm we simulate a decline to 49 percent from a maximum of 61, while in the rural north there is a decline from 63 to 55 percent. One explanation is that the share of singles increases most in Stockholm and least in rural Norrland and that the share of singles who live close to a child is lower than that of couples. Singles also tend to be older.

One implication of the general decline in proximity is that the regional migration and in particular the migration from the rural north to the metropolitan areas will lead to an increasing geographical mismatch between generations. This will increase the demand for public care of the frail elderly in all regions.

3. A model of the demand for old age care and mortality: specification, estimation, interpretation, and simulations

3.1. Introduction

In this section, we present an analysis concerning the interplay between the development of dependency in activities for daily living (ADL), the informal support from a partner, the mode of old age care (OAC) and the mortality among the very old. This analysis results in a model for the public OAC service choice among the very old that is used in the health module in SESIM, and a model for the excess mortality among the very old conditional on the choice of OAC. In the present study, we distinguish between three forms of OAC: independent living in ordinary home without public support (denoted state 0), independent living in ordinary home or special accommodations with home help and home health care (state 1), and living in special accommodations with round-the-clock care (state 2).

Population at risk for the OAC choice is everyone aged 65 or older. The OAC level of individuals entering the population at risk is simulated using an imputation model (a multinomial logit model). The OAC level of individuals above age 75, who were included in the population at risk in the previous year, is simulated using an estimated transition model (a separate multinomial logit model for each initial state). Because data are limited to individuals aged 75 or older (se below), we extrapolate OAC and ADL (using a model with a continuous age specification) to ages 65–74.

Data are from Kungsholmen, which is part of the inner city of Stockholm. The Kungsholmen study started in 1987 as a longitudinal population-based study with the aim of following a large number of elderly persons and study incidence and prevalence of disability with a special focus on dementia (Fratiglioni *et al.*, 1992). However, as the available data are limited in several respects, we had to make adjustments to the analysis. Because data were collected only at certain time points we do not have access to exact dates for the transfers between modes of care – only when a person died. The Kungsholmen study is furthermore from a rather special part of the country, and may therefore not be representative for the whole of Sweden. The first problem is addressed by using the elapsed time between observations as an independent variable. As for the second limitation, a comparison with national data, HINK/HEK from 1997 to 1998 (see below), shows that the transitions measured in the present study are not too different from those of the entire country. We did not have the possibilities to compare data along all dimensions, such as by health level.

Transfer between modes of care in a system of care for the elderly has been studied by many authors – both regarding utilization of home help and transfer to institutional care. The most important predictor of use of home help seems to be dependence in activities for daily living – instrumental (IADL) and personal (PADL) (Thorslund *et al.*, 1991; Larsson and Thorslund, 2002; Meinow *et al.*, 2005).

The impact of dementia and depression has been studied by Larsson using the same data from the Kungsholmen study as the present project (Larsson *et al.*, 2004). Also other studies using different data have confirmed the observation that demented persons are more likely to receive home help (Livingston *et al.*, 1997; Stoddart *et al.*, 2002). Other factors identified as associated with the use of home help are difficulties in moving outdoors (Sakari-Rantala *et al.*, 1995) and general health (Stoddart *et al.*, 2002).

Findings concerning the impact of gender are mixed. Controlling for the fact that women tend to outlive their spouses and consequently lack support from a partner at old age, gender does not seem to affect the use of formal home help (Larsson and Thorslund, 2002). Generally speaking access to informal care and having children has been shown repeatedly to reduce the likelihood of receiving formal in-home support (Stoller and Cutler, 1993; Lagergren, 1994; Szebehely, 1998).

Also when it comes to transfer to institutional care, ADL limitations and cognitive impairment stand out as the most important predictors (Willcocks *et al.*, 1987; Brown *et al.*, 1990; Kelman and Thomas, 1990; Aguero-Torres *et al.*, 2001; Larsson *et al.*, 2006). Access to informal care also seems to influence the probability to move to an institution (Tennstedt *et al.*, 1990; Pearlman and Crown, 1992; Larsson and Thorslund, 2002). However, it has further been argued that adult children act as advocates for their parents and often urge them to move (Thorslund, 2003). Connected to this is also the question of caregiver burden and "burn-out," which may prompt a decision to transfer (Brown *et al.*, 1990). Other predictive factors that have been discussed in this context are education and income, which at least in Sweden do not appear to influence the propensity to move to institutional care (Palme *et al.*, 2003). In other countries, however, the situation may be different (Mustard *et al.*, 1999).

3.2. Data

The Kungsholmen study followed elderly persons by the choice of OAC from age 75 until the person deceased. In total 2368 persons living in the parish of Kungsholmen and born in 1913 or earlier (aged 75 years or more) were included. Persons living in the community as well as in institutions were included. After an initial examination in 1987–1988 the involved persons were re-examined four times with intervals of 2–3 years until year 2000 (in the sequel denoted phase 1, 3, 4, 5, 6). The examination included among others estimation of dependence in instrumental and personal activities for daily life (IADL, PADL). A subset of 1810 of the above 2368 persons participated in all phases of the study.

One might be worried that data from the Kungsholmen study are not representative for the whole of Sweden, considering that they are drawn only from a quite small part of the country. We have, luckily, the opportunity to compare them with panel data from the Swedish Household Income Survey (HINK/HEK) from 1997 to 1998.[3] Unfortunately that data does not contain such variables as health or activities of daily life measures, aspects of the elderly population of particular interest in the present study.

A couple of things complicate a direct comparison with the HINK/ HEK study:

(1) The age distribution in subsequent waves of the Kungsholmen study is not representative of the original population, while the HINK/HEK data should be comparable to the overall population (see Figure 5). In order to increase comparability with HINK/HEK data, one might consider using only the transition between the first and second waves from the Kungsholmen study. We therefore included in Table 5 also the transition rates using the first transitions only (i.e., those between the first and second wave). As can be seen there are some minor deviations in the transition rates reported. We have split the sample into two samples above and below age 85.

(2) The duration between data collection points is on average about three times longer in the Kungsholmen study compared to HINK/HEK, which is annual. One can accomplish a comparable 3-year "translation" of the HINK/HEK transition matrix by using a Markov assumption. The original transition matrix along with the 3-year equivalence is also given in Table 5. Again we have divided the sample into two age groups (above and below the age 85).

---

[3] Conducted by Statistics Sweden, this is a large database containing both register-based income and wealth data and survey questions. For a broad description of HINK/HEK, visit the Internet address of Statistics Sweden, www.scb.se

**Figure 5.   Age distribution in the Kungsholmen study (top) and HINK/
HEK (bottom)**

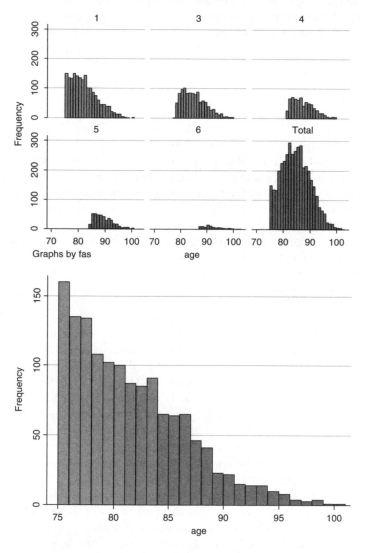

Table 5, top panel, gives the transition rates (percent) between two subsequent phases (denoted entrance state and exit state) in the Kungsholmen study. The typical pattern seems, not unexpectedly, to be that individuals went from having less care to more, although some move in the opposite direction. One can note that very few moved from having 24 h care (state 2) to less care (state 0 or 1). From the state of living in special accommodations with around-the-clock care, most exit to death. Hence, it seems unfeasible to model the transition for individuals in this mode of care as a multinomial

Table 5. *Transitions in the Kungsholmen study (top panel) and national data, HINK/HEK 1997–1998 (bottom panel), frequencies and percentages*

All waves

Age ≥75 & age ≤84, N=2146

Entrance state	Exit state			Death	Frequency
	0	1	2		
0	60.0%	9.1%	3.2%	27.7%	1644
1	15.4%	31.3%	8.7%	44.5%	402
2	2.0%	0.0%	32.0%	66.0%	100

Age ≥85, N=1904

Entrance state	Exit state			Death	Frequency
	0	1	2		
0	40.0%	15.0%	6.7%	38.3%	882
1	4.9%	30.8%	13.7%	50.6%	652
2	0.8%	1.1%	29.7%	68.4%	370

Waves 1 and 2

Age ≥75 & age ≤84, N=1900

Entrance state	Exit state			Death	Frequency
	0	1	2		
0	60.7%	8.2%	3.1%	28.1%	1460
1	15.8%	30.0%	8.3%	45.8%	360
2	2.5%	0.0%	33.8%	63.8%	80

Age ≥85, N=951

Entrance state	Exit state			Death	Frequency
	0	1	2		
0	37.8%	13.4%	5.5%	43.3%	418
1	6.9%	29.3%	14.2%	49.6%	379
2	0.6%	1.9%	23.4%	74.0%	154

(Continued on next page)

Table 5. *(Continued)*

1 year (raw data)

Age ≥ 75 & age ≤ 84, N = 1067

Entrance state	Exit state			Death	Frequency
	0	1	2		
0	87.7%	5.6%	1.8%	4.9%	891
1	20.0%	66.2%	1.4%	12.4%	145
2	12.9%	6.5%	58.1%	22.6%	31

Age ≥ 85, N = 335

Entrance state	Exit state			Death	Frequency
	0	1	2		
0	62.0%	19.3%	4.8%	13.9%	166
1	15.2%	63.6%	8.3%	12.9%	132
2	2.7%	5.4%	51.4%	40.5%	37

3-year equivalence (Markov)

Age ≥ 75 & age ≤ 84, N = 1067

Entrance state	Exit state			Death	Frequency
	0	1	2		
0	70.6%	10.4%	3.1%	15.9%	–
1	36.4%	31.7%	2.4%	29.5%	–
2	23.8%	9.1%	20.2%	46.9%	–

Age ≥ 85, N = 335

Entrance state	Exit state			Death	Frequency
	0	1	2		
0	29.7%	24.0%	7.7%	38.7%	–
1	18.9%	32.2%	9.9%	39.1%	–
2	4.2%	6.5%	14.6%	74.8%	–

choice. Another result is, not unexpectedly, that the mortality risk increases with higher mode of care.

Transitions in HINK/HEK are shown in the bottom panel in Table 5. A comparison with the Kungsholmen study shows that the transition rates are rather similar but also that some differences emerge: (a) the mortality risk is lower at the national level than at Kungsholmen; (b) the probabilities of changing from state 2 (24 h care) to state 0 (no home help service), and (c) changing from state 1 to state 0, are substantially higher at the national level than at Kungsholmen. However, the number of observations is low, and hence these differences may not be a big problem. Further, the Markov assumption is by no means harmless and the observed differences may be an artefact of this assumption. Also, with low frequent data, as in the Kungsholmen study, it is possible that states with a relative short duration are missed. It can be assumed that transitions from a higher to a lower state usually have shorter duration than the opposite. We conclude that the data from Kungsholmen can be used for our purposes.

3.3. Methodology

We have chosen to perform two separate analyses; one analysis concerning the transitions between OAC states and another one concerning the transition to death. The reason is that while the exact date of death is known, durations to transfer to the other states are interval-censored in data, as they do not contain the exact transition date. In case of transfer all that is known is that it occurred some time between two data collection dates. In the first analysis, we model the change from the current (entrance) state to one of states 0, 1, and 2 as a multinomial logit model (McFadden, 1973).[4] We estimate the exit state choice as a multinomial logit conditional on current (entrance) state. In the second analysis, we model the mortality risk conditional on current state using a piecewise constant hazard (PWCH) model.

3.4. Multinomial OAC choice analysis

3.4.1. Explanatory variables

The degree of ADL limitations (IADL and PADL) is constructed in four levels, (0) no ADL limitations, (1) only IADL limitations but no PADL limitations, (2) not so severe PADL limitations (1–2 PADL), and (3) severe

---

[4] The elapsed time between data collection dates is included as a covariate in this model.

Urban Fransson, Daniel Hallberg and Mårten Lagergren

Table 6. *ADL score (in three levels) and entrance state OAC in the Kungsholmen study, frequencies and percent*

ADL	Entrance state OAC			Total
	Independent living in ordinary home without public support	Independent living in ordinary home or special accommodations with home help and home health care	Living in special accommodations with around-the-clock care	
0	1024	140	12	1176
	87.1	11.9	1.0	100.0
1	1213	482	32	1727
	70.2	27.9	1.8	100.0
2	301	360	78	739
	40.7	48.7	10.6	100.0
3	35	99	368	502
	7.0	19.7	73.3	100.0
Total	2573	1081	490	4144
	62.1	26.1	11.8	100.0

PADL limitations (3–6 PADL).[5] Table 6 shows a cross tabulation between the ADL variable and the entrance state of OAC. The general impression is that individuals who are more dependent in terms of a higher *ADL* code also obtain a higher mode of care. The majority (73 percent) of the most dependent persons have 24 h care. Interestingly, there is also a group of individuals (7 percent) who were coded as very dependent (ADL = 3) but did not receive any public care service. The probable reason is that these persons receive their care from their families or another informal source. There might also be measurement errors in the ADL score.[6]

One expects the informal support and help that an elderly person is receiving to affect the transition between modes of formal care.

---

[5] IADL stands for instrumental activities in daily life and means that a person have difficulties to clean, cook, go shopping, etc. PADL stands for personal activities in daily life and means that a person has difficulties to handle her personal hygiene, and must have help with washing, dressing, getting out of bed, etc. Since it was partially missing, the incidence of IADL was imputed in phases 3 and 4, and for part of the sample in phase 1.

[6] Actually, a transition matrix of the health variable (not shown) shows unexpectedly that there was some substantial recovery rate among those with ADLi = 2. (However, individuals with severe PADL limitations were very unlikely to recover.) A closer inspection showed that the high recovery rate for these was mainly between phases 1 and 3 in the study. In subsequent phases the rates were what could be expected. One explanation for this, besides the obvious fact that individuals in the study becomes older by each phase, is that the questionnaire changed from phase 3 and onwards. A careful check of these differences revealed, however, that we unfortunately have no possibility to correct this problem.

For instance, a spouse, partner, or one's children should make individuals demand less outside home help. For a description of the importance of the informal care given by an adult child in Europe, see for example Börsch-Supan *et al.* (2005). Our Kungsholmen data do not have complete information about informal care, but we have possibility to control for living with a partner (*sambo*). This might, however, not catch all the effects of informal help considering that, an adult child might be giving more informal help than the partner.[7] Unfortunately, data on support from children were not available in the Kungsholmen database.

Spell length (in years, *ytid*) is included as covariate in the model to control for differences in time length between data collection dates.[8] We also consider gender (*man*) and age group dummies (age 75–79, 80–84,... 95+) as covariates in the model.

3.4.2. Results

Table 7 shows the estimated marginal effects from two multinomial logit models, with entrance states 0 and 1, respectively (and the coefficient estimates are given in Table A.1). Both allow 0, 1, and 2 as exit states (in other words, transition probabilities conditional on survival).[9] As noted above, very few change from having 24 h care

---

[7] We also tried to use another variable, which was a proxy for the distance to a relative by coding the telephone area code number to the next of kin reported in data. In a preliminary analysis this variable turned out significant but was, unfortunately, missing for a substantial part of the sample (around 65.1 percent in survey phase 1 was missing).

[8] One can note, however, as these spell lengths exaggerate the true duration; we will underestimate the effect of durations on separation probability. It is also possible that some individuals changed state more than once between data collection points. The analysis will not handle this problem.

[9] We make a few simplifications: (1) Individuals usually contribute with more than one transition, so observations may not necessarily be independent within observations from the same individual (they may well, however, be independent across individuals). We have, for simplicity, settled for an estimator that assumes independence. However, we use a robust variance–covariance estimator that allows for this type of observation clustering. (2) Although an ordered choice specification is conceivable for these data we have settled for a multinomial one. We have not performed any formal test of a multinomial (probit) model against an ordered one since such a test is quite cumbersome. Simulation of multinomial logit and ordered logit show very little differences in outcome. It matters some for the sign and the level of significance of the marginal effect whether we treat choices as ordered or unordered. The multinomial logit model is used since this is a more flexible specification. (3) We have not conditioned on state history longer than to the previous data collection point. It would of course be possible to include prior states, if we think it is likely that these would matter for the current transition (in other words, that the process is not characterized as a "Markov-chain"). The determining factor for not doing this, considering the limited sample size, is that we would then lose subjects who only participated in the starting phase of the study or contributed with only one phase observation.

Table 7.   *Alternative specification: marginal effects of the multinomial choice of care mode (exit state), conditional on current mode (entrance state)*

	Entrance state = 0; exit state = 0		Entrance state = 0; exit state = 1		Entrance state = 0; exit state = 2		Mean
Man	0.072*	(2.12)	−0.080**	(−2.73)	0.007	(0.43)	0.240
ADL1	−0.018	(−0.86)	0.013	(0.68)	0.005	(0.47)	0.463
ADL2	−0.081*	(−2.21)	0.028	(0.86)	0.053*	(2.24)	0.113
ADL3	−0.605***	(−4.37)	0.196	(1.22)	0.409*	(2.14)	0.006
Sambo	0.046*	(1.78)	−0.049*	(−2.08)	0.003	(0.21)	0.305
Sambo*man	−0.083	(−1.17)	0.100	(1.42)	−0.017	(−0.92)	0.152
Age 80–84	−0.159***	(−4.97)	0.102***	(3.50)	0.056**	(2.89)	0.390
Age 85–89	−0.330***	(−7.84)	0.180***	(4.40)	0.150***	(4.42)	0.255
Age 90–94	−0.509***	(−8.61)	0.238***	(3.24)	0.271***	(3.35)	0.059
Age 95 +	−0.637***	(−5.56)	0.287	(1.31)	0.350	(1.26)	0.003
Ytid	−0.069***	(−3.61)	0.031*	(1.85)	0.038***	(3.98)	3.191

	Entrance state = 1; exit state = 0		Entrance state = 1; exit state = 1		Entrance state = 1; exit state = 2		Mean
Man	0.002	(0.08)	0.148**	(2.51)	−0.150**	(−2.66)	0.131
ADL1	0.005	(0.29)	−0.013	(−0.22)	0.008	(0.14)	0.536
ADL2	−0.043**	(−2.87)	−0.052	(−0.76)	0.096	(1.39)	0.281
ADL3	−0.044**	(−2.35)	−0.167	(−1.23)	0.210	(1.53)	0.039
Sambo	0.037	(1.25)	0.145**	(2.36)	−0.182**	(−3.09)	0.135
Sambo*man	−0.020	(−0.65)	−0.364*	(−1.70)	0.384*	(1.65)	0.058
Age 80−84	−0.037**	(−2.56)	−0.153	(−1.39)	0.190*	(1.66)	0.287
Age 85−89	−0.070***	(−4.21)	−0.217*	(−2.14)	0.287**	(2.73)	0.384
Age 90−94	−0.078***	(−6.90)	−0.179	(−1.40)	0.257*	(1.99)	0.178
Age 95 +	−0.147***	(−7.87)	−0.138	(−0.75)	0.286	(1.55)	0.032
Ytid	−0.004	(−0.36)	−0.079**	(−2.36)	0.083**	(2.53)	3.022

Note: Except for the variable ytid, dy/dx is for discrete change of dummy variable from 0 to 1. Z-statistics in parenthesis. $^*p<0.05$; $^{**}p<0.01$; $^{***}p<0.001$. *ADL1*, only IADL limitations but no PADL limitations; *ADL2*, not so severe PADL limitations (1–2 PADL); and *ADL3*, severe PADL limitations (3–6 PADL).

(state 2) to a lower mode of care (state 0 or 1). Hence it seems not feasible to model this transition as a multinomial choice. Instead transitions away from 24 h care to death are handled within a duration model framework (see below).

The reference group consists of women aged 75–79 years of age without any ADL limitations (*ADL0*) and not married or cohabiting. The results show that men, both those who receive home help service and those who do not, have a higher probability of staying with the same care mode, and a lower probability to move to a higher care mode, compared to women. IADL limitations (ADL = 1) do not seem to have any significant effect on transition probabilities. It is rather persons with PADL limitations (either severe or not so severe) that have a higher chance of receiving more help in the next period, and significantly so. These ADL limitations also lower the chance of receiving less or the same amount of help in the next period. We furthermore find, although we control for IADL and PADL limitations, that higher age speeds up the transition to higher modes of public care.[10]

We interact *sambo* with gender. The results indicate that the partner effect differs by gender. For men the partner effect on moving is positive, i.e., men with a partner are *more likely to move* from home help service to living in special accommodation with 24 h care. It is negative for women, i.e., women with a partner are more likely to *remain* with the same care mode than women without a partner.

3.5. Mortality analysis

Mortality is analyzed within a duration model framework. We estimate an exponential model with intercepts varying with survival time, which is denoted as PWCH model.[11] This model uses a baseline hazard with a flexible functional form. The PWCH duration model can be written as follows: in a regression setting, let time for observation i, $t_i \geq 0$ be exponential, with probability density function

$$f(t_i|\mathbf{x}_i) = \theta_i \exp(-\theta_i t_i^{\alpha}), \tag{1}$$

where $\theta_i = \exp\left(\mathbf{x}_i\boldsymbol{\beta} + \sum_s \delta_s \mathbf{I}[a_s \leq t_i < b_s]\right) > 0$, $\mathbf{x}_i$ is a vector of regressors including the unit vector to accommodate an intercept, $\boldsymbol{\beta}$ a vector of parameters, δ_s an intercept parameter for time interval s, and $\mathbf{I}[a_s \leq t_i < b_s]$ an indicator function, which is 1 if the duration is equal to or longer than a_s but shorter than b_s, and 0 otherwise.

An advantage with the PWCH model is that it is possible to capture unobserved heterogeneity, which represents a particular complication in duration models. In duration models, it is most common to include unobserved heterogeneity, denoted v_i, multiplicatively in the hazard function

$$h(t_i; \mathbf{x}_i, \boldsymbol{\omega}, v_i) = \lambda(t_i; \mathbf{x}_i, \boldsymbol{\omega})v_i$$

where $\lambda(\cdot)$ is the original hazard, $\boldsymbol{\omega}$ the vector of parameters in that hazard, and v_i unobserved heterogeneity. v_i is assumed independent identically distributed, and independent of the included regressors $\mathbf{x}_i$. The unconditional distribution of t_i (obtained by integrating out v_i) is called the mixture

---

[10] Moreover, we get the expected sign of the spell length variable (*ytid*). It also comes out strongly significant in our models. We hence find support for the proposed estimation strategy. Longer time interval results in a higher probability that the individual will change state (e.g., positive marginal effects of going from state 0 to 1, from 0 to 2, and from 1 to 2) and a lower probability that the individual will not change state or remain in the same state.

[11] The hazard is the probability of an event occurring; in this application it is death, given that the event has not already occurred.

distribution, and if $g(v_i)$ is the density of v_i, then it is called the mixing distribution (thereby the notion *mixture models*).

A closed form solution of the marginal (unconditional) distribution of t_i is obtained by assuming that $g(v_i)$ is gamma. For the modified version of the PWCH model with "gamma-frailty" (exponential-gamma mix), the probability density function is

$$f(t_i|\mathbf{x}_i, \mathbf{\omega}, \sigma) = \theta_i(1 + \sigma\theta_i t_i)^{-((1/\sigma)+1)} \tag{2}$$

where $E[v_i]$ is normalized to unity and σ the variance parameter of the mixing distribution. The greater σ the greater the effect of heterogeneity. The exponential distribution is obtained as the limit of (2) when $\sigma \to 0$ (no unobserved heterogeneity).

To estimate the PWCH model, both with Eqs. (1) and (2), one needs to episode-split data at the time points when the hazard varies, and generate appropriate dummy variables to be included in the model. Estimation thus requires pre-specified intervals within which the hazard may be regarded as constant. A rough way of determining these is by studying the shape of the empirical hazards (not shown). Because the number of observations decreases rapidly by survival time we have chosen to partition the first 1825 days (5 years) into relatively short-interval units of 365 days, and then used longer intervals for longer durations; at 2500 and 4000 (maximum is 5348 days).[12]

3.5.1. Results

We use the same specification as in the multinomial analysis above – with gender-specific partner effects. Estimation results are given in Table 8A. For those living in special accommodation with 24 h care (entrance state = 2), the estimates strongly suggest that there is unobserved heterogeneity. Except for this subgroup the estimated coefficients change very little compared to the PWCH model without frailty.

Most slope estimates are what we would expect. The estimates clearly illustrate the importance of different models depending on the current care mode. For the group with either no assistance or home help (entrance states 0 and 1), we find that the mortality is higher among men, among those with severe ADL limitations, and among older persons. Further, the age gradient seems to be steeper among those who live in an ordinary home without public care compared to those who have home help. For those living in special accommodation with 24 h care, there are very few significant coefficients. Only when we control for unobserved heterogeneity in the exponential-gamma mixture model, we find some significant partial effects: there is a higher mortality risk among males (significant at 5

---

[12] Note that, due to the episode-splitting the number of observations increases.

Table 8A. **Estimates of a piecewise constant hazard (PWCH) model of mortality risk given current care (entrance state)**

Variable	No frailty			Model with frailty		
	Entrance state = 0	Entrance state = 1	Entrance state = 2	Entrance state = 0	Entrance state = 1	Entrance state = 2
Man	1.625***	1.472*	1.503	1.625***	1.472*	1.906*
ADL1	0.983	0.809	0.655	0.983	0.809	0.711
ADL2	1.214	1.049	0.99	1.214	1.049	0.997
ADL3	2.901***	1.509*	1.321	2.901***	1.509*	1.509
Sambo	1.134	0.513**	3.212	1.134	0.513**	4.549*
Sambo*man	1.004	1.473	0.513	1.004	1.473	0.336
Age 80–84	1.563***	1.134	0.985	1.563***	1.134	1.759
Age 85–89	2.303***	1.820***	0.872	2.303***	1.820***	1.871
Age 90–94	3.389***	2.633***	1.402	3.389***	2.633***	3.213
Age 95+	6.432***	2.536***	1.623	6.433***	2.536***	4.419
Time 0–365	0.125***	0.229**	0.438***	0.125***	0.229**	0.083***
Time 365–730	0.221***	0.328*	0.529*	0.221***	0.328*	0.129
Time 730–1095	0.303***	0.444		0.302***	0.444	
Time 1095–1460	0.288***	0.693	1.536	0.288***	0.693	3.40E + 176
Time 1460–1825	0.307***	0.254*		0.306***	0.254*	
Time 1825–2500	0.268***	0.366		0.268***	0.366	
Time 2500–4000	0.507*	0.444		0.507*	0.444	
Constant	0.001***	0.002***	0.003***	0.001***	0.002***	0.006***
ln(sigma)				−14.989	−14.354	−1.511
Z				−0.04	−0.05	−5.50
$P > |z|$				0.968	0.963	0.000
N	3716	1503	338	3716	1503	338
Log L	−1043.259	−645.033	−248.761	−1043.259	−645.033	−250.931
χ^2	227.109	134.912	33.023	227.109	134.912	28.683

Note: The estimates are displayed in exponentiated form. *$p < 0.05$; **$p < 0.01$; ***$p < 0.001$. *ADL1*, only IADL limitations but no PADL limitations; *ADL2*, not so severe PADL limitations (1–2 PADL); and *ADL3*, severe PADL limitations (3–6 PADL).

percent level) and among those who have a partner. This latter result goes in the opposite direction compared to those with home help services. In that subgroup, we find significantly *lower* mortality risk compared to not having a partner.

To study gender-specific effects, we have also estimated the duration model separately by gender. The estimation algorithm for the model with frailty did not reach convergence for all subgroups, presumably as a result of too few observations. We therefore present, in Table 8B, only the simpler specifications where we do not control for unobserved heterogeneity.

We see that many of the results in the aggregated model are in fact driven by females. This is presumably a result of the uneven distribution between men and women in the sample. One can also note that the age

Table 8B.   Gender-specific estimates of a piecewise constant hazard (PWCH) model of mortality risk by mode of care, no frailty

Variable	Males			Females		
	Entrance state = 0	Entrance state = 1	Entrance state = 2	Entrance state = 0	Entrance state = 1	Entrance state = 2
ADL1	0.896	0.614		1.045	0.802	0.667
ADL2	1.719**	0.816	3.153	0.989	1.064	1.015
ADL3	4.002***	1.311	5.795	2.524**	1.525*	1.283
Sambo	1.081	0.678	1.141	1.155	0.511**	3.774
Age 80–84	1.554*	1.644	1.724	1.610***	1.041	0.765
Age 85–89	2.402***	1.605	1.963	2.311***	1.872***	0.72
Age 90–94	3.419***	2.157	1.356	3.567***	2.722***	1.33
Age 95+	5.101*	1.37	12.322	6.980***	3.007***	1.407
Time 0–365	0.268***	0.871	0.082	0.113***	0.214**	0.321
Time 365–730	0.456*	1.194	0.075	0.208***	0.316*	0.424
Time 730–1095	0.709	1.293	0.153	0.269***	0.453	0.81
Time 1095–1460	0.655	2.351		0.266***	0.678	
Time 1460–1825	0.667	3.07		0.295***	0.215**	
Time 1825–2500	0.595			0.258***	0.369	
Time 2500–4000		2.636		0.494*	0.432	
Time 4000+	1.337					
Constant	0.001***	0.001***	0.004***	0.001***	0.002***	0.004***
N	975	216	45	2741	1287	293
Log L	−343.112	−112.669	−37.498	−694.532	−525.984	−207.468
χ^2	74.125	16.631	8.286	139.092	126.802	31.077

Note: See Table 8A.

gradient is about the same for both genders. The excess mortality among men without home help or special accommodations seems mainly to be caused by a steeper ADL gradient compared to women; both ADL2 (not so severe PADL limitations) and ADL3 (severe PADL limitations) affect men's mortality risk harder than that of women. The effects on mortality of having a partner that was found in the aggregated model (lower mortality among those with home help services and higher among those with special accommodation) seems to be about the same for both genders, however only significant for the female subsample.

In general, we would expect to find lower mortality rates among married or cohabiting men compared to single men, but the point estimates are positive and insignificanlty different from zero. First, there are rather few men in the sample. At higher ages, as one could expect, we find a higher rate of single women than single men, simply because men have a higher mortality rate and husbands usually are a few years older than their wives. Second, the variable which is used here – sambo – measures the present marital/cohabiting status, thus mixing widows/widowers with individuals never married. Third, the partner's health and age is unknown.

3.6. Simulation

The above-described models have been implemented in the SESIM model in order to simulate the demand for care of the elderly in Sweden. In the SESIM model, the individual level of health is simulated each year using probabilities derived from estimates obtained from ULF data (cf. Chapter 4). The first step is to use this health level together with age and sex to impute the degree of ADL limitations. This is done cross-sectionally for each year by an ordered probit model, i.e., there is no transition matrix for ADL as for the degree of ill health. As a result, ADL levels may shift from year to year in a way that is not entirely realistic. The imputation model was estimated using data from the SNAC study.[13] These estimates are given in Table A.2 in the Appendix.

Table 9 below shows the distribution of ADL limitations by degree of ill health, age group, and gender as calculated by running the simulation model according to the basic scenario. The basic scenario is described at the end of Chapter 3.

The next step in the simulation is to impute the level of assistance or mode of OAC. The initial level is imputed for each individual in the population using multinomial logit models estimated from the Kungsholmen data described above and with ADL level, age group, and sex as predictors. Population at risk for the OAC choice is everyone aged 65 or older. The OAC level of individuals entering the population at risk is simulated using an imputation model (a multinomial logit model). Because data are limited to individuals aged 75 or older (see below), we extrapolate OAC and ADL (using a model with a continuous age specification) to ages 65–74. Therefore, two different models were estimated: one with the effect of age represented by a step function (Table A.3), and another with age entering linearly (Table A.4) such that this model could be used for extrapolations into the age interval 65–74. The model with age entering linearily was calibrated to the care mode frequencies of the HINK/HEK study for the age group 65–74 (see Chapter 2).[14] The initial 1999 simulated distribution of mode of care is shown in Table 10 by ADL level, age group, and gender. This table demonstrates how increasing ADL transfers into

---

[13] The SNAC study (Swedish National Study on Ageing and Care) has four sites, one of which – SNAC-K – is an extended follow-up on the Kungsholmen study. In the SNAC study ill health and ADL limitations are registered for the same persons. The sample used here consisted of 891 observations from SNAC-K.

[14] The same model has also been calibrated to the HINK/HEK care mode frequencies for the entire age group 65+ and used for all imputations in a few base scenario simulations. If a step function or a linear function of age is used for people aged 75+ does not matter much to the simulation results.

Table 9. *Distribution of ADL-limitations by degree of ill health, age group and gender – SESIM, basic scenario, average 1999–2040 (percent)*

	No ADL limitations	Only IADL limitations	1-2 PADL limitations	Several PADL limitations	Total
Men					
65–74					
Severe ill health	75.3	20.5	2.9	1.2	100.0
Moderate ill health	95.5	3.8	0.5	0.3	100.0
Slight ill health	98.3	1.4	0.2	0.1	100.0
No ill health	98.9	0.9	0.1	0.1	100.0
All	95.3	3.9	0.6	0.3	100.0
75–84					
Severe ill health	41.2	42.0	12.0	4.8	100.0
Moderate ill health	84.2	13.1	1.8	0.9	100.0
Slight ill health	95.0	4.1	0.6	0.4	100.0
No ill health	96.6	3.0	0.3	0.2	100.0
All	82.1	13.5	3.1	1.3	100.0
85 +					
Severe ill health	16.1	41.2	25.5	17.2	100.0
Moderate ill health	43.8	41.4	9.9	4.9	100.0
Slight ill health	79.0	18.1	2.2	0.7	100.0
No ill health	88.6	9.6	1.5	0.4	100.0
All	49.3	30.8	12.4	7.6	100.0
Woman					
65–74					
Severe ill health	66.6	26.4	4.9	2.1	100.0
Moderate ill health	92.8	6.1	0.7	0.3	100.0
Slight ill health	97.8	1.9	0.2	0.1	100.0
No ill health	98.3	1.5	0.2	0.1	100.0
All	92.4	6.2	1.0	0.4	100.0
75–84					
Severe ill health	33.7	43.8	14.4	8.2	100.0
Moderate ill health	77.6	18.6	2.6	1.2	100.0
Slight ill health	93.0	6.1	0.7	0.2	100.0
No ill health	94.5	4.6	0.6	0.2	100.0
All	75.0	18.0	4.5	2.4	100.0
85 +					
Severe ill health	10.3	36.6	27.7	25.5	100.0
Moderate ill health	37.3	42.7	13.2	6.8	100.0
Slight ill health	73.7	21.3	3.5	1.6	100.0
No ill health	84.4	13.1	2.0	0.5	100.0
All	37.6	32.5	16.5	13.4	100.0

Table 10. Initial 1999 distribution on mode of care by ADL level per age group and sex – SESIM, basic scenario (percent)

	No help	Home help	Institutional care	Total
65–74				
No ADL limitations	98.8	0.2	1.0	100.0
Only IADL limitations	99.5	0.6	0.0	100.0
1–2 PADL limitations	87.7	10.5	1.8	100.0
Several PADL limitations	38.9	11.1	50.0	100.0
Total	98.6	0.3	1.1	100.0
75–84				
No ADL limitations	93.2	6.4	0.4	100.0
Only IADL limitations	84.1	15.6	0.3	100.0
1–2 PADL limitations	59.4	35.5	5.1	100.0
Several PADL limitations	26.5	20.6	52.9	100.0
Total	89.8	8.9	1.3	100.0
85+				
No ADL limitations	81.3	16.7	2.0	100.0
Only IADL limitations	60.0	38.1	1.9	100.0
1–2 PADL limitations	29.6	57.5	13.0	100.0
Several PADL limitations	6.1	20.2	73.7	100.0
Total	57.6	30.5	12.0	100.0

more care and that the care dependence of ADL limitations increases with increasing age.

The next step is the yearly dynamic simulation of the OAC level of individuals above age 65, who were included in the population at risk in the previous year, using the estimated transition model discussed above (a separate multinomial logit model for each initial state). The resulting total number of persons by mode of care as averages over time periods is shown in Table 11 and Figure 6.

The base scenario suggests that the 65+ population is expected to double, from 1.6 million in 2000–2004 to 3.0 million in the period 2035–2039. At the same time the number of individuals in institutionalized care is expected to almost triple from 49 000 to 138 000, the number of individuals with home help is expected to go from 130 000 to 197 000, while those who have no help increase from 1.4 millions to 2.6 millions. The base scenario hence suggests that there is a much quicker increase in institutionalized care compared to home help.

As can be seen from Figure 7, one finds quite dramatic non-monotonic changes in the share of people in institutionalized care among the very old (85+). In the first period, about 21 percent of 85+ receive institutionalized care. Around the year 2015, this share peaks at just over 28 percent. As the simulation progresses the share falls back to 23 percent. One possible interpretation is that there were changes in the age and health distributions within the 85+ group in the simulated period.

Table 11. *Simulated distributions of mode of care by marital status and gender 2000–2039*

	2000–2004	2005–2009	2010–2014	2015–2019	2020–2024	2025–2029	2030–2034	2035–2039	Total
Single men									
No help	90.5	90.4	91.4	91.6	91.3	90.7	90.4	89.8	90.7
Home help	6.5	5.9	5.2	5.2	5.1	5.7	5.6	6.1	5.6
Institutional care	3.0	3.8	3.4	3.3	3.5	3.6	3.9	4.1	3.7
Total	100.0	100.0	100.0	100.0	100.0	100.0	100.0	100.0	100.0
Single women									
No help	79.3	78.6	80.3	82.2	82.8	82.5	81.6	80.2	81.1
Home help	12.7	11.4	10.0	9.0	8.9	9.0	9.4	9.8	9.8
Institutional care	8.0	10.1	9.7	8.8	8.3	8.5	9.1	10.0	9.1
Total	100.0	100.0	100.0	100.0	100.0	100.0	100.0	100.0	100.0
Cohabiting men									
No help	94.0	93.6	94.5	94.7	94.7	93.9	93.3	93.6	94.0
Home help	4.0	4.3	3.7	3.5	3.5	3.9	4.3	4.2	3.9
Institutional care	2.0	2.1	1.9	1.8	1.8	2.2	2.3	2.2	2.0
Total	100.0	100.0	100.0	100.0	100.0	100.0	100.0	100.0	100.0
Cohabiting women									
No help	94.4	94.1	94.5	95.0	95.0	94.4	94.0	94.2	94.4
Home help	4.2	4.0	3.8	3.5	3.5	3.8	4.1	3.9	3.9
Institutional care	1.4	1.8	1.6	1.5	1.5	1.8	1.9	1.9	1.7
Total	100.0	100.0	100.0	100.0	100.0	100.0	100.0	100.0	100.0
All									
No help	88.2	87.6	88.7	89.6	89.7	89.2	88.6	88.1	88.8
Home help	7.6	7.1	6.3	5.9	5.8	6.1	6.4	6.6	6.4
Institutional care	4.2	5.3	5.0	4.6	4.5	4.7	5.0	5.3	4.8
Total	100.0	100.0	100.0	100.0	100.0	100.0	100.0	100.0	100.0

The importance of informal care, when it comes to demand for public care, is shown by comparing the distribution on modes of care for single-living persons and persons living with a partner. Table 11 shows the percentage distribution of mode of care as averages over time periods and by marital status.

As seen from Table 11 there is not a big difference between cohabitating men and women, but a large gender difference for singles. Table 12 shows that the larger part of the public services to elderly will also in the future go to singles. These estimates were obtained assuming that the amount of informal care had no effect on formal care. However, as shown above the share of the oldest elderly living in the proximity of an adult child will decrease in the end of the period both for singles and couples. Since adult children is the primary source of informal care this may lead to increased pressure on the formal care services for both categories.

Figure 6. Total number of individuals by mode of care and age group, 2000–2030 (in thousands)

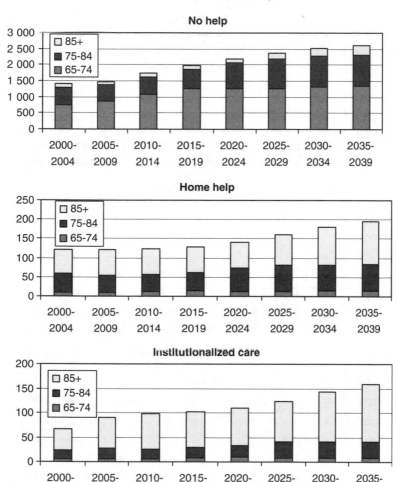

3.7. Conclusions

In this part of the chapter, we have specified, estimated, and simulated models for OAC and mortality for a population of elderly persons. Limitations in the data at our disposal have been discussed. The available data is limited in several respects: we did not have access to exact dates for the transfers – except in the case of death – and the number of observations is fairly small. The data are furthermore from a very small part of the country – Kungsholmen, a part of the inner city of Stockholm. The first problem was addressed by using the elapsed time between observations as an independent variable. Of course, this does not give ideal estimates and

Figure 7.   Population shares with no help, home help, and institutionalized care by age group 2000–2039

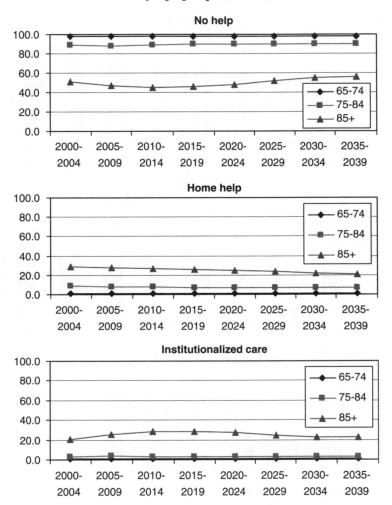

efforts will be made to improve the database in these respects. As for the third limitation, a comparison with national data (HINK/HEK) showed that the transitions measured in the present study do not deviate too much from those of the entire country. The imputation models for OAC were calibrated to these national data.

Variables explaining the choice of OAC and mortality were age, gender, ADL limitations, and having a partner (representing informal help or care). The results seem consistent with general beliefs and research results obtained from similar analyses. Thus, we find that the propensity to move to a more intensive mode of care was connected to gender, ADL – limitations, and age. As should be expected the probabilities also increased

Table 12.   Total number of single-living and cohabiting persons per mode of care 2000–2039 (in 1000s)

	2000–2004	2005–2009	2010–2014	2015–2019	2020–2024	2025–2029	2030–2034	2035–2039
Single men								
No help	231	276	362	437	506	566	645	692
Home help	17	18	21	25	29	36	40	47
Institutional care	8	12	14	16	19	23	28	31
Total	255	306	396	477	554	625	713	770
Single women								
No help	458	491	571	654	724	772	811	826
Home help	74	71	71	72	78	84	93	101
Institutional care	46	63	69	70	73	79	90	103
Total	578	625	711	796	875	935	995	1030
Cohabitating men								
No help	402	405	454	503	539	561	579	596
Home help	17	19	18	19	20	23	27	27
Institutional care	9	9	9	10	10	13	15	14
Total	428	432	481	531	569	597	621	637
Cohabitating women								
No help	315	312	345	390	430	459	484	499
Home help	14	13	14	14	16	18	21	21
Institutional care	5	6	6	6	7	9	10	10
Total	333	332	365	410	453	486	515	530

with time between observations. There was also an effect of the availability of informal care support, as measured by marriage or cohabitation.

Patterns of mortality could be studied with greater precision, since we in this case had access to the exact date of death. A model allowing for piecewise changes in the hazard function and unobserved heterogeneity clearly indicated neglected unobserved heterogeneity in our mortality model for those with 24 h care. Also for mortality the observed relations pointed in the expected directions – mortality increases with increasing ADL limitations and age and is higher for men than for women.

Gender-specific mortality estimates showed that the age gradient and the effect of having a partner are about the same for both gender (however, some of these effects are only significant for females). It seems, on the other hand, as if the excess mortality among men living in ordinary homes without home help is driven by a steeper ADL gradient compared to women.

The simulation shows that demand for OAC will increase substantially in the future. The estimated increase in the number of persons receiving public OAC in the period 2000–2039 – assuming unchanged service level –amounts to 88 percent, which is almost exactly the same as the projected population increase in the involved age groups (86 percent). The result reflects the assumption of unchanged levels of ill health in the basic scenario. The projected development of institutional care is much steeper than for home help, which means that the cost development will be more accentuated than the increase in numbers of helped persons. However, the result should be regarded with some caution as it is heavily depending on the estimated transition rates between levels of care, which – as mentioned above – were based on a fairly small and maybe not totally representative sample.

The increase regards especially the age group 85 years and above. Among all that receive home help, the share of this age group is, according to the simulation, expected to increase from 50 to 56 percent in the time period 2000–2040. For institutional care the corresponding increase is from 66 to 74 percent. Depending on changes in the age composition *within* the 85 + group the share of this group in institutional care will vary over time reaching a peak around 2015. As by present a much higher proportion of single-living persons than cohabitating will demand public old age services. Most of these singles are women. The possibilities for these women of receiving informal care services from nearby living children will decrease in the future (cf. Section 2 above). As a result the demand for public old age services calculated above may be somewhat underestimated. The discussions of these questions will continue in Chapter 12, where alternative scenarios are explored.

References

Aguero-Torres, H., E. von Strauss, M. Viitanen, B. Winblad and L. Fratiglioni (2001), "Institutionalization in the elderly: the role of chronic disease and dementia. Cross-sectional and longitudinal data from a population-based study", *Journal of Clinical Epidemiology*, Vol. 54, pp. 795–801.

Almqvist, A. (2004). "Drömmen om det egna huset", Sociology Department, Uppsala Universitet.

Bornefalk, A. and O. Yndeheim (2003), "Kan vi räkna med de äldre?" in: Långtidsutredningen 2003/2004, Ministry of Finance, Sweden.

Börsch-Supan, A., A. Brugiavini, H. Jürges, J. Mackenbach, J. Siegrist and G. Weber (eds.) (2005), Health, Ageing and Retirement in Europe – First Results from the Survey of Health, Ageing and Retirement in Europe. Mannheim: MEA, available at http://www.share-project.org

Brown, L.J., J.F. Potter and B.G. Foster (1990), "Caregiver burden should be evaluated during geriatric assessment", *Journal of American Geriatric Society*, Vol. 38, pp. 455–460.

Clark, R.L. and D.A. Wolf (1992), "Proximity of children and elderly migration", in: I.A. Rogers, editor, *Elderly Migration and Population Redistribution. A Comparative Study*, London: Belhaven Press.

Table A.2. **Imputation model of initial ADLi (0, 1, 2, 3), ordered logit estimates**

	Coefficients	Standard error
Age	0.114***	0.013
Health = 3	1.126**	0.484
Health = 2	1.773***	0.445
Health = 1	3.389***	0.468
Sex	0.2385	0.226
Ancillary parameters		
Cut1	12.455***	1.127384
Cut2	14.368***	1.16969
Cut3	16.659***	1.268012
N	891	
Log L	394.039	

Note: Estimation sample is ages 65 + . $^*p<0.05$; $^{**}p<0.01$; $^{***}p<0.001$.

Table A.3. **Imputation model of mode of old age care (states 0, 1, 2), age 75+**

	Coefficients	t ratio
Exit state = 1		
Age 80–84	*0.623*	*4.840*
Age 85–89	1.183	9.330
Age 90–94	1.603	11.050
Age 95 +	2.636	9.080
Man	−0.755	−7.190
ADL1	1.010	9.330
ADL2	2.124	17.090
ADL3	2.883	12.840
Constant	−2.683	−19.700
Exit state = 2		
Age 80–84	0.981	3.120
Age 85–89	1.904	6.310
Age 90–94	2.398	7.650
Age 95 +	3.886	8.990
Man	−0.767	−3.810
ADL1	0.692	2.010
ADL2	2.987	9.290
ADL3	6.539	18.820
Constant	−5.721	−14.460
N	4144	
Log L	−2562.49	

Note: Exit state 0 is reference.

Table A.4. *Imputation model and dynamic model for OAC (0, 1, 2), age effect in linear form*

	(1) Imputation model (reference is exit state 0)		(2) Dynamic model if entrance state = 0 (reference is exit state 0)		(3) Dynamic model if entrance state = 1 (reference is exit state 1)	
	Coefficients	t ratio	Coefficients	t ratio	Coefficients	t ratio
Exit state = 0						
Age	0.119	14.55			−0.155	−5.14
Man	−0.749	−7.12			−0.168	−0.35
ADL1					0.138	0.4
ADL2					−0.881	−2.14
ADL3					−1.15	−0.95
Sambo					0.347	0.87
Sambo*man					0.277	0.38
Ytid					−0.0575	−0.26
Constant					12	4.2
Exit state = 1						
Age			0.15	8.02		
Man			−0.7	−2.3		

ADL1	1	9.26	0.114	0.79
ADL2	2.12	17.06	0.307	1.34
ADL3	2.86	12.74	2.2	2.45
Sambo			−0.351	−1.66
Sambo*man			0.618	1.49
Ytid			0.354	2.7
Constant	−11.8	−16.95	−15.1	−8.25

Exit state = 2

Age	0.171	11.69	0.233	9.43	0.0538	2.22
Man	−0.769	−3.84	0.0547	0.15	−1.11	−2.09
ADL1	0.684	1.99	0.135	0.57	0.0473	0.14
ADL2	2.97	9.25	0.885	2.94	0.386	1.1
ADL3	6.5	18.74	3.51	3.33	0.711	1.27
Sambo			0.11	0.37	−1.36	−2.12
Sambo*man			−0.334	−0.64	1.85	1.84
Ytid			0.94	4.49	0.412	2.21
Constant	−18.8	−14.47	−25.1	−10.18	−6.88	−2.95
N	4144		1707		534	
Log L	−2556		−1049		−464	

CHAPTER 12

Simulating the Future of the Elderly

Anders Klevmarken*

Academic research as well as the public policy debate has in the last few years been much concerned with expected future increased demand for health care and social care which follows from the aging of the large baby-boom cohorts and the increased costs to provide such services in the future, whether they are provided privately or by the public. Will it become necessary to increase taxes and user fees and if so, how much? Would policy measures to encourage people to retire later, to encourage immigration, and to improve the general health status of the population alleviate the expected future burden of more health care and social care? These issues are at the core of this study and in this chapter we will address some of the issues using alternative simulation scenarios.

These alternative scenarios are compared to the base scenario all previous chapters have used to evaluate the model. The properties of this scenario were detailed in Chapter 3. The alternatives were chosen to address policy issues of relevance to the living conditions of the elderly. Thus, in one alternative we allowed an improved health progression with and without accompanying decreases in death risks, to analyze how these changes will influence labor force participation and the demand for health care and old-age care. Another alternative involves an increased pension age. As already described in Chapter 6, the working age ceiling was increased from 65 to 70. This change should both alleviate the burden of society to finance the pensions of the baby-boomers and increase the pensions of the elderly. Higher immigration is sometimes mentioned as another way to reduce the dependency ratio, and we have thus included

---

* Corresponding author.

CONTRIBUTIONS TO ECONOMIC ANALYSIS
VOLUME 285   ISSN: 0573-8555
DOI:10.1016/S0573-8555(07)00012-0

this as an alternative. Finally, we also investigate the sensitivity of our results to differences in growth rates by including one alternative with a high rate of wage growth and low unemployment and one with a low growth rate and high unemployment.

We would like to emphasize that our simulations of the future should not be interpreted as predictions. They are rather studies of the consequences of population aging using a model structure which primarily mirrors properties of the Swedish economy and the tax and benefit rules from the 1990s and the first few years of the 21st century.

As explained in Chapter 3, SESIM takes as exogenous input assumptions about inflation, the general rate of growth in wage rates, short and long-term interest rates, and the return on stocks and shares for the duration of the simulation period. In our base scenario, the annual real growth in wage rates is assumed to be 2 percent after an initial period and the inflation rate 2 percent. The assumptions about the return on real and financial assets harmonize with these assumptions as detailed in Chapter 3.

The demographic changes in SESIM are aligned to the main projection of Statistics Sweden. Our base scenario implies a population growth from 8.9 millions in year 2000 to 9.7 millions in 2020 and 10.3 millions in 2040. The share of people aged 65+ will at the same time increase from 17.5 to 21.1 and 23.9 percent, and the share of 80+ from 5.2 to 5.4 and 7.8 percent. The number of very old will thus not increase strongly until the end of the simulation period. The population growth and the increased shares of elderly imply that the number of people aged 65+ will increase by 58 percent from 2000 to 2040 and the number 80+ by 75 percent. The growth in the number of males exceeds that of females. For instance, the number of 80+ males will grow by 114 percent while that of females by only 54 percent. The number of elderly women will, however, still exceed the number of elderly males by 2040 (Table 2).

In the following, we will discuss one alternative scenario after another.

1. Improved health progression with and without decreased death risks

To allow for an improved health progression for the elderly, we adjusted the health index for those aged 40–90 proportionally to their age minus 40 and the calendar year minus 2000 in such a way that a 90-year-old person in 2040 will have the same health as an 80 years old in the base scenario. This implies that the improvement in health comes gradually and is largest for the oldest.

Because improved health should lead to decreased death risks and even higher longevity, we in one alternative simulation scenario let each individual after year 2010 and after the age of 35–40 have the death risks of a 5 year younger person in the base scenario. After the age of 100, the death risks were eased upwards toward the levels of the base scenario.

In this way people will live longer but we will avoid excessively old persons. The base scenario implies in itself an increased longevity. The expected life span of a newborn boy increases from 78 years in 2000 to 83 years in 2040, and for a newborn girl it increases from 82 to 86 years. The new assumptions almost doubled the increase in expected life span in 40 years compared to the base scenario, which is a rather drastic change. The reader might also like to note that the death risks and the corresponding longevity are imposed upon the simulations exogenously by an adjustment of the death rates to which SESIM is aligned. There is thus no functional relation from health status to death risk in the model. The implication is that lower death risks will not only keep healthy people alive longer in the simulation model but also unhealthy people.

An improvement of the health status by up to 10 years for those who are older than 40 might be seen as a major improvement in health. For the entire population, the health status distribution improves but not very much. Compared to the base scenario, the share with a severe health only reduces from 7.3 to 6.1 percent in year 2040. If the death rates are allowed to decrease as well, this share almost gets back to the base scenario level. The explanation is that now those who have a bad health do not die off as quickly as in the improved health scenario. The share with full health in 2040 is simulated to be 60.4 percent in the base scenario, 61.2 in the alternative with improved health, and 59.9 when the death risks are reduced as well. If we just look at the health distribution of people aged 40 +, i.e., those who got an improved health and lower death risks, the differences between the simulation scenarios become a little larger (see Table 1). All three alternatives imply deterioration in the general health status of the population. In the base scenario, the share with severe or bad health increases from 22.9 to 28.8 percent in 40 years, in the improved health alternative from 23 to 26.3 percent, and when health status increases parallel to a decrease in death risks the share increases from 23.2 to 27.9.

The simulations show that only improved health does not influence the age distribution, while the decreased death rates by year 2040 have increased the share of 80 + from 7.8 to 11.4 percent. In this scenario, the number of 80 + males increases by as much as 240 percent and that of women by 130 percent. But the share of 80 + women remains higher than that of men for the entire simulation period (Table 2).

When health improves one might expect labor force participation to increase. It does, but only marginally, and the whole effect comes from women in the age group 60–64 for which the labor force participation rate increases from 54.4 to 57.2 percent by 2040.[1] When death rates are allowed

---

[1] Remember that everyone is retired by the age of 65 in these scenarios.

Table 1. *Health distribution for the population 40+ by year and simulation scenario (percent)*

Year/health status	Base scenario	Improved health	Improved health and decreased death risks
2000			
Full health	45.3	44.9	44.5
Good health	31.8	32.1	32.3
Bad health	14.2	14.3	14.7
Severe health	8.7	8.7	8.5
Total population 40+	100.0	100.0	100.0
2020			
Full health	42.3	43.3	42.6
Good health	30.4	30.9	30.1
Bad health	15.6	15.2	15.2
Severe health	11.7	10.6	12.1
Total population	100.0	100.0	100.0
2040			
Full health	40.8	42.9	41.8
Good health	30.4	30.8	30.3
Bad health	15.9	15.5	15.7
Severe health	12.9	10.8	12.2
Total population	100.0	100.0	100.0

Table 2. *Population shares and number of 60+ by age class, gender, and simulation scenario in 2000 and 2040*

Gender/age group	Base scenario in 2000		Base scenario in 2040		Improved health in 2040		Improved health and lower death risks in 2040	
	Share (percent)	Thousands	Share (percent)	Thousands	Share (percent)	Thousands	Share (percent)	Thousands
Males								
60–64	4.8	211	5.5	276	5.5	281	5.3	288
65–79	11.4	500	16.1	821	16.3	837	16.7	900
80+	3.7	163	6.8	348	6.6	340	10.3	555
All males	100.0	4390	100.0	5178	100.0	5125	100.0	5393
Females								
60–64	5.1	228	5.3	272	5.4	276	5.2	280
65–79	13.3	596	16.0	828	16.4	839	16.1	871
80+	6.6	295	8.9	454	8.8	451	12.5	677
All females	100.0	4492	100.0	5125	100.0	5123	100.0	5418

to decrease as health improves, the female labor force participation rate in this age group drops back to almost the same level as in the base scenario. A possible explanation is that some of those who die in the improved health scenario now live but get disability pension.

Improved health should imply that the demand for health care and social care decreases. Tables 3–5 give the results of our simulations. The average number of hospital days per person for people aged 65+ only improves marginally as a result of better health. Changes in the age distribution have a much stronger impact. If the improvement in health leads to more people surviving we will by year 2040 get so many elderly that will need hospital care that the average number of hospital days increases from 3.2 in year 2000 to 4.0 in year 2040 for people 65+. At the same time, the size of the population of elderly will increase and the result of both effects is that the total number of hospital days will increase by a

Table 3. Average and total number of hospital days for people aged 65+, by year and scenario

Year	Average number of days			Total number of days (1000)		
	Base scenario	Improved health	Improved health and lower death risks	Base scenario	Improved health	Improved health and lower death risks
2000	3.2	3.3	3.2	4954	5068	4990
2020	3.2	3.1	3.5	6495	6270	8117
2040	3.4	2.9	4.0	8396	7241	12087

Table 4. Share and total number of people aged 65+ with assistance at home, by year and scenario

Year	Share (percent)			Total number of individuals 65+ (1000)		
	Base scenario	Improved health	Improved health and lower death risks	Base scenario	Improved health	Improved health and lower death risks
2000	8.4	8.7	8.6	131	135	132
2020	6.6	6.2	8.0	135	128	185
2040	8.0	7.8	10.5	196	193	317

Table 5. Share and total number of people aged 65+ with all day surveillance, by year and scenario

Year	Share (percent)			Total no of individuals 65+ (1000)		
	Base scenario	Improved health	Improved health and lower death risks	Base scenario	Improved health	Improved health and lower death risks
2000	7.0	6.3	6.7	109	98	102
2020	6.5	6.4	8.2	133	132	190
2040	8.2	8.1	12.0	200	199	359

factor of 2.5! This compares to the base scenario in which the total number of days will increase by "only" 70 percent.

The same pattern is repeated in the case of assistance at home. Only an increase in the health status of the elderly will reduce the utilization of assistance at home marginally, but if the death risks decrease as well the share of people 65+ with assistance will increase from 8.6 percent in 2000 to 10.5 percent in 2040. In the base scenario, only 8.2 percent will have this kind of assistance in 2040, and the total number of people will in this scenario increase from just above 130 000 to 196 000. If the death risks decrease as assumed the total number with assistance at home will, however, increase to 317 000.

The differences between the three scenarios become even more extreme in the case of old-age care in the form of all day surveillance, which is primarily given to the very old. In the base scenario, the share that gets this kind of care increases from 7 to 8.2 percent. When, however, both the health status of the elderly improves and the death risks decrease, the share increases from 6.7 to 12 percent. If one also takes into account that the population of the elderly increases the implication is that the total number of people with surveillance 24 h increases from just above 100 000 to 359 000 in year 2040. In the base alternative, the number only doubles.

Given that the simulated age distribution does not strongly depend on the health status of the population, one cannot expect the dependency ratio to improve very much as a result of the improvements in health, and it does not. Defined as the ratio between total population and those working, there is virtually no difference between the base scenario and the scenario with improved health. In both cases, the ratio increases from 2.2 in year 2000 to 2.4 in 2040 while the share of retired to working increases from 0.5 to 0.7. When the death rates decrease, these numbers get worse, by 2040 they have increased to 2.5 and 0.8, respectively.

The cost of inpatient hospital care and social care will increase as a function of the increased utilization. But it is also reasonable to assume that unit cost will increase as well because these activities are very labor intensive. New treatments and technical improvements might give productivity gains, but it is hard to guess their future magnitude. In calculating the future care costs, we have disregarded any productivity gains and assumed that the cost for a day in a hospital, help at home, and surveillance for 24 h all increase by the assumed real increases in the average wage rate and in the CPI. The cost of an average day in a hospital in year 2000 was estimated to 6800 SEK,[2]

---

[2] According to the annual yearbook of health and health care statistics (Hälso-och sjukvårdsstatistisk årsbok) 2002 Chapter 3, Table 21, footnote 4, the total number of care days produced was 9 430 278, and according to Chapter 5, Table 3, the total cost was 64 145 milj. SEK.

Table 6. *Total costs of inpatient hospital care and social care for people 65+, by year and scenario (prices of year 2000, milj. SEK)*

Year	Total cost	Share of total cost			Total cost as a share of total direct taxes paid by all households (percent)
		Inpatient hospital care	Home help	All day surveillance	
Base scenario					
2000	92 231	0.365	0.240	0.395	20.5
2020	166 719	0.396	0.204	0.400	24.9
2040	339 297	0.363	0.211	0.426	36.2
Improved health					
2000	90 014	0.383	0.253	0.364	20.1
2020	163 678	0.389	0.208	0.403	24.6
2040	320 301	0.332	0.220	0.448	34.2
Improved health and reduced death rates					
2000	90 301	0.376	0.244	0.380	20.2
2020	224 394	0.367	0.208	0.425	33.2
2040	552 594	0.321	0.209	0.470	57.8

the annual cost of help at home per individual to 169 100 SEK and the annual cost for surveillance 24 h per day to 335 100.[3] The result is displayed in Table 6. Total cost in fixed prices for all three kinds of care will increase in the base scenario by a factor of 3.7 from year 2000 to 2040. In the scenario with improved health status, the increase is just marginally smaller, a factor of 3.6, but when people also are assumed to survive longer the increase in total costs almost double compared to the other scenarios. In this case, total cost in 2040 will become six times that in 2000! Even if these increases are rather impressive one also has to recognize that incomes and taxes increase too. A relative measure might thus be more informative. Ideally one would like to simulate all income and expenditure accounts of the public sector to evaluate the relative importance of the increased costs for health care and social care of the elderly. Unfortunately our model does not allow this. All we can do is to simulate and add up the total of all direct taxes paid by the household sector. The last column of Table 6 gives total cost as a share of the sum of all direct taxes paid by all households. Also with this measure we find a substantial increase in costs. In year 2000, they amounted to about 20 percent of total direct household taxes, but the share increases to 36 percent by 2040 in the base scenario, 34 percent in the improved health alternative, and to 58 percent when there is both an improvement in health and a reduction of death risks. Even if the direct taxes paid by the household

---

[3] Source "Aktuellt om äldreomsorgen 2006," www.webor.se

sector are just part of the income of the public sector, these results suggest that it will become difficult to finance increases in these public services at the magnitude we have simulated.

Table 6 also gives the cost shares of the three kinds of services. In all scenarios, the share of all day surveillance increases as a result of the increase of the very old. The share of hospital care decreases in the two scenarios with improved health status, while it remains more or less stable in the base scenario. The share of help at home decreases.

All these simulations assume that the utilization of health care and social care follow the same pattern as in the 1990s which generated the data we have used to estimate our models. If policy changes and these public services provided according to new principles or if the share of private services increases, our models no longer hold. Our simulations should only be seen as indicative of what might be needed if public policy is unchanged in these respects.

2. Increased immigration

Increased immigration has occasionally been mentioned as a policy that can mitigate the consequences of an aging population. It would bring into the country people in working age that do not need much health care or old-age care. On the other hand, demographers have pointed out that immigration to Sweden has not changed the age distribution very much and that an increased immigration, within reasonable bounds, is not likely to influence much the burden of supporting the elderly and the young.

To investigate these issues, we have run a simulation scenario with increased foreign immigration to Sweden and compared to the base scenario. These two scenarios are rather close to two scenarios from Statistics Sweden.[4] Table 7 gives an outline of these two alternatives in thousands of migrants. The columns give emigration of Swedes, return migration of foreigners, return immigration of Swedes, immigration of foreigners, and net migration to Sweden. The main difference between the two alternatives is that the immigration of foreigners is increased from almost 60 000 individuals per year after 2010 to about 80 000. As a consequence, return migration also increases a little. The net effect of these streams is that net migration increases from about 25 000 per year to between 35 000 and 40 000.

---

[4] See the publication Sveriges framtida befolkning. Befolkningsframskrivning för åren 2003–2050, Demografiska rapporter 2003:4, Statistics Sweden, Örebro, ISBN 91-618-1188-2. Our base scenario is close to "huvudalternativet" (medium alternative) in this report and our alternative with a higher immigration is close to the high alternative (Table 3.7).

Table 7. **Two immigration scenarios (thousands of individuals)**

Year	Em_Sw	Em_for	Im-Sw	Im_for	Net migration
Base scenario					
1999	17	19	10	40	14
2010	19	24	13	58	28
2020	21	27	15	59	25
2030	21	28	15	59	25
2040	22	29	16	59	24
High immigration scenario					
1999	17	19	10	40	14
2010	19	26	13	72	40
2020	23	36	16	80	37
2030	24	38	17	80	36
2040	25	39	18	80	34

SESIM is aligned to these immigration assumptions. First, emigrated Swedes are exposed to re-immigration risks. Second, the remaining number of immigrants needed to meet the assumptions made is determined as the difference between the total number of immigrants from Table 7 and the simulated number of re-immigrated Swedes. This number of immigrants is allocated to age groups and household sizes proportional to the frequencies of new immigrants in 1997 from LINDA. Finally, the demographic properties and the schooling of each new immigrant are copied from randomly chosen individuals within each respective age and household size group in the SESIM population. Most other variables, such as incomes, pension rights, and assets, are put to zero.

Already in the base scenario, the share of foreign-born will increase from about 12 percent to almost 20 percent (Table 8). The share of immigrants among those in working age is even higher and will increase a little faster. Comparing the two scenarios, we find that the number of foreign-born will become more than 50 percent higher in 2040 in the high-immigration alternative. Most of this increase is rather evenly divided between working age and pension age. By 2040, the elderly will thus have increased in number due to an increased immigration.

The dependency ratio will increase also in the higher immigration alternative, but not as much (Table 9). By year 2040, it is 2.38 in the base scenario but 2.33 in the high-immigration alternative. The number of retired relative to the number of working also increases somewhat less in the high-immigration scenario. In 2040, the two simulated values are 0.67 and 0.64, respectively, an increase from 0.49 in year 2000.

There is almost no difference in hospital care, as measured by the number of hospital days, between the two scenarios (Table 10). The total number of days is simulated to increase by 75 percent in both cases. Utilization of social care at home will also increase about as much in both

Table 8.   Number of foreign-born in SESIM by scenario

Year	Age			Total	Population share of foreign-born	Population share of aged 20–64
	≤19	20–64	65+			
Base scenario						
1999	1498	8450	1632	11 580	0.111	0.139
2000	1492	8729	1706	11 927	0.114	0.142
2010	1666	11 578	2406	15 650	0.144	0.182
2020	1886	13 446	3465	18 797	0.166	0.211
2030	1923	14 844	4558	21 325	0.181	0.232
2040	1870	15 641	5884	23 395	0.194	0.243
High immigration scenario						
1999	1498	8451	1791	11 740	0.112	0.139
2000	1517	8792	1919	12 228	0.117	0.144
2010	1920	12 656	3431	18 007	0.162	0.196
2020	2576	16 123	6550	25 249	0.210	0.244
2030	2677	19 086	9520	31 283	0.244	0.282
2040	2636	21 188	11 847	35 671	0.267	0.306

Table 9.   Dependency ratios by year and scenario

Year	Base scenario		High immigration scenario		High pension age	
	Total/ working	Retired/ working	Total/ working	Retired/ working	Total/ working	Retired/ working
2000	2.21	0.49	2.21	0.49	2.19	0.47
2020	2.28	0.59	2.25	0.57	2.21	0.54
2040	2.38	0.67	2.33	0.64	2.30	0.61

Table 10.   Number of hospital days for people 65+ by year and scenario

Year	Base scenario		High immigration scenario	
	Average number	Total number (1000)	Average number	Total number (1000)
2000	3.3	5115	3.2	5123
2020	3.2	6515	3.3	6862
2040	3.6	8908	3.5	8952
Change 2000–2040 (percent)	9.1	74.2	9.4	74.7

scenarios, approximately 60 percent. The share of 65+ who are cared for 24 h a day becomes, however, somewhat lower in the high-immigration scenario, but the population increase that follows from higher immigration implies that the total number of people who needs care 24 h a day becomes

Table 11.   *Utilization of old-age care by year and scenario*

Year	Base scenario				High immigration scenario			
	Share (percent) with		Total number (1000) with		Share (percent) with		Total number (1000) with	
	Care at home	Institutional care	Care at home	Institutional care	Care at home	Institutional care	Care at home	Institutional care
2000	7.7	3.4	119	53	8.1	2.2	126	34
2020	6.6	5.2	135	105	6.4	4.7	132	95
2040	7.9	6.7	192	164	7.8	5.8	193	146

approximately the same (Table 11). We simulate an increase in the number of people with this kind of care by a factor of 3.

In conclusion, we thus find that increased immigration will improve the dependency ratios a little while the burden of the care systems will become about the same as in the base scenario. Immigration will thus to some extent increase the number of persons who can help to provide for the old, but at the same time the number of elderly and in need of care increases by immigration. If immigration could be more restricted to guest workers than we have assumed in our high-immigration scenario, the positive effects of immigration might increase, but immigration is not likely to become a major solution to the problem of providing for the old baby-boomers even in this case.

3. Delayed retirement

In the policy debate, a higher pension age has been seen as one of the most effective means to reduce the dependency ratios and ease the burden of providing for the elderly. In Sweden, the pension system was reformed in the beginning of the 1990s with this in mind. Postponing retirement should result in at least an actuarially fair increased compensation, and early retirement should be discouraged. The same policy has been aimed at in other countries. As already explained in Chapter 6, we have thus simulated an alternative in which the retirement ceiling was lifted from the age of 65 to 70. The option to retire early was kept but the age pattern of retirement in the age interval 60–65 was stretched to cover ages up to 70.[5] The result was that the average age at retirement increased by a few years. Table 12 shows how the increased window of work opportunities successively

---

[5] The model includes a dummy variable for each year of age in the interval 60–64. The corresponding parameters determine the probability to retire early. The parameter for the age of 60 was now assumed to apply also for the age of 61, the parameter for 61 now applies to the ages of 62 and 63, etc. (see Table 6 in Chapter 6).

Table 12. ***Labor force participation rates (percent) by age, gender, year, and scenario***

Year and age group	Females				Males			
	Base scenario	Increased retirement age	High growth	Low growth	Base scenario	Increased retirement age	High growth	Low growth
2000								
20–50	88.9	89.0	88.9	88.9	92.2	92.3	92.2	92.2
51–59	85.1	85.1	85.1	85.1	90.5	90.5	90.5	90.5
60–64	61.8	65.7	61.8	61.8	68.3	70.9	68.3	68.3
65–69	0.0	5.9	0.0	0.0	0.0	8.6	0.0	0.0
2020								
20–50	90.5	90.7	90.6	90.3	92.9	93.1	93.1	92.9
51–59	87.7	87.5	87.2	87.5	90.8	91.1	91.0	90.2
60–64	53.4	57.4	54.5	51.2	62.4	66.4	63.6	62.3
65–69	0.0	17.6	0.0	0.0	0.0	25.1	0.0	0.0
2040								
20–50	90.7	90.5	90.1	90.2	92.8	92.9	93.0	93.0
51–59	86.9	87.1	87.2	86.7	90.4	89.8	90.0	90.1
60–64	54.4	59.0	55.9	51.9	63.7	66.2	64.2	63.3
65–69	0.0	19.5	0.0	0.0	0.0	27.2	0.0	0.0

increases the labor force participation rate in the age bracket 65–69 for both males and females. By 2040, almost 20 percent of the females in this age group are simulated to work and 27 percent of the males. Labor force participation also increases in the age group 60–64 compared to the base scenario, because now labor force participation in this age group is determined by the higher rates of participation among the youngest sample members of the age group. These increases in the labor force participation rates also explain why the dependency ratios do not increase as much (Table 9), but the increase in pension age and labor force participation is not sufficient to maintain the dependency ratios at the levels of year 2000.

Postponement of retirement will also increase the median disposable income of the Swedish society because higher work incomes replace pensions during the additional years of work and pensions also increase. By year 2020, median equivalized disposable income is about 4 percent higher in this scenario than in the base scenario and by 2040 the difference has increased to 5 percent (Table 13). For the same reasons, the incomes of the age group 65+ relative to the group 20–64 increase. As already discussed in Chapter 8, the relative income of 65+ decreases from 71 percent in 2000 to 55 percent in 2040 in the base scenario, but in the scenario when retirement is postponed the decrease is smaller and relative income only reduces to 62 percent. The income changes that follow from a higher retirement age also imply that income inequality decreases a little, see Table 13.

Table 13. ***Equivalized disposable income (median income and Gini coefficient), and relative income of 65+ by year and scenario***

Year	Base scenario	High retirement age	High immigration	High growth	Low growth
Median income (1000 SEK current prices)					
2000	133	133	132	133	132
2020	277	289	277	311	221
2040	548	577	552	733	320
Gini coefficient					
2000	0.272	0.270	0.273	0.273	0.270
2020	0.325	0.316	0.321	0.321	0.344
2040	0.318	0.308	0.314	0.315	0.348
Relative income					
2000	0.709	0.711	0.712	0.710	0.713
2020	0.634	0.693	0.634	0.610	0.692
2040	0.552	0.623	0.558	0.505	0.680

Note: Disposable income was equivalized by the square root of the number of family members. The unit of analysis is the individual and every adult individual was given the equivalized income of its family. Relative income is the median equivalized income of 65+ relative to that of the age group 20–64.

4. Changes in growth assumptions and in unemployment

Average real growth in wage rates is in the base scenario assumed to be 2 percent annually. To investigate the consequences of changes in this assumption, we simulated one alternative with 1 percent growth and another alternative with 3 percent. It is reasonable that a change in the growth of the economy also should imply that unemployment is adjusted accordingly. For this reason, the intercept of the unemployment model (probability to become unemployed) was adjusted upwards for the low-growth alternative and downwards for the high-growth alternative. The resulting unemployment rates are displayed in Table 14. Compared to the base scenario, the alternatives have an unemployment rate 1–2 percent higher and lower, respectively. The model simulates a rather high-unemployment rate in the age group 60–64. The difference between the two extreme alternatives becomes striking in this age group. The explanation is that the probability to become unemployed in our dynamic model depends positively on lagged unemployment status. A higher general unemployment accumulates over the life-cycle.

The differences in growth and unemployment also have a marginal effect on the labor force participation rates, in particular in the age group 60–64. In our model, a high-unemployment rate will increase the probability to take up and remain in higher education. It will also increase the incidence of sickness, which will imply that more people go into

Table 14. *Unemployment rates by year, age group, and scenario (percent)*

Year, age group	Base scenario	Low growth and high unemployment	High growth and low unemployment
2000			
All	7.6	8.3	6.8
50–59	6.1	6.9	5.5
60–64	15.0	16.8	13.2
2020			
All	6.3	8.3	5.0
50–59	5.0	7.1	3.2
60–64	12.3	20.1	7.9
2040			
All	6.6	8.2	5.2
50–59	4.7	6.8	3.4
60–64	10.4	18.8	6.0

disability pension. The income differences generated in the alternative growth/unemployment scenarios will also influence withdrawal from the labor market. By 2040, the male labor force participation rate in the base scenario is 63.7, but 64.2 in the high-growth scenario and 63.3 in the low-growth alternative. The corresponding rates for females are 54.4, 55.9, and 51.9, respectively. The dependency ratios also differ accordingly. The number of individuals for every working individual has in 2040 increased to 2.35 in the high-growth scenario and 2.43 in the low-growth alternative compared to 2.38 in the base scenario.

The difference of about two percentage points in growth between the high- and low-growth scenarios will in about 30 years time make a major difference in income level. Median equivalized disposable income in the high scenario becomes by 2040 more than double the income of the low scenario. Also small differences in annual growth will during such long periods have a substantial effect on the living standard of people. However, contrary to what many might believe income inequality increases when growth becomes low. Contributing to this result is the increase in unemployment and in the number of people on disability pension, which after 65 is transferred into relatively low old-age pensions. Another explanation is an increased relative importance of incomes from capital. In this scenario, the return to financial wealth is kept at the same level as in the base scenario.

The relative income of those 65+ also increases in low growth. This is also a result of the increased relative importance of capital incomes in the right tail of the income distribution. In the high-growth scenario, the median equivalized disposable income of those who are 65 or older will in 2040 only become 50.5 percent of the median income of those aged 20–65, while in the low-growth scenario it becomes as high as 68 percent.

Finally, we might note that our model does not simulate any differences in the utilization of health care and social care due to differences in growth and unemployment. This is perhaps not what one might have expected and could be an unrealistic property of our model. High unemployment should lead to a higher incidence of sickness and early retirement and thus a higher demand for health care and social care.

5. *The incomes and wealth of people in old-age care*

We have found that the utilization and costs of old-age care will increase considerably and that direct taxes paid by the household sector, using the tax system of 2005/2006, will increase in a much slower pace. An alternative way of financing these (public) services is to increase user fees. In this perspective, it is of interest to know if those who use old-age care will have the means to cover increased user fees. We have already found that the incomes of the elderly will decrease relative to the working population. Will this be true in particular for those who will need old-age care? We have also found that the baby-boom cohorts have become relatively wealthy and our simulations suggest that they to a large extent will stay wealthy even when they age. Even if incomes are relatively low, will the baby-boom generations have assets that can be liquidized to cover old-age care? Even if it is not possible to give definite answers to these questions, we will try to address them by a closer look at the income and wealth distributions of people aged 65 +.

To study the position of the elderly in the income and wealth distributions, we first need the percentiles of these distributions for the entire population. Tables 15 and 16 give them for the distributions of equivalized disposable income and equivalized net worth, respectively. Like in previous chapters, we have used the square root equivalence scale.[6] The unit of analysis is the individual. In year 2000, the distribution of equivalized disposable income is virtually the same across all simulation scenarios as it should be. The small differences are due to simulation randomness. Median income is about 150 000 SEK and the 90th percentile is almost three times the 10th percentile. Depending on the growth assumption of each scenario, median income will increase more or less. In the base scenario, it increases to 650 649 in nominal terms by 2040, which is a real increase by almost 100 percent in 40 years. In the high-growth scenario, the real increase is about 170 percent and in the low-growth alternative only about 13 percent. These numbers might seem low

---

[6] Disposable income and net worth of a household were divided by square root of the number of adults + 1/2 the number of children, and the result ascribed to each household member.

Table 15. Percentiles of equivalized annual disposable income, by year and scenario (current prices, SEK)

Year/percentile	Base scenario	Increased retirement age	High growth and low unemployment	Low growth and high unemployment
2000				
10	87 180	87 786	87 082	87 613
25	109 487	110 371	110 247	110 256
50	149 411	150 155	149 722	149 036
75	198 419	198 916	198 553	197 762
90	254 258	255 349	253 782	253 996
2020				
10	158 792	164 049	176 854	128 846
25	221 846	230 509	249 210	178 181
50	319 155	327 733	358 908	251 300
75	429 837	434 883	484 868	359 985
90	543 764	546 534	615 582	425 745
2040				
10	302 886	315 520	390 233	184 526
25	440 163	463 573	585 842	257 613
50	650 649	670 798	889 733	363 978
75	888 016	900 351	1 219 854	488 774
90	1 119 693	1 130 164	1 533 924	621 246

Note: The equivalence scale used is the square root of the number of adults + 1/2 the number of children. The unit of analysis is the individual.

compared to the assumed growth in wage rates, but one must keep in mind that the incomes of those who do not work increase less. This is in particular true for those who have retired.

Income inequality as measured by the ratio of the 90th and 10th percentiles increases from 2.9 to 3.7 in 40 years according to the base scenario. In the high-growth alternative, inequality becomes even higher in 2004, 3.9, while it only becomes 3.4 in the low-growth scenario. In all scenarios, income inequality thus increases.

The distribution of net worth differs from the income distribution in that it is almost invariant to scenario (Table 16) and that inequality decreases rather than increases (cf. Chapter 9). With the assumptions we have made median equivalized net worth increases in real terms by a factor of 5 in 40 years.

Table 17 displays the income distribution for people aged 65+ by kind of old-age care. Depending on scenario about 50 percent of the 65+ belong to the first income quartile. This share is even higher for those who have old-age care, about 70 percent. The number of people with help at home or all day surveillance is rather small, which implies that random simulation variability will influence the income shares of these groups. Some of the differences across scenarios and over time in Table 17 are thus due to random variation. It is, however, clear that income poverty among those who have old-age care

Table 16. Percentiles of equivalized net worth, by year and scenario (current prices, 1000 SEK)

Year/percentile	Base scenario	Increased retirement age	High growth and low unemployment	Low growth and high unemployment
2000				
10	−143	−146	−145	−144
25	−1	−1	−2	−1
50	223	223	225	224
75	708	708	7089	716
90	1547	1542	1550	1556
2020				
10	−154	−143	−167	−144
25	324	320	301	318
50	1249	1242	1242	1251
75	2303	2301	2302	2311
90	3871	3920	3931	3954
2040				
10	−191	−189	−241	−131
25	665	621	618	659
50	2392	2376	2375	2426
75	4186	4163	4185	4206
90	6503	6525	6515	6505

Note: The equivalence scale used is the square root of the number of adults + 1/2 the number of children.

will increase over time (cf. the discussion in Chapter 8). In the scenario with high growth, the share in the first income quartile becomes as high as about 80 percent. In this case, their real income standard increases more than in all other scenarios, but their relative poverty is highest! The explanation is that high-wage growth will increase the incomes of the working generations more than the incomes of those who have retired. As explained in Chapter 8, this is primarily a result of the design of the public pension system. We can now conclude that most of those who have old-age care have very low incomes and their situation is not likely to improve.

Table 18 gives the distribution of wealth by type of care. There are very small differences between the alternative simulation scenarios, and for this reason the table only displays the results from the base scenario. In year 2000, almost 40 percent of those who were 65+ had wealth in the fourth quartile and very few belonged to the first quartile. The share for those who used old-age care was lower, about 30 percent were in the fourth quartile. By 2040, all these fourth quarter shares are simulated to increase to almost 50 percent independently of kind of care. There is thus a large share of those who have old-age care who will have relatively high wealth. An interesting issue then becomes to what extent low income is compensated by high wealth. To address this issue, we will first look at the

Table 17. **The distribution of equivalized disposable income for people aged 65+ by type of assistance for elderly, year and scenario (percent)**

Scenario/year/type of assistance	Income quartiles			
	1	2	3	4
Base scenario				
2000				
No assistance	46.7	30.8	14.1	8.4
Help at home	68.6	18.7	7.1	5.6
All day surveillance	65.5	22.2	8.0	4.3
All 65+	49.9	29.1	13.1	7.9
2040				
No assistance	53.1	30.7	10.9	5.3
Help at home	75.4	17.6	3.8	3.2
All day surveillance	76.4	14.7	4.6	4.2
All 65+	56.8	28.4	9.8	5.0
Increased retirement age				
2000				
No assistance	47.7	29.5	13.8	9.0
Help at home	70.5	18.7	6.8	4.0
All day surveillance	73.6	17.4	5.7	3.3
All 65+	50.2	28.3	13.1	8.4
2040				
No assistance	47.6	27.7	14.2	10.4
Help at home	68.0	21.6	5.9	4.5
All day surveillance	74.4	16.1	5.0	4.5
All 65+	50.8	26.6	13.0	9.6
High growth and low unemployment				
2000				
No assistance	48.1	29.6	13.8	8.5
Help at home	70.8	18.8	7.1	3.3
All day surveillance	72.2	17.2	6.3	4.2
All 65+	50.6	28.3	13.1	8.0
2040				
No assistance	57.8	30.6	7.6	4.0
Help at home	78.9	15.6	3.0	2.5
All day surveillance	83.0	12.2	2.2	2.6
All 65+	61.2	28.1	6.9	3.7
Low growth and high unemployment				
2000				
No assistance	47.9	29.7	14.0	8.4
Help at home	70.1	17.8	7.5	4.5
All day surveillance	74.2	16.3	6.1	3.4
All 65+	50.6	28.3	13.2	7.9
2040				
No assistance	43.9	28.3	16.5	11.2
Help at home	63.7	22.1	7.6	6.6
All day surveillance	72.1	16.5	5.5	5.9
All 65+	47.4	27.1	15.0	10.5

Table 18. **The distribution of equivalized net worth for people aged 65+, by type of assistance and year; base scenario (percent)**

Year/type of assistance	Wealth quartiles			
	1	2	3	4
2000				
No assistance	4.7	28.0	27.4	39.9
Help at home	2.5	40.2	27.4	29.8
All day surveillance	2.0	39.9	25.8	32.3
All 65+	4.3	29.9	27.3	38.5
2040				
No assistance	12.0	17.4	20.8	49.9
Help at home	12.4	20.1	18.2	49.3
All day surveillance	11.1	21.6	19.9	47.4
All 65+	12.0	17.9	20.5	49.6

Table 19. **The distribution of equivalized net worth by quartile of equivalized disposable income for people aged 65+, by year and base scenario (percent)**

Year/income quartile	Wealth quartiles			
	1	2	3	4
2000				
Income quartile				
1	5.2	41.9	27.0	25.9
2	4.0	22.8	32.2	41.0
3	2.7	12.1	22.4	62.7
4	2.7	9.4	19.2	68.7
All 65+	4.3	29.9	27.3	38.5
2040				
Income quartile				
1	16.7	20.5	20.7	42.0
2	5.8	15.1	21.4	57.7
3	3.7	12.1	18.2	66.0
4	8.8	15.9	17.2	58.1
All 65+	12.0	17.9	20.5	49.6

distribution of wealth by income quartile in Table 19. For the same reason as above we only give results for the base scenario.

Even if a large share of all people 65+ is wealthy, there is a clear positive correlation between income and wealth. In the fourth income quartile, the share of people in the fourth wealth quartile is as high as 69 percent in year 2000, while in the first income quartile it is only 26 percent. These differences even out somewhat to year 2040, but there is still a positive correlation. To more specifically analyze joint income and asset poverty, we define poverty as having less equivalized disposable income than 50 percent

Table 20.   ***The incidence of poverty among people aged 65+ by type of***
assistance, year and scenario (percent)

Scenario/year	Type of assistance			
	No assistance	Help at home	All day surveillance	All 65+
Base scenario				
2000	1.5	1.4	2.5	1.6
2020	11.1	10.8	13.2	11.2
2040	14.3	15.1	16.3	14.5
Increased pension age				
2000	1.7	2.6	2.2	1.8
2020	6.8	7.2	10.1	7.0
2040	7.9	9.8	12.0	8.3
High growth and low unemployment				
2000	1.7	2.1	2.4	1.7
2020	7.7	9.0	10.5	8.0
2040	10.4	13.8	13.8	10.9
Low growth and high unemployment				
2000	1.6	1.4	2.5	1.6
2020	12.6	12.0	13.9	12.6
2040	16.5	16.0	16.9	16.5

Note: Poverty is defined as having an equivalized disposable income less than 50 percent of the median equivalized income of the entire population and an equivalized net worth less than 50 percent of the median equivalized net worth of the whole population.

of the median equivalized disposable income for the whole population, and less equivalized net worth than 50 percent of the median equivalized net worth for the entire population. The result is displayed in Table 20.

In year 2000, only between 1 and 2 percent of those 65+ were poor. In this year the incidence of poverty was marginally higher for those who had all day surveillance. The poverty rates then increase as the simulations proceed and reach by 2040 the high figures of 14–16 percent. Those who have care all day around continue to have a little higher poverty. The alternative scenarios give the same general picture, but the magnitude of the poverty rates vary. They become lower if pension is delayed and also when income growth is high and unemployment low. The highest poverty is reached when growth is low and unemployment high. The poverty rates do not increase more than they do in this scenario because we have kept the same return on financial and real wealth in this scenario as in the other scenarios. We can thus again conclude that poverty will increase and that there will be a rather large share of those who will use old-age care that will not have the means to pay for these services. However, there will also be a relatively large share that is asset rich. Much of this wealth will be tied up in homes, which will need to be liquidized, if this group will be able to pay for old-age services.

CHAPTER 13

Evaluation and Conclusions

Anders Klevmarken*

1. Summary of findings

The predicted increase in the population share of elderly in Sweden is rather modest compared to some of the central and south European countries. The share of 65+ will, in our base scenario, increase from 17.5 to 23.9 percent in the period 2000–2040. Yet, this implies a major increase in the number of elderly. The number of 65+ will increase by 58 percent. The very old and care intensive group 80+ will increase even more, by 75 percent, and their share of the population will increase from 5.1 to 7.9 percent in 40 years. This is likely to put an increased pressure on the political system to match the expected increased demand for health care and social care by an increased supply. In some countries, the increase in the number of elderly will become balanced by a decrease in the number of children, and thus a natural reallocation of resources from children to elderly is possible. This is, according to our simulations, not the case in Sweden. The population share of those below 18 will stay rather stable between 21 and 22 percent.

When evaluating the future need for health care and social care of the elderly and how it can be met, we first have to look at the demand side and consider any competing demand, then to the size of the working population and its productivity, and finally to the relative incomes and wealth of the elderly to be able to discuss who can bear the increased burden of financing more care.

---

* Corresponding author.

CONTRIBUTIONS TO ECONOMIC ANALYSIS
VOLUME 285   ISSN: 0573-8555
DOI:10.1016/S0573-8555(07)00013-2

In international comparisons, we have been used to find the Swedish population of elderly in better health than in most other countries, with less life-style health risks and more time for physical exercise. We have no reason to believe that this relative advantage would change in the nearest future, but we have found that the historical trend toward an ever more healthy elderly population might be broken and we simulate a minor decrease in the health status of the population, in particular among the young old. The explanation seems to be an increase of allergy, asthma, diabetes, and obesity and its consequences among the current middle aged. According to this scenario, there is thus no help to find in a further improved health status of the elderly population.

However, if the decrease in health status is just a temporary set back, or if the technology of medicine improves to balance the observed changes, people might continue to improve their health relative to previous generations and the expected survival time will continue to increase. It is not obvious that this would decrease the demand for care; it might just postpone it for a few years. In our scenario with increased health status among the oldest, the effect on the demand for care was marginal. More important were changes in the death risks. If improved life-styles, nutrition, and medical technology continue to decrease death risk among young old and increase expected life time, we might well at the same time find an increased share of the oldest old in need of extensive care.

Our simulations suggest that the number of inpatient hospital days for people 65 + will have to increase by 70 percent, the number of elderly in all day care by 83 percent, and the number of elderly with home help by about 50 percent. If survival increases, these numbers will increase even more. These estimates primarily reflect the increase in the number of elderly while we only predict a modest increase in utilization. This is a natural consequence of our methodology through which we take forward current levels and trends in utilization into the future. In this sense, we assume that the current standard of health care and old age care is maintained in the future.

Children and the working population compete with the elderly about public resources for health care and social care. We have already noted that the share of children will remain more or less stable, which implies that no resources will be freed from child care, schooling, and health care of children, if the standard of these services will remain unchanged, but on the other hand there is no need to increase resources either to maintain the current standard. Our simulation model does not allow us to simulate all uses of public services by the working population, but for three relatively large items, i.e., sickness benefits, disability pensions, and inpatient hospital care. According to our simulations, the number of compensated sickness days reached a maximum by 2003 and then gradually decline as the large baby-boom cohorts retire out of the sickness benefit system. The result is that the number of compensated days in 2040 will become approximately as many as in 2000. The number of inpatient hospital days for people younger than 65 only increase by a modest 10 percent, and the number on disability pension are simulated to increase by 8 percent. These findings suggest that any increase in total resources for health-related purposes can be allocated toward the elderly.

Using the assumption that the cost of care will increase at the same rate as an average wage rate and that there is no productivity gain in these labor intensive activities, we found that total cost in fixed prices for inpatient care, home help, and all day care will increase by a multiple of 3.7 in 40 years. Ideally one would like to compare this increase to the increase in the total budget of the public sector and to competing public expenditures. Within our model, this is not feasible. All we have been able to do is to compare to total direct taxes paid by Swedish households, and we found that the expenditures for these three items that goes to the population 65+ as a share of total direct taxes will almost double, from 20 percent in 2000 to 36 percent in 2040. Judging from this comparison, the increased demand for care of the elderly is so large that adjustments in one form or another will be needed, i.e., a reallocation of public expenditures toward the elderly, increased taxes or increased user fees, or decreased supply of public services. As suggested above, the changes in the age distribution give some leeway for a reallocation within the public budget, but this will most likely not become enough. We therefore turn to focus on alternatives.

One alternative is to have spouses, children, and relatives help to care for the elderly. Parents and adult children do not live as closely in Sweden as in some of the south European countries, but still much of the care elderly need is provided by spouses, children, relatives, and neighbors. Spouses help each other. Usually it is a wife, who typically is younger than her husband, who helps him. Singles are more dependent on children and other relatives. A necessary requirement for a child to be able to help its parents is that they live rather close. There are clear regional differences in this respect. In the rural and in particular northern part of the country, there are fewer elderly living close to their children compared to the large metropolitan areas. One explanation is that distances are larger in the rural areas and another that children have tended to migrate to urban areas in the southern part of the country. The share of singles, in particular women, without children at commuting distance is higher than that of couples. One reason is of course that some of them never had a child, but also that they tend to be older and have survived their children. Old-olds single women will find it most difficult to get help from children. Our simulations show that the share of people 65+ with children at commuting distance will decrease from about 60 percent in 2000 to 53 percent in 2040. Most of this decrease is due to an increasing share of singles in high ages. This tendency holds for the whole country but it is a little stronger in the large metropolitan areas, in which the share of singles increases most. These simulations thus suggest that the future large groups of very old cannot count on their children but will have to find help and care elsewhere.

The continued migration from rural to metropolitan areas will contribute to the mismatch between generations. Around year 2000, about one-third of the Swedish population lived in one of the three large metropolitan areas, while we now simulate that this share will increase to 45 percent in 2040. Migration from urban to metropolitan areas is predominantly by young people, which implies that the aging of the population goes much faster in the rural areas. The dependency ratio is already higher in the rural areas but it will also increase more than average in the future. The rural communities, in particular in the northern part of the country, will thus face a much more difficult problem in caring for their elderly than metropolitan Sweden.

Our studies of the distributions of incomes and wealth have its intrinsic interest as an analysis of the standard of living of the elderly. They also tell us something about the means elderly will have to pay for care services.

A most striking property of the new Swedish pension system is what we have called "front loading," i.e., young pensioners receive a higher pension than an actuarially fair annual rate would suggest. To compensate for this, future pensions are not indexed by the average annual growth rate in nominal wages, as many believe, but with this average less 1.6 percent. The implication is that pensions will lag behind the earnings of the working cohorts, and if the real increase in wages is less than 1.6 percent, pensions will not maintain their real value. While the replacement rate, defined as the age-specific mean taxable income of retired to the mean taxable income of people 20–64 years old, is 75–80 percent for someone who is 65, it drops to below 50 percent at the age of 90. Because pensions make such a large share of the incomes of retired, this decrease in relative incomes with increasing age also shows up in the disposable income. Median disposable income of people 65+ relative to the median disposable income of those in the age bracket 20–64 was just above 70 percent in 2000. In our simulations, the ratio decreases to 63 percent in 2020 and to 55 in 2040. Most of this decrease is a result of the aging of the pensioners, but also a result of younger cohorts getting lower replacement rates because they are assumed to live longer.

Another result of the design of the Swedish pension system is that the share of poor pensioners will increase. While poverty, defined as having a disposable income less than 50 percent of the median disposable income of the adult population, is less than 5 percent before people start to retire, and about 10 percent the first years after retirement, it then increases as people age. For the birth cohorts we have analyzed, poverty varies between 20 and 35 percent at the age of 90.

When considering increasing user fees (or taxes) to cover the increased costs for health care and social care, it is of interest to know how high incomes the elderly in need of care will have. In year 2000, we found that 65–70 percent of those who needed home help or all day surveillance had disposable incomes in the first quartile of the income distribution, while only 47 percent of those who did not have any social care and also were 65+ were in the same quartile. By 2040, these shares will increase to just above 75 and 53 percent, respectively. There is thus a large and increasing share of elderly in need of care that will have so low incomes that they hardly will be able to pay any major increase in user fees.

Future changes in the wealth distribution will to a large extent depend on the growth in real estate prices and in the prices of stocks and shares, and on their relative magnitude. In our base scenario, own homes and other real property will take a larger share of total wealth and the inequality of the wealth distribution will decrease. But if we instead allow the value of financial assets to grow relatively faster, inequality will increase. We have found that the large baby-boom cohorts are relatively wealthy. At the time of retirement, the baby-boom cohorts will have wealth amounting to about eight annual incomes. The wealth buffer is relatively more important for the income poor than for those who have high incomes.

Our simulations then suggest that they will keep their wealth as they age. By the end of our simulation period, the very old will have about the same wealth as those in the age bracket 60–69. The share of elderly living in owned homes decreases with increasing age, and they thus liquidize their wealth when they sell their houses. But still much of this wealth will be tied up in owned homes and thus not very liquid. Compared to year 2000 the share of elderly in owned homes is simulated to increase with a peak in the middle of the simulation period around 2020. A recently developed market for reversed mortgages might, however, help to liquidize this kind of wealth.

When we correlate wealth and the utilization of social care, we find no strong correlation. In year 2000, about 30 percent of those who had home help or all day surveillance belonged to the fourth quartile of the wealth distribution, while about 40 percent of those who had no social care belonged to the same quartile. Those who needed care were thus not quite as rich as those who had no needed but there was no major difference in distribution of wealth, and our simulations suggest that this difference will become eliminated completely by end of the simulation period. In year 2040, about 50 percent of all 65+, independently of their care status, will belong to the fourth quartile of the wealth distribution. A large share of the elderly thus has a wealth buffer that could be used to finance health care and social care, but at the same time there will be a fair share of elderly who are both income and wealth poor. In 2000, only about 2 percent of those who had social care were poor in this sense, but by 2040 this share is simulated to increase to between 15 and 16 percent.

Which policy changes could reduce the need for care and ease the burden to provide for the elderly? We have analyzed the effects of improved health, reduced death risks, higher immigration, delayed withdrawal from the labor market, and changes in the growth rates of the economy. We find no major effects on the utilization of care of improved health of the elderly. One might have expected that the demand for care would have decreased but we only find very marginal effects. This might be a result of our model specification not allowing health improvements to work through strongly enough into reductions in care, see below, but it is also possible that it takes much stronger improvements in health than we have assumed.

When we exogenously reduced the death rates, the result was a major increase in the utilization of care. Our model simulated that more people with poor health and various limitations survived, and thus that the demand for health care and social care increased. It is possible that we exaggerate this effect because there is no direct functional relation in our model between health and survival with the exception of the excess mortality of those who have around-the-clock surveillance. Even so these results illustrate the importance of healthy ageing. If the expected life span continues to increase but without improvement in age-specific health, the result will become ever more elderly in need of care.

Our simulations with assumed higher immigration to Sweden confirms what demographers previously have told us, namely that immigration is not the solution to the dependency burden. Although immigrants are younger than the average Swede, they have poorer health and will more frequently experience unemployment and go into disability pension. Initially they have higher fertility, but tend to adjust toward Swedish behavior when they stay in the country. They will, of course, also age and eventually become retired. Immigration will only have a long-term effect on the dependency ratio if the immigration rate continuously increases.

Of the alternative scenarios we have tried, that with postponed retirement is the most effective to reduce the dependency ratio and to improve the income standard of the retired. When we lifted the upper retirement age from 65 to 70, the labor force participation rate of the age group 60–69 gradually increased. As a result the labor incomes of these age groups increased and they also increased their pensions. At the end of the simulation period, the relative income of 65+ increased to 62 percent compared to 55 percent in the base scenario. All groups of elderly, independently of care status, will experience this increase in relative incomes but most of it will go to those who do not need any social assistance. Among those who use home help or all day surveillance, there will be an overrepresentation of people who will not able to take advantage of the opportunity to postpone retirement.

The incidence of poverty becomes much lower when people work longer. This is primarily a result of a reduction in the number of income poor, because the wealth distribution is not much influenced by people postponing retirement.

Changing the assumptions about the growth in real wage rates and in the general unemployment rates primarily influences the incomes of people.

We also find changes in the labor force participation rates among those above 60, higher wage growth implies higher participation and lower growth lower participation rates, but the effects are smaller than those in the postponed retirement scenario. There are no effects on labor force participation in the age bracket 20–59. It is possible that our model underestimates the effect of increases in wage rates on labor supply, because there is no proper labor supply function in the model.

Assuming a constantly higher growth in wage rates will of course in about 30 years results in much higher incomes, primarily for those who are in the labor market, but also for retired. In our high-growth alternative, the relative income of 65+ decreases because the incomes of the working cohorts increase faster than those of retired, while in the opposite scenario with a lower growth the relative income of retired increases. To this result contributes that relatively more pensioners now receive the guaranteed basic pension and that the capital incomes of retired become relatively more important. The latter effect also implies that income inequality among 65+ increases in the low-growth scenario.

In a final evaluation of the ageing of the Swedish population, we suggest that the consequences of the ageing are not alarming, but adjustments are needed to meet the expected increase in demand for health care and social care. A policy that gives people incentives to postpone retirement is important. We also expect resources within the public sector to become reallocated from the working population toward the elderly. Our methodology does not allow a proper analysis of the need for increased user fees or tax increases, but we cannot exclude it. Perhaps even more important than the issue of financing future care is our demonstration of the relatively low future income standard of the elderly. It is a good prediction that relatively wealthy elderly will run down their stocks of wealth to compensate for low incomes when they age, and that young generations will increase their life-cycle savings when they discover the consequences of the pension system design. Unfortunately our simulations tell us that we will get an increasing share of both income and wealth poor elderly.

2. Methodology issues

In view of the large resources need for the development of a completely new microsimulation model, we decided to use an already existing model and within our resources add the new modules needed to analyze the problems of population ageing. Aside from the issue of resources, this approach had its pros and cons. We got an already functioning model structure with a good interface, a demographic model, and most importantly, the whole tax, benefit and pension system included. The model is also a working tool at the Ministry of Finance, which implies that there is someone who is updating it and someone who might be interested in using the modules we have developed after our project is completed. The other side of the coin is that the already existing structure put constraints on what we could do. For instance, the status concept of SESIM (see Chapter 3) made it difficult to allow for part-time work and part-time retirement. We might have preferred to have a proper labor supply model.

With the experience we now have, we should probably have made the death rates health dependent so we had been able to endogenously capture the effects of health changes on survival and then simulated survival without the current close alignment to the official predictions of Statistics Sweden. These predictions embed assumptions about an increased expected life duration which might contradict our own simulated mild decrease in health status.

SESIM is a household sector model and it does not include any markets or mechanisms for market clearance. There is thus no automatic feed back on changes that takes place in the household sector. We found this particularly troublesome when analyzing domestic migration and its consequences for house prices. The historical and predicted future migration to the metropolitan areas have and should in the future drive up prices of owned homes in these areas more than in other areas in the country, and the resulting increase in the cost of housing should restrain migration. We considered introducing a price mechanism along the lines suggested in Creedy and Kalb (2005), but it turned out that relative housing prices had an insignificant effect on the choice of region to migrate to, and housing prices were also insignificant in the tenure choice model. This result might cause thoughts about the model specification, but we decided to avoid the hazel of introducing a price mechanism. House prices are now indexed with a nation wide index, which implies that we maintain current regional differences in house prices in our simulations into the future.

There are almost no private markets for health care and social care in Sweden and thus no price mechanism that clears the market. Supply of the publicly provided services is determined in a complex political process and excess demand results in queues and rationing. Our simulations are based on the observed utilization of publicly provided services in the 1990s and the beginning of the current century. This implies that observed levels and changes in this period are carried forward in the simulations. We thus simulate the consequences of population ageing assuming that the frequency of utilization and in this sense the standard of care is maintained unchanged. This is probably the only practically feasible approach. The alternative, to model how the political and administrative processes react to changes in demand, would become more adventurous.

There is no macro economic feed back in the model either. Indicators like CPI changes, returns on financial assets, and unemployment rates are fed into the model exogenously. The model thus does not generate any business cycles, but it is possible to make the model react to exogenously imposed cycles and it is of course possible to adjust the exogenous indicators to the outcome of the simulations in an interactive simulation strategy which switches back and forth between simulations and changes in the exogenous indicators. A disadvantage with such a strategy is that it is labor intensive and time consuming. It might also be difficult to know exactly which changes one should make in each iteration. We have chosen just to run a few distinct alternatives without attempting to replicate business cycles. We leave a study of the sensitivity of our results to cycles in the exogenous variables to future research.

Data problems are legion in microsimulation. In our study, we have been forced to make stochastic imputations to the start data set in a number of cases because LINDA does not have all the data needed. For the same reason, we have also found it necessary to estimate models using other data sets than LINDA. In all these cases, one has to make sure that the models, both for imputation and for simulation, are estimated so it is possible to draw inference to the LINDA population. As long as we use register data, this is not a great problem because all these data sets are based on the same population register. The samples of ULF and HINK/ HEK were drawn from the same register too. The only sample we have used that does not permit a statistical inference to the whole Swedish population is the Kungsholmen study, which only covers a parish in the down town area of Stockholm. At the time when we estimated our models for social care there was no other data set that included both ADL scores and information about care. By calibrating the estimated imputation model to national estimates of care frequencies by age and gender from the HINK/HEK survey, we made sure that the start values were at the right level. (HINK/HEK does not include information about ADL.) The Kungsholmen study might also deviate from a national sample in its transition frequencies between modes of care but it is not as obvious as the difference in initial levels.

The calibration techniques have in this study also been used to make the model simulate demographic changes, which coincide with the official demographic forecasts of Statistics Sweden. The demographic models of SESIM then primarily serve the purpose of assigning events such as marriage, separation, and death to single individuals. We have also used calibration to introduce alternative scenarios with respect to death risks and immigration frequencies, and finally also, as explained in Chapter 3, to reduce simulation uncertainty.

In a simulation model like SESIM, there are both direct causal links and indirect links. For instance, the utilization of social care is primarily determined by ADL, and ADL is determined by health status in addition to age and gender. A change in the health status of an individual or in a group of individuals will thus work on the demand for care indirectly via the ADL. Because all models are stochastic and they have unexplained residuals, the variance of which is not unimportant, the relation between health and social care becomes "smoothed." In retrospect, we now suspect that the effect of changes in health status on social care is too weak. There is a similar problem with respect to the relation between health and wealth. Our model does not include any direct causal effects of health on wealth or vice versa, but any correlation would have to be generated by indirect relations through age, unemployment, disability, income, etc., and it turns out to be rather weak. Contributing to this result is of course also that we had to impute initial health status rather than observe it.

The greatest advantage of microsimulation is probably that it is such a good tool for studying distributional issues and comparing subpopulations to each other. We have used our model for this purpose, in particular when we have analyzed poverty and the income standard of people in need of social care. This kind of analysis requires, however, that the model is designed such that it replicates well the conditional distributions of interest. As suggested above, one cannot always trust a microsimulation model to do so if it has not been designed for this purpose from the beginning.

For a few variables, we have observed that the model in the first few years moves rather quickly toward a new (dynamic) equilibrium. This initial adjustment might be the result of observed relatively large changes in the exogenous variables in the first years of simulation, and then the adjustment has an observable equivalence in reality. But it can also be an artefact arising from bad imputed start values or lack of coherence between start values and the dynamic model. If our start year 1999 was extreme, the model tries to bring the simulated path back to a more normal course, but depending on model structure it might not react strongly enough to do it in one or 2 years but needs more time. A simple Markov type model with just one estimated parameter for the effect of the lagged dependent variable might not be fully realistic. To estimate a richer dynamic structure, one will, however, need longer panels of data than we have been able to use.

To build and to keep a microsimulation model alive is not one man's job. It requires a team. We have been fortunate in having a team representing different disciplines. Given the topic of our project, the complementing competences have been very useful, although we initially had to bridge differences in "research culture." In a project like ours, it is very important to have a skilled programmer who is not only interested in technical solutions but also in the scientific problems the simulation model is designed to solve and understands the environment in which the model is to be used. A programmer who does not have these skills cannot communicate with the scientific team efficiently and will most likely find technical solutions, which later will be found suboptimal. Our project has been fortunate in this respect. Even if some of our project members have been able to program Visual Basic, the language of SESIM, there is need of coordination and of having someone who has both complete overview and detailed knowledge of what the model contains and does.

Microsimulations is data demanding and needs relatively large resources in terms of scientific competence. It used to need the best computers one could get, but modern standard PCs have become so powerful that computing capacity is no longer a great problem. Most of the simulations in this project have been done on good PCs and sometimes even on notebooks. Running SESIM, even if one used the whole sample, was no great problem. Turn around time was acceptable, but to write out large data sets of simulation output on a hard disk or external media was rather time consuming. The size of these data sets also meant that conversion to, for instance, STATA or SAS data sets and analysis within these packages took time and needed some planning.

Fifty years after Guy Orcut presented his path-breaking ideas of mirroring natural experiments in a microsimualtion model, microsimulation has become an accepted approach. In particular, government agencies have seen how useful this approach is in policy making and an increasing number of models, both static and dynamic, are now in use around the world. Resistance have been stronger in the academic community, in particular among economists, who favor small neat *ceteris paribus* type models which focus on a few conditional mean relations. About 10 years ago, the Panel of Retirement Income Modeling of the U.S. National Research Council (Citro and Hanushek, 1997) expressed the view that our theoretical and empirical understanding of how society works was not good enough to motivate a microsimulation approach to study the problems of an ageing population. We hope that we in our project and through this book have demonstrated that microsimualtion is a useful and viable approach for this and similar purposes. There is no reason why social scientists should refrain from using and developing microsimulation when this is a standard tool in science and technical science. In doing so, we must of course maintain our high standards of model building and rigorously test our models against data using conventional methods of statistical inference. Plugging in desk-top models into large microsimulation structures without good empirical foundation will just give critics of large black box models of doubtful scientific quality new wind and not produce useful tools for policy analysis.

References

Citro, C.F. and E.A. Hanushek (eds.) (1997), *Assessing Policies for Retirement Income. Needs for Data, Research and Models*, Washington DC: National Research Council, National Academy Press.

Creedy, J. and G. Kalb (2005), "Evaluating policy reforms in behaviour tax micro-simulation models", Paper presented at the 34th meeting with the Economic Society of Australia, September 26–28, Melbourne.

Subject Index